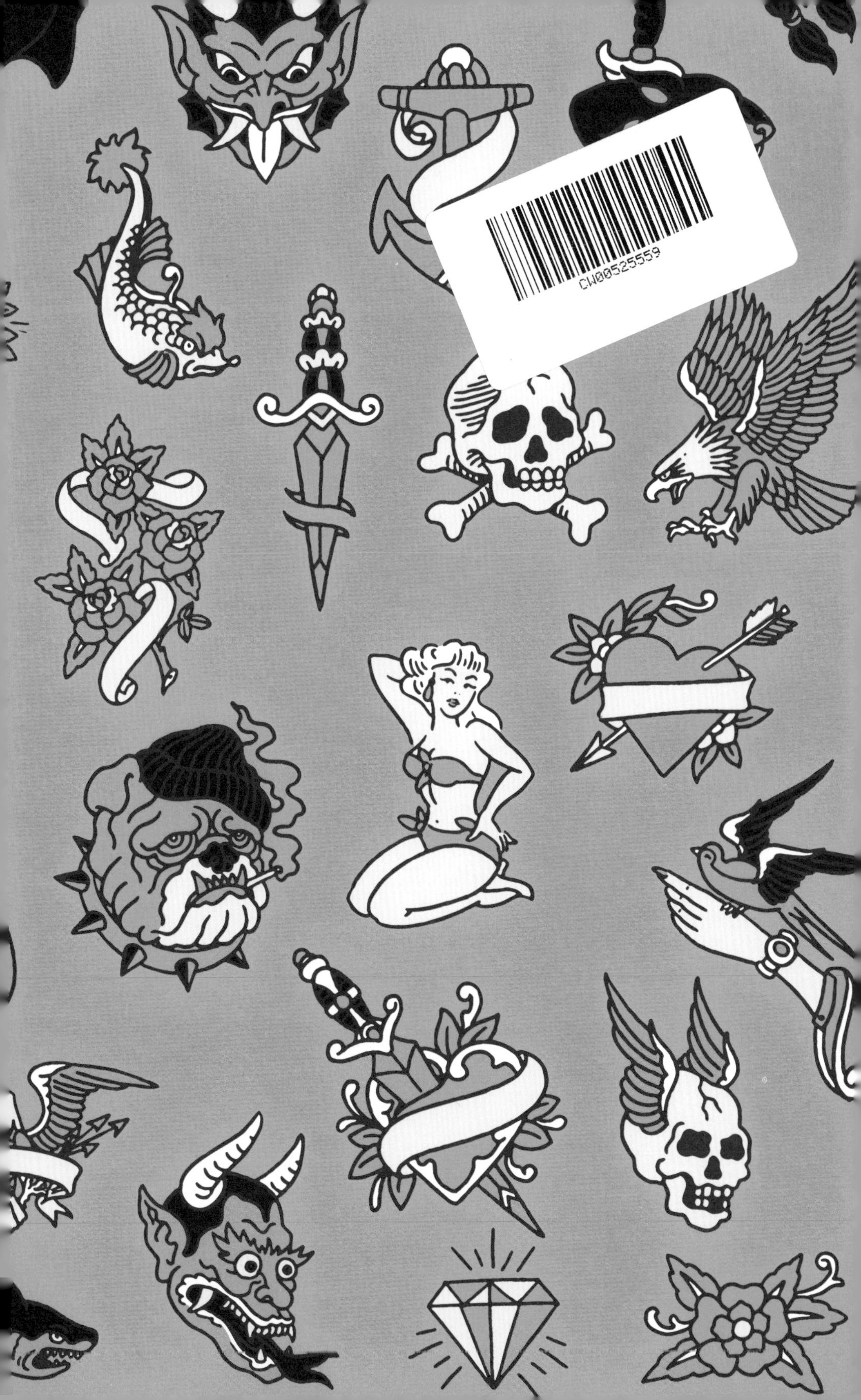

PAINTED PEOPLE

PAINTED PEOPLE

HUMANITY IN 21 TATTOOS

MATT LODDER

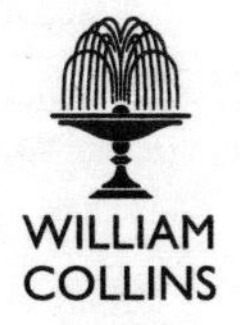

WILLIAM
COLLINS

William Collins
An imprint of HarperCollins*Publishers*
1 London Bridge Street
London SE1 9GF

WilliamCollinsBooks.com

HarperCollins*Publishers*
1st Floor, Watermarque Building, Ringsend Road

First published in Great Britain by William Collins in 2022

2023 2025 2024 2022
2 4 6 8 10 9 7 5 3 1

A catalogue record for this book is available from the British Library

ISBN 978-0-00-840206-8 (hardback)
ISBN 978-0-00-840207-5 (trade paperback)

Typeset in Sabon and Agenda One by Jacqui Caulton
Printed and bound in Great Britain by CPI Group (UK) Ltd, Croydon

For Lal Hardy

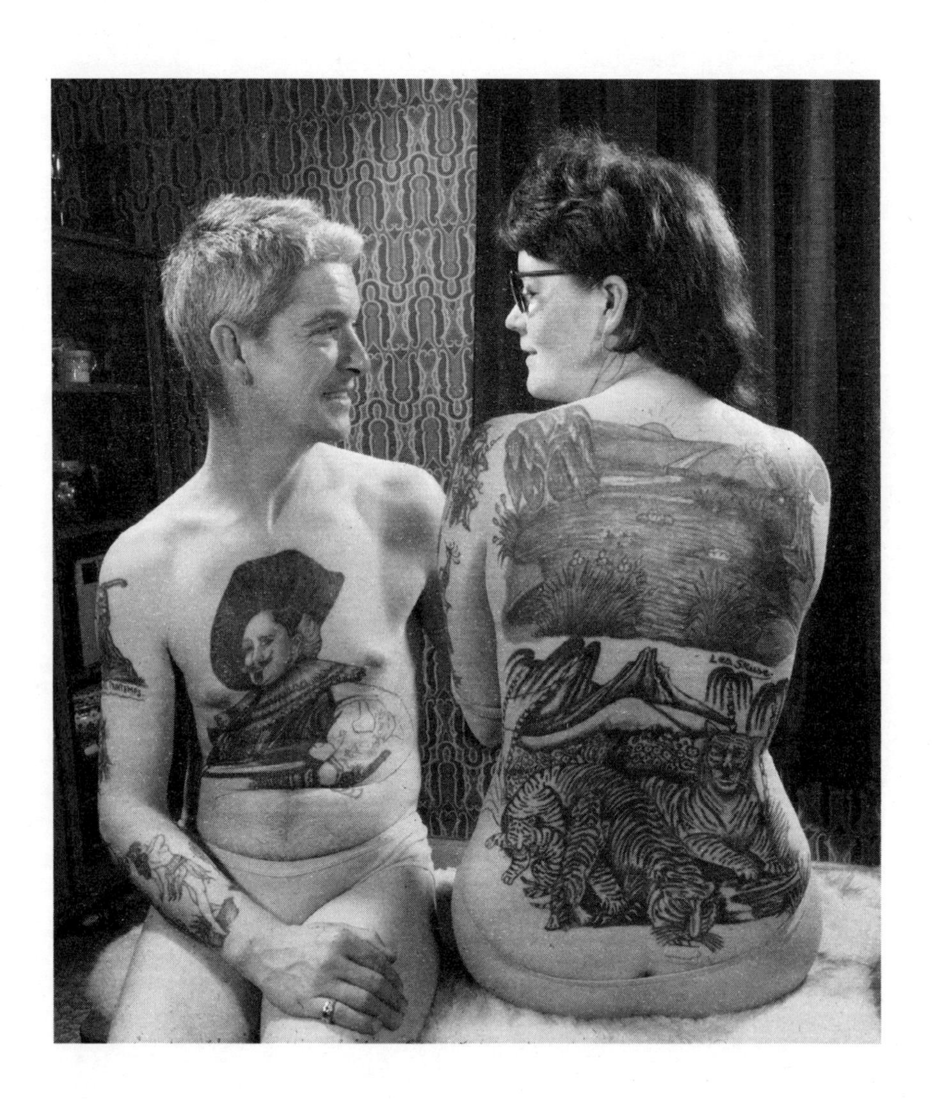

'Tattooing . . . is an art without a history. No one, as far as we are aware, has made it the business of his life to study the development of tattooing from its rude beginnings to the consummate forms we are [now] invited to admire.'

—*Saturday Review* (1881)

'Tattooing is one subject that – to be written about – demands a plunge into the waters, not a comfortable observer's beach chair at the side of the ocean.'

—Dr Samuel Steward, aka Phil Sparrow (1990)

Left: Ivor and Marianne Collier, tattooed by Les Skuse of Bristol, UK, *circa* 1970

CONTENTS

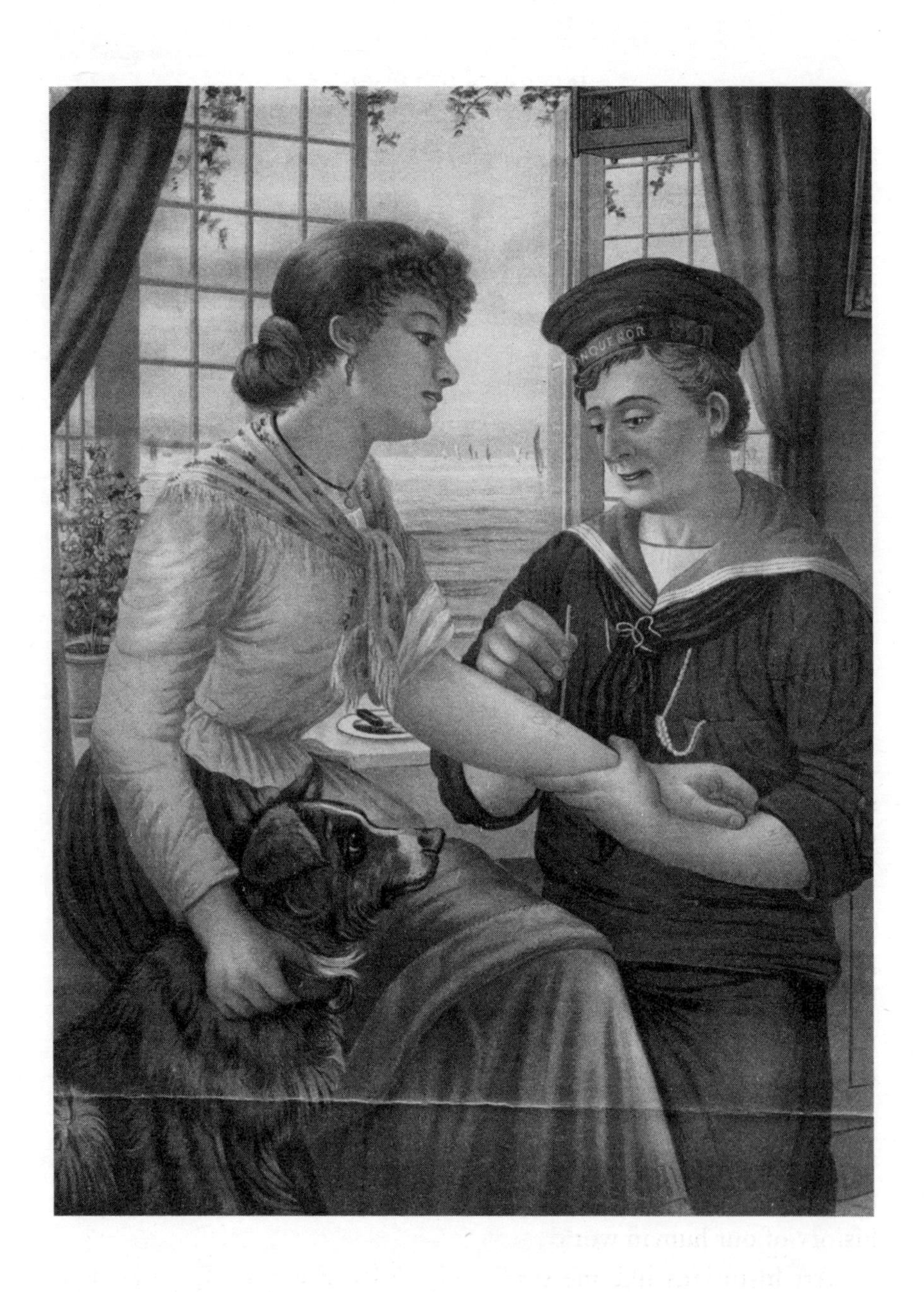

INTRODUCTION:

'TATTOOING OUR SKINS AND CALLING IT PAINTING'

'Suffering and ecstasy and despair belong most wholly to sensitives. It is they who carry the treasure, it is they whom life should nourish and protect, for it is because of them that man rises from clay to potter. Strike out the great people of history and we would still be tattooing our skins and calling it painting.'

—Advert for Elizabeth Arden cosmetics, *Ladies' Home Journal*, 1930

The Louvre gets thirty thousand visitors a day to its collections of sculptures, drawings and Old Master paintings. Few in this number would deny the power of standing in front of the 'Mona Lisa'. We gaze adoringly at her quixotic smile and radiant beauty, surrounded by others in equal rapture. By contrast, the tattoo marks on my own skin get, most of the time, just the one person viewing them – me, when I look in a mirror. But they are a symbol of their moment of creation as much as the 'Mona Lisa' is. Some of them are pieces created by artists of supreme talent and imagination; some of them I simply find fun; others are markers of a specific moment in my personal history. But my tattoos, like those of hundreds of millions of other people both in the present and the past, are a vital and fascinating portal into the history of our human world.

Art historians like me study old works of art not because they are beautiful, but because they are fascinating and necessary anchor

Left: Sweetheart tattooing, late nineteenth-century print

points through which we can begin to make sense of the past. Paintings, sculptures and the other objects made by human hands that we broadly call 'art' tell us things about the people and communities who made them, about the times and places they were made and about the lives of the people who were present when they were created. Most importantly, they also tell us about ourselves, now. How can we, in our own time and with our own unique experiences, understand the times and experiences of others?

All images are therefore meaningful and hold significance in some way. But tattooed images, which are acquired slowly and painfully, and which permanently change the bodies of the people who wear them, are perhaps the most meaningful and the most significant of all. As a form of image-making, tattooing seems to get closer to both inner and communal lives than any other.

* * *

This book tells the stories of twenty-one tattooed people from history. Well, twenty people from history, to be precise, plus my great-grandmother Ethelwynne. The tales come from across the globe, and date from more than five thousand years ago to the turn of the twenty-first century. And whilst you will learn a lot about the history of tattooing from this book, it is not really a history of tattooing, per se. Rather, it is a series of diverse histories told *through* tattoos. The thread that binds the following chapters together is a basic claim that we can understand people, places and moments in time by looking at the permanent marks humans make on their skin, and the responses of others to those same marks.

Each chapter explores an individual story and articulates its place geographically and historically, though it is important to be clear that there are deep, contingent stories to be told about the histories and the present circumstances of tattooing in every corner of the globe. I do not pretend or intend to offer accounts of tattooing in every possible cultural context. It is important, too, to note that rather than seeking to explain the intricate details of tattooing practices, this book is primarily a book about the *reception* of tattooing, and about how Western historians have understood and misunderstood tattoo cultures in the present, in their own pasts, and in the places they encountered and colonised.

Tattooing is a medium, not a phenomenon. To those who have never been tattooed, the simple, painful act of inserting an ink-soaked needle into the skin seems like the most salient fact about the practice. Thought of in this way, a tattoo mark made by a sharpened turkey bone in ancient North America and the elaborately decorative backpiece tattoo on a wealthy traveller to Japan in the 1880s are usefully thought of as the same thing, at some basic level. The things non-tattooed people too often ask tattooed people about our tattoos – Did it hurt? What will you do when you're older? – reveal some basic anxieties about the process of tattooing, which has remained basically unchanged throughout all human history.

But just as prehistoric cave painting, Renaissance frescos and toilet wall graffiti are not directly comparable simply because they are paint on vertical surfaces, tattoos in one place and time are also not directly comparable with those made elsewhere simply by virtue of the way they are produced. The stories in this book are connected not just by the fact that they involve ink in skin, but because in each case we can take those ink marks as indicative of something more. Tattoos are intangible cultural heritage. They offer deeper insights into the people who made them, the people who bore them and the cultural contexts in which they were produced.

* * *

Permanently marking the skin with ink has often been understood as something which differentiates the present from the past. In 1930, for example, cosmetics firm Elizabeth Arden published a long advertorial in the *Ladies' Home Journal* promoting their range of soothing moisturisers, tonics, and anti-wrinkle creams: 'Strike out the great people of history and we would still be tattooing our skins and calling it painting.' By embracing and nourishing her sensitive side, the modern woman could join a long and storied history of similarly sensitive people who together had dragged humanity into the twentieth century. Soft skin, by this account, is what separates us from our barbarian past. That, and the absence of tattoos.

Similarly, tattooing has been thought of as a practice that separates individuals from wider societies, or – more profoundly – that distinguishes one culture from another. In 2022, for example, it is still remarkably common to read, as I did recently in *The Times*, that tattooing was 'once confined to rough sorts such as navvies, convicts or soldiers', that tattoos 'are far from being decorative or artistic', and that the popularity of tattoos indicates such a profound departure from civilised cultural norms that the 'existential crisis of humanity in the post-religious West would seem to be a plausible explanation for the ubiquity of tattooing.'

This idea, that tattooing demarcates peoples from one another, has recurred frequently throughout human history. Across many cultural traditions, millennia apart, we find groups of tattooed people being categorised differently due to their tattoos. For example, one theory about the derivation of the European name 'Arapaho', given to the Native American Hinono'ei who originally lived near the headwaters of the Mississippi River, is that it means 'the tattooed people'. Anthropologist Hugh Lenox Scott once claimed that the chief of one of the Arapaho's rival tribes, the Piegan Blackfeet, told him that their word for the Arapaho meant 'people who were tattooed on the breast'. In a similar vein, stories from seventh-century China make mention of a place called Wén Shen, meaning 'Land of Marked Bodies', seemingly referring to the islands in Northern Japan inhabited by the indigenous, heavily tattooed Ainu people. In another seventh-century Chinese source, a state-sponsored poet called Liu Zongyuan bemoans having been sent to the southern region of Zhuang as part of a bureaucratic mission: 'this is where they have sent us, this land of tattooed people, and not even letters to keep us in touch with home'.

In 1526, Spanish colonial explorer Alonso de Salazar dubbed a group of islands in the Western Pacific 'Islas de Los Pintados', Islands of the Painted Ones, because the native population were heavily tattooed. Many English-language scholars used to believe that Văn Lang, the name of the ancient kingdom of Vietnam, translated to something like 'Land of the Tattooed People', even though today the consensus is that it was named after a particularly revered species of wading bird. And because historians have long believed – likely erroneously – that tattooing was a common cultural practice amongst the ancient Britons, it has been suggested by linguistic scholars that the very name 'Britain' might actually mean something like 'Land of the Painted People'.

But rather than understanding tattooing as something that divides us from one another and separates the modern West from its own past, I want to show you that tattooing *connects* us across historical time and geographical space, revealing details about human experience in the process.

Through the individual tattoo tales told here, we will gain brief insights into topics as diverse as: colonial attempts to extinguish cultural traditions in North America and the Pacific; ancient Greek medicine; the Persian imperial postal system; the horrors of children's homes in early twentieth-century New York; contemporary copyright law; the height of beach fashion in interwar France; and even the machinations of the international beef trade during the Cold War.

With this approach, *Painted People* does not straightforwardly ask the other reductive question which has so often been asked of tattooed people: 'What does that tattoo mean?' That question presupposes a specific, narrow answer, interpreting tattoos as a kind of code to be deciphered, signifying individual or cultural meanings in a linear way. But even when a tattoo is intended to have a clearly legible meaning, as might be the case in contexts where tattoos indicate social hierarchy or familial connection, marks on the skin always speak far beyond themselves.

Unless we read tattoos as the complex indexes of art and culture that they are, connecting inner lives with social fabrics and wider cultural contexts, we can only draw restricted conclusions about individuals, cultures or traditions, which, simply by being tattooed, are understood as somehow separate from wider society.

Nothing could be farther from the truth.

PART ONE

TATTOOS FROM THE ANCIENT WORLD

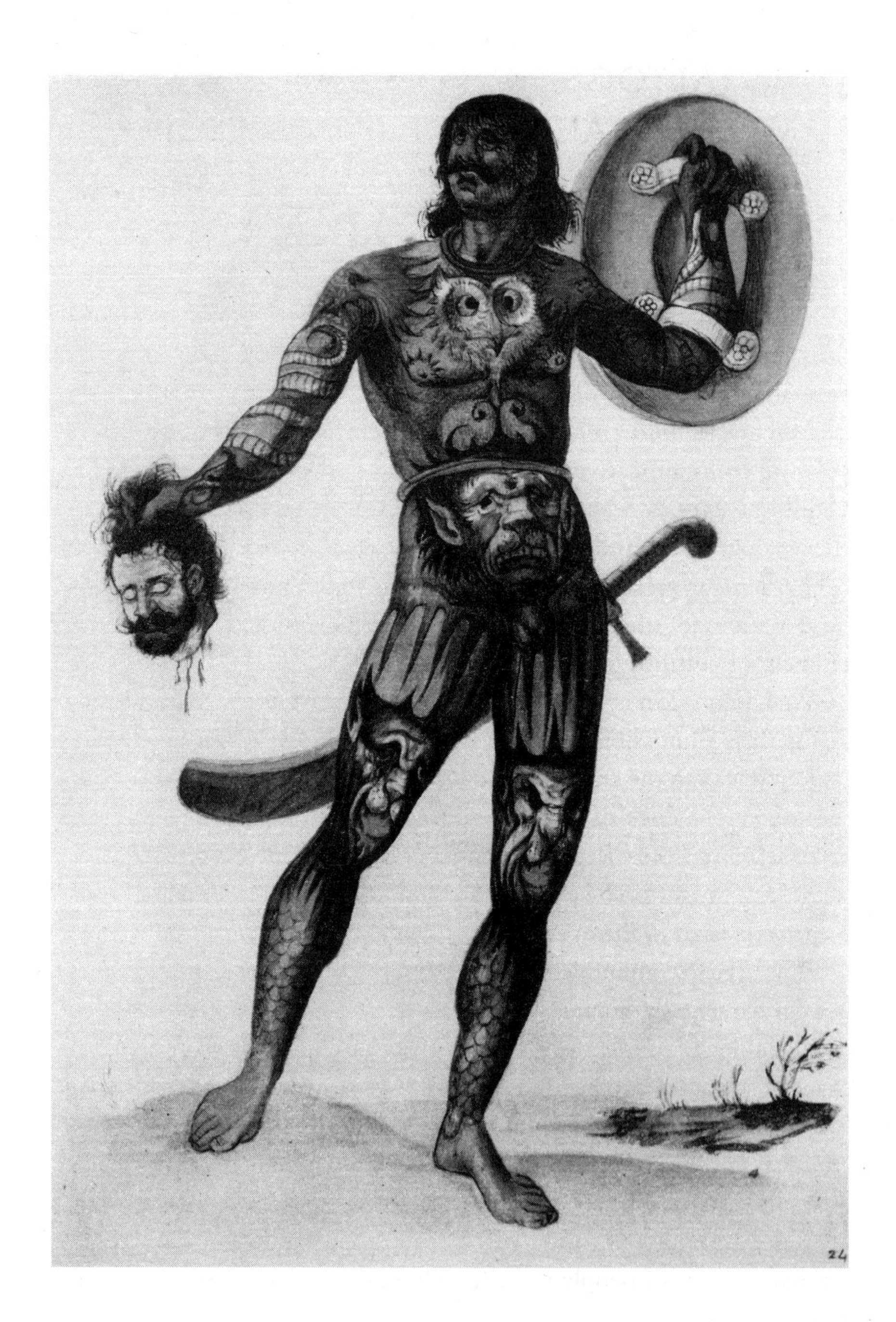

TATTOOS FROM THE ANCIENT WORLD: LANDS OF PAINTED PEOPLE

Current estimates place the sporadic emergence of creative art practices amongst modern humans at around a hundred thousand years ago. Some paleoanthropologists have argued that proto-human species such as *Homo erectus* may have been making decorative, symbolic, or communicative marks on objects such as shells for up to half a million years. It seems from the evidence of artefacts such as jewellery, stone tools and musical instruments that consistent symbolic behaviour was present in modern humans from about forty-five thousand years ago, and it is likely that tattoos emerged alongside this moment of cultural invention.

As human skin is much less durable than cave paintings and ornaments, it is impossible to tell how close tattooing's first appearance on Earth was to the emergence of other kinds of creative practice, but secondary evidence of ancient tattooing from objects like figurines and tattooing tools is well documented. The best current evidence suggests a longer prehistory of tattooing in the Eastern and Southern continents than in Europe.

The urge to communicate through mark-making, art and adornment is a fundamentally human characteristic, so it is unsurprising that tattooing, along with other practices that produce images and designs on a range of surfaces, is to be found across disparate human cultures back at least several millennia. The daubing of cave walls feels familiar to modern ideas of art, of course, but there is something immediate and fundamentally recognisable about the intimacy of inserting ink into the skin.

Since antiquity, tattooing has often been a useful shorthand to distinguish groups of people from their neighbours, their peers and their

Left: Picitsh Warrior, painted by John White, 1585

adversaries. As such, tales of outrageous tattooing from 'elsewhere' have often been exaggerated, and strong claims for tattooing's scarcity in a particular culture have been asserted contrary to the evidence. As we shall see over the coming chapters, each of which focuses on a particular tattoo tale from prehistory and antiquity, the truth of the matter is always more complex than might initially be imagined.

* * *

If we want to make better sense of the ancient world, we must make sense of its tattooing cultures. In this regard, the job of a tattoo historian comes with a particular set of nuances that historians of more conventional artistic practices do not often have to face. Tattoos, unlike paintings and sculptures and ceramic vases, are rarely to be found in dusty museum store cupboards, or long forgotten in your grandmother's attic. Though they are stubbornly permanent in the context of a human lifespan – as horrified parents have often reminded their freshly tattooed progeny – their existence and that of their bearer tend to be coextensive, bar a quiet period of posthumous decomposition.

Tattoos last, as one tattoo artist once put it, 'for life, plus six months'. To study the history of tattooing, then, we must usually resort to secondary representations – photographs, paintings, carvings, figurative sculpture – or to the artefacts and ephemera of tattooing that can transcend individual human lives, such as preparatory drawings or tools. In some cases, either due to particular funerary practices, bizarre collecting habits or the dumb luck of circumstance and environment, tattoos can survive through centuries and even through millennia. Inevitably, though, the traces of verifiably ancient tattoo history that reach into the present are faint, indistinct and frequently indecipherable. Precisely because they are so rare, fragile and inscrutable, tattoos that have survived the ravages of time, and outlived their bearers, are particularly precious threads linking the past to the present.

Fortunately, scientific tools that allow us to uncover evidence of ancient tattooing are developing rapidly, and, as we will see in the coming chapters, modern imaging and scanning techniques are increasingly being used to reveal tattoos on ancient bodies, some previously hidden in plain sight. Despite these advancements, modern research into prehistoric (and even modern) tattoo cultures has only recently been able to begin extracting itself from a mire of poor scholarship, prejudice, misunderstanding and even deliberate falsehood.

* * *

Let us return to an illustrative example, the deep, tattooed past of the rainy islands I call home, Great Britain, the 'Land of the Painted People'. The exact timescale of tattooing in Britain is hard to estimate, and it remains contentious. Roman histories make frequent mention of the Picts, a confederation of tribes in Scotland who appear as a clearly identified group in third-century Roman accounts and who have come to stand as the most iconic of the ancient, tattooed British tribes.

In surviving histories, several classical authors including Claudian, Herodian, Solinus, Pliny, Martial and Pomponius Mela make reference to earlier groups of Britons whose bodies were adorned with colours or figures, but the only account by any of these writers that actually describes having seen them first-hand was Julius Caesar's in 54 BCE. He wrote in his chronicles of the Gallic wars that '*Omnes vero se Britanni vitro inficiunt, quod caeruleum efficit colorem*' – 'all the Britons dye themselves with woad, which produces a blue colour'. Most of the accounts of tattooed Brits in the following centuries of Roman writing seem to be more-or-less fanciful and exaggerated versions of this original description. And given that he speaks of 'all Britons', but makes no further reference to these supposedly ubiquitous, blue-painted warriors elsewhere in his chronicles, it seems likely that Caesar himself was mistaken on this point.

Syrian-born historian Herodian's much later account from the third century CE does describe body-decoration practices amongst the northern British tribes in a manner that indicates tattooing more than painting, describing the presence of specific designs and images, as opposed to the covering of the body with a single colour as prior authors had described. By the time Solinus was writing in 235 CE, though, almost two hundred years after Caesar, the blue-painted Britons had become 'barbarians', who from childhood had different pictures of animals skilfully implanted onto their bodies, so that as the man grew, so grew the marks painted on him: 'there is nothing more that they consider as a test of patience than to have their limbs soak up the maximum amount of dye through these permanent scars'.

Though based on little primary evidence, these classical sources became the foundational descriptions of ancient Britons in the early modern imagination, and despite the lack of a solid base of evidence to support them, the myths they created have proved to be formative over the centuries in how modern Britons viewed themselves, and how they viewed peoples from elsewhere on the globe. In the eleventh-century *Chronicles of the Kings of England*, for example, William of Malmesbury remarks that the prehistoric English had skin 'adorned with punctured designs', a habit that they 'imparted to their conquerors' at the time of the Norman invasion. Similarly, the English chronicler and monk Ranulf Higden wrote in the fourteenth century that 'inhabitants of Scotland are called Scots in their own language, and also Picts, because their bodies were painted in the following manner: they used to incise and prick their own bodies with a sharp-edged tool, marking out various figures and shapes on them which they stained with ink, or with other pigments and colours, so that they were called "Picti", which means "painted men" in Latin'. In 1480, this tale, in translation, featured in one of the first English-language books ever printed by William Caxton, and is thus indelibly etched into the foundational fabric of early modern British identity.

In the face of the unreliability of these classical texts, several archaeologists have argued that there *is* physical evidence to prove that ancient Scots were indeed tattooed, including discoveries of pigmented tools and the means of making a woad-based tattoo ink; the analysis of preserved 'bog bodies'; and secondary evidence in depictions, particularly on coins. However, when examined more closely, none of these sources seem to yield particularly convincing conclusions.

Actual evidence that the various tribes of Ancient Britain were permanently tattooed (rather than, say, temporarily painted for particular occasions) is scarce and circumstantial. It appears that stories of ancient British tattooing are primarily myths. No preserved bodies of tattooed Pictish warriors have been discovered, and the evidence from elsewhere in the British Isles is just as thin. Rather than providing positive support for these legends of fearsome tattooed warriors, what little evidence we do have actually casts doubt on the idea that the Britons were tattooed at all.

Unlike the preserved tattooed bodies from Egypt, Siberia and the Northern Alps which feature in the coming chapters, there have also been no discoveries of preserved ancient Britons bearing tattoos. In a 1991 study, for example, archaeologists analysed pigment traces on an Iron Age human body recovered from a bog at Lindow in Cheshire. The analysis revealed that the body had been decorated on the surface of the skin with a pigment of mineral clay. Moreover, the same study suggested that the translation of the Latin word '*vitrum*', as used by Caesar, to the blue flowering plant 'woad' in English is likely an error, and that there is no good evidence or reason to believe that the pigments used were plant rather than mineral in nature. In light of all this, the bulk of the current evidence points primarily to a culture of body painting with clay rather than permanent tattooing. There is as yet no unambiguous way to determine if any discovered traces of clay pigments were used for tattooing or painting, or to definitively identify tattooing tools or paraphernalia such as grinding bowls from potentially identical objects used to carry out body painting. No coins showing faces with plausible tattooing have ever been found in Britain (though, intriguingly, they have been discovered in Northern France). And although occasional needles and toothed bronze objects have been discovered at British Iron Age sites in Lincolnshire, Hampshire and Kent, there is no good reason to think any of them were used for tattooing rather than medical, clothes-making or cosmetic purposes. Indeed, other sources suggest that some of these tools were likely for leather-working or the production of fishing nets.

Unfortunately, as hard evidence of ancient British and European tattooing has been hard to come by, some unscrupulous academics have resorted to simply inventing it. In 1990, two young postgraduate students from Germany and the Netherlands were attempting to make sense of research from the 1970s by the eminent archaeologist Alfred Dieck, who had supposedly documented extensive tattooing on bodies dug up from bogs in Germany and Austria over the preceding century, stories that have given succour to many who still assert the truth of the tattooed Britons. Despite Dieck having catalogued nearly two thousand bog bodies at sites across Europe, describing many of them as vividly tattooed, these modern scholars could find no extant evidence of any tattooing at all. Indeed, when checked, it turned out that many of the bodies themselves did not even exist, and those that did were frequently rather different from the way Dieck had described them.

One of Dieck's most celebrated cases was that of two preserved bodies from the bogs of Upper Austria, supposedly discovered in 1884. A medical doctor and gentleman archaeologist named Reiber, Dieck said, had recorded in his diary that he had discovered two well-preserved ancient bodies, a fat elderly lady with tattoos on her head marked out vividly in red, and a rather tall man with tattoos all over his body. When he had discovered the diary, Dieck had taken care to copy sketches from Reiber's manuscript of the tattoo marks, providing compelling illustrative evidence of a Northern European tattoo tradition dating back a thousand years or more. Curiously, by 1990, no trace of this diary could be found, Dr Reiber himself seemed invisible in the historical record, and these bodies had seemingly vanished after their discovery, having never been recorded anywhere else.

In Dieck's files, discovered after his death, the researchers hit upon the truth. Amongst his papers, they found a clipping of a text which described tattooing in nineteenth-century Bosnia and illustrated several examples taken from life by anthropologists working in the region. Whilst tattooing in the Balkans is likely of some antiquity as a tradition, the drawings in that clipping were scarcely eighty years old by the time Dieck copied them, line for line, onto an outline sketch of this supposedly 'ancient' bog body.

However, as definitive evidence for ancient tattooing in Britain and Northern Europe has ebbed away, elsewhere in the world, new techniques are pushing the lacuna of tattoo history much farther back into the past than anyone had previously imagined. For example, whilst images of tattooed Native American people in North America once placed its practice within the first century CE, archaeologists working at the Fernvale site in Tennessee, on lands traditionally occupied by Cherokee, Chickasaw, Shawnee and Yuchi peoples, drew on complex microscopic scanning, pigment mineral analysis, and an innovative method of disambiguating tattoo needles to show that indigenous American tattooing dates to at least a thousand years earlier.

At several sites in Tennessee, archaeologists had long discovered needles fashioned from turkey bones, though these had primarily been catalogued as medicinal or leather-working tools. Cleverly, this new generation of experts realised that the wear-patterns which result on the soft bone needles used for tattooing would be rather different, at a microscopic level, to the patterns of use visible on other sharp tools. By fashioning new needles from turkey bones and tattooing themselves with them (in what appears to be a bold act of gonzo archaeology), they were able to realise that bone tattoo needles, uniquely, would bear pigment remnants only at a particular position on the tool, and would wear to a distinctive, rounded, polished end unseen when put to other uses. Armed with new tattoos and a new methodology for re-examining previous finds, it was possible to compare these ancient needles with their modern control examples and conclude that they constituted hitherto unknown evidence for a much older set of traditions than previously understood.

Given the limitations of the medium, we will never be able to fully trace the full extent of tattooing across the wide span of human histories. But as more work is undertaken, it is becoming increasingly clear that the desire to mark our bodies is almost a universal human impulse, which has been known about on every continent, even if not always part of mainstream cultures, for thousands of years.

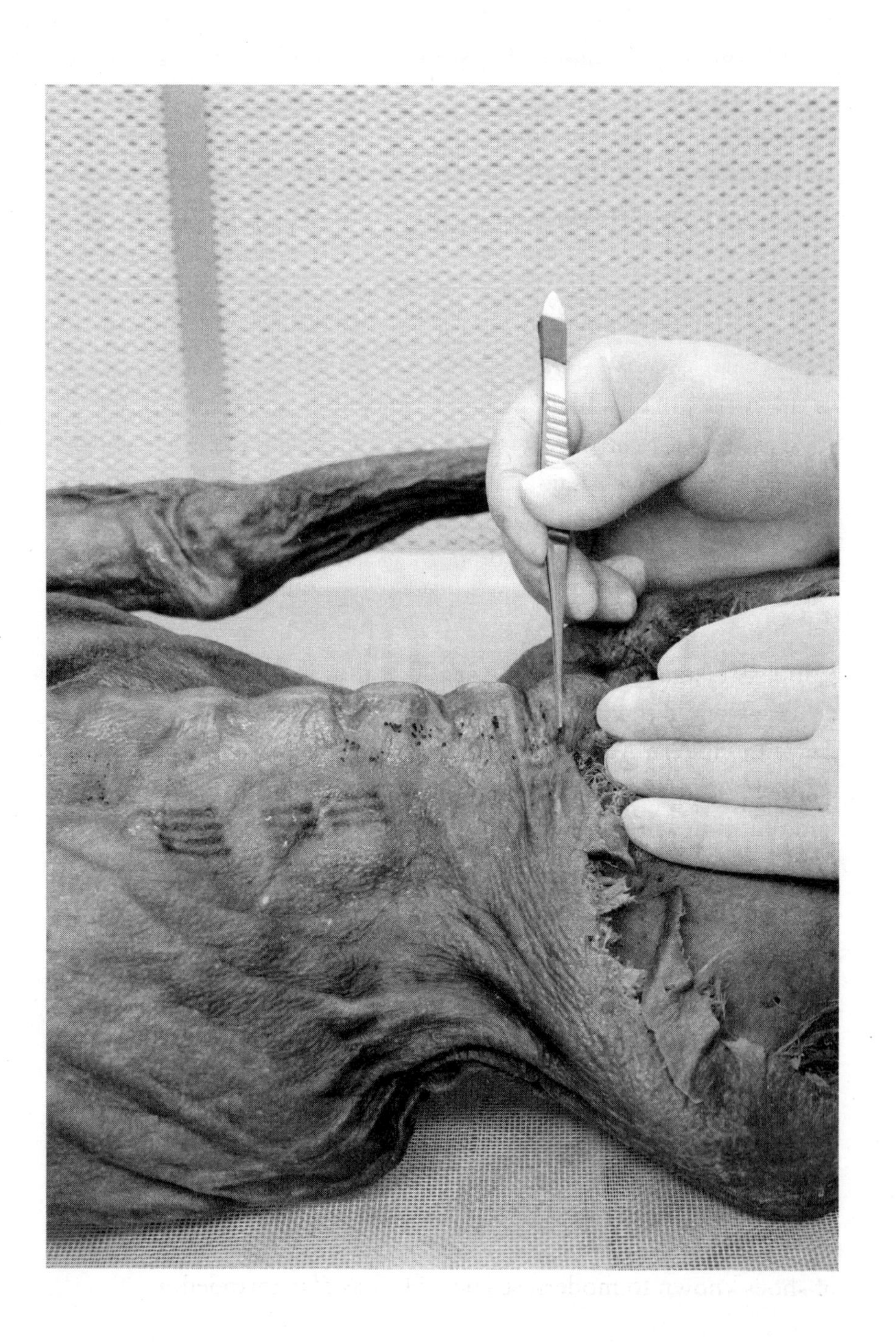

CHAPTER 1

Crosses and Dashes: Ötzi the Iceman, c. 3,400 BCE

> 'Mystery still surrounds the age and identity of the presumably historical glacier corpse recovered below the glacier . . . On the dead man's back there is said to be a kind of tattoo in the shape of ten lines arranged in three rows one above the other.'
>
> —*Tiroler Tageszeitung*, 21 September, 1991

5,500 years ago, a forty-five-year-old man was shot in the back with an arrow while travelling in what is now the Italian Alps, on the border with modern Austria. He had been murdered and left to die on a cold, remote and windswept mountainside. In 1991, climbers chanced upon his immaculately preserved body, newly revealed from beneath millennia of snow and ice as the planet warmed. On his fateful trip up the mountainside, he had carried an elaborate copper axe and a variety of sharp tools made of flint, wood, bone and deer antler, as well as a kit for lighting fires. Ötzi the Iceman, as he is known to the modern world, is the oldest mummified European man and the oldest tattooed human body yet to be formally identified.

Since this discovery, archaeologists, anthropologists and historians have meticulously examined his frozen corpse. His body has revealed details of the Neolithic diet, inspired filmmakers to turn his death into something resembling a modern-day murder mystery and revealed Ötzi to be the proud owner of one of the oldest pairs of shoes known to modern science. He was also tattooed.

Left: Examination of Ötzi the iceman, South Tyrol Museum of Archaeology, Bolzano, Italy

* * *

Ötzi's icy corpse and the artefacts of his perilous life are revelatory discoveries in themselves, but his tattoos are particularly surprising. Many people imagine the practice of tattooing as something distant and alien to European cultures, but Ötzi undermines this assumption. Though much about these black marks and the circumstances of their application will be forever unknown, they do reveal an embodied continuity between his ancient frozen body and our own.

Ötzi has sixty-one discrete lines tattooed on him. They are primarily in the form of short black tally marks and crosses and are found in nineteen groups at fifteen locations on his body. Seven closely spaced lines are tattooed on his lower left leg, for example, and fourteen short lines are tattooed on his lower back, placing Ötzi several millennia ahead of his time in predicting a late 1990s craze for cute, fashionable tattoos in the same spot. The marks were created using a pigment made of soot – the simple carbonic remnants of the burning of organic material – and flecks of ash also survive in some tattooing sites. Close spectrographic analysis reveals other traces of minerals amongst the carbon: surviving microscopic crystals from the stones Ötzi or his tattooer had used to build the fireplace from which this soot was taken. Minute variations between the chemical compositions at different tattoo sites suggest that they were applied over several occasions rather than in one single session. The carbon pigment found embedded in Ötzi's skin is essentially of the same chemical composition as black tattoo inks used in modern tattooing, and the very basic use of burned organic soot as a tattoo pigment has been documented in traditional tattoo practices across the globe.

* * *

The locations of the tattoo marks do not entirely rule out the possibility that Ötzi partly tattooed himself. His left wrist is tattooed, but there are no tattoos on his right arm at all; they appear only where a right-handed tattooer could easily reach. However, the marks on his lower back are as neat and sharply drawn as those elsewhere on his corpse: strong evidence that they were tattooed by someone else. It is possible that he sat alone by a smouldering fire, painfully puncturing or slicing his skin with a sharpened implement before gathering soot and ash to rub into his wounds. More plausibly, he sat with a member of his community whose social role empowered them to perform tattooing in a magical, ritual or medicinal context and, as people getting tattoos today still do, our Iceman gritted his teeth and breathed slowly and purposively as the outer layer of his skin was painfully broken to allow the pigment to enter his body. As those microscopic particles of soot were inserted into his skin, his blood ran and his endorphins and adrenaline kicked in, and once the brief operation was complete, the wound was washed and left to heal. Over the next week or two, his immune system worked to heal his skin, his cells absorbed the particles of blackened soot, and, unable to remove them through his lymphatic system, they remained there, visible through the newly healed skin for the rest of his life.

At its most basic, tattooing is the insertion of the right kind of pigment into the right layer of skin during a wounding process. Tattoos remain permanently on the body when pigment particles are inserted into the dermis, the collagen-rich layer of skin that sits about one or two millimetres under the very thin and regularly renewed upper layer called the epidermis. When the dermis is injured during the process of tattooing, cells called macrophages surround any foreign matter as part of the body's healing immune response. Unable to remove granular pigment particles through the lymphatic system, as they are simply too large, the pigment particles are absorbed into the cells that surround them and keep them stable, and are visible under the skin newly healed above them. As the body ages and these pigment-containing cells themselves die off, the ink particles are assimilated by nearby cells, causing the fuzziness and hazing visible in older tattoos. If the ink is deposited too deeply, this spreading will happen much more quickly (even almost instantly), as the cellular regeneration process differs in the subdermal tissue. Too shallow, and too much of the ink will have been deposited in the rapidly regenerating upper epidermal later, sloughing away most of the pigment as the skin heals, resulting in a tattoo that is indistinct and rapidly fades.

Throughout history, tattooists have used various technologies to help them break the skin to the correct depth. Though needles are synonymous with modern-day tattooing, similar results can also be achieved with a blade, opening the skin to the right depth before rubbing the pigment particles in afterwards. This method is less precise and predictable than fine-pointed needles, but no less successful. Archaeologists are unsure if Ötzi's tattoo marks were made by rubbing pigment into a freshly cut wound or piercing the skin with a needle-like implement, but essentially, any sharp object able to break the skin to a sufficient depth would have done.

As prehistoric humans transitioned from the Stone Age to the Bronze Age, their knowledge of metalworking gradually improved. Ötzi lived between these two periods in an era known as the Copper Age. At this time, soot could have been inserted into the skin with a sharpened stick, a metal sliver (though no such copper needles have been discovered in the Alps), or most plausibly, an animal bone fashioned into a pointed tool.

As for why his skin was marked, archaeologists believe the marks' location offers a possible clue: most of Ötzi's tattoos are located where there is evidence of degenerative joint conditions, so perhaps the tattoos were magical or medicinal rituals believed to relieve inflammation. Others have argued that the presence of another set of marks on his chest largely discredit this theory.

What we do know is that Ötzi suffered from a variety of painful ailments including gallstones, clogged arteries and intestinal worms, which could have caused chest pain. So perhaps the process of tattooing was understood by Ötzi's community to be healing, and the marks indicated some religious or spiritual ritual through which ailments might be alleviated. Perhaps the crosses indicate one kind of ritualistic mark, and the lines another. It is possible that in sites such as his left leg, which bear seven short parallel lines, each individual tally is evidence of an ongoing course of treatment, with each line applied separately over time as his pain subsided or returned. Perhaps there is some cultural significance to the number of lines at each site, indicative of a particular theory of magical medicine. Perhaps these lines reveal a theory of medicine akin to that of acupuncture, where specific points on the body were believed to have therapeutic value when needled directly.

It seems unlikely that Ötzi was the only tattooed man in his community, but without further evidence, we cannot know how widespread tattooing was at the time, nor to what degree this system of medicinal tally marks was representative of tattooing in general. Were these tattoos the only kind of tattooing undertaken by Ötzi's community? Or was more decorative tattooing undertaken by women, perhaps, or individuals of a different social or hierarchical status? It is impossible to know for sure.

* * *

Commenting on the widespread distribution of tattooing throughout the globe in 1925, anthropologist Wilson Dyson Hambly wrote that no 'investigator would claim that tattooing by puncture is a simple and obvious practice which might reasonably be expected to occur spontaneously in a large number of widely separated areas'. It seems Hambly was so baffled by the worldwide prevalence of permanent marks on the skin – and so awed by the various ways in which they were created – that he could only imagine that tattooing was the novel invention of a single individual, from whom news spread throughout the disparate peoples of the Earth, from Alaska to Australia, Egypt to Samoa, and from China to the Americas, via every corner of the planet. 'The very ingenious invention of making small separate punctures, possibly with pygmy flint implements and introducing coloured matter,' he wrote, 'I regard as a deliberate attempt of some thoughtful individual seeking consciously to impart a more enduring symbol of vitality than that afforded by mere surface painting.' Although the image of some prehistoric human becoming the proto-tattooer is compelling, like some adorned Prometheus stealing tattooing from the gods, it simply cannot be true. Hambly considered that tattooing was not an obvious procedure, but the reverse is clearly the case: fundamentally, there is nothing technologically complex about puncturing the skin with a blackened instrument which will leave a permanent mark.

It certainly is true that tattooing emerged and persisted as a practice in different cultures at different times, and that contact between them will have transmitted ideas about it. Though Ötzi's black-marked skin is unambiguous evidence of tattooing in Southern Europe during the very early Bronze Age, it is highly unlikely that the oldest tattoos to have survived into the present age were the first tattoos ever performed. The desire to alter and modify the body is present in every human culture ever documented, and whilst the precise details of the profusion of tattooing in prehistoric societies are not known, the practice was certainly geographically widespread in the ancient world.

Some of the other oldest surviving tattoos are also from northerly latitudes: sites from the so-called 'Catacomb Culture' of the Russian Bronze Age, where tattooed bodies that are approximately six hundred or so years younger than Ötzi have been identified. But to date, no evidence of European tattooing has been found any farther north than Ötzi's icy grave in the Alps from any earlier than the Iron Age, about four thousand years later. In the southern stretches of Europe, though, tattooing seems to date back over ten thousand years from the present day to the Neolithic period. Bone needles from archaeological sites in Romania indicate that tattooing was happening a thousand years before Ötzi's death; from the same period, sculptural figures found in modern-day Bulgaria show what may be geometric, ornamental tattooing on female bodies.

Anyone who has been tattooed is able to empathise with Ötzi's experience, despite the inordinate passage of time. Even though his motivations, cultural beliefs, attitudes and ideas are opaque to us, the biological reality of undergoing that painful procedure, patiently dealing with the healing process, and living out the rest of his life with a body that has been visibly altered is consistent across the millennia.

That thread of embodied human familiarity links his ancient life with ours.

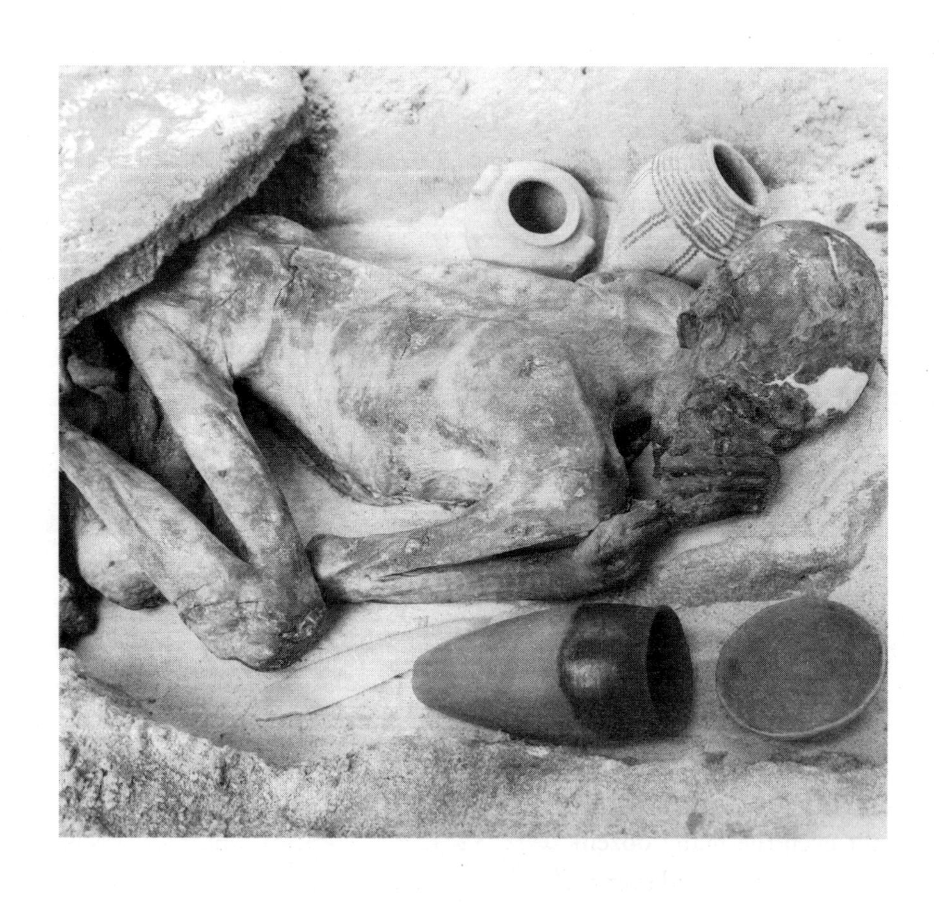

CHAPTER 2

Raging Bull: The Gebelein Man, c. 3,300 BCE

> 'I saw lying in the grave, with pots and flints about it, the body of a man . . . The body was quite naked and complete . . . We broke away bit by bit the sandstone bed of the grave, and thus the body dropped down by degrees to the bottom of the pit we had made. We then lifted out the body uninjured, and after that the other contents of the grave. We found the body quite dry, and some of its skin was cracked.'
>
> —Sir E. A. Wallis Budge, 1920

In the British Museum's vast Egyptian galleries, nestled within a carefully staged recreation of an ancient sandy grave, lies the curled, shrivelled body of a mummified young man. His body has been almost constantly on display since he was first brought to London in 1899.

Over the past century, millions of visitors have gazed in wonder at it as they shuffled past his display case. Only the most diligent will have stared long or closely enough to have noticed a small, greenish smudge on his upper right arm, almost imperceptible in natural light. Nobody, not even the many dozens of scientists and curators who had closely examined him, had ever realised that this smudge was actually a tattoo. Tattoos fade over time, and this one has had a long time to do so. It was only in 2014, as part of complex process of re-examination, that modern imaging techniques were able to make visible again a mark that had first been inserted into his skin over five thousand years previously.

* * *

Left: The Gebelein Man, British Museum, London

Once affectionately nicknamed 'Ginger' due to his shock of red hair, the mummy is now known more respectfully as 'Gebelein Man', the colonial name of the town in which he was discovered. The Gebelein Man was alive in about 3,300 BCE and lived in the predynastic period of Egyptian civilisation, just prior to the rule of the first Pharaoh. Unlike many of the museum's younger mummies, whose cloth-wrapped corpses were diligently and deliberately preserved as part of complex funerary rites, this man was spared the normal course of human decomposition due to the hot and arid conditions of his shallow desert grave. His body is dried out and dehydrated, but otherwise remarkably well preserved, with his skin, hair, teeth, bones and even internal organs essentially undisturbed by the passing millennia. Archaeologists speculate that chance discoveries of well-preserved ancient bodies like the Gebelein Man may have inspired the Ancient Egyptian spiritual belief in the afterlife, and led to the development of the later, purposive mummification processes which are now one of the most emblematic clichés of ancient Egyptian culture.

Victorian archaeologists discovered a total of six naturally mummified bodies in the grave site at Gebelein, all of which were taken to the British Museum. Recently it was revealed that the lone adult female of the group is also tattooed, making her the oldest surviving tattooed woman yet discovered. Though almost exactly contemporaneous with our tattooed Tyrolean, Ötzi, the artistic complexity of the tattoos on both these individuals are remarkable in comparison to the simple tally marks and crosses that adorned the Iceman's aching body.

The presence of tattooing in ancient Egypt and the adjacent Nubian kingdom has been attested for many decades, though evidence has been sparse. Until these recent discoveries, our understanding of the history of Egyptian tattooing was based on a very few surviving mummies, all much younger than the Gebelein bodies, as well as circumstantial clues found in various artistic representations of human bodies. By 2017, only about thirty tattooed Egyptian and Nubian mummies had been identified. Of these, only four were men, with the next oldest male tattooed mummy some 1,500 years younger than the Gebelein Man. No items that can be definitively identified as tattooing tools have been discovered, though bound bunches of copper needles have been documented in several grave sites, conventionally identified as tweezers for removing thorns but bearing a striking resemblance to the implements used in modern poke tattooing. As such, the cutting-edge scientific processes used on the Gebelein mummies and elsewhere proves that the prevalence of tattooing is much more widespread in antiquity than had previously been imagined.

* * *

The infrared technology which identified the smear of dark green as a tattoo also revealed the image itself to be of two horned animals. The animal figures overlap, giving an illusion of perspective and animation, as if they are prancing close to each other. One, more distinctly and heavily rendered than the other, with a particularly long tail, seems to represent a species of wild bull; the other, a fainter image, has curved horns, and is likely a Barbary sheep, a hardy species familiar across the Egyptian deserts. As the sheep is much more hesitantly inscribed in the skin, it seems likely that it was tattooed at a different, earlier moment in time from the more confidently drawn bull in front. By contrast, the woman's tattoos are not figurative but consist of patterns or symbols. Though her tattoos are also invisible to the naked eye, these new imaging techniques have revealed that she sports a series of S-shaped marks on her shoulder and a short L-shaped line on her upper right arm.

The Gebelein tattoos are fascinating because the designs are familiar motifs within the wider visual cultures of the period. The Barbary sheep on the Gebelein Man's upper arm, for example, is a common motif in art and decorative objects from across Egypt in the immediate predynastic period. The distinctive curved-horned animal has been depicted at rock art sites, carved into sandstone hills; etched into ivory; displayed on knife handles and decorative flints; and it has been found inscribed into pottery, including some unearthed at Gebelein. Horned sheep also appear painted onto female figurines and dolls thought to represent ritual dancers, suggesting that this was a tattoo design also liked and appreciated by women.

Given that these animals were part of this young man's everyday life, the tattoos may simply have been decorative designs reflecting familiar scenes from his everyday life, but it is likely that there was some culturally specific meaning associated with the image. Bulls, as in contemporary culture, connote masculine strength, aggression and power, and in ancient Egypt signified the power of hierarchical rule. In this context, getting a tattoo of a bull's head might have been a way for young men to commemorate a great, successful hunt, or to show off how tough he (thought he) was. The tattoos may also have magical or ritual significance, in which the act of tattooing and the wearing of this aggressive image was believed to confer power or protection. If this was the case, they weren't particularly successful – the man died from being stabbed in the back (literally)!

By the time of the Gebelein Man, hunting Barbary sheep was not necessary for subsistence and survival. Knowledge of this fact has led archaeologists to argue that representations of these animals on walls and pots indicate the importance of hunting as a social activity, where men could practise their prowess with weapons. Unlike the bull, Barbary sheep do not appear to have held particular ritual significance, nor do they seem to have held any particular importance over other animals. By the beginning of the Egyptian dynasties in about 3,100 BCE, the sheep design seems to have disappeared from the visual lexicon, as it rarely appears on objects from the dynastic period.

The Gebelein woman's tattoos are even harder to decipher. As with the animal images found on the male body, her tattoos resonate closely with similar designs that survive on contemporaneous pottery. When painted on pots, the four staggered S symbols across her collarbone have been interpreted as abstract representations of birds in flight, or even as arrows that connect to different parts of a scene. The hooked line on her upper arm seems to resemble ceremonial staffs which are frequently depicted being carried by male figures in scenes of ritual gatherings, or dances. In other media, though, these designs have never been found in isolation, and are always depicted as part of larger and more complex scenes.

Whatever significance these symbols may have held to the individuals and their culture, this continuity of form, style and iconography illustrates something that appears rather obvious, in some senses, but which has often been missing from historic writing about tattoos and the ways in which anthropologists and the general public understand them. Times, places and cultures have specific visual styles which transcend one single creative discipline. The nineteenth-century art historian Heinrich Wölfflin once remarked that there is often to be found in history an aesthetic spirit particular to a time and place – a remarkable continuity of style between enormously diverse cultural forms, with shapes and ideas reflected across disparate types of human creativity. In thirteenth-century Europe, he said, the Gothic sweep of the grandest cathedrals' arches was matched by the fashion for extravagantly pointed shoes.

In the same way, tattooing is intimately intertwined with the visual cultures from which it emerges. Customers in tattoo shops in the twenty-first century often download their designs from social media sites; in the 1940s, many American tattoo studios had walls filled with sheets of designs taken from popular Disney cartoons; and old sailor tattoos reflect the iconography of naval images they also etched into their snuff boxes and embroidered onto scraps of fabric. Though the pain and permanence of tattooing often adds symbolic significance to the act of mark-making, it should not be surprising that the visual forms that tattoos take are continuous and familiar.

Over the centuries, historical understanding of tattoos on ancient Egyptian bodies has been influenced by European cultural prejudices against tattooing, particularly towards women. In 1891, for example, the mummified, bandaged body of woman named Amunet was discovered in a richly appointed tomb in Thebes, now known as Deir el-Bahari. When her bandages were unravelled, her four-thousand-year-old body was discovered to be adorned with extensive tattooing forming dot-dash patterns on her upper chest, abdomen and stomach, her right forearm and her right thigh. It is now known that Amunet served as a priestess, and bore a title indicating that she was a high-ranking lady-in-waiting to the queen of King Nebhepetre Mentuhotep. Initially, though, her role was interpreted by archaeologists as that of a 'concubine', and her tattoos were taken to have specifically sexual and erotic symbolism. This presumption was reinforced by the appearance of tattoo-like marks on figurines sculpted from clay that were understood at the time to be 'Brides of the Dead', erotic companions for the deceased.

Scholars concluded that if these tattooed figurines were 'Brides for the Dead', then perhaps they were avatars of real women whose intimate tattooing signified their sexual availability and erotic appeal. As most mummies did not appear to have tattoos, and because tattooing had been primarily observed on female mummies, archaeologists of the 1940s concluded that tattooing was a marginal practice or perhaps something specific to sex-workers. More recent scholarship suggests that far from being straightforward erotic avatars intended for the posthumous pornographic titillation of a dead king, the 'Bride' figurines are in fact complex ritual objects, and the tattooed women they represent held important roles in the worship of a goddess called Hathor, the major female deity in the ancient Egyptian pantheon.

* * *

In 2014, archaeologists were examining sites in the Egyptian town of Deir el-Medina, built to house the workers who cut and constructed the famous Valley of the Kings, home to the elaborate necropolis network of tombs that housed the bodies of Egyptian kings and nobles. During their painstaking work, they came to re-examine a headless, carefully eviscerated torso of a young woman found amongst a pile of ancient body parts, intermingled centuries earlier as a result of careless and haphazard looting. The body was unwrapped, save for a small sliver of bandage on her right arm.

Her body dates from around 1,200 years BCE, during the later centuries of the period of Egyptian history known as the New Kingdom. As with the predynastic bodies at the British Museum, it is only new photographic techniques that have fully revealed these remarkable marks to modern eyes.

The woman was approximately thirty years old when she died about three thousand years ago. Her surviving torso bears at least thirty tattoo marks on her arms, lower back, and most significantly, on her throat, nearly all of which would have been visible even when she was clothed.

The tattoos are figurative, and inscribed with hieroglyphs, symbols and images which directly connect her to the cult of Hathor. As a nurturing mother goddess, Hathor is strongly associated with

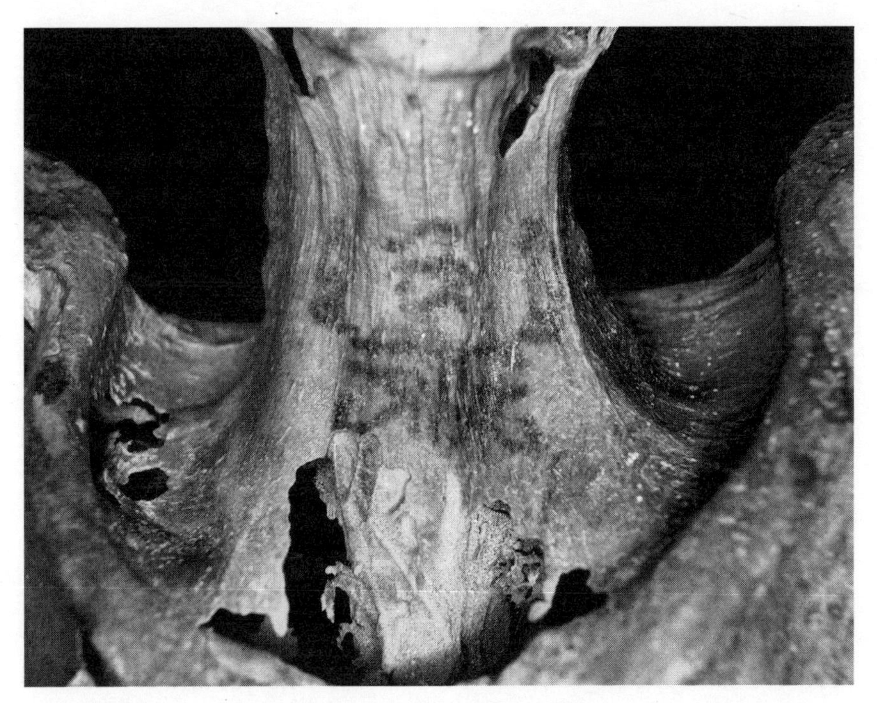

Deir el-Medina mummy, French Institute of Oriental Archaeology, Cairo, Egypt

the symbol of a cow, two of which are tattooed prominently on this woman's wrist. On her left shoulder, a bent clump of papyrus can be found, suggesting a connection to a story about Hathor raising her child Horus in the reedy marshes. Hathor is a mother-goddess, often represented as a nurturing mother cow whose spots take the form of celestial symbols. A four-petalled design on each of this woman's arms perhaps refers to a legend in the famous *Book of the Dead*, in which a four-leafed design, resembling a star, appeared on Hathor's hide as she descended from a mountain in the form of a cow.

Although her connection with Hathor is clear enough from the symbolism of these tattoo designs, her precise role within the temple and the wider community is decidedly less so. Conventional scholarship has argued that by this period in Egyptian history, women were no longer considered able to hold roles as priestesses, but this woman does appear to have held a religious or magical role within temple life. A tattoo on this woman's right arm seems to depict a sacred staff called a 'Hathor Handle' or sistrum which would be shaken during rituals. Every movement of this woman's arm, then, becomes a symbolic act of ritual worship, with the tattoo mark becoming animated as she gesticulated.

Given the ritual significance of these symbols when taken as a whole, it is perhaps plausible that the tattoos were intended to heal some illness from which she was suffering. Unlike Ötzi, though, there is no real suggestion that her tattoos were directly placed at sites where she was suffering from illness. Nevertheless, some relationship between these symbols and the healing of others can perhaps be deduced. Alongside the devotional and practical symbols linking her to Hathor, the stark symbolism of some of her other tattoos suggests that she may have held some kind of medical role as a healer or 'scorpion charmer' who was sought out in the event of scorpion stings or poisonous snake bites, or as a *rhyt* – a 'wise woman' ritualist or some kind of magical coroner, who would be consulted to determine the cause of someone's death.

On her upper arms, for example, she bears two tattooed cobras; near her armpits, one on either side of her body; and she sports two further coiled serpents hanging from suns. On her right arm, a tattoo inscribes an image of a snake goddess called Wadjet, wearing a red crown. Wadjet has also been understood by scholars as another manifestation of Hathor in places where Hathoric beliefs merged with older legends.

Inscribed with so much symbolism, this tattooed woman may have been a performer of sorts, embodying the goddess in ritual activity. The hieroglyphs tattooed on her throat are particularly interesting in this context, seeming to work as a collection of symbols which resemble a series of magical amulets, and permanently marked at a site on the body where protective jewellery or magical spells written on papyrus were often worn. Most prominent amongst these symbols is a series of hieroglyphs which take the form of a spell reading 'Do Good. Do Good', framed by a magical Eye of Horus symbol and seated baboons symbolising a god called Thoth, who was associated with the supernatural and the afterlife. Perhaps, then, this woman was a musician, or ritual singer, whose throat tattoos bestowed power on her voice, and whose similar shoulder tattoos served to further empower her magical gestures.

Tattooing is not necessarily directly indicative of a particular profession, however. Individuals or subcultures at a particular time and place may share similar tattoo designs through shared cultural interests or practices, not simply because any specific design is narrowly connected to a social role. For example, as with the Gebelein mummies, there is a clear continuity between the images tattooed on her skin and the wider visual culture in which she lived. Lotus flowers tattooed on her lower back mirror graffiti on the floor of the Hathor temple in which her body was discovered; a similar design was found represented on another Egyptian sculptural figurine. Cow motifs are also common graffiti at the Deir el-Medina site, where they seem to have been drawn by both worshippers and by idle workmen. Snake designs similar to this woman's tattoos are frequently found on household objects such as headrests, where they are believed to have served as symbols of magical protection. As in the case of the Gebelein mummies, some of this woman's crosses also resemble designs on figurines and dolls, adding further weight to the argument that such representational figurines mirror the tattoos of real humans.

* * *

New research into tattooed mummies continues. The Gebelein mummies will yield further secrets, and more thorough investigation of them is likely to push the dates of our earliest tattooed specimens back even earlier than Ötzi the Iceman. As with the new documentation of Hathor's do-gooding singer, such discoveries not only tell us about tattooing, religion and magic in ancient Egypt but reveal the richness and variety of ancient lives.

These new discoveries also show us that we need to be careful about making assumptions about who was tattooed, and in what circumstances. Most importantly, perhaps, they remind us that we should resist the temptation to impose our contemporary prejudices on the distant past.

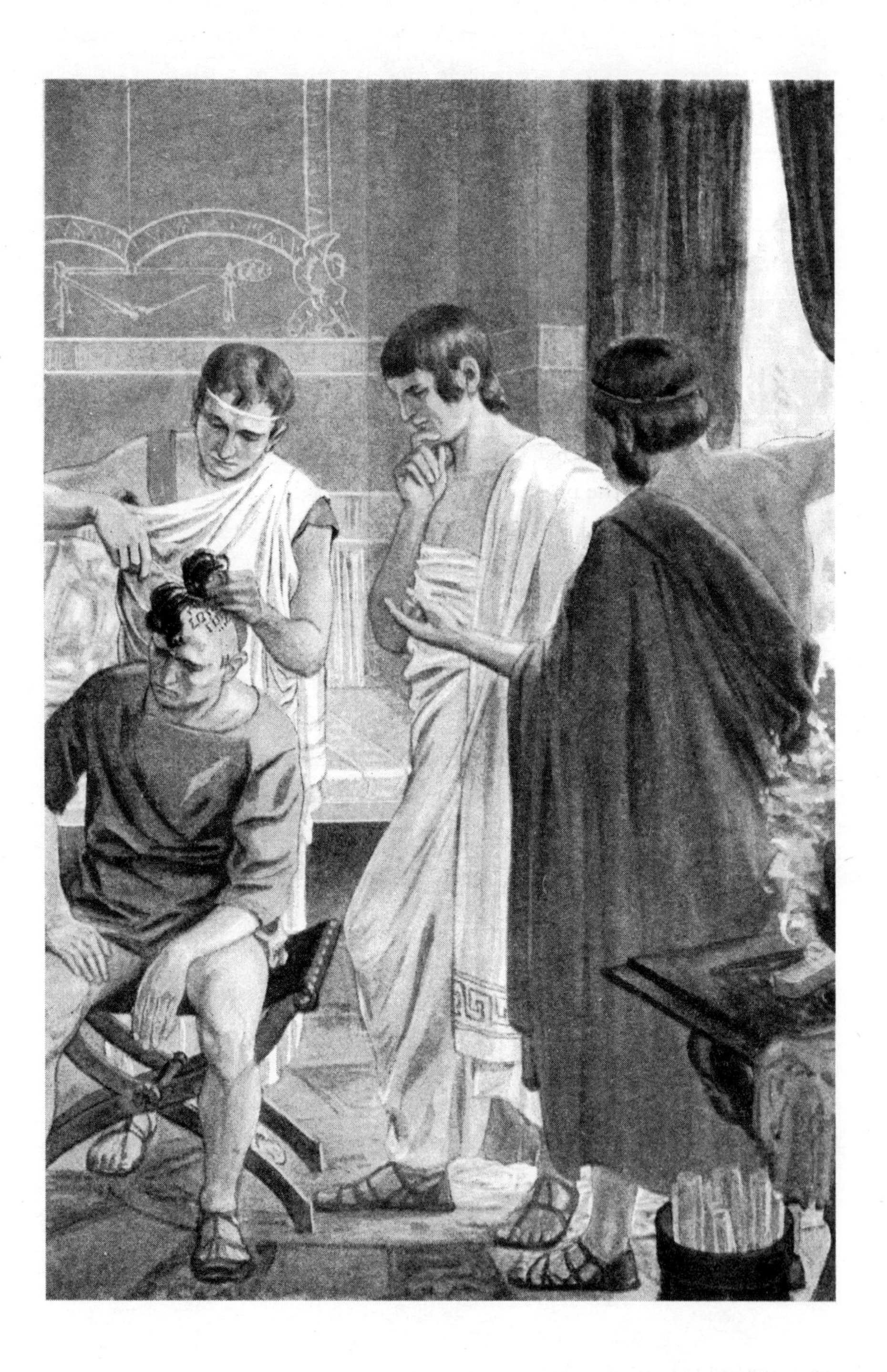

CHAPTER 3

'Call for the revolt of Ionia': Histiaeus' Slave, 499 BCE

> 'He shaved the head of his most faithful slave, tattooed him, and detained him until the hair had grown again . . . and gave the tattooed man no other orders except that when he had come to Miletus, under the presence of Aristagoras, he should request him to shave his head and examine it.'
>
> —Aeneas Tacticus, 31. § 28-29

Histiaeus had been a trusted confidante of Persian King Darius the Great during military victories over the Scythians in the late sixth century BCE. Darius had installed him as a puppet governor of the city of Miletus during his campaigns to conquer the Aegean, which had expanded the Persian Empire by suppressing revolts and conquering both nomadic tribes and Greek cities alike. As a reward for his service, the King had also appointed Histiaeus to take command of Myrcinus, a strategically vital settlement in Ionia, rich in silver, gold and timber.

The tattoo in this tale is not one that was part of dominant Greek culture – the Greeks did not have any tradition of mainstream tattooing, and as was also the case in Persia, the technology of making permanent marks in the skin was used primarily for penal purposes. Even where stories of tattooed Greeks are told by classical authors, they are often a narrative device used to suggest antisocial behaviour or countercultural strangeness: according to one legend, for example, the body of the mystic philosopher-god Epimenides was said to have been

Left: The story of Histiaeus' Slave, illustrated by Max Wulff, 1908

covered in tattooed recitations from his own shamanic incantations. His skin was preserved after death for its magical properties.

Rather than culturally significant or socially strange, however, Histiaeus' clever use of tattooing was instead part of a cunning political plot.

* * *

Histiaeus was Greek, and many of Darius' Persian generals were distrustful of him, and jealous of his proximity to the king. They were especially concerned that he had been granted power over Myrcinus, believing it to be a grave mistake to put a Greek commander in charge of such an important city. One of them, Megabazus, was determined to convince Darius that his Greek confidante was secretly plotting against him, allowing him to win the King's favour. Once the king trusted Histiaeus, Megabazus hoped he would be allowed to rule over Myrcinus instead.

On Megabazus' advice, Histiaeus was ultimately stripped of his power over Myrcinus. Darius had invited him to serve as his trusted confidante in the imperial capital of Susa instead. Sources disagree about whether Megabazus was actually able to convince the king of Histiaeus' treachery, and thus that this invitation was a trick by Darius, or if the Persian general simply bluffed, convincing the king that bringing Histiaeus with him to Susa was a good idea in its own right. But whether Darius was in on the ruse or not, the end result was the same – Histiaeus was dragged to Susa, against his wishes. Megabazus was given command in Myrcinus. Histiaeus' son-in-law Aristagoras, who was also loyal to Darius, was put in charge in Miletus.

In Susa, far from being hailed as Darius' most loyal strategic adviser, Histiaeus quickly found himself isolated and humiliated, a virtual prisoner. In his frustration and his homesickness, desperately looking for a way to win back power in the Persian empire, he formulated a conspiracy: he planned to revolt against the King.

If he could incite rebellion in Miletus, perhaps Darius would send him back at the head of a suppressive force, after winning back the king's favour in victory. Histiaeus had to hope the request would be heeded, but fortunately Aristagoras too had his own motives for rebelling. Whilst in charge of Miletus, he had bungled a military operation and was left fearing reprisals. He was looking also for a way out from under Darius' rule and rapidly running out of options.

To spark the rebellion, Histiaeus urgently needed to send a message to Aristagoras. Susa and Miletus were some 3,000 km apart, and communication between the two men was difficult, and fraught with risk. Persian monarchs had built the world's first transcontinental postal system, a vast network of interconnected way stations, but they thus held a monopoly on the dispatch of mail throughout the empire. Messages could be sent relatively quickly and efficiently over vast distances, but, just like modern governments, the Persian kings were able to use their control of the network strategically to intercept and spy on the communications sent by their subjects.

The roads between Susa and Miletus were heavily guarded by Darius' forces, and the journey would take several weeks. Watchmen along the mail routes were specifically empowered to investigate, read and report on any messages they seized. Any emissary carrying a seditious note or other physical message would risk being stopped, searched, and perhaps killed. Even if it was well concealed, seizure of any evidence that a plot was afoot would scupper the whole plan, and very quickly, both Aristagoras and Histiaeus would also find themselves executed. Clay tablets were cumbersome. Parchment was delicate. The messenger himself might betray the secret to the king. So how might Histiaeus send his message, ensuring that it was kept secret until it was safely in Aristagoras' hands?

In a stroke of ingenuity, Histiaeus developed a cunning plan to conceal his command. Perhaps inspired by the tattoos he must have seen adorning neighbouring cultures, he realised that he could inscribe his instruction permanently onto his messenger's scalp. The tattoo would be hidden by the messenger's hair once it had regrown. The message could not easily be lost, destroyed or altered, and even the most curious of guards wouldn't think to look for a secret seditious note on someone's head.

One last problem presented itself, though. For maximum secrecy, Histiaeus wanted to hide the message from even the messenger himself. Because it was to be written on the top of his head, the slave could not straightforwardly even read the message, reducing risk of disclosure in a moment of loose-lipped indiscretion. But if he knew that his head bore a valuable message whose discovery put him at risk of death, he would perhaps be empowered to betray his master, an all-too-common occurrence in these times of fragile allegiances and shifting loyalties. Histiaeus would thus need to find a way to inscribe the message without the slave knowing he bore a message at all. To convince the young messenger boy to shave his head and undergo the painful procedure without revealing the plan to him, he needed a plausible excuse.

At that moment, Histieaus noticed that the boy's eyes were red and swollen. In ancient Greece, diseases of the eye were thought to be caused by build-ups of fluids in the head. Usefully, for Histieaus' purposes, scarification and bloodletting of the scalp were standard treatments at the time for disorders of the eye, and it was therefore fairly simple to convince the naive servant boy that the ordeal of shaving his head and poking needles into his scalp would be an appropriate remedy for his ailment. As Hippocrates himself would later say, 'Those diseases that drugs do not cure, the knife cures.'

Histiaeus undertook the task himself, shaving the boy's head back to smooth baldness, before taking a needle and using it to poke ink into the thin, white skin he had revealed. Slowly and deliberately, he pricked his message in clear, black letters: 'Histiaeus to Aristagoras, call for the revolt of Ionia.' Skin on the head is delicate, and tattooing it is painful. The frequent needle impacts necessary to drive the ink into the correct layer cause the skull to rattle disorientatingly. As he grimaced, blood ran down the boy's face. Unsurprisingly, it also did very little to improve his eyesight woes.

For Histieaus' purposes, though, the plan had worked perfectly. The boy was bandaged up, in order to conceal the message as it healed. After a week or so, the marks had scabbed over, and boy's hair had regrown sufficiently. He was sent on his way. 'When you come to him,' Histiaeus said, 'say that my son-in-law should shave your head, as I did a little while ago.'

The boy's journey was arduous, but he reached his target without having been discovered, or worse. When he arrived at Miletus, Aristagoras was understandably rather confused by the instruction, unused to impetuous barbering requests from recent arrivals. Nevertheless, he did as the boy requested and called for a razor and a pair of scissors and began cutting away. As the boy's hair fell again to the ground, the message was revealed, etched in now bluish pigment visible through a dry and healing layer of skin. Aristagoras was at first confused, then astonished, and finally emboldened. After consulting with his council, he made his decision. He would call on his forces to take up arms against the king. He would declare Miletus a democracy, free from tyranny. He would spark the Ionian Revolt.

As Darius' forces pushed back over the course of a bloody and protracted series of conflicts, Aristagoras fled fearfully to Thrace, falling in battle at the hands of the Thracian army. Histiaeus' plan did work, at least initially. Pleading ignorance as to the cause of the uprising, he was able to fool Darius, and Greek historian Herodutus reports that the king did decide to send his former right-hand man Histiaeus back to Miletus to help stem the rebellion. When he arrived, however, the people of Miletus were understandably unhappy at the thought of being returned to the yoke of tyranny, and expelled Histiaeus from the city to which he had schemed so hard to return. Enraged, and running out of options, Histiaeus ultimately joined fading rebel Ionian forces in their battles against the Persians, but was captured on the battlefield in a last stand. Pleading for his life, Histiaeus begged to be sent back to Darius' court as a prisoner, perhaps hoping to scheme his way back into the king's affections and save his own skin. Suspecting his plot, Histiaeus' captors instead chose to return him to Darius rather less intact than he had hoped. Fittingly, for a revolt that had begun with a bloody message inscribed onto the top of someone's head, the Persians decided to keep Histiaeus' body to display impaled on a stake, and to send his decapitated head back to Darius in a box. No further message was required. A disembodied skull speaks clearly enough.

* * *

The story of Histieaus' tattooed message comes as part of many similarly apocryphal tales about military strategies and tactics adopted throughout antiquity, including several tales involving cunning ways of hiding messages. Even during the years before the First World War, a story about a duplicitous spy called Elsie Pfitzer, with striking echoes of the ancient Greek tale, appeared in newspapers around the world. Pfitzer, also known by her alias, Ida Müllerthal, reportedly fell in love with a young officer in the German army, who did not have the means to marry her. In his desperation, the officer offered to sell strategic plans of the fortress at which he was stationed to the Russians, who were threatening an invasion of the German empire's eastern borders. Pfitzer offered to smuggle the plans to Russia herself, but in order to transport the plans safely, and without discovery, her lover suggested that he tattoo them permanently across her shoulders. Though she successfully delivered the plans, she was discovered on her return to Germany, and both she and her betrothed faced imprisonment or even execution. (This story seems to have begun in the French satirical magazine *Le Rire* in 1911, and is therefore unlikely to be true, though it graced the pages of *The Washington Post* as a serious news report and was frequently mentioned in the British and Australian press for several months during the summer of 1912, often accompanied by a large illustration of the woman's tattooed shoulders, adorned with diagrams of gun emplacements and the orientation of moats.)

* * *

Elaborate tattooing was practised by many neighbouring tribes with whom the Greeks frequently came into conflict. These tribes included the Scythians, as we will see in the next chapter, as well as the Sarmatians and the Thracians. As such, in an aesthetic tradition still familiar in American and Western European media today, tattooing was a useful shorthand in Greek writing and art to signify barbarianism and exotic otherness. For example, male and female Thracians are often depicted on Greek vases with extensive geometric and animal designs drawn on their arms, necks and feet. As one ancient Greek text explains, 'for Thracians, it is as an adornment for girls to be tattooed, but for other people, it is punishment for wrongdoers'. Indeed, the word 'stigma', which in modern English refers to a metaphorical stain of disgrace or low bearing, comes from ancient Greek, where it referred first to spots on snakeskin, and then to tattoo marks or (later) branding on animals, slaves and criminals.

On enslaved people, tattoos served as marks of ownership and diminished social status, to discourage delinquency and attempts to escape. Tattooing slaves primarily took the form of writing on the face, in order that it would be visible to everyone with whom they

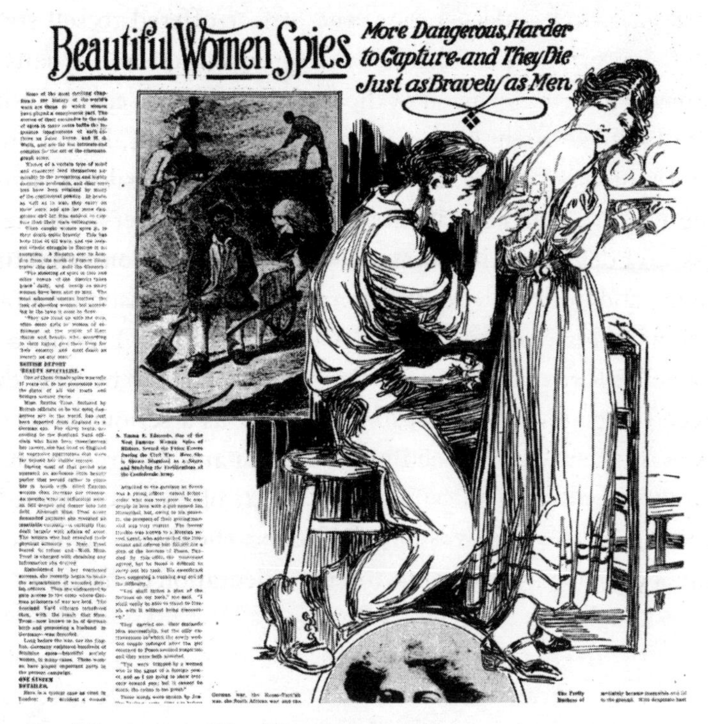

Beautiful Women Spies

More Dangerous, Harder to Capture—and They Die Just as Bravely as Men

Sensationalised illustration of Elsie Pfitzer's story, 1915

came into contact. Such tattoos would send a clear message that the slave, branded as disobedient and cowardly, was to be considered even more abject than slaves in general. In one account purportedly from the fourth century BCE, a slave was forced to bear 'Stop me, I'm a runaway!' on his forehead, a clear indication to onlookers that the man should be apprehended. Facial tattoos could also serve to present a litany of transgressions: in the third century BCE, Herodas Bion described how his father, a freed slave, was left with 'less of a face than a narrative', such was his captor's cruelty in noting his disobediences in tattooed disfigurements. Histiaeus' cryptographic innovation is continuous with this custom of permanently inscribing text on the bodies of lowly men, only with the hope of hiding rather than revealing the message's meaning.

This practice of punitive tattooing is found throughout the Hellenistic period into Roman and Byzantine penal cultures, with criminals forced to wear descriptions of their misdeeds prominently on their faces, enslaved people marked as possessions, and prisoners of war humiliatingly defiled with the iconic symbols of those who had defeated them. Through the early centuries of Christian Europe, tattooing was a commonly codified consequence of law-breaking, and even though the early Christian Emperor Constantine softened the use of the practice in the fourth century, he only ruled that criminals should not be tattooed on their faces, in order to preserve God's image, and not that they be spared being forcibly tattooed in general. Even into the modern period, sixteenth-century Italian polymath Giambattista della Porta wrote that readers of his stories on cryptography and secret messages would find the story of Histiaeus familiar, because slaves in Naples and elsewhere had the names of their masters indelibly inscribed on their faces 'with the point of a needle, or [they] opened it with a razor, and cast in the powder of burnt pine resin'. Branding of deserters and criminals was also common in both nineteenth-century France and Britain, with the marking of men who had fled their enlistments to the British army not fully eradicated until as late as 1879.

Horrifically, in the twentieth century, a teenage girl, one of thousands like her from Korea and China, told the UN Commission on Human Rights that she was captured, taken into sexual slavery and systematically raped by the Imperial Japanese army during the Second World War. As part of her brutal and dehumanising treatment, she was forcibly tattooed 'on the inside of the lips, the chest, the stomach and the body' before being dumped on a mountainside and left for dead. Several elderly survivors in Korea still bear similar tattoos on their skin today. During the Korean War of the 1950s, prisoners of war from the North and from China were often tattooed with anti-communist slogans and pro-Southern imagery whilst in captivity. Across these diverse moments in history, even if these marked men and women were freed from captivity, their tattoos would continue to stigmatise them for the rest of their lives, as they were almost impossible to cover or remove without trace.

Several classical writers describe recipes and tinctures by which tattoo marks might be removed, often through the painful application of searing, caustic substances to the skin, but this would have been in vain – the scar would speak as loudly as the tattoo as to the social status of its bearer. Even if attempts were made to tattoo over the specific descriptions of crimes and misdemeanours, the very presence of heavy tattoo marks on someone's face would serve to ostracise their bearers all the same: one freed slave attempted to obscure his penal marks on his forehead with more aesthetically pleasing stars, but by all accounts, this simply ensured he would forever be subjected to mockery and suspicion. The permanence, of course, was fundamental to tattooing's punitive and shaming character. In a note of hope for Histiaeus' slave, though, one Greek legend does explain that a man named Pandarus did succeed in fully removing what appeared to be tattoo marks on his head. Unfortunately, the solution was not some meticulously mixed tincture or long-forgotten Hellenistic laser technology, but magic: Pandarus miraculously erased his tattoos by visiting a healing cult. In a vision, he saw a god wrapping his tattooed head in a bandage, which lifted the marks away with it when it was removed.

* * *

On receiving Histiaeus' head, Darius was reportedly enraged at his generals in the field for not sending Histiaeus back alive. Refusing to accept the truth of Histiaeus' treachery, he wrapped the embalmed head in fine cloth and ordered it to be buried with military honours to commemorate his prior service. Perhaps if the messenger boy's tattooed head had been sent back at the same time, Histieaus' duplicity ineffaceably inscribed in ink, Darius' reaction might have been rather different. Not every transgression leaves a visible mark.

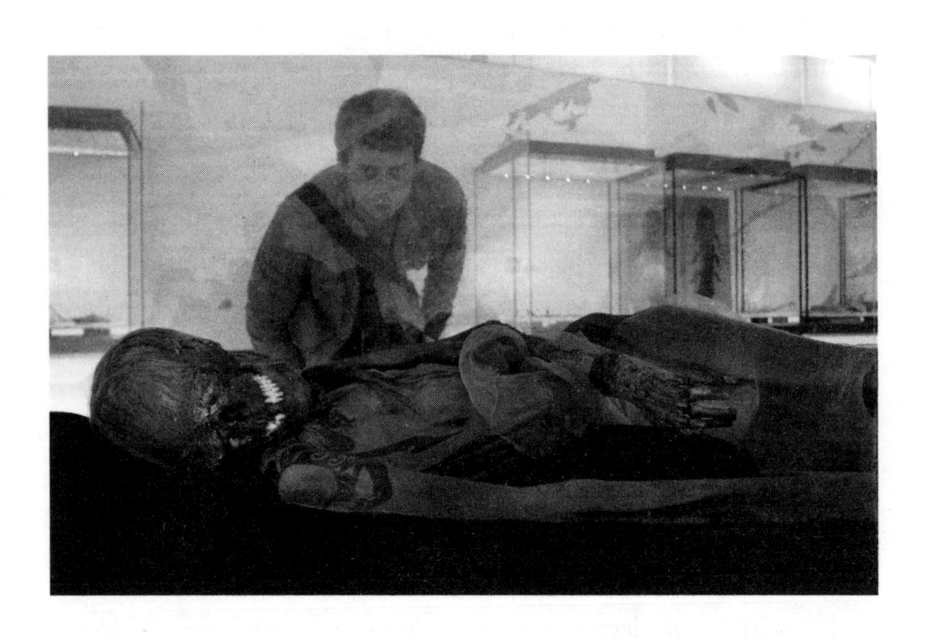

CHAPTER 4

A Lady's Tattoos: Ochy-Bala, the Altai Princess, 277 BCE

'In the crook of the Lady's knee was a red cloth case containing a small hand mirror of polished metal with a deer carved into its wooden back. Beads wound around her wrist, and more tattoos decorated her wrist and thumb. She was tall, about five feet six. She had doubtless been a good rider, and the horses in the grave were her own. As we worked, the fabric gradually revived around her limbs, softening the outline of her legs, the swell of her hip. And somehow, in that moment, the remains became a person. She lay sideways, like a sleeping child, with her long, strong aristocratic hands crossed in front of her. Forgive me, I said to her.'

—Natalia Polosmak, *National Geographic*, October 1994

'The skin bears an ancestral imprintation. The skin is the first boundary, first place of contact, with the past, with one's tribe, with another.'

—Kim Trainor, *Ledi*, 2018

The Lady had died in January during the grip of a cold Siberian winter at the end of a long season herding sheep for winter pasture, but it was June before she was finally buried. Only in the summer, as the weather warmed, had the ground thawed enough that her tomb could be dug sufficiently deeply into the permafrost.

Left: The Lady, or Pazyryk princess, German Archaeological Institute, Berlin

She was in her mid-twenties, and was already riddled with cancer when a bone-shattering fall from her horse brought her short life to an end. Hers was a reverent and extravagant burial, as befitted a woman of high social status within Pazyryk culture. She was buried alone, suggesting celibacy, and her grave, for all its richness, contained no weapons to mark her out as a warrior of any kind. Though she had frequently been called a 'princess' in the years since her discovery, it now seems that she was more likely to have served a shamanic, soothsaying or ritual role. Whatever her profession or position, extreme care and solemnity had been taken to ease her passage into the afterlife. Her internal organs had been removed, replaced with horsehair and fragrant grasses, and her body was carefully embalmed in a waxy ointment to preserve it until it could be properly buried. Her companions had constructed an elaborate and deep funeral barrow to contain her ornate wooden sarcophagus, which was wrapped in decorative tooled leather and held shut with long bronze nails. Inside, she was dressed in fine Chinese silk, and beautifully embroidered boots. She wore a wig on her head; jewellery and a mirror lay by her side. Archaeologists also found the remains of six horses in the tomb, ritually killed at the grave site and themselves finely appointed with bridles, embellished harnesses and felt-covered saddles embroidered in a rainbow of coloured threads with fantastical designs of animals and mythical beasts.

Sometime after burial, when winter returned to the steppes, rains and snow had filled the barrow with water, which then froze solid. Generations later, a man from a rival cultural tradition was buried just above the princess in the same barrow – his kin perhaps intending a great disrespect to the Pazyryk by repurposing their burial mounds – but it is this act of desecration that ultimately ensured her body would lie undisturbed into the late twentieth century. Looters had stripped this man of all his grave goods at some point in the decades or centuries that followed his death, but they had not realised that under him, concealed by stone slabs, another, much richer body lay, as yet undiscovered. To all future visitors, this grave appeared already picked bare of everything worth taking; all that lingered was a lone skeleton, some sheep bones, the remains of three further dead horses and some worthless iron knives. The Pazyryk buried their noble dead with coriander fruits, perhaps as an offering, or to sweeten the smell as the bodies decayed. In the Lady's tomb, though, the coriander had been frozen in a saucer, its decay as arrested as that of the body it accompanied. After several days of painstaking work, more than two millennia after her death in the Altai Mountains of Southern Siberia sometime in 277 BCE, just ten yards from where a fence now crudely demarcates the borderlands between the modern Russian Federation and China, her body was again exposed to the clear summer skies.

Natalia Polosmak, the lead archaeologist on the team who discovered her in 1993, wrote that the Lady's body 'emerged from the ice like a temple rubbing', a tangible image of the past slowly becoming discernible as boiled water was carefully poured over the ice to melt it away. As the ice thawed, more than two millennia later the process released the smell of a meat offering, still laid on a dish in the tomb, impaled with an elaborate knife.

Her jawbone was revealed first. As work continued, the rest of her body began to appear, initially her shoulder, its skin still intact under a fur cape. Polosmak gasped. Pulling the cape aside, she saw that the shoulder bore a tattoo, still bright and vivid after twenty-five centuries, depicting a strange, beaked, deer-like animal with a cascade of antlers. The beast's front hooves are raised in a gallop. Its rear legs curl behind it, almost as if it is leaping from the woman's skin.

Assuming Polosmak's voice for her conceptual poem, *Ledi*, writer Kim Trainor asks: 'Isn't our skin like a photograph? It carries the trace of others. It develops in time. A scraped knee. A tiny scar below the lip. Fingerprints of a lover's grasp smudged blue, then ochre.' This lady's tattooing largely covers her left arm, from shoulder to wrist and onto her hand. The thick lines tracing each image were seemingly as clear and well defined as they were on the day she was buried. Each is tattooed in a carbon-black ink which over time had taken on that murky blue tone still familiar to anyone who had elderly, tattooed relatives in the 1970s. Below the leaping creature with antlers, usually identified as a griffin or horse chimera, is a snow leopard locked in mortal combat with a horned ram. On her forearm sit the hindquarters of another chimeric mammal with a tiger's tail and fearsome claws, and on her wrist, she wears a realistic outline of antlers. The outline of a ram, its hind body also twisted, curves across her left thumb. Her right arm is not so well preserved as her left, but there, too, fragmentary indications of tattooing survive.

* * *

The Pazyryks were from the Altai Mountains of Southern Siberia, and formed part of a broader transcontinental cultural grouping known to the Greeks as Scythians, nomadic and semi-nomadic people who roamed across territories which spanned from the Black Sea to the Ural River between the sixth and the third centuries BCE. Scythian tribes traded along the Silk Road from Greece, along the southern borders of modern-day Russia, through to China, India and Persia, frequently coming into contact with neighbouring cultures, and earning a reputation as fearsome warriors. Writers from adjacent empires, including the Greeks and the Chinese, told of the fearsome, heavily tattooed nomads from across the steppes of Central Europe who wielded spears, arrows and axes in bronze and gold. Hippocrates, for example, wrote that the Scythians 'cauterised their shoulders, arms and hands, chests, thighs and loins, for no other purpose than to avoid weakness and flabbiness and to become energetic'.

Pomponius Mela wrote several centuries later that Scythians 'tattoo their faces and limbs, each more or less in proportion to the prominence of their ancestors, but they all do so with the same marks and in such a way that they cannot be washed off'. Scythian women were described particularly fearfully, and the realities of Scythian culture inspired, at least in part, Greek legends about the mythical Amazons, a race of powerful warrior women. Despite the legends, though, the extravagance and extent of Pazyryk tattooing was never recorded, as none of these ancient authors accurately or adequately described the bestiary of leaping and fighting creatures that Pazyryk men and women actually wore.

The discovery of tattooed bodies in the icy tundra has therefore been revelatory. The Lady's tattoos were particularly well preserved, and thus surprising to Polosmak and her team, but to date, the remains of seven Pazyryk mummies have been found, every one of them tattooed. The first two were discovered in 1947. It was immediately obvious that one, a sixty-year-old man, was extensively tattooed. He bore amongst other images an almost comical-looking rooster on his hand, its tail nestling in the crook of his thumb as its body stretched out to his perfectly preserved thumbnail. The second, a slightly younger woman, did not seem to be tattooed at all, leading to theories that Pazyryk tattooing was perhaps restricted by sex, class, or social role, but in 2004, novel imaging techniques revealed her shoulder, wrist and arm tattoos which had become invisible over the centuries, just like those worn by the Gebelein mummies from Egypt.

The evidence now shows that Pazyryks of both sexes, spanning social hierarchies, all bore elaborate, pictorial tattoos across their bodies. The eldest man whose body is preserved seemed to have been a chieftain, though another was a simple, ordinary warrior. There is no clear difference between the tattooing habits of men and women in either extent or motif, though the female mummies do not have tattooing on their legs. There are such remarkable iconographic and stylistic similarities between them that they clearly form a distinct cultural tradition. Most amazingly of all, it seems likely that several of them were tattooed by the same artist, given how consistent the style is across the Pazyryk bodies.

The designs are almost all of animals, though one woman wears designs that appear to be floral and the first man to be discovered has dots tattooed around his lower back, perhaps therapeutically. Alongside the griffin-horse on the Lady's arm, which recurs on four of the mummies and seems to have been of particular importance, other designs include a veritable bestiary of wildfowl, ungulates, big cats and fish, each depicted with varying degrees of realism and fantasy. One woman, a young noble discovered in 1949, sports on her lower right arm an astonishing scene of three striped cats ambushing and devouring two broad-antlered animals, perhaps an elk and a deer. The design is picked out in graphic black linework, and wraps artfully around her forearm. The scene is so brilliantly and effectively composed that it almost appears as if it is a cell from an animation: a mortal combat frozen in time forever on her arm.

Archaeologists surmise that the images are so consistent in style, and so eloquently placed on the skin in concert with the flow of the wearer's body, that the designs must have been drawn on the skin prior to being tattooed. This ancient master was not working freehand, but perhaps to some ancient equivalent of the design sheets hanging in modern tattoo studios.

As elsewhere, Pazyryk tattooing is intimately intertwined with the wider visual cultures from which it emerges, and the narrow but consistent pictorial vocabulary of Scythian art suggests that the designs form part of a legible iconography – that is to say, the specific tattoos communicated specific and determinate meanings, with close relationships to particular features of mythological and social belief. In nomadic or semi-nomadic traditions, tattooing often takes on particular importance, as tattoos are easier to transport than more tangible indicators of status or affiliation, and cannot be lost or broken. It is therefore not surprising that the same visual languages found in Pazyryk tattoos also appear in their physical objects and artefacts.

In the Lady's case, her tattoos reflect a recognisable and consistent set of designs found on other grave goods, including leatherwork, bronze, felt, embroidered carpets, clothing and objects, some made from wood, some from horn. It is possible that this animal language is heraldic, with specific animals representing particular roles or social groupings, but the current consensus is that the designs are glimpses into spiritual and metaphysical theologies within Pazyryk culture. The mix of real and fantastical animals depicted reveals a belief system that encompasses a realm beyond the mundane realities of conventional animal biology, and as the Scythians also made use of cannabis in ritual contexts, some archaeologists have speculated that the strange beasts may even be representations of hallucinatory visions induced by ingestion of psychedelics. Confusingly, though, even sacrificial horses are frequently buried with headdresses that give the impression of antlers, much like the elk or deer-type creatures seen in Pazyryk tattoo art. Even the tattoos of apparently mystical beasts may thus be reasonably accurate representations of actual Scythian horses wearing decorative masks!

Paying close attention to the visual metaphors contained in many of these images can give us insights into Pazyryk cosmology. Most interestingly, many of the scenes are elaborate depictions of deadly combat between predatory and prey species, indicating a sustained interest in death and rebirth. These fighting beasts perhaps indicate a combative social hierarchy, or represent combative relationships with neighbouring traditions. In particular, the twisted and inverted hindquarters on the Lady's chimeric griffin, which are also found on many other of the animalesque designs, show the creatures at the precise moment between life and death, suspended between this realm and the next, never quite dead, always somehow still living. This is referred to as 'the defeated pose'. The Pazyryk and wider Scythian cultures clearly practised animal sacrifice, including of the horses with which the Lady was buried, and their funeral rites also suggest a complex understanding of afterlives and a sense that Pazyryk burials were a process of passage into another life or realm.

From Pazyryk tattooing, we can also begin to speculate on the wider art history of their culture. The designs, and the flowing, curvilinear style with which they are rendered, are comparable to similar compositions in a range of art forms from Western Asia, China and Northern India, suggesting that the Siberian Scythians engaged in creative contact with the East. Of course, the simple, legible resonances of images of fighting beasts in mortal combat have long featured in – and remain – popular in Western and Asian tattooing, because they speak to something quite fundamental about human experience. Tattooing, like many folk art and indigenous artistic practices, is conservative, preserving imagery and iconography over centuries, if not millennia. Designs are repeated and deployed frequently, often communicating quickly and bluntly rather base and universal emotions about fear, hope and familial ties. Stylistic evolution accentuates and exaggerates the most clearly expressive parts of the image, simplifying meanings and styles in harmony with each other over time, and turning them into a recognisable set of symbols.

* * *

Pazyryk tattooing was poked with a needle using inks made from organic pigments fashioned from burnt plants. After tattooing, the wound would have been rubbed with an ointment of soot and fat, to darken the design and protect from infection during healing. Technologically, the precise details are hard to discern. No objects that can be definitively identified as Scythian tattooing kits have been found, and unlike the bone needles of North American tattooing, it is harder to differentiate metal tattooing needles from needles used for other purposes. Recently, however, presumed tattooing tools have been identified in burial sites of neighbouring cultures, giving us the closest possible glimpse to date of how Pazyryk tattoos might have been produced.

The Sarmatians were a nomadic community of Scythians whose history is intertwined with rival Scythian groups across the steppes. The Sarmatians are also recorded in Greek sources as undertaking tattooing. Between 2004 and 2007, archaeologists excavated several funeral barrows containing the skeletons of Sarmatian women at a site north of the modern border between Russia and Kazakhstan, discovering an incredible set of tools. The kits – or 'complexes' of objects – comprised everything these women would have needed to draw a design on the skin, produce a pigment and undertake a tattoo, all in a handy, portable format. For drawing, the kits included a broad stencilling marker carved from bone or fashioned from bronze, and were paired with a leather pouch for carrying pigments. Pigment traces suggested that Sarmatians tattooed with inks made from minerals including ochre and charcoal, as well as with organic compounds from plants. Wonderfully, these pigments are not just in black, but also in red, yellow and pink, suggesting that Sarmatian tattooing may have been multicoloured.

The kits also include stone palettes for holding pigment during tattooing, small bowls made from horse teeth or walnut shells for grinding pigments into inks, and specialised spoons for transferring pigments from the pouches to the palettes and for stirring the ink mixture during the process. The needles themselves are fashioned from gold or from iron, and feature twists along their length to aid grip, as well as tapered edges, useful perhaps for scraping blood from the surface of the skin as the artist worked.

Unfortunately, however, other identifications are equally likely for these toolkits, and they may just as likely have been cosmetic kits, kits for needlework, or a range of tools for ritual or medico-magical purposes. Most problematically for the tattoo tool hypothesis, many of the presumed Sarmatian tattooing needles feature eyelets at their end, which rather works against their identification as tattoo tools and suggest instead a utility for sewing with thread. Pazyryk tattooing was certainly not sewn in in the same manner as Arctic tattooing might have been, for example, and whilst it is not inconceivable that a rival, but closely related group tattooed in a radically different manner, new discoveries and new forms of analysis will be needed if we are to be able to be more definitive.

* * *

In light of the narrow range of evidence available to us, the secrets of the Lady's tattooing are likely to remain mysterious and opaque into the future. Climate change has accelerated the melting of the Siberian permafrost, which will ultimately mean fewer bodies are preserved for future discovery. More importantly, though, shifting and contentious questions of both geopolitical identity and museum ethics have rendered archaeological work in the Altai region and the display and investigation of ancient bodies controversial.

Since her discovery in 1993, the Lady has gone by a number of names in both the media and academic literature, each ascribing to her a geographic place of origin and a social role. Aside from simply being 'the Lady', she has also variously been called a princess and a maiden. She has been claimed to have hailed from Siberia, from Ukok (after the plateau where she was buried), or from Altai, after the mountain range and its associated ethnic republic.

In the turbulent debates about ethnonationalist identity after the fall of the Soviet Union, she became the subject of increasingly acrimonious arguments about her identity in relation to the contemporary inhabitants of the region. Locals call her 'Ochy-Bala', identifying her specifically as a legendary figure of Altai epic folklore. The Altai people saw her incautious exhumation by Russian and international scientists as an act of desecration, and she has become an enduring symbol of their ethnic and national identity, distinct from Russia. Russian scientists, by contrast, argued on the basis of DNA analysis that she was not directly genetically related to the contemporary populations in the region, and should be understood instead as Russian, undermining contemporary Altai claims to indigenous rights over their land in the process. This struggle over the Lady has become a microcosm of a much larger set of conflicts over Altai identity, and, as one indigenous politician has claimed, 'sometimes it is difficult to openly talk about politics, so we use her as a metaphor to discuss the difficult position of Altaians in Russia. Claiming her is claiming our land.'

After twenty years being studied and displayed elsewhere in the Russian Federation, the Lady's body was ultimately returned to the Altai Republic to much fanfare and ceremony. Her body is now housed in a purpose-built museum curated by indigenous specialists. The museum takes a proudly activist stance on Altai nationalism, and the return of the Lady was a particular symbol of emboldened identity and increasing sovereignty and regional autonomy from the Kremlin. Nevertheless, as part of an arguably cynical game of necropolitics – the politics of the dead – the museum was financed by donations from the oil giant Gazprom, which was seeking legitimisation and local political support for pipeline construction across Siberia.

The Gazprom-financed institution has become a cultural and political hub for indigenous rights, and has empowered regional indigenous politicians to raise their status and win elections. Nevertheless, this activism has arguably bought Gazprom important political influence in the region. It has also resulted in the banning of future excavations of funerary sites and a commitment to the protection of the vast pastures of the Ukok plains, and to the increasing understanding that it is unacceptable to treat these ancestral bodies simply as loci of curiosity. Tattooing has often been used to signal otherness, but for the Lady, it is deeply meaningful and important to articulate where she belongs.

PART TWO

TATTOOS IN THE EARLY MODERN WORLD

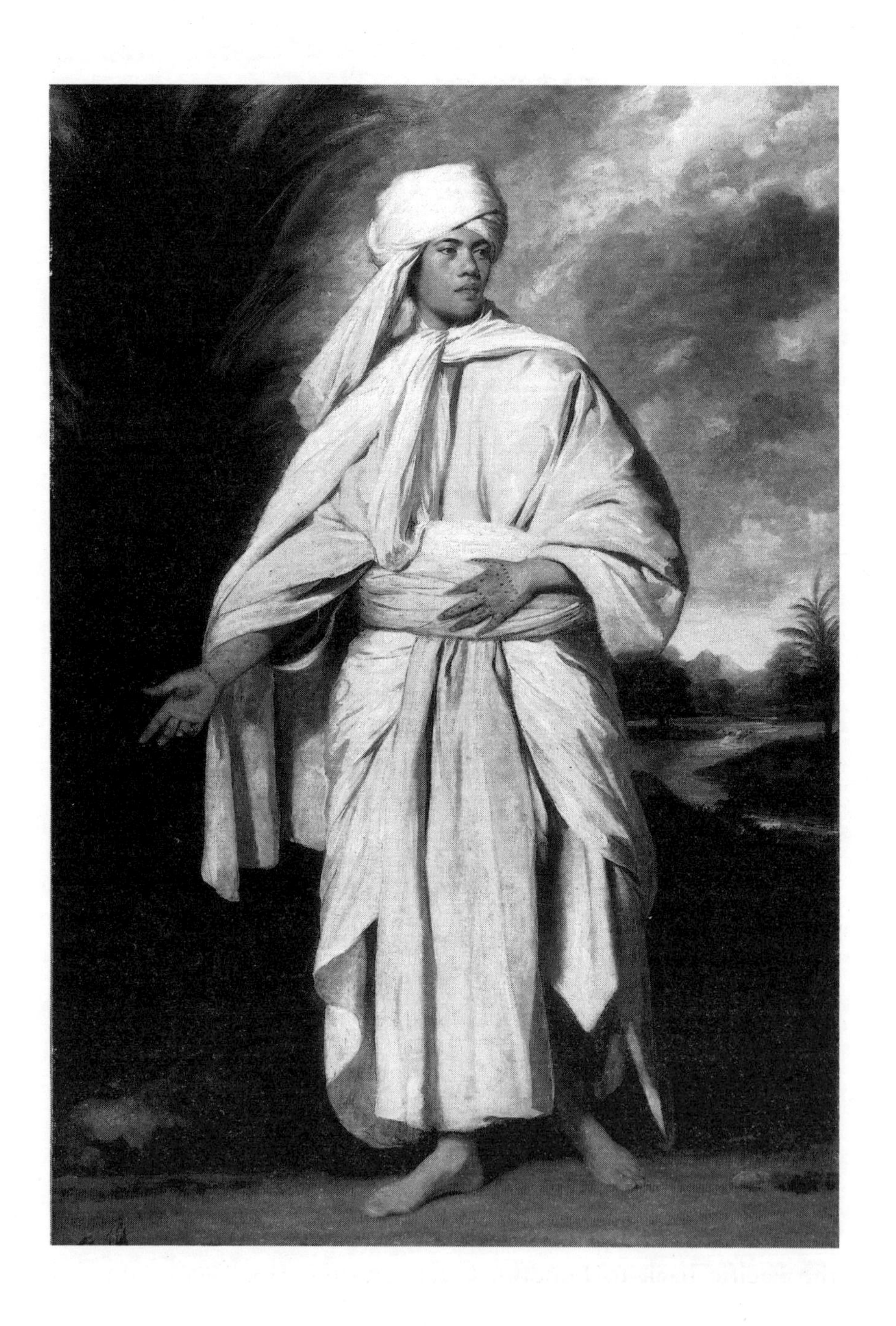

TATTOOS IN THE EARLY MODERN WORLD 'FROM TIME IMMEMORIAL'

'Both sexes paint their bodys, tattow . . . This is done by inlaying the Colour of black under their skins in such a manner as to be indelible.'

—Captain James Cook, 12 July 1769

'The European seamen also, particularly in the Northern kingdoms and the British Islands, have from time immemorial marked themselves with a kind of tattooing, by pricking on their arms, legs and sometimes on other parts of their bodies, single figures, for instance, the cross, letters, or names.'

—*Literary Gazette*, 1819

The earliest use of the word 'tattoo' in its modern English sense and spelling is in a letter written by English novelist Fanny Burney to playwright Samuel Crisp. Burney's brother James sailed with Captain James Cook on his second and third voyages to the Pacific, and as such, she was afforded something of a front-row seat for the objects, stories and even people that had returned with Cook to London.

On 1 December 1774, Burney was invited to have dinner with Omai, a man from Ra'iātea in the Society Islands whom Cook had met in Tahiti, and who had travelled with the fleet from the Pacific back to London. Omai was feted in London for his

Left: Omai, painted by Joshua Reynolds, 1776

charm and intelligence, and though treated as something of a curiosity in the English press, he was not subjected to the indignities and violence to which people taken captive in the Americas in previous decades and centuries had been. Instead, he was invited to theatre showings and social gatherings at grand houses in the city, and it was at one such evening that Burney recorded that Omai's hands were 'very much tattooed, but his face is not at all'.

In her letter, 'tattoo' is effaced, and scruffily overwritten with a correction to 'tattow'. Cook had recorded in his own journal that the practice of skin-marking which he documented on Tahiti was called '*tattow*' in the indigenous language, where it also refers more generally to the practice of writing, and several early sources did adopt that particular spelling. Now rendered as 'tatau', though, the word evokes the sounds made by traditional Tahitian tattooing tools, as a mallet beats out repetitive tapping sounds on a hafted, comb-toothed tool to insert pigment into the skin. Ta! Too! Ta! Too!

Burney's confusion about the term was understandable. The word, like the practice itself, was at once familiar and bizarre. Though it was not used to refer to skin-marking, 'tattoo' had existed in English since at least 1644 to denote a military drumbeat, a meaning whose roots are also clearly onomatopoeic. As such, the new term from Tahiti took on the more familiar English spelling, and 'tattoo' became the all-encompassing word to describe permanent, inky marks in the skin, whether from the Pacific, or anywhere else.

Cook's voyages thus impose a linguistic lacuna on tattoo history and its historiography. There are no 'tattoos', in some sense, before 1769. It has often been suggested that tattooing was discovered in the Pacific, and that Europeans in general, and the English in particular, did not ever know, or had perhaps simply forgotten, about permanent skin-marking technologies before the late eighteenth century. In 1908, US Navy Surgeon A. Farenholt wrote that 'the custom probably originated among the natives of the South Sea Islands . . . whence it was carried by admiring voyagers to home ports and in turn imitated by the envious', and the idea also features prominently in Hanns Ebensten's book *Pierced Hearts and True Love* from 1953, a seminal work on the history of tattooing ('With the Voyages of Discovery Europeans rediscovered this form of personal adornment'). In 1971, *Newsweek* wrote that 'as Christianity spread in Europe, the craft of the tattoo . . . died, even in cultural memory' and that 'it came back in the seventeenth century through contact with Polynesian peoples in the Pacific.' This belief survives in many academic and popular accounts right through to the present day. But as we have already seen, and will further explore over the course of the following chapters, tattooing was common around the world throughout human history, but fascinatingly, it was also well known from descriptions of mainstream and marginalised practices closer to home.

* * *

Before the word 'tattooing' came to define the permanent marking of skin, these practices and the marks in which they resulted were called things like 'pricking' or 'staining' or 'marking' in English. Without a specific word for the habit of marking the skin permanently with ink prior to the late eighteenth century, it has been difficult for historians to assemble a full picture of how widely tattooing was practised and how commonly it was known about in Europe. Nevertheless, evidence is now rapidly amassing that tattooing was continually present, and continually documented, in Europe throughout the early modern period.

One of the best attested and longstanding uses of what would become known as tattooing in Europe was to mark children for the purposes of identification. In late sixteenth-century Italy, for example, foundling children who were abandoned into the care of hospitals in Rome, Venice and Siena were routinely marked with an identifying insignia on one of their feet, pricked out in carbon-black with a lancet. Such a tattoo would ensure that if a baby died in the care of a wet nurse, she could not substitute the body of the poor deceased infant with an abducted, live impostor. Of course, these marks had the effect of literally stigmatising foundlings throughout their lives. Similarly, in 1754, an English anthropologist recorded that parents in the Austrian alps used to 'mark some image' on their children before sending them away to work for rich farmers in Germany, sometimes for years on end. These 'Swabian children' endured a long, arduous period of toil many hundreds of miles from home and would often be unrecognisable to their families when they eventually returned. Their tattoos were familiarly made 'with a needle, or with the point of a knife; and these marks being rubbed over with a particular black ink, they never wear out, but many years after prove the means of evincing their consanguity'.

Even when not explicitly applied for the purposes of identification, tattooing proved useful in tracking down miscreants and runaways. 'Indian Ink' marks crop up relatively frequently, for example, in record books of dockworkers, and in descriptions of indentured servants in the American colonies during the eighteenth century who had fled their masters and who were now on the lam.

Many of these marked men and women seemed simply to bear their own names or initials: for example, in January 1769, a transported convict called John Abbot fled captivity soon after having arrived in Virginia, identifiable by his initials 'marked with Indian Ink' on his left arm. In another story from 1748, landowner Matthew Hopkins was seeking the whereabouts of a British servant, John Kent, a cabinet maker. Kent, Hopkins' advert tells us, 'has on one of his arms the letters JC, with several flourishes round it, done as he says by a Turk, who instead of putting a K put a C'. In the eighteenth century, just as today, it was important to find a tattooist who could spell!

Beyond the marking of names, though, many of these servants also had extensive pictorial designs, primarily of a religious nature. In one striking example from 1739, landowner Benjamin Fendall was offering a reward for the return of John Headford, an escaped English servant, sailor and cook thus described: 'on one of his Arms is represented, our Saviour upon the Cross between two Thieves; and on the other, the Image of Adam and Eve'. In 1766, one Francis Power, born in Dublin, was similarly marked 'with Indian Ink or Gunpowder on both his arms, under his shirt, with the figure of our Saviour crucified, and upon the upper part of his right thumb, has the date of the year 1761 on it'.

In these decades before the Pacific encounters, we must presume that people like Headford, Power, Abbot and €Kent were tattooed, or tattooed themselves, in England, in America, at sea, or, at least in Kent's case, in another cultural context entirely. And it is clear, too, that this pre-Cook tradition of religious tattooing on ordinary people was not a phenomenon confined to British subjects: a similar image was documented by the Spanish Inquisition in 1743 on the arm of a rose and lemon seller named Lorenzo. Lorenzo was reported to the Inquisition after a witness spotted that the tattoo of Christ on his arm also blasphemously featured the word *carajo*, a slang term for 'cock'. Even though Lorenzo had sought to obscure the profanity under thick black lines, he was imprisoned for the offence.

* * *

As had also been the case for the Ancient Greeks, Persians and Han Chinese, European discourse came to conceptualise tattooing as indicative of the supposed degeneracy of other cultures as compared to their own. Pseudo-scientific narratives of cultural evolution began to use tattooing as just one signifier of 'primitiveness', 'otherness' and 'savagery', and by the early twentieth century such perceptions had ossified into a deep-seated belief that tattooing was the most visible indication that colonised peoples were fundamentally different in character from Europeans.

But these marks on servants, foundlings and dockworkers prove without a doubt that tattooing was present on European bodies and in the European consciousness in the months, decades and even centuries before the colonial voyages to Tahiti, Hawaii, Samoa and New Zealand. Moreover, they demonstrate that tattooing was not, or at least not straightforwardly, a practice alien to European life and imported from elsewhere.

That leaves us with something of a conundrum. Given that tattooing was well attested in Europe and on European bodies throughout the seventeenth and eighteenth centuries, the question remains as to why the idea that tattooing was fundamentally something foreign became so pervasive in the contemporary imagination. It is also unclear how so many centuries of accumulated information about tattooing at home and abroad evaporated from common knowledge in the West, and why the resulting amnesia about tattooing's historical circumstances largely persisted throughout the twentieth century, and even into the twenty-first.

In earlier centuries, antiquarian writers had understood tattooing as a shared element of diverse human cultures, and even in times and places where tattooing was not part of the dominant cultural practice, had at least acknowledged its existence. In the wake of the colonisation of the Pacific, however, a shadow fell over historical research, and very quickly any clear sense of European tattoo history faded into obscurity, strengthening and perpetuating perceptions of cultural hierarchies.

Widespread understanding of tattoo history became so untethered from the historical evidence, and even from institutional and cultural memories, that the ways in which dominant narratives about tattooing in Western writing shift over successive centuries reveal as much about attitudes to cultural difference and colonial ambition as they do about the history of tattooing itself. Descriptions of tattooing in this sense become a lens through which we can understand developing ideologies about the relationships between cultural traditions across time and geography, and when we can juxtapose the claims made about tattooing's history with a more fulsome account of what was actually undertaken, it becomes possible to shine light on some of the blind spots and the cynical intellectual manoeuvres that sustained colonial power.

Tattooing was not an early modern discovery for Europeans. As we saw in previous chapters, tattooing in Europe had been practised for millennia and documented for centuries prior to Cook's trip. And yet, as we'll see in the following section, European writers had also documented, depicted and marvelled at tattooing in Asia and in the Americas since the thirteenth century.

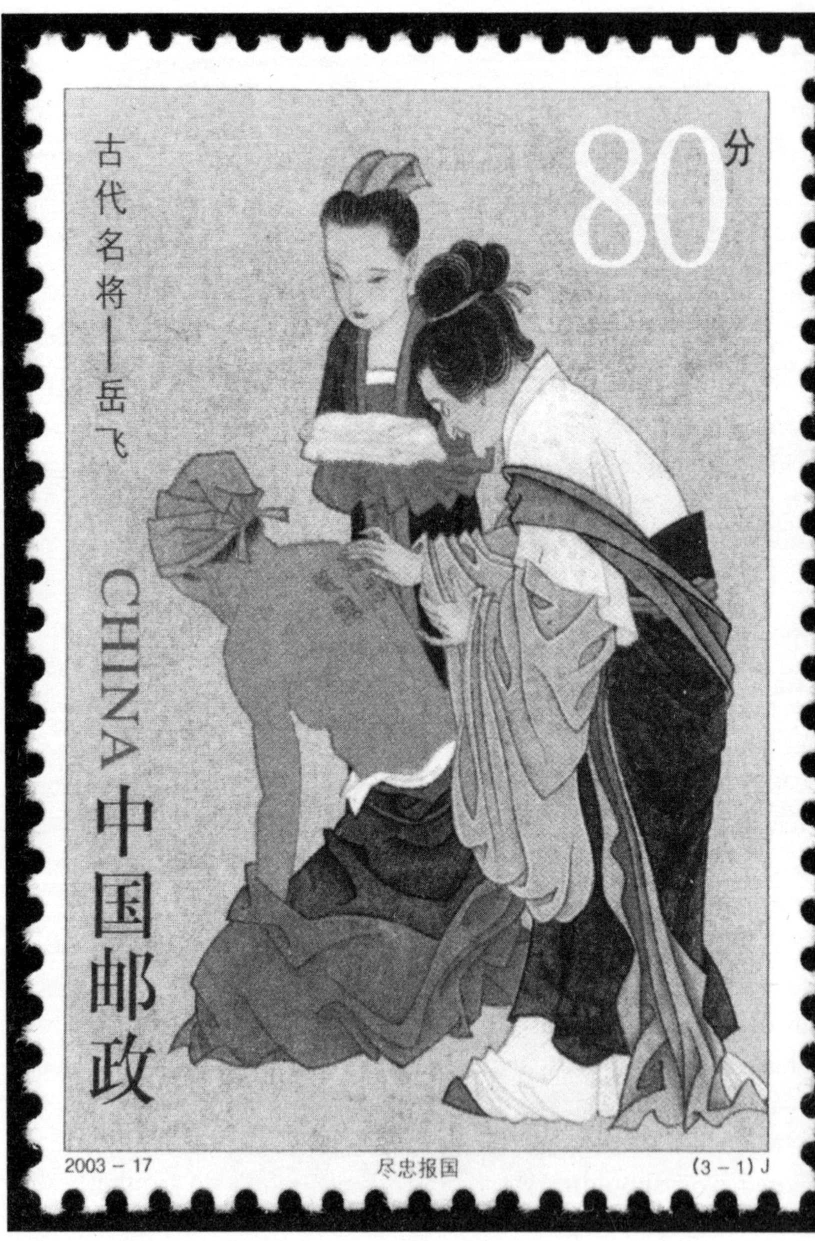
古代名将——岳飞
80分
CHINA
中国邮政
2003-17
尽忠报国
(3-1) J

CHAPTER 5

'Serve the nation with utmost loyalty': Yue Fei, 1122

> 'I raise the embroidery needle but cannot carve. The skin is blue and white. Lines of words and drops of blood make the heroic text all line up as loyalty and filial piety. So solid and permanent that even Heaven can take it as a standard.'
>
> —Madame Yue, in Zhu Liangqing's *Duo Qiu Kui,* 1957

Madame Yue proved to be a somewhat reluctant tattooer. Her son, Yue Fei, lay prone on the table in front of her, his broad, muscular back unclothed and damp with sweat.

War was raging at the far edges of the Song Empire, as northern Jurchen tribes rebelled. Yue was deeply afraid that the Song court was at risk of falling, and that the country he held so dear could be lost imminently. He wanted to fight. He needed to fight.

As he prepared to head to the battlefront, he pledged to inscribe his resolve, his patriotism and his loyalty to the emperor into the very skin of his back. 'I want you to mark four characters on my skin,' he had told his mother, 'as a vow not to follow treacherous people. What do you think?'

'My child!,' she replied, incredulously. 'If you really are so devoted, you shouldn't worry that things won't go to plan! Why on earth would you want to be tattooed? It's not very patriotic to hurt yourself!'

Left: Yue Fei being tattooed, Chinese postage stamp

Yue Fei insisted. His proud mother tattooing a nationalist slogan onto his back would itself be symbolic. Familial loyalty would be transferred to the nation. With her blessing, in this act, her son would become connected not just to his family, but to the whole country.

Chastened, she reluctantly agreed. So reluctantly, in fact, that as she brought the embroidery needles down towards her son's body, she was crying gently. She did not want to hurt him, and she did not want to lose him. With hesitation and gentle concern, her hands were shaking as she began to mark him as he'd asked her to. Slowly, she pricked out four large characters on his skin. Yue's wife watched nearby, playing her own role in the ceremony by grinding soot into a fine, powdery pigment which Madame Yue could rub into her son's freshly bleeding wounds.

At the end of the ordeal, blue lines on Yue's back spelt out *jin zhong bao guo*: serve, nation, utmost, loyalty.

* * *

Yue Fei is a famous twelfth-century Chinese military general. Between 1122 and 1141, he fought for the armies of the Southern Song dynasty against rebellious uprisings of northern Jurchen tribes during the Jin-Song Wars. In legends, he is frequently depicted as almost superhuman, with extraordinary strength and mastery of archery, spear-fighting and hand-to-hand combat. His martial prowess and unwavering loyalty to the territorial integrity of his nation have made him a legendary folk hero to generations of Chinese people, and over the centuries scenes from his life have been made into plays, operas, contemporary television dramas and even video games.

As a military hero, an unwavering patriot and a martyr against treachery, Yue Fei has become one of the most recognisable, powerful and enduring embodiments of Chinese national allegiance in the modern cultural imagination. His life story is both fable and parable, teaching honour, loyalty and commitment in the context of national struggle. At the centre of his legend is the fierce and proud nationalism signified by his tattoo, which acts as a poetically expressive distillation of political ideas that have underpinned Chinese national identity for centuries.

The tale of his tattooing has become more elaborate over the centuries, so that it best serves the mood and the message of each storyteller. In most versions of his life story, the scene where Yue is tattooed serves as a vivid and pivotal moment of the narrative, with the painful ordeal and its associated bloodshed testifying to his sincerity and fortitude, as well as foreshadowing his martyrdom at the hands of a traitor.

Many years after being tattooed, the story goes, having won fame and glory on the northern battlefields, Yue was arrested by a political rival named Qin Hui on false charges of treason. Facing death, he pleaded with the judge to understand that he was a true patriot, and that the charges against him were scurrilous lies. Just as the judge was poised to pass sentence, in a moment of high courtroom drama, Yue's shirt ripped open to reveal his true convictions proudly etched into his skin, just as his mother had made them. The judge was aghast. No traitor would have such a nationalistic slogan on his body! Yue Fei proudly wore an oath of indelible commitment to his country! Thwarted and embarrassed in the courtroom, Qin Hui and his wife nevertheless plotted to ensure that Yue would be put to death anyway, and in different versions of the story, Yue is judiciously executed on a trumped-up charge, poisoned, stabbed or strangled at the hands of Qin's men.

Other versions of the narrative have his mother actually present in a courtroom scene where Yue is set to be executed not for treason, but for unjustly killing another man. In desperation, she pleads with the judge to take notice of his tattoo, a clear sign of his evident moral character. Miraculously, in these tellings the judge takes Madame Yue's pleas to heart and is convinced to spare the sainted Yue from the death penalty because of the marks on his skin. 'I almost accidentally killed a pure-hearted lowborn hero,' the judge exclaims, before setting him free.

In other versions of this tale, Madame Yue decides to give him a tattoo not in preparation for war, but instead as a commemoration of Yue's decision to renounce a pirate chief who had offered him riches to betray the national army. In this telling, the tattoo she applies *after* the event is intended to ensure that he does not forget the lessons about fidelity she had taught him as a child, with the permanent patriotic oath ensuring that her maternal wisdom endures in him long after her death. In every version, the fact that tattoos are indelible, painful to acquire, and strikingly legible to observers are vital both to the progression of the plot and to the encoding of the story's moral messages.

* * *

In modern China, the story of Yue Fei's patriotism and the national commitment that he literally embodies continues to animate cultural conversations. Since the 1950s, teaching about Yue Fei's legend has on occasion struggled to reconcile his status as a national hero with the fact that his enemies, the Jurchen, are now understood to be part of the nation themselves. A unified, pan-ethnic conception of Chinese identity evolved over the twentieth century, and so a figure who represents ethnic division at the expense of national unity within the borders of the modern Chinese nation state has often been controversial. The tattoo on his back relates to a rather different conception of Chinese nationhood than that promoted by many contemporary nationalists. Nevertheless, despite occasional protests to the contrary from some public commentators, the government do continue to hail Yue Fei in their pantheon of important national heroes.

However, the celebration of Yue Fei's tattoo is somewhat unusual in Chinese history. Though tattooing seems to have been fairly common in the Han military as marks of either identification or filial association, tattooing has been generally stigmatised in Han culture since antiquity. In common with Greeks, Persians, Romans and others, tattooing was a useful shorthand to demarcate social deviance and foreignness. As such, tattooing has been particularly associated in Chinese texts with the 'barbarian' cultures of China's distant borderlands, with the marking of slaves and with the forced stigmatisation of criminals as part of a long list of punishments.

For the culturally dominant Han, who did not have an indigenous tattoo tradition of their own, tattooing has served as a deeply ingrained marker of otherness, demarcating particular ethnic groups from their own 'civilised' culture dominated by Confucianism's ideas of bodily integrity and purity. Minority ethnic groups throughout China have carried out various kinds of tattooing on their bodies and faces since antiquity, and several island communities including in Taiwan have also undertaken the practice. To accentuate this cultural distance, different tribal groups across China were frequently described as manifesting their differences from the Han through dress, culinary habit, hairstyle and tattooing. Song-era texts often sweepingly describe all southern tribes as being tattooed, though later ethnography begins to be more specific: the Yi and Yue people, in the southeast, tattooed their bodies and cut their hair short; the Man people from modern-day Vietnam apparently tattooed their foreheads and blackened their teeth; and in a more positive depiction, the Li people on the island of Hainan off the mainland's southern coast 'embroidered' the faces and necks of women as marks of status and maturity.

Records of this indigenous tattooing in the Far East reached medieval Europe in the writings of Marco Polo. In the account of his travels through Asia between 1271 and 1295, readers learn about tattooing in southern China and northern Vietnam. In the area of modern-day Quanzhou in the southeast of China, for example, Polo describes a veritable tattooing trade on visitors who flock from far and wide to be 'painted with needles'. In the southwest, he claims that men 'take five needles tied together, with which they prick their flesh until the blood flows; then they put a black dye on, which cannot come off'. The bands of black dots they etch into their arms apparently served as markers of nobility and elegance.

In Vietnam, Polo presents an elaborate description of the process, vividly writing in detail about how the tattooing there was done:

> All the people, both men and women, are painted from head to toe in the way I will tell you. They have pictures made with needles all over their skin, depicting lions and dragons and birds and many other forms and done in such a way that they are indelible. They have them on their faces, their necks, their bellies, their hands, their legs and everywhere else. This is the procedure. To begin with, the person being painted has the various images he has chosen sketched out in black all over his body. This done, he is tied hand and foot and

> held down by two or more men. Then the artist takes five needles, four fastened together in the form of a square and the fifth in the centre, and starts pricking the client all over, following the outlines of the drawings. The instant the pricks have been made ink is applied to them, and eventually the figure as sketched appears in these pricks. Meanwhile the client suffers such agonies that they might be thought sufficient to serve out purgatory. In fact many of them die while they are under the needle, for they lose a great deal of blood. But they go through with it in the name of gentility; for the more pictures they sport, the more refined and desirable they are held to be.

Tattooing is in fact so central to the folk history of Vietnam that the patriarch of the nation's founding dynasty, Hung Vuong, is said to have told his people to tattoo their bodies so as to ward off crocodiles. Medieval Chinese writings claim that the tattoos in Vietnam were supposed to prevent harm from 'flood dragons', and even as late as the fifteenth century, a chronicle records a conversation with a Vietnamese man who claimed that 'we tattoo our bodies with the designs of the Dragon Lord, so that when we swim in the river, serpents will not violate us'. Though modern scholars disagree, the name of Hung Vuong's kingdom, Văn Lang, had even long been claimed to translate, much like the Celtic name for Britain, to 'Land of the Tattooed People'.

The first Italian trader to visit the Far East after Polo's return, Italian merchant Niccolò de' Conti, also explains Eastern tattooing to a wide audience, writing that 'both men and women of this country prick themselves, making diverse marks, and of diverse colours, on their bodies'. Versions of Conti's 1444 tale were amongst the most influential late medieval accounts of the Orient, and were translated and read across Europe, inspiring generations of explorers and merchants to head east. John Frampton even included Conti's text alongside the first English translation of Polo's *Travels* in 1579.

* * *

As tattooing in ancient and medieval China was largely considered a marker of ethnic otherness and primitive savagery, its use as an active mode of social stigmatisation held a particular cultural resonance. Indeed, accounts of the history of tattooing also functioned in later Han texts as a way of indicating cultural progress, as the apparent abolition of the brutal punishments of the past signalled that modern readers were living in more enlightened times.

As these writers sought to minimise accounts of the use of penal tattooing in the distant past, it is difficult to know with any certainty just how widespread the practice was, though penal codes and legal texts make frequent mention of it. For example, a first-century book on the history of punishments in ancient China asserts that during the Zhou dynasty, which ruled swathes of China between 1050 BCE and 771 BCE, over five hundred crimes were considered 'ink crimes', or *mo zui*, for which prisoners were subject to forcible punishment by tattooing before being sent to guard the city gates. A wound was gouged into the prisoner's forehead and ink rubbed into it as it bled, marking these criminals as 'people of knife and ink' for the rest of their lives.

Despite having been legally abolished by Emperor Wen in 167 BCE, evidence of the tattooing of criminals, or in lieu of the payment of a fine, continued for several centuries, and eventually returned as a legally sanctioned punishment. One dramatic story of such a punishment from the seventh century CE concerns a high-ranking Tang Dynasty court official called Shangguan Wan'er, a young woman who had been enslaved by the Empress Wu Zetian since birth but who had risen to such prominence due to her skill as a writer and political aide that modern historians have occasionally referred to her as China's first female prime minister. Historical texts record that Shangguan disobeyed the empress's will, which should have seen her beheaded, but Wu Zetian chose instead to spare her, tattooing her face as an alternative, disfiguring punishment.

Sources are divided on the exact nature of her crime, but one suggests that she had fallen in love with a man who was also a lover of Wu Zetian's, which explains the desire to mar her beauty. In a fictionalised version of this tale told in 1960, Shanggaun is involved in hiding details of a political conspiracy. In this retelling, the tattoo is a plum blossom inked squarely on her forehead, which in the story's narrative binds her closer to the empress. In an echo of Yue Fei's legend, this modern retelling sees Shangguan's tattoo as marking her as the property of the imperial family, cementing her commitment to the dynastic cause.

The pigment in Shangguan's tattoo may have been made from a mixture of a peacock's gallbladder and verdigris, the green-coloured carbonate that forms on copper as it weathers. Tang-era texts describe the use of peacock gallbladder for the purposes of tattooing ink, as do earlier writings from the fourth century. In the later Tang period, author Duan Chengshi documented a range of tattoos that might even be described as fashionable: so-called 'flower makeup', supposedly inspired by stories of Sangguan's tattooed face, and more delicate red beauty spots pricked with cinnabar, inspired by the legend of the third-century courtesan Lady Deng. Lady Deng's cheek had been scarred accidentally as her husband Sun He flailed drunkenly about, and a physician sought to heal the wound with an unconventional tincture of otter marrow, jade and amber. A small red scar formed, and legend has it that all Sun He's future paramours marked their cheeks with red tattoos in order to win his affections.

* * *

During Yue Fei's lifetime, the list of 'ink crimes' was reduced to two hundred, and punitive facial tattooing was usually only carried out on soldiers who had tried to desert, and habitual criminals who had already been convicted on several previous occasions. Before such drastic disfigurement was undertaken, small, half-inch tattoos were placed behind the offender's ear – a ring for a robber, a square for someone sentenced to be banished, and a round design for someone convicted to be flogged. By the thirteenth century, though, punishment tattoos had become more elaborate, with adulterous men forced to be tattooed with the words 'Committed licentious acts twice' on their faces if caught in flagrante a second time.

One final, innovative use of facial tattooing was found to have been practised by the Liao, a dynasty that ruled a kingdom spanning northern and northeastern China, Mongolia, North Korea and areas of eastern Russia during the tenth and eleventh centuries. Emperor Deguang is said to have tattooed the faces of prisoners of war with the phrase 'By imperial command: do not kill' before releasing them back to their homes. The soldiers would forever bear evidence of both the power and the mercy of the Liao.

Amongst these tales of criminality, savagery, slavery, betrayal and martial masculinity, one particular exception shines out. Whilst tattooing in ancient China never reached any widespread social acceptance, it is clear that there were at least brief periods where it began to percolate beyond bandits and soldiers. In Jingzhou during the late eighth century, Duan Chengshi writes, 'there were tattoo vendors in the street. They had imprinting stamps into which they would press needles together closely into the shapes of all kinds of things, like toads and scorpions, mortars and pestles, or whatever people wanted. Once they'd imprinted the skin, they would brush [the pricked area] with black lead. After the wound had healed, the tattoo was finer than [the picture] on the pattern from which the customer had originally ordered.'

This scene is so reminiscent of modern tattoo shops, and written so similarly to the ways in which today's media write about tattooing, that it scarcely feels like a description of life over a thousand years ago. As will become a theme in this book, Duan is quick to caution his readers that tattooing is likely much more common and widespread than many ever suspected. Whilst they might find tattooing shocking, if they paid more attention to the details of ordinary life, they would surely discover a rich social tapestry just waiting to be revealed.

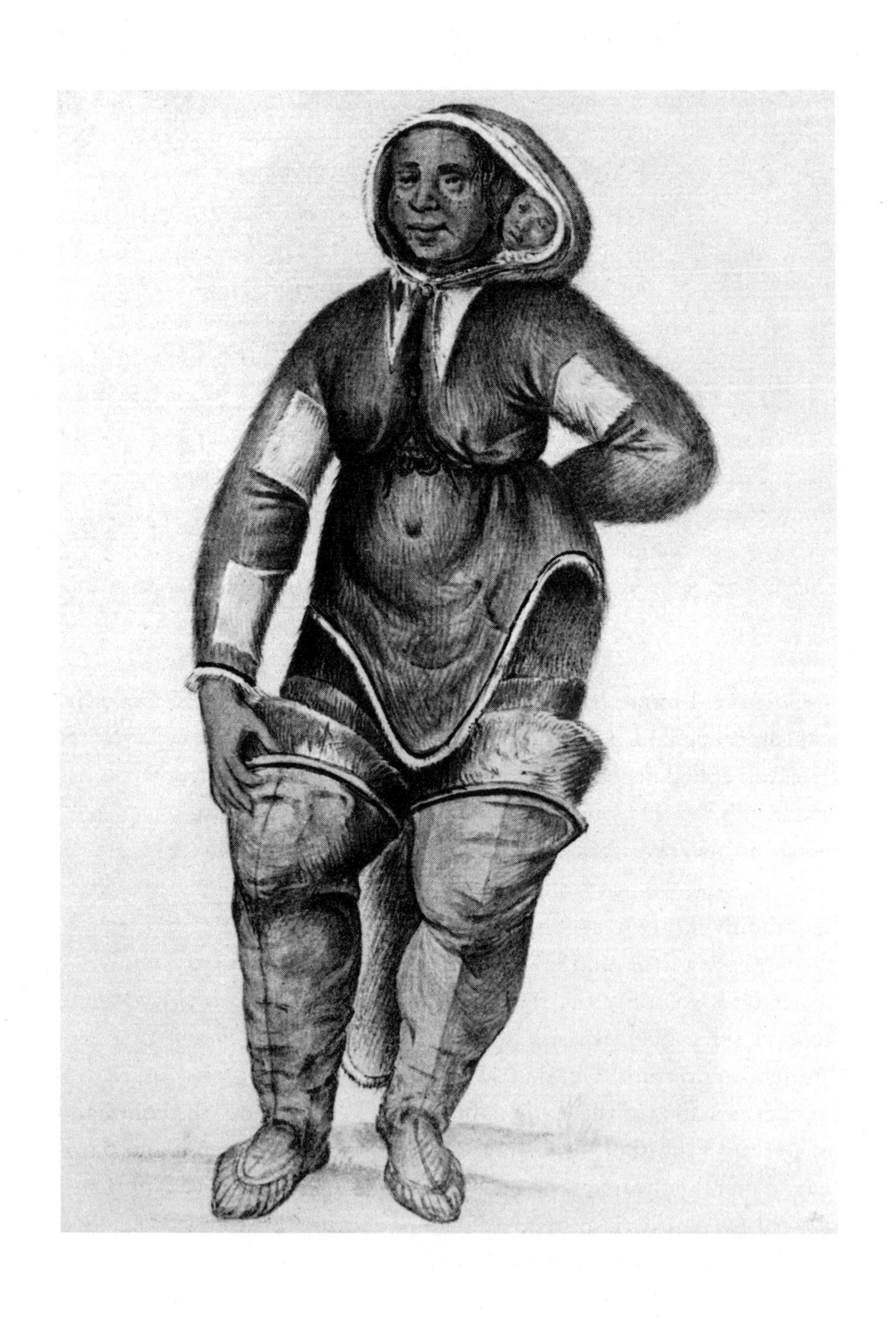

CHAPTER 6

Facial Tattooing on the Unknown Shore: Arnaq, 1577

'. . . hee found men of blacke hayre, broad faces, flat wry noses, of a swart and tawny colour, clothed with Sea-Calves skinnes, and the women were painted about the eyes and the balls of the Cheeke with a deepe azure colour, like the ancient Britans.'

—William Camden, Annales, *The True and Royall History of the famous Empresse Elizabeth Queene of England*, 1625

Arnaq's real name has been lost to written history. The men who captured her and her infant son, Nutaaq, and transported them to England called her 'Egnock', 'Egnoge' or 'Ignorth'. The history books eventually settled on 'Arnaq', which, as well as being a common name, is also the word in her native Inuktitut language for 'woman'. Like all Inuit women from her community on Qikiqtaaluk, now more commonly known as Baffin Island in the northeast of Canada, Arnaq bore tattoo marks on her cheeks, forehead and chin.

Arnaq was only the sixth person from the American continent to ever set foot on British soil, and the first indigenous American woman to do so. In October 1577, she and Nutaaq arrived in Bristol as captives aboard the *Ayde,* a hulking tall ship under the command of Martin Frobisher. Frobisher was a rakish, ill-tempered and hard-edged merchant and privateer. On behalf of the Muscovy Company, a wealthy consortium of merchants, Frobisher had embarked on a gruelling search for the fabled northwest passage – a route through

Left: Arnaq and Nutaaq, painted by John White, 1577

the Arctic ice to the rich trading wealth of Asia on the other side of the continent. With the explicit and visible patronage of Queen Elizabeth I, who had personally waved Frobisher's first voyage off from a balcony at Greenwich, the Company understood that economic and political dominion over the northern spans of the American continent would prove to be strategically valuable as colonial conflicts with Spain began to boil over. On the occasion of Frobisher's successful return, with the English flag flying on newly charted islands, Elizabeth took the opportunity to formally name the landmass *Meta Incognita* – the unknown shore.

The cold, open tundra that Frobisher encountered was wild and virtually unmapped. The people living there, too, were equally unknown to the wider world. Without a specific name for their culture, Frobisher called them simply 'the countrie people', a population of coastal Inuit who subsisted on hunting and fishing, thriving in environments in which English sailors struggled to survive comfortably. The languages of the indigenous people and the newly arrived Europeans were mutually unintelligible, and each culture's habits, practices and beliefs were opaque, and even terrifying and disgusting on both sides.

The narrative accounts of Frobisher's voyages record that their initial entreaties to trade with Inuit were met with recognition, suggesting that although no prior encounters had been recorded in England, some independent European sailors must have made contact with them in the recent or even distant past. Nevertheless, the first descriptions of Inuit by members of Frobisher's parties belie a wide-eyed, almost incredulous tone, particularly in their descriptions of the men and women they met. Initially, perhaps excited by the possibility that the northwest passage was soon to be discovered, shipmaster Christopher Hall wrongly imagined that the Inuit were from Central Asia. *Meta Incognita,* remember, was thought to be the boundary landscape between Europe, Greenland and the East. 'They bee like Tartars,' he wrote, 'with long blacke hair, broad faces, and flatte noses, and tawnie in colour.' In particular, Hall noted that Inuit dressed in sealskin clothes, and that both men and women dressed similarly, save for the fact that 'the women are marked in the face with blewe streekes downe the cheekes, and round about the eyes'.

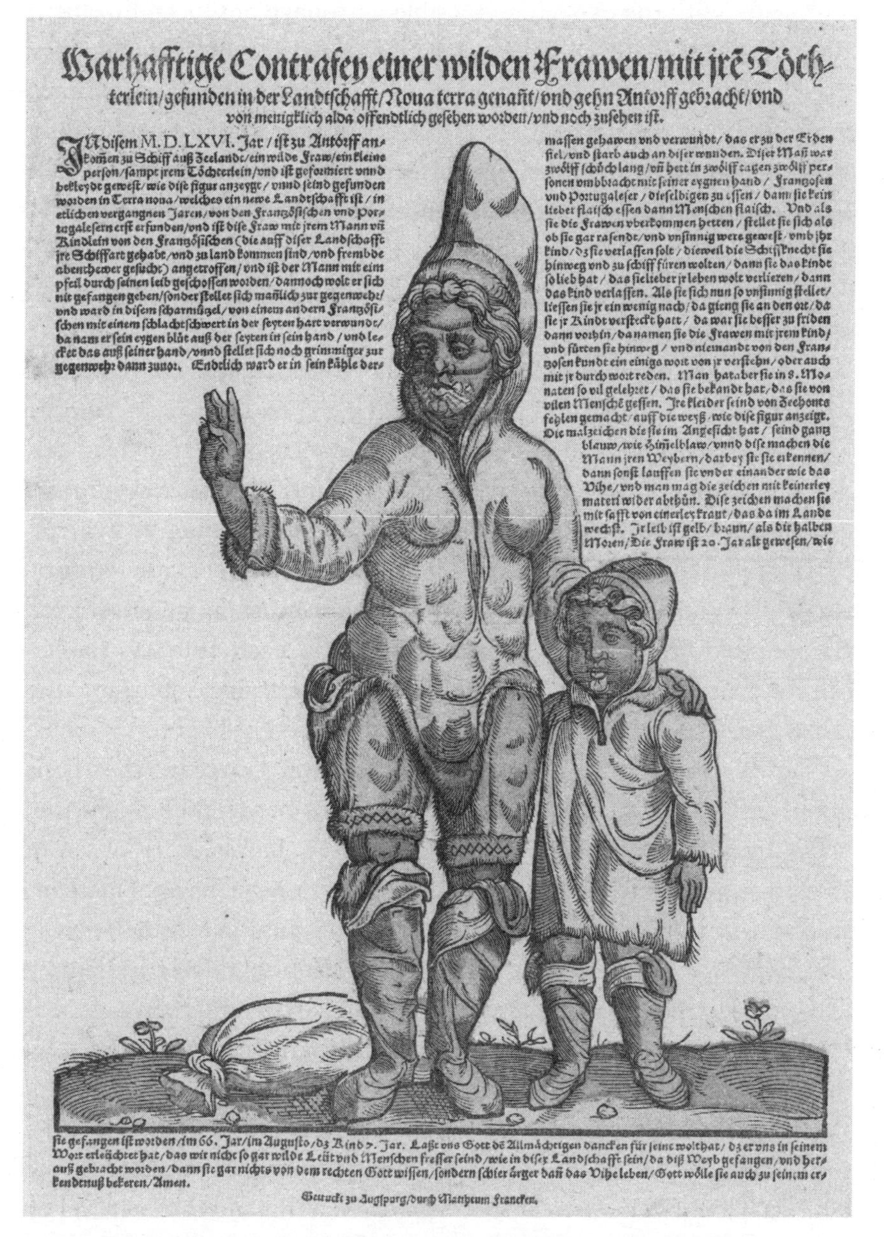

Warhafftige Contrafey einer wilden Frawen/mit irẽ Töchterlein/gefunden in der Landtschafft/Noua terra genañt/vnd gehn Antorff gebracht/vnd von menigklich alda offendtlich gesehen worden/vnd noch zusehen ist.

JN disem M.D.LXVI. Jar/ist zu Antorff ankomen zu Schiff auß Zeelandt/ein wilde Fraw/ein kleine person/sampt irem Töchterlein/vnd ist geformiert vnnd bekleydt gewest/wie dise figur anzeygt/vnnd seind gefunden worden in Terra noua/welches ein newe Landtschafft ist/in etlichen vergangnen Jaren/von den Frantzösischen vnd Portugalesern erst erfunden/vnd ist dise Fraw mit irem Mann vñ Kindlein von den Frantzösischen (die auff diser Landschafft jre Schiffart gehabt/vnd zu land kommen sind/vnd frembde abenthewer gesucht) angetroffen/vnd ist der Mann mit eim pfeil durch seinen leib geschossen worden/dannoch wolt er sich nit gefangen geben/sonder stellet sich mañlich zur gegenwehr/vnd ward in disem scharmützel/von einem andern Frantzösischen mit einem schlachtschwert in der seyten hart verwundt/da nam er sein eygen blůt auß der seyten in sein hand/vnd lecket das auß seiner hand/vnnd stellet sich noch grimmiger zur gegenwehr dann zuvor. Endtlich ward er in sein kähle dermassen gehawen vnd verwundt/das er zu der Erden fiel/vnd starb auch an diser wunden. Diser Mañ war zwölff schůch lang/vñ hett in zwölff tagen zwölff personen vmbbracht mit seiner eygnen hand/Frantzosen vnd Portugaleser/dieselbigen zu essen/dann sie kein lieber flaisch essen dann Menschen flaisch. Vnd als sie die Frawen vberkommen hetten/stellet sie sich als ob sie gar rasendt/vnd vnsinnig were gewest/vmb jhr kind/dz sie verlassen solt/dieweil die Schiffknecht sie hinweg vnd zu schiff füren wolten/dann sie das kindt so lieb hat/das sie lieber jr leben wolt verlieren/dann das kind verlassen. Als sie sich nun so vnsinnig stellet/liessen sie jr ein wenig nach/da gieng sie an den ort/da sie jr Kindt versteckt hatt/da war sie besser zu friden dann vorhin/da namen sie die Frawen mit jrem kind/vnd fürten sie hinweg/vnd niemandt von den Franzosen kundt ein einigs wort von jr verstehn/oder auch mit jr durch wort reden. Man hat aber sie in 8. Monaten so vil gelehret/das sie bekandt hat/das sie von vilen Menschẽ gessen. Jre kleider seind von Zeehonts fehlen gemacht/auff die weyß/wie dise figur anzeigt. Die malzeichen die sie im Angesicht hat/seind gantz blaw/wie Hĩmelblaw/vnnd dise machen die Mann jren Weybern/darbey sie sie erkennen/dann sonst lauffen sie vnder einander wie das Vihe/vnd man mag die zeichen mit keinerley materi wider abthůn. Dise zeichen machen sie mit safft von einerley kraut/das da im Lande wechßt. Jr leib ist gelb/braun/als die halben Moren/Die Fraw ist 20. Jar alt gewesen/wie sie gefangen ist worden/im 66. Jar/im Augusto/dz Kind 7. Jar. Laßt vns Gott dẽ Allmächtigen dancken für seine wolthat/dz er vns in seinem Wort erleüchtet hat/das wir nicht so gar wilde Leüt vnd Menschen fresser seind/wie in diser Landschafft sein/da diß Weyb gefangen/vnd herauß gebracht worden/dann sie gar nichts von dem rechten Gott wissen/sondern schier ärger dañ das Vihe leben/Gott wölle sie auch zu seinem erkendtnuß bekeren/Amen.

Getruckt zu Augspurg/durch Mattheum Francken.

Inuit woman and her daugher, illustrated by Matthäus Franck, Belgium, 1567

* * *

Though Inuit were unstudied and unknown to Frobisher's men, they were correct to deduce that other Europeans had likely been in the region in the recent past. In fact, whilst Arnaq was the first tattooed woman from the Americas to come to England, another Inuit woman had been abducted and brought to Europe a decade earlier.

In 1566, a handbill was circulated in Belgium and in Germany. The flyer depicted a woman in sealskins alongside her infant son. Very little is known of this woman, her story or her ultimate fate, but an accompanying text described how she had been captured by French sailors, who had killed her husband as he tried to defend her. The Frenchmen kidnapped her and transported her to Antwerp, from where she was put on display in a grotesque spectacle before braying, paying customers. Visitors were told she was a cannibal, a description frequently and erroneously given to people from the New World, and were invited to marvel at her tattooed face. 'The paint marks she has on her face are entirely blue,' the text gawped, 'like sky blue, and these the husband makes on his wife [when he takes her for his wife] so that he can recognise her by them, for otherwise they run among one another like beasts, and the marks cannot be taken off again with any substance.'

Beyond these descriptions of Inuit tattooing, wider skin-marking traditions in the Americas had been recorded almost immediately after Christopher Columbus arrived in 1492. Columbus' travels were greatly inspired by the stories of Marco Polo's expeditions to the Far East, and as Polo had described the body-decoration practices amongst various cultures he had encountered across Asia, perhaps Columbus was not surprised to observe tattooing on the native people of the Americas. On 11 October that year, Columbus first observed body decorations on San Salvador in the Eastern Caribbean, and on his second voyage, in 1493, Dr Diego Álvarez Chanca, a physician on the mission, wrote to authorities back in Spain that the fleet had seen men and women who 'paint their heads with crosses and a hundred different devices, each according to his fancy; which they do with sharpened reeds'. Interestingly, another of Columbus' retinue, Michele da Cuneo, described these Taíno people as having 'flat heads, and with faces *atartarato* ("like the Tartars")', making the same analogy as Hall would about the Inuit a century later. Ten Taíno people who were kidnapped during this voyage survived the trip, setting foot as tattooed captives in Europe on their arrival in Lisbon on the 4 March 1493.

On the continental mainland, between contemporary Delaware and Nova Scotia, Italian diplomats Alberto Cantino and Pietro Pasqualigo wrote as early as 1501 of men who 'have their face marked with great signs', and who were 'marked on the face in several places, some with more, others with fewer lines'. As with Columbus' trips, some of these tattooed men were kidnapped, and also transported back to Lisbon, where they were treated more as objects of curiosity than as human beings. In 1509, an unverified report also suggests that 'seven savage men' were brought to Rouen in France. The men were 'the colour of soot, with thick lips and *stigmata* on their face from their ears to the middle of their chins, like a little blue-coloured vein'. These men were presumed at the time to be from 'Terra Nova', Newfoundland, but full details of their origins and eventual fate remain mysterious.

* * *

Current research suggests that tattooing on the North American continent dates back over five thousand years, based on analysis of bone needles from a site in Tennessee. In the Arctic, the discovery of masks and figurines bearing facial tattoo designs suggests that in the northernmost regions of the Americas, tattooing is at least 3,500 years old. However, much of what is known about pre-contact traditions in the wider literature is filtered through the lens of centuries of colonial writing, rendering the details opaque, particularly to outsiders. Indigenous people in the Arctic have endured centuries of genocide and concerted efforts to extinguish their cultural practices, and as such, the deep histories of many traditions are occluded.

European writers described tattooing, filtering what Inuit told them through their preconceptions and prior assumptions. As such, Christian writers often misinterpreted the relationship between tattooing and these spirits as a devotional practice, or form of deity worship. However, Inuit cosmology does not recognise 'gods', nor conceive of the relationship between the Invisible World of the Spirits (*silam aapaa*) and the Visible World of Humans (*sila*) as a hierarchical one. For example, Inuit men are tattooed only in response to moments where they have broken taboos, in order to prevent revenge from angered spirits. They might, for example, be marked with a tattoo after failing to properly carry out a ritual following a hunt. This kind of tattoo does not genuflect to a god, but rather signals a particular kind of connection to the spirit world.

Tattooing young women like Arnaq, by contrast, was systematic. Colonial writing frequently understands its application as a 'fertility rite'. Young Inuit girls begin to be visibly tattooed from about eight years old onwards as they take on gendered tasks and spiritual responsibility in their communities, but although tattooing is first carried out in the years before a young Inuit woman reaches puberty, it is not specifically performed in relation to menstruation or sexual maturity. Rather, tattooing serves as a gender marker. In Inuit social systems, gender is not strictly bound to biology or physiology, but to social role, and thus tattooing's role in distinguishing gender is particularly significant.

Although Inuit women bore tattoos all over their bodies, including as amulets for hunting or during pregnancy, it is tattooing on the hands and face of women that was predominantly visible to the colonial writers. Dionyse Settle, for example, who accompanied Frobisher on his voyages, noted that 'some of their women race [or scar] their faces proportionally, as chinne, cheeks and forehead, and the wristes of their hands, wherevpon they lay a colour, which continueth darke azurine'.

While there are localised differences in tattoo patterns and mythology across modern-day Greenland, Alaska and Canada, it is possible to connect the practice to two fundamental origin myths. The first myth concerns tattooing on the face. For Inuit women, facial tattooing on women represents the myth of a woman named Maliina, the most revered spirit in Inuit religions. Maliina had been violently raped in the dark over the course of several evenings, following great feasts. In order to discover the identity of her violator, she secretly rubbed soot from an oil lamp on her fingers before retiring once more in the dark, knowing that when he came to rape her again, she could rub a blackened mark on his shoulder and thus identify him come morning. Discovering that the rapist was her own brother Aningaaq, in violation of the deep taboo of incest, she fled to the sky, holding a tuft of burning moss from her lamp to light the way.

According to one ethnographic summary, Maliina burst into flame and became the Sun. As she ran past the fire 'she seized an ember and ran beyond the earth'. Her brother pursued her, though his own tuft of moss left a trail of embers across the sky, which became the stars. His own light dimmed, Aningaaq became the Moon, and continued to chase his sister through the heavens. The myth explains that this endless, sorrowful pursuit drives the tides, determines the rhythms of menstruation and reproduction, and in turn, the persistence of this World.

So whilst Aningaaq is understood as a fearsome spirit of great strength and temper, Maliina, by contrast, is kind, gentle and respected. More than that, she is deeply loved – unhappily but tirelessly, she flees across the sky, now unable to fulfil her role as a mother, but dutifully propelling the very survival of the world by cyclically ending the polar winter, bringing plants and berries in the spring, and ensuring that, as her brother pursues her, reproductive cycles are perpetuated.

To reflect Maliina's unhappiness, Inuit women's forehead tattooing takes the form of a V-shape to symbolise her frown – which, in opposition to her brother's grinning smile, reminds us that the siblings' unending chase creates the conditions for the world to exist as it does. Her mournful visage is also frequently represented on carvings and masks, where it serves as a reminder of her sacrifice, encourages kindness and warmth, and celebrates the giving of life.

Tattoos around the mouth and chin, which are visible on the portrait of Arnaq and on the woman depicted on the Antwerp handbill, are the first to be applied to young girls. Some ethnographers have clumsily analogised breath in Inuit metaphysics with the Christian concept of the 'soul', or something like a 'life force'. By this analogy, tattoos on the chin and around the mouth symbolise a woman's role in giving life and her connections to the community's past and its perpetuation into the future. This connection continues even after death, where tattooed faces and bodies permit passage into the spirit world and make Inuit recognisable to their forebears. Women with poorly executed tattoos or none at all are not able to enter the world of their ancestors.

The second myth explains that tattooing on the hands and arms is a practice symbolic of the mythology of the Sea Woman. The Sea Woman, who goes by a vast number of names, is the spirit and sentience of the ocean itself. An incredibly powerful spirit, she is said to have been taken to sea by a father figure, who was angry with her, though the reasons for his fury vary between traditions. In his rage, he threw her overboard, though she clung desperately to the side of his kayak to avoid drowning. To release her grip, her father chopped off her fingers, joint by joint. As she sank deep into the sea, she became the spirit of the sea. In many versions of the story, her severed digits spawn or become the first sea mammals. When the wind blows, it is sometimes possible to hear her screaming.

In the Visible World, when a woman is unclean, due to a taboo such as still-birth, or the death of her partner, she is hidden away, as taboos anger the spirits and lead to famine and death. Without her fingers, the Sea Woman cannot comb her hair, nor cleanse herself. As such, she is turbulent, angry and frustrated by humans breaking taboos, which also contaminate her. As the consciousness of the ocean and the source of the animals who are the primary food source of humans, she must be appeased.

In this context, the tattooed lines that Inuit women mark across their finger joints and hands commemorate the creation of animals on the earth and in the sea. In different parts of the Arctic, myths differ over how many fingers the Sea Woman lost, and thus the number of tattooed fingers vary. Crucially, these marks do not honour or celebrate the Sea Woman as such, but act as a reminder of the interconnectedness of human behaviour and the natural world, and the relationship between taboos and survival in the Arctic landscape.

* * *

Arnaq's capture came during a brutal conflict with Frobisher's crew. Several of his men had failed to return from a trading trip, and

Frobisher furiously concluded that they must have been captured or killed by Inuit. In a subsequent mission to rescue his missing men, or at least to avenge their deaths, Frobisher led a further skirmish that resulted in the death of five or six Inuit. The encounter was so vicious that its location became known afterwards as 'Bloody Point'. Following the massacre, Arnaq, Nutaaq and an old woman were taken captive.

Arnaq and her child were brought to England along with another captive called Kalicho and greeted with prurient and invasive social, anthropological and medical fascination. News of their being trafficked spread rapidly through Europe. Tragically, Kalicho died within six weeks of arriving. Arnaq contracted a disease which caused her skin to break out in boils, dying just a few days later. Both were buried at St Stephen's Church in Bristol. Little Nutaaq barely survived a week or two more, and his body was transported to London to be buried at St Olave's Church in Hart Street.

With her tattooed face, Arnaq was certainly able to pass into the land of her ancestors with fire in her heart.

* * *

Despite the suddenness of their deaths, and the cruelties inflicted upon them as they were dragged from their homes and families to die in an unfamiliar land, both Arnaq and Kalicho played a romanticised role in English and other European descriptions of the New World. All three were drawn and painted, and though the extensive reportage and documentation of their lives and habits do not reveal their own voices, opinions or lives, we can learn a great deal about the colonial mindset from the way in which they were described.

Under the influence of deep-rooted myths, Frobisher and his men falsely believed that the Inuit were cannibals and literal devils, even violently removing an old woman's boots to confirm to their satisfaction that she did not have cloven hooves. In the immediate decades after Arnaq and Kalicho's time in England, however, early modern humanist descriptions began to understand people of the Americas as ethnographically connected to Europeans, rather than separate from them. In particular, the visible tattooing on Native

Americans and Inuit reminded English antiquarians of the Roman tales of the tattooed Picts, and the presence of tattooing helped place European cultures in an evolutionary timeline as compared with those elsewhere.

In the aftermath of these New World encounters, William Camden's *Britannia* (1586) explicitly reminded his readers that the ancient Britons marked their bodies with 'small needle points and the juices squeezed from grasses'. In 1590, Theodor de Bry wrote in a volume compiled by Thomas Hariot titled *America* that 'the Inhabitants of the great Bretannie have bin in times past as savvage as those of Virginia'. Hariot included in his book engravings by de Bry of watercolours by John White, an Oxford contemporary of Camden's who had compiled a large set of depictions of Native Americans from up and down the eastern seaboard of North America, many of which depict tattoo traditions with detail and fidelity. White also drew fantastical images of the Picts based on the Roman sources, which were juxtaposed in order to allow readers to make the visual comparison for themselves.

Both Arnaq and Kalicho feature in watercolour drawings by John White, though these were not published in Hariot's volume. White had perhaps been on Baffin Island with Frobisher, but he more plausibly copied his depictions from those painted from life in Bristol by Flemish artist Cornelius Ketel. Ketel's paintings were given to Queen Elizabeth and survived in the Royal Collection until at least the time of James I, though they are now lost. Whatever its source, in White's image of Arnaq, her facial tattoos are clearly visible, including the traditional V on her forehead, curves around her mouth and dots encircling her eyes. White's is a gentle, empathetic depiction, and these images and others like them, allowed a moment of cultural recognition for English writers, who were seeking to readjust their own understanding of the world in light of recent discoveries. The peoples of the New World, though clearly presented as 'strange' in some senses, were often depicted in ways which clearly connected them to Europeans.

As we will see in the next chapter, this social-evolutionary thinking, which understood human civilisations as existing on a trajectory from 'primitives' in the Americas, Africa and Asia through to modern

Europeans, soon hardened into an explicitly exterminatory logic over the centuries of colonial violence that followed. Rather than representing common ground between colonised and colonisers, by the late eighteenth century tattooing in the Arctic and elsewhere was presented by European writers as symbolic of cultural difference.

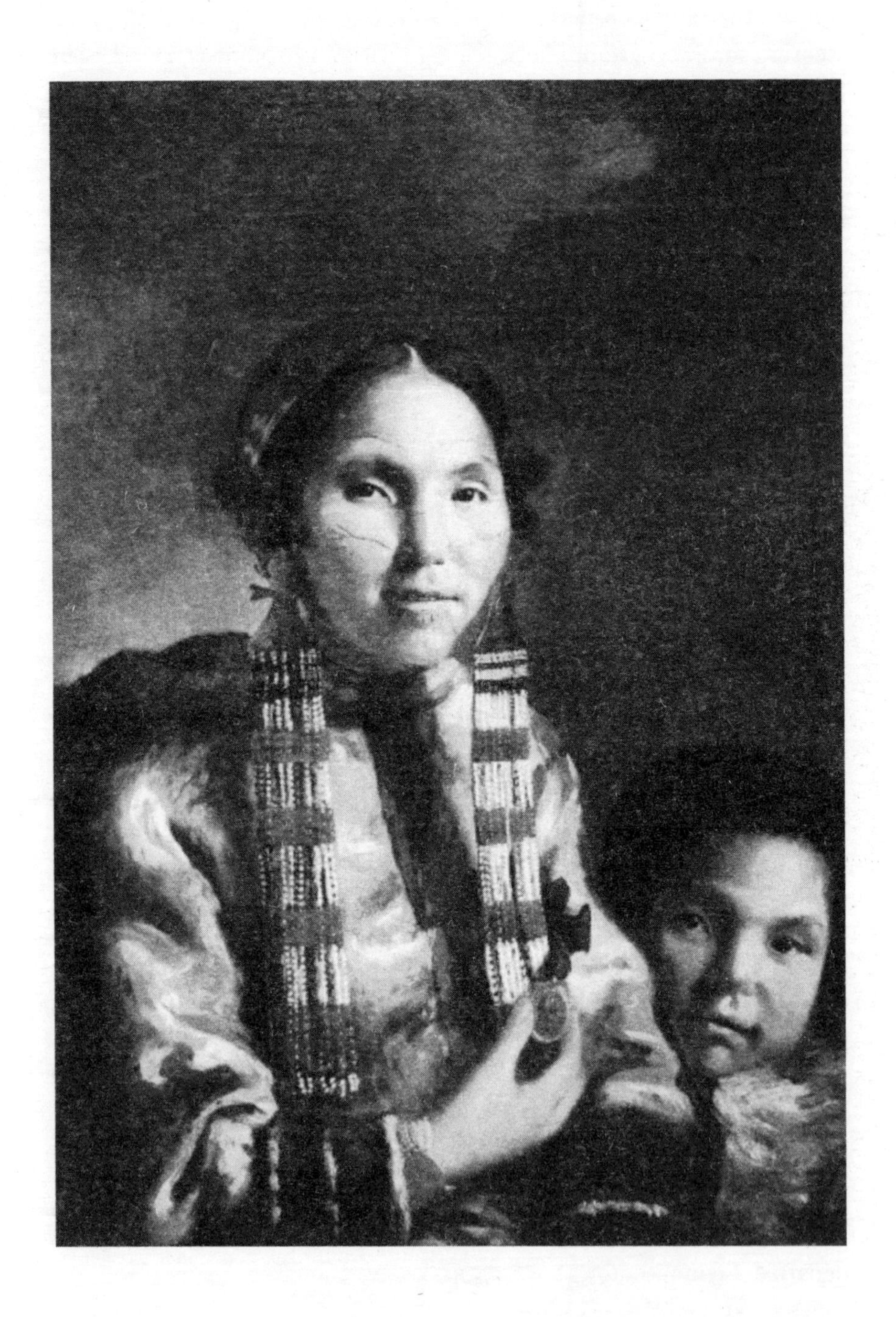

CHAPTER 7

Kakiuineq Hiding in Plain Sight: Mikak, 1768

'Her face and hands, with tattoo rich,
By women work'd in careful stitch,
And fashion'd into pattern neat,
Renders the toilette quite complete.'

—'A Lady', *A Peep at the Esquimaux*, 1836

The first ever Royal Academy Summer Exhibition, which opened on 26 April 1769, featured a painting by society portraitist John Russell of a tattooed woman named Mikak and her infant son, Tutauq. Given that in 2022, it is still possible to read newspaper accounts, popular books and even academic scholarship confidently stating that Captain James Cook 'discovered' tattooing in the South Pacific only a matter of weeks later, that may come as something of a surprise. Mikak's journey puts her tattooed face at the centre of English high society at a moment when many have long claimed that tattooing simply did not exist outside of the Pacific, or if it ever had done, it had long since been forgotten. Her story then is not just an account of its prominence in the middle decades of the late eighteenth century, but perhaps offers clues as to why the tattoos of Mikak and Arnaq, and all tattooing in the Americas, faded so powerfully from European consciousness in the centuries that followed.

Mikak had left Labrador on the east coast of modern Canada in the autumn of 1768, only a few months after Cook's HMS *Endeavour* departed Plymouth for the Pacific. She was brought to England by

Left: Mikak and Tutauq, painted by John Russell, 1769

Governor Hugh Palliser, and arrived in November of that year to some fanfare as the first native 'Esquimaux' to come to English shores in nearly two hundred years. Many who reported on her visit did not even seem to know about the fateful and fatal arrival of Arnaq with Frobisher two centuries earlier, hailing her as the first 'Esquimaux' to ever visit England. Mikak was famed in society circles for her grace, beauty and intelligence, and was presented to the Queen, the Princess Dowager of Wales and the Duke of Gloucester. In January 1769, she was even taken to the theatre, an experience that a patronising press reported she very much enjoyed.

Russell's portrait is a remarkably sensitive picture. A wide-eyed Mikak kindly gazes out of the composition as her son nestles in the crook of her arm. She holds in her hand a small gold medal that had been presented to her by the royal family, indicative of the welcome and the esteem she received at court. Spidery, stitched lines of traditional Nunatsiavut women's facial tattooing are clearly visible on her chin and around her eyes, picked out by Russell in blue, and as she cracks a gentle smile, the tattoo marks animate her features.

In many respects, Mikak's relaxed countenance and coy smile in the painting seem surprising, given what we know about the circumstances of her sitting. Russell was a notoriously melancholic zealot, more given to documenting his ongoing existential and spiritual crises in his journal than showing any genuine human warmth towards his sitters. In typical fashion his diary on the day of Mikak's appointment is frustratingly light on details of their interaction, and of her personality. In a characteristically wailing tone, he notes only his frustration that his attempts to proselytise the Christian God to her were limited, given the inevitable language barrier. 'I had the Esquimaux Indian woman to sit for me,' he wrote, sparsely. 'I longed to have had power to have preached Christ to her, but she could not understand a word of English.'

The portrait of this smiling woman, though serenely presented as a willing imperial subject, obscures the violence and bloodshed with which her long voyage across the Atlantic had begun. Mikak had been captured at the age of about twenty-five with her son and several other Inuit in August 1767, after a bloody skirmish with British colonial merchants at a heavily fortified sealing station called Cape Charles. The previous day, three Englishmen had died during what has usually been reported as an Inuit raid attempting to steal whaling boats.

The resulting combat led to a brutal massacre of twenty Inuit men and a retaliatory chase of the fleeing survivors. The following morning, a crew of English sailors encountered two boats carrying Inuit men, women and children. They remorselessly opened fire with muskets and blunderbusses. In a bloody echo of Frobisher's battle two centuries earlier, four Inuit men were murdered, including Mikak's husband.

Mikak's capture came at a time of rising tensions between European colonists and the Inuit who lived on northernmost parts of the Americas. Having recently wrested Labrador away from French control, the British were keen to once again exert territorial and economic power over the region. To the administrators, local Inuit populations were becoming frustrating impediments to the smooth commercial operation of the colony's fishing industry, and they thus sought to evict them from the coast through a combination of economic enticement and technologically enhanced violence. Whilst longstanding histories of the encounter at Cape Charles predictably relayed a story of savage, thieving and ungrateful Inuit having to be regretfully tamed through violent suppression, other documents reveal a different story entirely. According to missionary records, the initial clash was triggered not by Inuit stealing English boats, but by colonial traders trying to steal oil and whalebone from Inuit stores. Rather than an act of aggression, the Inuit dispatch of arrows against the colonists was an act of self-defence.

Colonialism presented itself to the Inuit as an iron fist in a threadbare velvet glove. Missionaries had made efforts to learn the Inuktitut language, and through them Governor Palliser had made several increasingly fragile entreaties to the Inuit to settle for peace. Palliser was frustrated and at times even apparently horrified by the treatment of Inuit by Europeans, and so he hoped to achieve his commercial goals of inducing Inuit to move inland whilst simultaneously avoiding bloodshed. The ruthless plundering and cruelty dealt out by his men against Mikak and the other victims was precisely the kind of behaviour he wished to stamp out through more diplomatic means. Against this backdrop, the capture of prisoners was an attempt to calm hostilities. His goals were not altruistic, of course, but cynical. Palliser imagined that by speaking with his captives, by treating them well and then ultimately returning them to their homes and communities, he could establish what he considered a 'fair trade' with the local population whilst being clear that theft and killing would be severely punished.

Mikak was immediately of great use to Palliser's strategy. In a letter to Lord Hillsborough, the Secretary of State for the Colonies, Palliser happily reported that Mikak had proved herself intelligent and useful to him, though she did not fully trust that her captors were not saving her for some public sacrifice. Unwilling to risk returning her home after a summer of captivity, Palliser decided that he would instead send her to London along with her son and a young orphan boy called Karpik. Palliser hoped that she would become a diplomatic tool in his hands, able to inform him of the details of her community and, in turn, convince those closest to her that the English were trustworthy trading partners after all.

Francis Lucas, who led the attack that had resulted in her capture, accompanied her on the voyage, along with a missionary, Jens Haven. Lucas had begun to teach Mikak English and had learnt some rudimentary words in her language in return. In missionary reports, at least, she was also said to have already begun to become interested in Christian theology, having offered protection to a group of missionaries from a howling storm some years earlier, of which Jens Haven was one. During colonisation, many Inuit communities took on Christianity syncretically in combination with their traditional spiritual and religious beliefs, and missionary descriptions often report that Mikak made lengthy enquiries about particular details of the Christian tradition. One account describes her admonishing Lucas for patronising her on issues of doctrine. Rather than being unable or unwilling to hear John Russell's painterly sermons, then, it seems perhaps she simply didn't warm to them. In any case, Russell's inability to preach the word of God to her foretold a greater set of challenges to come.

The London newspapers were apparently surprised by Mikak's grace and politeness, and dismissively reported that she was overwhelmed by urban life. In these reports, she was depicted more as a curiosity than a human being, allegedly being confused by English dining habits and baffled by painted nudes, while onlookers were embarrassed by her lack of sophistication at court. Articles made frequent mention of her exploits, and members of high society to whom she was introduced wrote extraordinarily warmly about her in their letters and journals. The Earl of Bathurst was particularly verbose in his praise, writing that 'there is so much to be said in relation to the Esquimaux lady that I shan't be able to go through it'.

Strangely, one thing that does not feature prominently in the extensive coverage of Mikak's time in London are details of the facial tattoos visible in her portrait. As outlined in the previous chapter, Inuit women tattooed their faces, hands and other parts of their bodies, most frequently using a technique that involved pulling an ink-sodden sinew through the skin on the end of a needle, much like that used for sewing skin and pelts. Though often called 'skin stitching', the method better resembles the embroidery technique of basting. Another technique described as a 'double-poke' method – only recently deduced from research into archival tools and oral histories – first pierced a fold of skin with a copper awl. Thick grass, bone splinters or wooden points soaked in pigment were then threaded through the piercing, depositing ink subdermally. The resultant patterns of both methods, which vary across different communities throughout the Arctic, are distinctive series of staccato dots or dashes marked out in thin, spreading, blue-black ink.

* * *

From a slightly later account, that of Captain George Francis Lyon, we can perhaps envisage the technological process – though certainly not the cultural contexts – through which Mikak's own tattoos were made. Lyon acquired a tattoo from an Inuit woman he clumsily and patronisingly calls 'Mrs Kettle' in 1822, describing how, having furnished her with a fine needle,

> she tore with her teeth a thread off a deer's sinew, and thus prepared the sewing apparatus. She then, without a possibility of darkening her hands beyond their standard color, passed her fingers under the bottom of the stove pot, from whence she collected a quantity of soot. With this, together with a little oil and much saliva, she soon made a good mixture, and taking a small piece of whalebone well blackened, she then drew a variety of figures about my arm ... She commenced her work by blackening the thread with soot, and taking a pretty deep but short stitch in my skin, carefully pressing her thumb on the wound as the thread passed through it, and beginning each stitch at the place where the last

> had ceased. The colour which the *kakeen* assumes when the skin heals is of the same light blue as we see on the marked arms of seamen.

The word Lyon uses, *kakeen* – a corruption of a word in several Inuit dialects, *kakiuineq* or *kakiniit* – did not catch on in English. In some alternate version of the present, I might be writing a book about kakeening. Beyond the descriptions of 'blewe streekes' from Frobisher's voyages in 1576 and 1577, French writer Georges de Buffon described the same marks on the foreheads of women on Baffin Island in the 1740s, for example, and in January 1767, about a year before Mikak arrived, German missionary Daniel Cranz published the wildly influential English-language edition of his *History of Greenland*, which explained that women there 'have a thread blackened with soot drawn betwixt the skin of their chin, and also their cheeks, hands, and feet, which leaves such a black mark behind when the thread is drawn away, as if they had a beard'. Cranz also attempts some account of the meaning of tattooing in Greenland, summarising that 'the mother performs this painful operation on her daughter in her childhood, for fear she might never get a husband'.

By the time of Mikak's move to London, tattooing had been long documented in English sources, and as we saw earlier, she was far from the first tattooed individual from the Americas to make waves in English high society. In the immediate decades before her capture, many Native Americans had arrived either as captives – as in the case of two tattooed Choctaw and Creek 'Princes' who were captured and cruelly displayed to spectators in 1719 – or on diplomatic business. The heavily tattooed 'Four Kings', a party of one Machian and three Mohawk chiefs, for example, were received by Queen Anne in 1710, from whom they sought military aid against the French. Just a few years before Mikak's visit, a delegation of three Overhill Cherokee leaders arrived in London in 1762 to meet with George III. These men bore tattoo marks on their throats, and contemporary engravings further imagined cross-hatched lines tattooed across their faces, as well as cruciform designs prominently visible on their necks, inspired by the earlier Mohawk visitors.

As is common in anthropological and ethnographic texts both historically and today, these colonial, patriarchal accounts underestimate, flatten and misstate the spiritual complexity of tattooing in the life of

Inuit women. Across the vast range of cultural traditions amongst Inuit groups, tattooing was deeply embedded in a set of spiritual, cultural and religious beliefs for women, which, for example, marked the moment of transition to womanhood or served as apotropaic symbols within a dense system of spiritual beliefs. These marks cannot be distilled into simple explanations to be read as straightforward signs, but must instead be understood, like all cultural heritage, as part of an embedded tapestry of knowledge connecting deep time and specific geographies and communities through an opaque fog of colonial history.

This deep connection to Inuit belief systems and traditions and the intercession of colonial, missionary zeal is the solution to the mystery of our Western cultural amnesia about tattoo history and the idea that tattooing had been imported recently from the Pacific. Cranz's account of Greenlandic tattooing in 1767 already noted that 'our baptised Greenlanders have relinquished this practice long ago', and through the eighteenth and nineteenth centuries, enforced religious education for Inuit had suppressed and shamed Inuit skin sewing almost to extinction, along with vast swathes of other Inuit cultural tradition. As missionary work and colonial violence conspired to tear Inuit from their heritage, Inuit tattooing slipped from view.

* * *

It was important for Palliser that Mikak appeared to both the English and to her own community not as a so-called 'noble savage', but simply as noble. On her return, her father found her so transformed by her experiences that he renamed her Nutarrak, meaning 'newborn', though she was quickly able to regain the trust of her family and community, and assumed a key diplomatic role, negotiating the establishment of a new missionary outpost when Jens Haven, perhaps her closest European ally, returned to Labrador in 1770. She was so successful in her diplomacy that the missionaries were initially scared it was a trap. Mikak calmly explained that she was offended that they would have such suspicions about her countrymen and women, and that, though there might admittedly be some rogue elements, there were of course plenty of those amongst the English too. She facilitated Christian proselytising by the missionaries and worked closely with the mission for several years, giving them use of her tent, working as an interpreter for them and consistently playing an ambassadorial role. Nevertheless, she maintained a traditional way of life with her husband, travelling inland to hunt in the summer and back to the coast in the winter. This frustrated the missionaries, who feared that the further Inuit communities ventured from their oversight, the more likely they were to regress into what they saw as dangerous, pagan practices.

By 1773, trust between the missionaries and Mikak's family had eroded to such an extent that when her husband and his brother requested passage to England on a trade expedition, the leader of the Moravian Church, James Hutton, wrote an excoriating letter back to London to discourage it. Mikak and her family were, by Hutton's account, exploiting English goodwill and largesse. The riches she had seen in England had spoilt her, he wrote, and had created jealousy and ill-feeling. All her countrymen would come to expect similar generosity from the British state, and perhaps her time abroad even made the Church's job of converting her to Christianity harder. 'She must have much to unlearn,' he wrote scornfully.

Despite Hutton's scepticism and the souring relationships of the whole project, in 1772 another Inuit woman called Caubvick was brought to London with her husband and several members of her family. There she was introduced to John Hunter, the famous anatomist and surgeon, as well as to Joseph Banks. Like Mikak, her portrait was painted. Unlike Mikak, though, her facial tattoos were not depicted. Careful restoration of the portrait in 2003 did reveal that the tattoo marks had in fact been rendered by the original, unknown artist, but only extraordinarily faintly, before being over-painted for the final version, and were likely never intended to be seen in the finished picture.

As we will see, the exotic allure of Polynesian tattooing immediately captured the European imagination in 1770, but it seems that by 1768 Arctic tattooing had become so well known in Europe as to hardly be worth mentioning, and then very quickly seen so rarely that it was basically forgotten beyond travel journals. Some Pacific travellers at the time did note the connection – French Pacific explorer Louis-Antoine de Bougainville explicitly remarked that the indelible marks he'd seen in Tahiti reminded him of what he'd read about a similar habit in Canada, and Banks and Cook also certainly understood the similarities.

Both Banks and Cook owned copies of Cranz's *History of Greenland*, with its clear account of the process of Arctic tattooing, and Banks also owned one of two copies of the Mikak portrait, likely the one which had hung in the Royal Academy. It is possible that he even commissioned the portrait directly, hoping to finally be able to see an Inuit woman, after having failed to do so when he was in Labrador in 1766.

The picture, now in a German museum, was proudly on display in his library until 1797. It seems likely, too, that Banks would have later been told about Mikak in some detail drawn from a first-hand account, as officer James King, who had travelled on board ship with Mikak on her journey from Labrador, was a correspondent of Banks' and later served on Cook's third voyage. The cultural 'forgetting' of Inuit tattooing is therefore not an accident of history, but the result of centuries of concerted colonial effort to eliminate Inuit cultural practice through missionary conversion. So much of the cultural specificity of Inuit tattooing was erased in such a short space of time that even the word 'tattoo', imported from Tahiti, swiftly expunged from European vocabularies the precise and various indigenous terms used to describe different kinds of skin markings for different purposes within different communities across the Arctic. Moreover, as I think Caubvick's over-painted portrait demonstrates, for a few years at least, every Inuit facial tattoo was perhaps a stark and even embarrassing illustration of the limits of missionary work, and a sign that the wild Arctic was not yet quite tamed by Christian proselytising.

Mikak's final years seem to bear this out, to some extent. After being somewhat ostracised by Hutton, Mikak made several unsuccessful requests over the following decade to be baptised with her son, who had by 1774 taken the name 'Palliser', after Governor Hugh, the man who had taken them to England. She had continued to hunt and fish itinerantly in the traditional fashion, much to the missionaries' frustration, and had suffered ignominy at the hands of her husband, Tuglavina, who had abandoned Mikak for several other women, including her own sister. Mikak struck up a long-term relationship with one of these women's abandoned husbands, Pualo. She disappears from the historical record for a decade between 1780 and 1790, before resurfacing for her hard-fought baptism in 1795, just prior to her death at the age of fifty-five.

303

NAME. White Jane No.

Trade - - - Nursery Maid

Height without shoes 5-1

Age - - - 22 [illegible]

Complexion - Dark [illegible]

Head - - - Long

Hair - - - [illegible]

Whiskers - - —

Visage - - - Long

Forehead - - High

Eyebrows - - [illegible]

Eyes - - - Hazel

Nose - - - [illegible]

Mouth - - - [illegible]

Chin - - - Short

Remarks - - [illegible]

[illegible]

CHAPTER 8

'Pricking various figures on their flesh with the point of a pin': Jane White, Mary Cunningham and the Forty Thieves, 1838

'Tattooed people who are not in prison are either latent criminals or degenerate aristocrats. Sometimes, they do reach the end of their life without reproach, but that is only because they died before they committed their crime.'

—Adolf Loos, *Ornament et Crime*, c. 1910

'This custom is a completely savage one, which is found only rarely among some persons who have fallen from our honest classes, and which does not prevail extensively except among criminals, with whom it has had a truly strange, almost professional, diffusion.'

—Cesare Lombroso, *The Savage Origins of Tattooing*, 1896

When the police arrived to investigate a robbery at the house shared by Jane White and Mary Clifford, they initially found no trace of William Giles's cash, which had been taken from him earlier in the evening. They did find White, her fingers blackened from soot, and in the hearth, the remains of Giles's purse, burned to ashes. The coins were an arm's length up the chimney, concealed on a small ledge.

Left: Transportation record of Jane White, 1838

Caught red-handed – or, I suppose, black-thumbed – White and Clifford were both found guilty, their extraordinarily flimsy alibis of having been with their respective mothers at the time of the theft failing to convince the judge. As punishment, both women were sentenced to be transported to Australia, and to be held there for seven years each.

At the gaol, both women were stripped and revealed to be tattooed. Clifford was pricked on her left arm with the initials MJ, perhaps indicating the name of a current or former boyfriend. White was more extensively marked, bearing tattooed pictures of a woman, a man and a heart on her left arm, and the initials JLL on her right. Her hands were tattooed, too, marked with small dots of ink. To Inspector Derwing, the policeman who took them down to the cells, the presence of these ink-marks could indicate only one thing – that White and Clifford were not simply wayward rogues chancing their luck as they took advantage of an innocent pensioner, but rather members of a notorious gang of pickpockets, robbers, sex workers and ne'er-do-wells who had been terrorising London for years.

Yes. The tattoo on her hand gave it away.

It was the Mark of the Forty Thieves.

* * *

The crime had not been one of preordained malice, but the circumstances which led up to it did suggest perhaps a degree of forethought on the young women's part.

Jane White was already exuberantly drunk on gin when she encountered William Giles wandering the streets of east London. Giles, an elderly military pensioner up in London from Oxford, was lonely, and trawling London's Smithfield district in search of company and shelter for the night. Falling out of a pub after a day's drinking, he caught White's attention as she passed him in the street.

'Wench! Wert thou going?' he called after her in his broad rural accent.

'I'm looking for a sweetheart,' she replied.

White suggested he might want to accompany her back to the home she shared with her friend Mary. He eagerly agreed.

Giles would later implausibly insist to the Old Bailey that he planned only to 'sleep until morning', and that he had not made any improper bargains with the young women for anything other than lodgings, even though, he boasted, 'she said she had taken quite a fancy for I'. Whatever his intentions, the evening quickly turned from a quiet night of rest and became increasingly raucous, with White and Clifford persistently demanding Giles furnish them with more booze. He gave them the last of the gin he had with him, and when that had been hastily consumed, he pressed some coins into White's hand, insisting she head out to buy more, plus a pint of porter for himself.

After her return, the trio continued drinking until their bottles were once again dry. Giles gave White some more money, and once more sent her out into the night to buy gin, as well as some meat for supper. Clifford and White, canny and streetwise even at the tender ages of nineteen and twenty-one, clearly sensed they had an easy mark in Giles, and continued to ply him with booze and press him for cash as the night wore on.

Giles realised he was being robbed. He had secreted his money-purse inside his shoe for safekeeping, but White had seen where he'd stashed it, and passed it to Clifford, who stuffed it down her top in a clumsy attempt to hide it. The old man realised what was happening and grabbed White in anger, prompting her friend to pick up the dinner knife and threaten to stick him with it. She'd 'Burke' him, she said, – murder him and sell his body for cash in the manner of famed Victorian killer Edmund Burke. The two women fled and he gave chase, clumsily pulling on his clothes as he ran after them, stumbling down the stairs and shouting for help.

He had – he later said – already 'headed' to sleep when the young women snatched his coin purse from him. He had already retired to bed when Clifford pulled the knife on him, which explained quite clearly and innocently, of course, why he wasn't wearing any trousers at the time.

* * *

By the time of Clifford and White's arrest in October 1838, stories of the fearsome tattooed gang of Forty Thieves had been appearing in the papers for more than a decade. The Forty were 'the terror of the Borough . . . in the habit of committing the most daring depredations'. They were an infestation, violent, dangerous.

As most famously depicted in Charles Dickens' *Oliver Twist,* which was being serialised at the time of White and Clifford's arrest, poor young boys and girls in Victorian London frequently turned to petty crimes to survive, and as a result a veritable moral panic had developed around the criminal habits of apparently degenerate inner-city youth. Everyday stories of children and teenagers arrested for stealing cheese, boots or silk handkerchiefs, for fighting in the streets, or even simply for loitering, were frequently given an extra layer of salaciousness with the description of tattoo marks which proved at a glance that these kids were part of a ferocious organised crime operation.

In *Oliver Twist,* Dickens has the villainous gangmaster Fagin worried that the eponymous orphan might shop him to the authorities, bringing his whole crooked enterprise to an end:

> Suppose that lad was to peach – to blow upon us all – first seeking out the right folks for the purpose, and then having a meeting with 'em in the street to paint our likenesses, describe every mark that they might know us by, and the crib where we might be most easily taken.

Fagin's immediate concern is the police recognising him by a distinctive burn on his neck, but his worry about the indexing of visible marks on his gang of thieves would have resonated with Dickens' audience, given the frequency with which pickpockets' tattoos were mentioned in public reports and official paperwork.

A decade earlier, in September 1828, the *Evening Standard* had reported on the story of William Creamer, a 'tall, stout lad' caught stealing flannel from a tradesman. On his hand, proving he was one of the Forty, was a mark between the thumb and forefinger, and on his arm, he was tattooed with a heart pierced through with an arrow, plus the initials of a woman, reportedly 'a prostitute with whom he cohabited'. That same month, a dozen girls all under seventeen years of age had been found to be bearing the dot marks when they were arrested for singing lewd songs in the street.

Earlier that same summer, too, a boy under the age of twelve called Rutledge had been caught pickpocketing. In his trial, the magistrate had attested that 'the thieves belonging to the gang had peculiar marks on their hands and arms, by which they were known to each other'. Rutledge was ordered to roll up his sleeve and pricked out in gunpowder were a set of initials – his own, and again those 'of a prostitute', as every juvenile member of the gang reputedly bore the name of his 'fancy woman'. Like Creamer, he too had a dot between his forefinger and thumb, much to the delight of the magistrate, who realised that he would be able to use these tattoos to distinguish these hardened and formidable gang members – children, remember! – from ordinary prisoners, and thus stop them from fraternising in gaol.

Throughout the 1830s, news reports assiduously tracked the Forty Thieves and their 'mark' in their headlines and their court reporting. Many stories describe initials and dots, often alongside images of women, but close inspection also reveals something rather odd: the supposedly determinative 'mark' shifted frequently over the years both in design and the body part upon which it was inscribed.

For example, in the same month as Rutledge's arrest, 'two little urchins' had the 'private mark of the Forty Thieves' not on the backs of their hands, but on their palms. This time, rather than dots, each boy had a number marked on him – five and eight, respectively – 'pricked with a pin and rubbed over with gunpowder'. A year later, a thirteen-year-old arsonist was distinguished as a member of the gang by a 'triangular mark' on his hand, which he claimed to have had done at the Naval School in Greenwich, but whose grandmother attested was acquired whilst the lad had been held at the notorious Coldbath Fields House of Correction. In 1830, pickpockets were identified as members of the Forty by three blue stripes tattooed on their thumbs; in 1831, two brothers, one sixteen, the other just ten, bore the mark on their wrists. In the most shocking example, a five-year-old orphan boy called John Jones was found at his trial for shoplifting to have been tattooed on his hand with a black cross, 'the same mark used by a band of little fellows who went by the name of the Forty Thieves. The boy said it was not put there by his own desire, but by some boys who did it with soot and a needle, and told him it would soon rub out.'

In many cases, including that of Jane White, the single 'mark of the Forty Thieves' was often simply one of many tattoos an individual prisoner had acquired. In one striking instance, a fourteen-year-old, George Freeman, was clearly identified by arresting officers as being a member of the gang by the dots on his hands, but his prison records describe a number of tattoos all over his body, including an anchor, a mermaid, a half moon, a sun and seven stars. As such, the linking of tattooing and the Forty became a common prosecutorial shorthand throughout the 1830s, and the very presence of tattoo marks, particularly on the hands, was enough to signify gang affiliation. It didn't seem to matter if the mark was a dot, a cross, a number, a set of initials or a triangle, or if it was on the hand, palm, wrist, or even elsewhere on the body – the Forty Thieves were a gang of tattooed miscreants, and any tattoo would be enough to inevitably link you with the gang as far as the police and the courts were concerned.

* * *

The common sight of tattooed ruffians in Victorian courthouses and prisons allowed policemen, judges, gaolers and the general public to begin to build up an image in their minds of the kind of person who got tattooed. Though, as we have seen in the introduction to this part, tattooing had been present in ordinary populations in Europe dating back to the seventeenth century or even earlier, the practice was not frequently visible to the general public. Where pricking or tattooing *was* mentioned in the Georgian and early Victorian eras, it was almost always in reports about sailors, about 'savages', or in the context of an official record about a criminal, runaway or wanted suspect, where the marks described could offer an identificatory clue.

In a vivid, early example of this phenomenon, amongst a motley collection of thieves and other sundry criminals tried at the 1738–9 Christmas Quarter Sessions for the County of Surrey, one stood out. At the session, five men were convicted of petty larceny, and four of them were sentenced to be stripped to the waist, tied to the back of a cart and publicly whipped as they were pulled from the county gaol on Borough High Street to the gates of St Thomas' Hospital.

> One of them, a Rogue of about 15 years of age convicted of stealing Weights out of Salter's Shop in the Borough, from a Natural Propensity to Villainy, had on his Breast, mark'd with Indian ink, the Poutraiture of a Man at length, with a Sword drawn in one Hand and a Pistol discharging Balls from the Muzzle in the other, with a Label from the Man's Mouth, *G-d d-amn you, stand.* This the Rogue would have conceal'd, but a Discovery being made thereof, he was order'd to shew his Breast to the Court, who were all shock'd at so uncommon a Sight in so young a Ruffian.

The scale of this boy's tattooing, as well as that of the marks on the Virginian colony servants described in the introduction to this part, suggests a thriving subculture of tattooing in England which seemingly barely changed in style or technique for more than a hundred years through the eighteenth and nineteenth centuries.

Aside from brief glimpses in rare examples such as this one, however, that subculture is almost invisible. Because Georgian and Victorian tattooing was predominantly carried out behind closed doors and worn hidden under clothing during daily life, it would have been unknown to all but the most intimate of one's acquaintances. Furthermore, without any comprehensive picture of tattooing in the general population, it is impossible to properly address just how widespread marking of the skin really was, resulting in a sense that perhaps the only people who ever got tattooed at all were those, like Jane and Mary, of a rather dubious character.

* * *

In 1864, an Italian military doctor, Cesare Lombroso, was studying the supposed relationships between the character of his patients and their physical appearances. 'I was struck,' he later wrote, 'by a characteristic that distinguished the honest soldier from his vicious comrade: the extent to which the latter was tattooed and the indecency of the designs that covered his body.'

To make sense of this apparent connection between tattooing and viciousness, Lombroso began a systematic programme of studying the bodies of soldiers, patients, criminals and the dead, keen to combine psychology and physiognomy to understand how character was expressed in and on the body. And in the 1870s, whilst studying the cadaver of arsonist Giuseppe Villella, he realised that the man's skull had a deep indentation, making it more 'apelike' than human.

'This was not merely an idea,' he wrote, 'but a revelation.'

> At the sight of that skull, I seemed to see all of a sudden, lighted up as a vast plain under a flaming sky, the problem of the nature of the criminal – an atavistic being who reproduces in his person the ferocious instincts of primitive humanity and the inferior animals. Thus were explained anatomically the enormous jaws, high cheekbones, prominent superciliary arches, solitary lines in the palms, extreme size of the orbits, handle-shaped or sessile ears found in criminals, savages, and apes, insensibility to pain, extremely acute sight, tattooing, excessive idleness, love of orgies, and the irresistible craving for evil for its own sake, the desire not only to extinguish life in the victim, but to mutilate the corpse, tear its flesh, and drink its blood.

Physiognomy – the pseudoscientific idea that moral character is reflected in someone's physical appearance – is a very old and deeply entrenched idea. There was a longstanding belief in popular culture and discourse, even before Lombroso's revelation, that criminals *look different* from law-abiding citizens, and that by extension anyone whose appearance differed from cultural norms through race, disability or deformity was prone to criminality. As Irish political prisoner John Mitchel observed of his fellow inmates in 1854, for example, misquoting Shakespeare's *King John*, 'many of them have evil countenances and amorphous skulls – poor fellows! – burglars and swindlers from the womb. *By nature marked, coted and signed to do some deed of shame!*'

Lombroso's additional insight – if that really is the right word for it – was that the evolutionary theories of the mid-nineteenth century could add a new scientific layer of explanation to such physiognomic ideas when applied to the study of antisocial behaviour.

Villella, as he noted, was similar to an ape or a 'savage' in both his character and his body. Many evolutionary thinkers of the period believed that non-white people were behind whites on an evolutionary timeline back to non-human ancestors, and that this relative primitiveness explained (indeed, proved) the superiority of European cultures over those from elsewhere in the world. Physiognomy had long argued that as moral character could be divined by studying the body, cultural differences between human populations were correlated with – or perhaps even caused by – physical differences in groups of people across geography and through time.

If that was the case, Lombroso argued, then certain physical features that were seen to be more prominent in non-white people would be indicative of a degraded, primitive character if exhibited in a white European. Tattooing was thus an excellent signifier of something much more than simply a desire to mark the skin. Tattooing marked savagery, and with savagery came criminality and degeneracy.

In his book *The Criminal Man*, the foundational text of modern criminology, Lombroso calls tattooing 'one of the most singular characteristics of primitive men and those who still live in a state of nature'. Over the course of a chapter, he explains that he has compared rates of tattooing 'among normal individuals for the sake of comparison'. However, his initial control set was a group of soldiers in the Italian army, and so there was no attempt to assess rates of tattooing in the general population at all. This, of course, results in an entirely circular argument: if you're only studying tattooing in criminals, soldiers and sex workers, you will inevitably find a great deal of tattoos on criminals, soldiers and sex workers, and thus be able to claim the singular presence of tattooing amongst those groups. Moreover, without any sense of tattooing outside the military, you will be unable to account for any cultural reason – deference to authority or uniform rules, say, or the simple popularity of tattooing in prison as a pastime rather than an atavistic endeavour, which might explain disparities between different sub-populations of enlisted men.

By the latter part of his career, in 1896, Lombroso was sufficiently distressed by an increasing uptake of tattooing in the fashionable corners of London – a phenomenon we will discuss later – to pen an article entitled 'The Savage Origins of Tattooing'. In it, he presents the final form of the prejudiced argument he had by then been developing for over three decades:

> The influences of atavism and tradition seem to me to be confirmed by the fact that we find the custom of tattooing diffused among classes so tenacious of old traditions as shepherds and peasants.
>
> After this study, it appears to me to be proved that this custom is a completely savage one, which is found only rarely among some persons who have fallen from our honest classes, and which does not prevail extensively except among criminals, with whom it has had a truly strange, almost professional, diffusion; and, as they sometimes say, it performs the service among them of uniforms among our soldiers. To us they serve a psychological purpose, in enabling us to discern the obscurer sides of the criminal's soul, his remarkable vanity, his thirst for vengeance, and his atavistic character, even in his writing.
>
> Hence, when the attempt is made to introduce it into the respectable world, we feel a genuine disgust, if not for those who practice it, for those who suggest it, and who must have something atavistic and savage in their hearts. It is very much, in its way, like returning to the trials by God of the middle ages, to juridical duels atavistic returns which we can not contemplate without horror.

Because the wider and deeper histories of tattooing were invisible or had been forgotten and suppressed, the result of Lombroso's theorising was a fertile intellectual soil in which new theories about tattooing could grow. Watered by racism, colonialism, ableism, the fruits of these academic labours produced a tenacious set of assumptions about tattooing which still persist.

The idea was wildly influential across Europe, inspiring adaptations and responses from thinkers such as Alexandre Lacassagne in France and Havelock Ellis in England. Lacassagne and others even built anatomical collections of tattooed skins taken from criminals as resources through which to access the workings of the criminal mind. In some senses, we even live with the echoes of these ideas into the twenty-first century, with systematic recording and profiling of tattoos by law-enforcement agencies still common, and a mass media culture that still so often uses tattooing as a visual signifier of moral decay and criminal association.

* * *

Jane and Mary were sentenced to transportation to Australia, and each lived a rebellious life in the colony, frequently absconding. In the newspaper accounts following their trials, however, the inevitable association between tattooing and crime that Lombroso and his fellow criminologists would seed into the public consciousness several decades later was already revealed to be not only utterly misconstrued, but also based on the rudimentary mistake of conflating what is visible with what is actually occurring.

After Inspector Derwing had proudly identified Jane White as the latest of the Forty Thieves to have been taken off the streets, it was left to the gaoler, Mr Waddington, to patiently explain the policeman's error to the court. 'No such gang ever existed,' he said. Whilst there were undoubtedly lots of tattooed people in London, and some of them happened to be criminals, not every tattooed person is a criminal, and certainly not every tattooed person knows everyone else who happens to be tattooed.

Thirty years before Lombroso's observations on the Italian Army, a humble gaoler from London had, in a handful of sentences, exposed the basic error of more than a century of criminological study of tattooing before it had even begun.

'Such marks were frequently found on persons who were never connected with thieves,' Waddington explained, patiently. 'It originated some years ago in the Mint, Borough, where a set of loose and idle characters were in the habit of pricking various figures on their flesh with the point of a pin, and rubbing in gunpowder, or Indian Ink, and it was impossible ever to remove the marks. Some would prince rings around their fingers and make five dots about their hands, whilst others would have the names of fancy men and women about their breasts.'

'He had heard a great deal about the Forty Thieves,' the report concluded, 'but he never knew of such a gang, and it was all nonsense.'

PART THREE

TATTOOING AFTER 1853

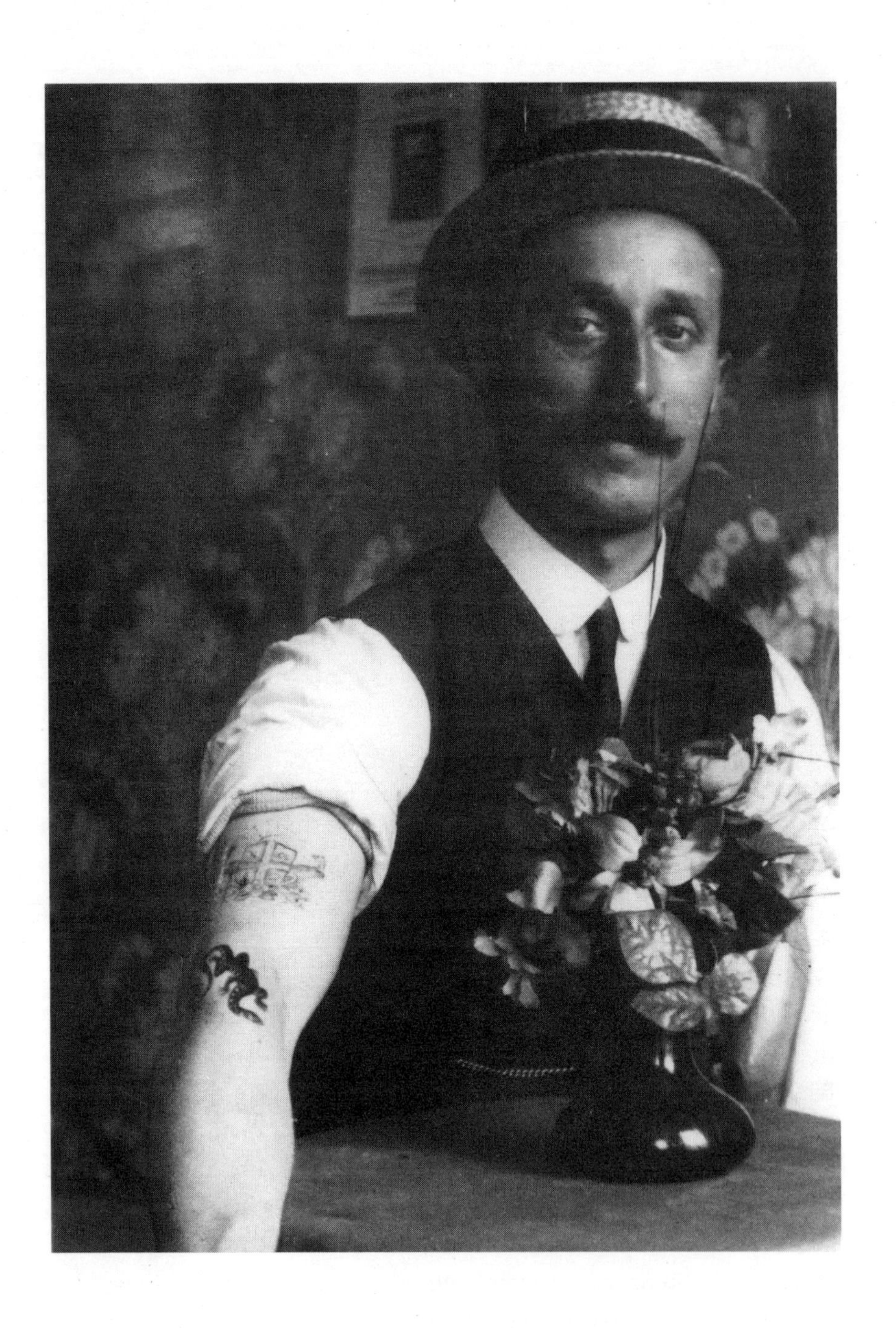

TATTOOING AFTER 1853: 'A PERFECT FRENZY'

'If you are like some children I know you have a perfect frenzy for decalcomania, a mania it is indeed with you. Now take my advice and don't adorn every available vase and door handle and even tattoo your hands and face with them.'

—*Indiana Herald*, 22 December 1875

There is a lovely but increasingly obscure word in the English language, 'cockamamie'. It has come to mean something like 'foolish'. The OED defines its noun form as 'an absurd, muddled, or crazy situation or thing' or a 'ridiculous, crazy, or wildly eccentric person'. More commonly these days, it is an adjective, meaning 'implausible' or 'hare-brained'. It first appeared in American English children's slang in about the 1920s, but its roots go back to the early 1860s.

As cockamamie as it may initially sound, the cultural and linguistic changes that formed the meaning of this strange multisyllabic word during the second half of the nineteenth century are directly connected to the changes that transformed tattooing in the West from a subcultural habit, mainly involving close friends, comrades and confidantes, into a recognisably professional art. The stigmatised and intimate marks made in these decades connect past centuries of historical practice to the impending future moment when tattoo shops began to dot urban landscapes across Europe and North America. The chapters in this part show Western tattooing at a pivotal moment, as the custom of pricking symbols amongst thieves, sailors and schoolboys morphed from the

Left: Tattooed man, UK, nineteenth century

marginalised and hidden, to the fashionable and visible. And as the public perception of tattooing's present changed rapidly, the misconceptions about tattooing's past needed to be re-evaluated at the same time.

* * *

Before 'cockamamie' came to be a term indicating derision and confusion, kids in New York during the 1920s used it to describe little motifs printed onto sheets of self-adhesive paper, the kind that were given away in packs of bubblegum and sold over the counter in corner stores and bodegas. Cockamamies! You could stick them all over your house to brighten the place up a bit, though they were so extraordinarily hard to remove that one frustrated housewife described them as 'the equivalent of getting your house tattooed'.

Alternatively, rather than permanently decorating your bedroom walls, you could use them as temporary tattoos, beautifying your body with cockamamies to make yourself look like a haggard, swarthy sailor. 'Painted strips of paper,' they were 'applied to your wrist, and rubbed with spit until the image was transferred to your hand.' A writer in Oakland recalled in 1948 how when he was a child, he and his playmates 'followed the craze of plastering our hands, arms, legs and even our faces with colored transfer pictures purchased for a dollar a sheet at the neighborhood candy store. We pretended, as children still do, that we were tattooed men in a circus sideshow.' As a character in Henry Roth's 1934 novel *Call it Sleep* more evocatively put it, 'I could buy fuh two cends cockamamies and pud em on mine hull arm.'

The term was still in use to describe these novelties far into the 1960s. In a 1967 issue of *Playboy*, for example, a short story imagined a man whose mother had sent him a box full of childhood junk for Christmas. Alongside a battered doll of a character from *Popeye*, a ragged teddy bear and a grimy space helmet, it was some small scraps of self-adhesive paper that sparked the most evocative of memories. He was 'sucked bodily into this sobering and edifying dissection of [his] formative years.

'I returned to my investigation, fishing up next a collection of thin sheets of paper bound together with a crusty old rubber band that broke in my hand immediately, spilling the crinkly slips out over the floor,' the narrator explained. 'Cockamamies! I hail unearthed some unused gems from the precious collection that I had bought over the years at Old Man Pulaski's. He really hated the times when we would come in to buy these tissue-paper tattoos that dissolved in water.'

The sheets were printed with violent designs from his youth during the Second World War, evoking popular tattoo themes from the period. (Of course, the stickers almost seemed to beg to be finally detached from their backing paper after all these years.) 'I licked the ancient decal, tasting the old familiar glue flavor that I knew would not leave my mouth for a month,' he described, 'and meticulously smoothed the soggy cockamamie onto the back of my left hand, blowing on it expertly, as I had done so often in the past, to dry it off. Now for the delicate part. With the skill of a surgeon, I slowly peeled off the moist backing.' He was disturbingly proud of the finished result, a blunt and bloody depiction of an impaled enemy soldier sitting brightly on his fist.

* * *

These adhesive tattoos had directly and linguistically evolved from an earlier decorative hobby first popularised in the early 1860s called 'decalcomania', or 'decalcomanie', from which we also got the more familiar word 'decal'. (Its root is French – *décalquer*, meaning to trace, and *manie*, a mania. Decalcomania: a craze for decoration.)

Amongst Yiddish speakers in interwar New York, so the story goes, no one knew how to spell 'decalcomania', and thus 'cockamamie' was coined. Decalcomanias were designs printed on paper, intended to be cut out and glued onto flat surfaces. They had become extraordinarily fashionable during the 1860s and '70s, spawning a whole industry selling books packed full of images, as well as specialist application brushes and glues, depending on what precisely you might want to decorate. As one newspaper advertisement from 1866 boomed: 'DECALCOMANIA, the art of ornamenting China, glass, earthen and woodenware, jewel or other fancy boxes, marble, ivory, papier-maché goods, tinware, bindings of books, cigar cases, fans, leatherwork of every description, and in short every possible article considered worth while to be beautified and made attractive, and thus increased in value by this new process.' Even back in the 1870s, though, newspapers were already commenting on kids' propensities to stick them on their hands as if they were tattoos.

It is easy to imagine why, as a list of the popular motifs reads much like the list of designs you might find hanging in a stereotypical tattoo shop window. An 1876 catalogue of decalcomanias and transfer ornaments published in Boston, for example, allows us to imagine young children playing as tattooed sailors, covering their arms with scrolls, lions, tigers and grizzly bears, American eagles and shields, birds on branches, bouquets of flowers, cupids, muses and portraits of women.

The practice was taken up in Europe and America with great gusto in the aftermath of the forcible opening of Japan to the West in 1853. As we will discuss in greater detail in the coming chapters, Japan had been closed to most foreign visitors and trade for more than two centuries, but was forced to rapidly transform into a modern society and become part of the global order after an American gunboat fleet arrived, threatening the ruling Shogunate with invasion if they did not allow foreign access to Japanese goods and resources.

After the subsequent political turmoil, known as the Meiji Restoration, Japanese arts, decorative goods, textiles and furniture flooded westwards. Japanese arts were so novel, so inspiring, so beautiful and so stylistically disconnected from Western trends that artistic tastes and fashions across Europe were rapidly transformed. The decalcomania craze is a direct result of this process.

* * *

In 1866, French ceramics dealer Eugene Rousseau commissioned the designer Félix Bracquemond to design a set of porcelain for the Paris World's Fair the following year. Searching for inspiration, Bracquemond claimed to have been unwrapping imported pieces of tableware from Japan and noticed that the packing paper in which the pieces had been wrapped was covered in extraordinary designs of animals, frogs and flowers.

These ornamented pages had been carelessly torn from books by the now-revered Japanese artist Hokusai: his *manga*, or collections of 'random drawings', which had been produced in great numbers in Japan in the decades before the Americans had arrived. In a flash of creativity which has been hailed as transformational for art and material culture in Europe, Bracquemond was inspired to carefully cut individual pictures from Hokusai's pages, and to delicately transfer them onto white porcelain plates, cups, bowls and saucers. The resulting dinner service – the *Service Rousseau* – was an immediate, seismic hit in the most fashionable corners of Parisian high society, and has been hailed as the moment when Japanese art and European popular culture collided, sparking the cultural movement known as *japonisme* and, in its wake, modernism.

Ordinary consumers had been trying to cheaply replicate the kind of fine Oriental porcelain that had been newly arriving in grand homes and museums since the earliest moments after the Americans had threatened invasion. The first of these trends – called 'potichomania' after the French term *potiche* given to a particular type of Oriental vase – involved painting Orientalist patterns and pictures directly onto European ceramicware. This quickly morphed into decalcomania around 1865, as the cut-and-stick process was more accessible to those without much artistic ability to draw designs themselves. But once Bracquemond had used similar transfer techniques to graft Japanese paper pictures onto high-end crockery, the humble hobby took on great new energy, acquiring a particular social cachet in the process.

* * *

In the aftermath of the Meiji restoration, tattooing was also part of this craze for all things Japanese. Many early foreign visitors to Japan were tattooed by local artists, including the Duke of Edinburgh, and as authentic decorative arts became harder to come by as supplies dwindled, tattooing remained a way by which a wealthy traveller to Japan could acquire a unique piece of local art. Photographs, drawings and stories of Japanese tattooists were eagerly consumed abroad, and the tattoos produced both in Japan and by Japanese artists working in other countries transformed the way in which the general public understood tattooing as a whole. Before the encounter with Japan, most tattooing which ordinary people in Europe knew about was small, indelicate and crude. Afterwards, though, as *Cassell's Magazine* in London explained in 1873, the Japanese influence had come to define tattooing as an art-form in the Western imagination. By 1891, Japanese tattooing was so revered that an English-language guidebook explained to travellers that it had 'become an art indeed – an art as vastly superior to the ordinary British sailor's tattooing as Heidsieck Monopole [champagne] is to small beer'.

It is in these decades following the Meiji restoration in 1858, then, that tattooing becomes associated with the wealthy and the fashionable in Europe and North America, and it is a desire by the moneyed classes to be tattooed back home which makes tattooing, for the first time, a viable, permanent career in European and American towns and cities. As tattooers set up fixed establishments in order to work commercially and take advantage of this trend, they also frequently drew on fashionable Japanese designs for their tattoos – literally many of the same designs from Hokusai, for example, that Bracquemond had transferred onto his porcelain, and the same set of Oriental motifs that often featured so prominently in the decalcomania books.

In turn, this moment where duchesses, kings and captains of industry were getting proudly and openly tattooed also forced the European and American publics to reassess their own tattoo histories, and to begin to acknowledge tattooing as more refined, more socially acceptable and more visible than it had been in prior centuries. This process necessarily involved a re-evaluation of popular and scholarly perceptions about tattooing, and how the long history of tattooing on Europeans had been written about in the first half of the nineteenth century, following encounters with the much less aesthetically influential tattooing in the Pacific.

* * *

Decalcomania and tattooing are thus fundamentally connected as decorative arts that reimagine and reinterpret Western traditions through the lens of Japanese influence. When young children were stealing their mother's prized decals to play 'dress-up', they were doing so because real, professional tattoo artists were doing something similar when they transferred Japanese designs to skin, albeit more permanently. And, as we will see over the coming chapters, as the fancy and fashionable decalcomania hobby becomes first a childish mischief and then, by the 1940s, literally nonsensical and absurd, something rather similar happens to tattooing, too.

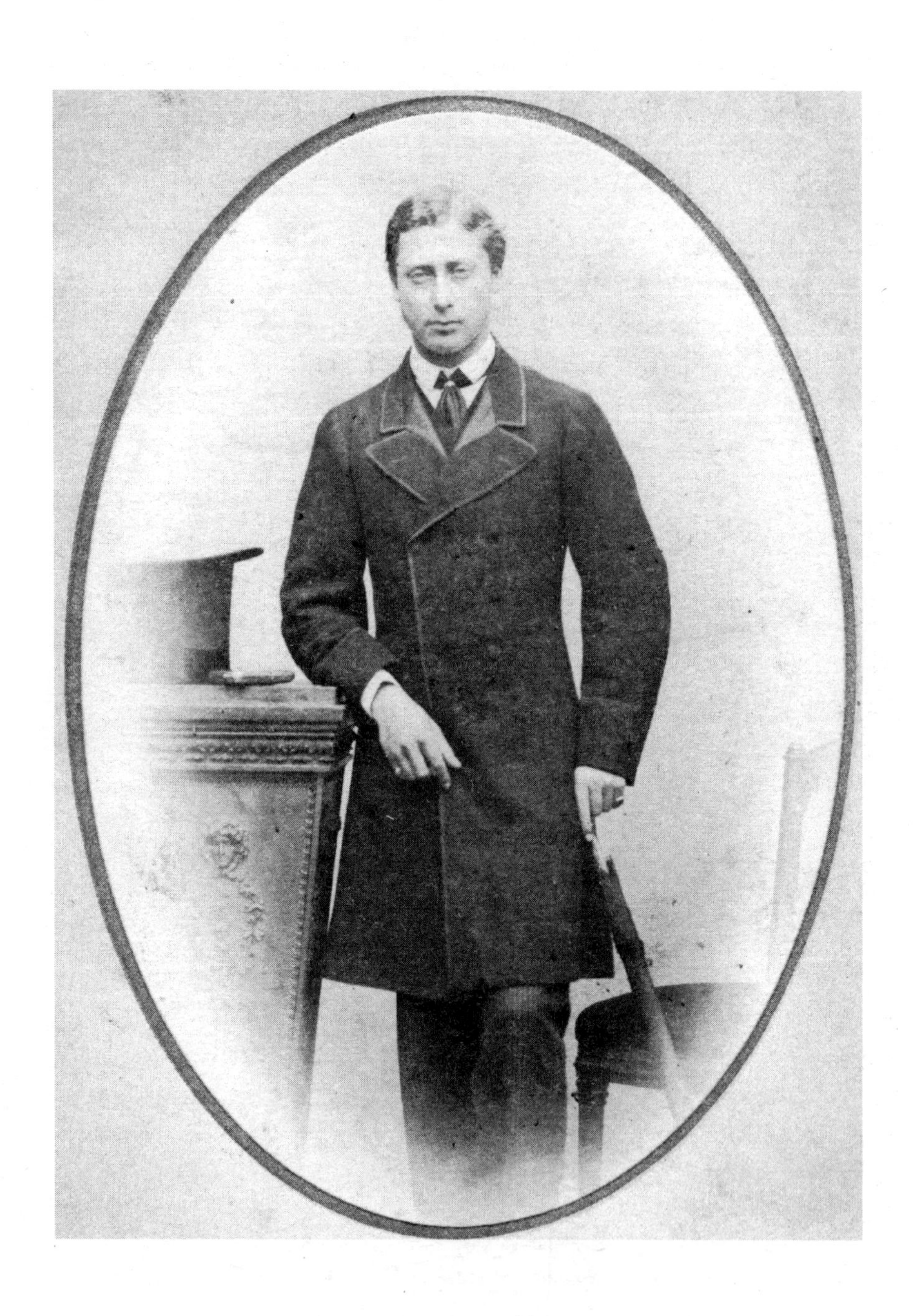

CHAPTER 9

'Gather up some good feelings, some more than merely passing pleasure, from these sacred scenes': Albert, Prince of Wales, 1862

'It must be observed that, although most prevalent among the lower classes, tattooing is by no means confined to the ignorant or debased. It is not long since the English papers rather indignantly commented upon a statement in the *Revue des deux mondes* that the Prince of Wales, when at Jerusalem, had permitted an anchor to be tattooed upon his arm.'

—Robert Fletcher, *Tattooing Amongst Civilised People*, 1882

On 1 April 1862, Queen Victoria's eldest son Albert, the future King Edward VII, recorded in his diary that he had been tattooed. 'In the evening,' he wrote, 'I was tatooed [sic] by a Native, and so was [one of my party], Keppel.' This tattoo begins the story of what would eventually become today's thriving British tattoo industry. It is but a trickle, but it is the stream from which much of the expansion into today's torrent can be traced. Like many streams, it is simply the manifestation of a much deeper well whose source lies buried deep in historical time.

Bertie was a callow youth (at least in his mother's estimation). He had spent his teenage years cultivating a life as a rakish playboy, seduced while an undergraduate at Oxford into a life of well-cut suits,

Left: Albert Edward, Prince of Wales, later King Edward VII, 1870

large cigars and rich, fattening food, as well as drinking, hunting, gambling and womanising. He was, by the accounts of his tutors, rude, lazy and intemperate, though well-liked by his peers. He had toured Canada and America in 1860, aged eighteen, where he was immediately welcomed as a celebrity, greeted by cheering crowds and invited to countless balls, dances and social occasions, and it is reported that before departing Boston he and several of his entourage were fitted with pairs of fashionable alligator skin boots. Following the death of the Queen's Consort, Prince Albert, in 1861, however, Victoria was insistent that her son calm his boisterous lifestyle and begin to live in a way more suited to the presumptive heir to the throne. A pilgrimage had already been planned, and despite his father's death, Bertie, future head of the Church of England, was dispatched on a low-key and rather austere journey to the Holy Lands of Egypt, Syria and Palestine, ostensibly to learn discipline, humility and spiritual purpose.

The Jerusalem of the 1860s was a strange, exotic place in the minds of many travellers. In the British imagination, it was the grand, almost mythical site of the Bible stories. Those who made a pilgrimage to the Holy Land, though, particularly by the nineteenth century, often found the disjunction between the stories of a place of sacred contemplation and the reality of a busy, noisy, bustling city at the meeting point of cultures somewhat jarring. From an account of a pilgrim who visited in the same period, it is possible to imagine the scene that greeted the prince that April morning. 'I can say nought of Jerusalem save lamentation, and mourning, and woe,' moaned a Mrs Augusta Mentor Mott, just two years after the prince's visit. Her report for 7 April 1864 describes the thronging city and its crowds of bizarre inhabitants. 'Truly her crown is fallen from her head; she sits silent in the dust, covered with sackcloth and ashes! . . . You can scarcely imagine how despoiled, dirty and dilapidated this city is. Then, too, it is the strangest medley of human beings ever congregated in one spot, all having their particular interests and feelings, animosities and predilections, besides, what is so strongly marked and diversified, their nationalities, costumes, and occupations.' In a remarkable, lengthy list, run through with explicitly racist descriptions, Mott describes a cast of characters including 'a group of half-naked, savage-looking Arabs playing at cards or dominoes', in states of dress and of apparent wealth from the ragged to the finely appointed, most of whom seem, by her descriptions, to be selling, hawking, or begging for money from travellers in this dirty, bustling bazaar. Amongst the women she describes, horrified, 'a party of Bedouin women – so hideously ugly! their thin lips dyed deep blue; their mouth, nose, and eyes tattooed with a circlet of blue spots.' It is not hard to imagine the prince's tattooist in this noisy marketplace, eagerly beckoning pilgrims into what we might today call his tattoo studio to receive a mark of their journeys.

In the spring of 1881, almost twenty years after Bertie's visit, a French journalist and travel writer by the name of Gabriel Charmes travelled to Jerusalem on assignment for the journal *Revue des Deux Mondes*. In one of his expansive reports, he relays how he was stopped in the bustling streets around the Holy Sepulchre by a friendly man offering to give him a tattoo on his arm to commemorate his pilgrimage to the Holy Land and to mark his religious devotion, a practice that had been common amongst Protestant pilgrims since the medieval period. 'He gave me various designs to choose from,' he explains, 'a Greek cross, a Latin cross, a Fleur-de-Lys, a spearhead, a star, and a thousand others. He told me it wouldn't hurt a bit, and I could smoke a hookah, drink coffee and chat to his wife and daughter whilst he did it.'

Despite the tattooist's comely wife and beautiful daughter beckoning him into the workshop, Charmes left Jerusalem without a tattoo, but not before noticing that on the walls of this makeshift studio hung several certificates and letters, one of which stood out. 'The Prince of Wales was clearly weaker than me when he gazed into the beautiful eyes of the tattooist's daughter,' Charmes writes. 'There was no doubt as to the authenticity of the certificate, which read "Let this be proof that Francis Souwan marked the cross of Jerusalem on the arm of His Royal Highness, the Prince of Wales. His Majesty was so pleased with the operation that he would certainly recommend it. Signed, Vane, emissary to HRH the Prince of Wales, Jerusalem, 2nd April, 1862".' 'I don't know how much the Prince paid,' concluded Charmes, 'but us mere mortals can acquire one of these designs to wear on our arms, or anywhere else on our bodies, for the very reasonable sum of five or ten francs.'

Bertie's taste for women was well known, so perhaps his first tattoo had more to do with the charms of Souwan's daughter than some innate desire to get tattooed (though as twenty years had passed and Charmes gives no indication of Souwan's daughter's age, this must naturally remain speculation). It is impossible, of course, to assess Bertie's thought process, and he seems never to have spoken of his tattoo again in any documentary source (nor does any public photo or portrait painting of him exist where it is visible).

As a rebellious young man who clearly enjoyed playing with his clothing and appearance, the tattoo may simply have been a moment of youthful recklessness. Nevertheless, 1 April 1862 had been an important moment in the young prince's trip, and a particularly momentous one in religious terms. That morning, he had paid a visit to various key religious sites including the Dome of the Rock, the Mosque of Omar, and the Dome of the Chain, and reputedly became the first Christian given permission to set foot inside the Mosque of Hebron at the biblical site of the Cave of Machpelah. Aboard HMS *Osborne* a couple of days before, Bertie had heard from the ship's priest, Arthur Penrhyn Stanley, that (as per John 6:12) the party arriving in Jerusalem 'cannot but gather up some good feelings, some more than merely passing pleasure, from these sacred scenes', and following a sermon urging Stanley's itinerant congregation to take some grain of this place's holiness into their hearts and home to England, it is perhaps not surprising that Bertie had his body marked – not, as Robert Fletcher had it with an anchor, but with the Jerusalem Cross, a large central cross surrounding four smaller ones, which symbolises the religious message of Christ emanating throughout the world and which featured prominently on the arms of the Franciscan custodians of the pilgrimage sites.

* * *

The modern history of tattooing on Europeans begins in the records of Christian pilgrimages to the Holy Land in the early modern period. Explicitly religious tattooing of Christian iconography has formed a key part of devotional and cultural practice in the region for centuries. Tattooing amongst Coptic Christians in Egypt, which persists to the present day, is very well documented, with early evidence of Christian religious tattooing existing back to the fifth and sixth centuries. As well as the Gebelein mummies, the British Museum collection includes an eighth-century, naturally preserved body of a woman from modern-day Sudan who bears a tattoo of the monogram of St Michael on her inner thigh. During the caliphate of Hisham, which stretched across the Middle East during the eighth century, both Christian and Muslim sources report that Egyptian Christians often wore tattoos or brands of lions on their hands, and that the presence of this mark acted as a kind of licence, as it was required to be able to engage in trade. Rogue traders without these tattoos risked having their hands amputated as punishment.

The tattooing of both Christian and Islamic pilgrims to the Holy Land and other sites including Loreto in Italy is therefore a practice with a long pedigree. From the late sixteenth century onwards, published accounts from Western Christian travellers to Jerusalem and elsewhere provide detailed evidence of a thriving practice of souvenir tattooing by local, largely Christian tattooers, including a remarkable continuity of technique and design over the centuries. As early as 1587, pilgrims to Bethlehem were marked – as Bertie would be centuries later – with the Jerusalem Cross.

By the late sixteenth century tattooing was such a central marker of pilgrimage that when it was published in a new edition, at least one published pilgrim narrative from the fifteenth century had a tale of tattooing inserted where none existed previously. The likely fictional tale of a pilgrim named Jan Aerts of Melchelen, who supposedly visited Jerusalem in 1484, features no mention of the prominent tattoos he supposedly witnessed on a recently deceased knight in its early iterations, but includes in a later edition from 1595 descriptions of both an image of St Catherine's martyrdom and, yes, a Jerusalem Cross. 'When this knight was deceased,' the late edition of Aert's travelogue tells us, 'were found burnt on his body two whole wheels with an oblique palm passing through them, and two double crosses usually worn by the knights of Jerusalem, one wheel in front

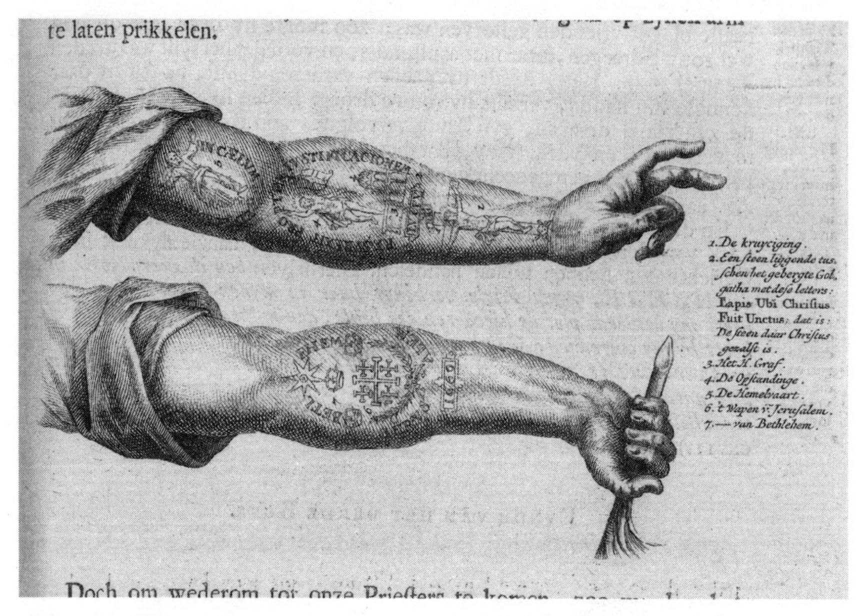

Engraving of the tattooed arms of German pilgrim Ratge Stubbe, 1726

on his chest, the other on his back; one cross on his right shoulder, the other on his left shoulder, which neither his first nor his second spouse, nor his father nor his mother, nor anyone had ever seen or also known about.'

Several pilgrim accounts are illustrated with pictures of the chosen tattoo designs. Various editions of the stories of German pilgrim Ratge Stubbe, for example, depict his complex of designs, including a three-part scene of Christ's Passion on one arm, and a Jersualem Cross and the date 1669 on the other. In an earlier example, Scottish Protestant William Lithgow proudly showed off his Jerusalem Cross design in published accounts of his 1612 pilgrimage, to which he asked the artist to add a crown of the anti-Catholic monarch King James VI/I. Years later, in 1620, Lithgow was captured by the Spanish Inquisition in Malaga, accused of espionage and heresy during a period of intense political tension between Britain and Spain. They considered the addition of James' crown to the religious mark so blasphemous and provocative that the Inquisitors forcibly excised the tattoo from Lithgow's arm whilst they had him stretched on a rack.

Some rare examples of paintings of tattooed pilgrims also survive, including one anonymous early eighteenth-century oil portrait of

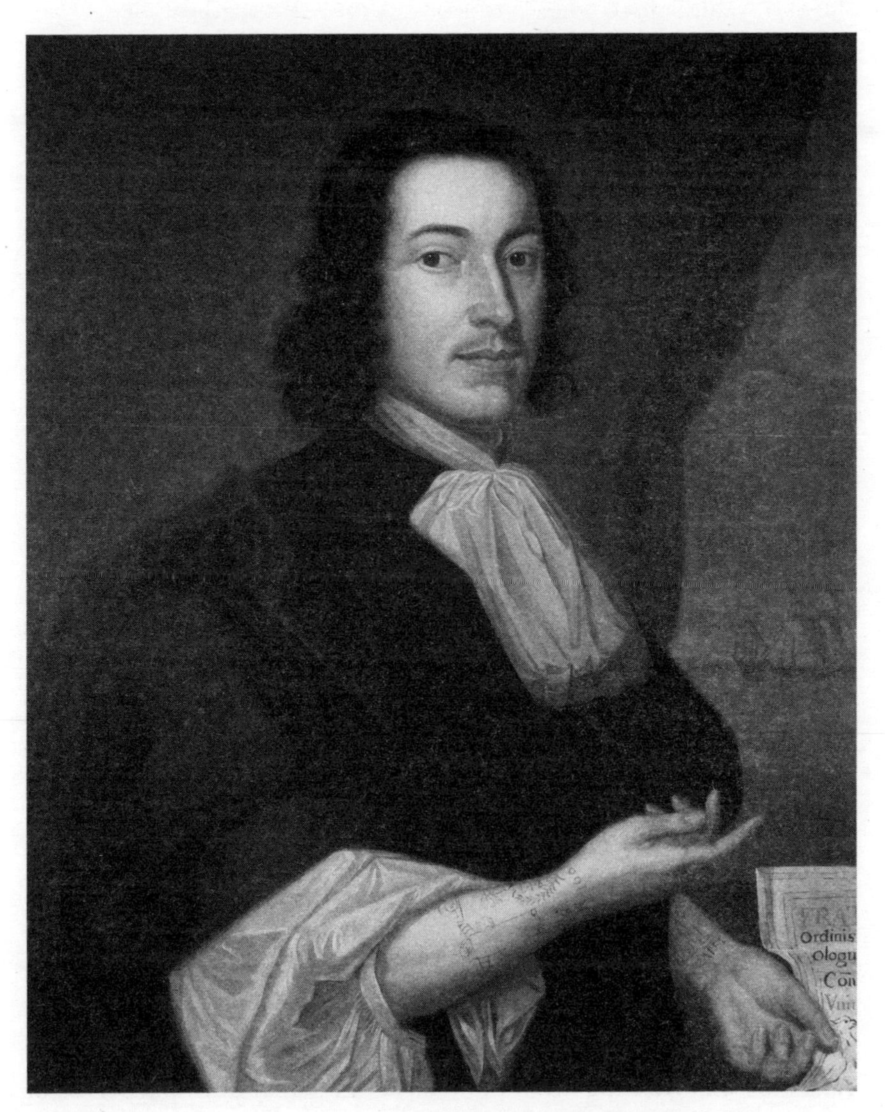

Portrait of an unknown pilgrim who travelled to Palestine in the 1660s

German diplomat Heinrich Ludolf, secretary to the Danish embassy at the Court of St James, in which his large 1699 tattoo depicting Christ's passion forms a key part of the scene. Another English portrait shows a wealthy man whose arms bear a 1660s date, a Jerusalem cross, the inscription NAZARET and the floor plan of Bethlehem's Grotto of the Nativity. In a sign that Lithgow's experience hadn't halted the practice of the inscription of crowns during times of political and religious turmoil, this crown also appears to be marked with the initials of a British king, likely Charles II in the aftermath of the Restoration.

There are a number of records of Jerusalem tattoos on the arms of sailors, criminals and runaways from the late seventeenth century onwards, and even a tantalising glimpse in the transcripts of the Old Bailey in London that some men who had returned from the Holy Lands had made a living applying religious tattoos to others in England, making them amongst the first professional tattooers in the Western world. In 1719 the trial transcript of two housebreakers called John Woodward and Thomas Williams, both of whom were marked with a cross tattoo, reveals that 'one of them said [it] was his Business to make the Jerusalem arms'.

The most elaborate accounts of pilgrimage tattoos, though, come from travellers who were from the aristocratic and clerical classes. One seventeenth-century account, by French traveller Jean de Thévenot, is particularly vivid: the design was stamped on the body using a carved wooden block dipped in ink, and then traced over several times by piercing the skin with a grouping of needles bound together with thread and dipped in an ink mixture of carbon black and ox bile, or 'gall', a naturally acidic substance also used for centuries as a solvent by watercolourists and engravers. 'We spent all Tuesday, the Nine and twentieth of April [1658],' de Thevenot writes, 'getting Marks put upon our Arms, as commonly all Pilgrims do; the Christians of Bethlehem (who are of the Latin Church) do that.'

> They have several Wooden Moulds, of which you may chuse that which pleases you best, then they fill it with Coal-dust, and apply it to your Arm, so that they leave upon the same the Mark of what Is cut in the Mould ; after that, with the left hand they take hold of

> your Arm and stretch the skin of it, and in the right hand they have a little Cane with two Needles fastened in it, which from time to time they dip into Ink, mingled with Oxes Gall, and prick your Arm all along the lines that are marked by the Wooden Mould: This without doubt is painful, and commonly causes a slight Fever, which is soon over; the Arm in the mean time for two or three days, continues swelled three times as big as it ordinarily is. After they have pricked all along the said lines, they wash the Arm, and observe if there be any thing wanting, then they begin again, and sometimes do it three times over. When they have done, they wrap up your Arm very streight, and there grows a crust upon it, which falling off three or four days after, the Marks remain Blew, and never wear out, because the Blood mingling with that Tincture of Ink and Oxes Gall, retains the mark under the Skin.

These accounts reveal a great deal about the actual practice of the working pilgrim tattooer in the seventeenth-century Holy Land. The first thing to note, perhaps, is the framing of the clearly common procedure as a transaction involving a degree of aesthetic choice, with the pilgrim choosing a favoured design from a selection made available to him. Key to this is the use of 'wooden moulds' or 'stamps', small blocks employed to create an outline of the chosen design on the skin for the tattooer to trace with his needles. Museum collections preserve several of these stamps, and a survey by John Carswell in 1956 describes and reproduces a collection of several hundred examples owned by a tattooer and coffin-maker by the name of Jacob Razzouk, 'the head of a family belonging to the small Coptic community in Jerusalem, where his ancestors settled in the eighteenth century, coming from Egypt'. Razzouk, whose family continues to tattoo in Jerusalem today, explained to Carswell that his clients at that time were largely Copts from Egypt, and that none would dare return home without a tattoo marking their trip. The seasonal trade, predictably centred around the major Christian pilgrimages at Easter, kept Razzouk busy, and he tattooed upwards of two hundred Egyptian Copts and members of other Christian denominations every year. Whilst Carswell visited, a queue of twenty customers waited patiently.

Razzouk had kept and continued to make use of a collection of stamps from his ancestors, carved by a variety of hands. Though certainly predating his own lifetime, Razzouk was unable to confirm when any of them had been made; Carswell argues that some dated back to the seventeenth century, though the earliest bearing a date showed 1749. They are remarkable objects.

Ranging from between a quarter of an inch to an inch in size, they are carved in cameo-relief from olivewood, chiselled to leave the design as a raised outline against the body of the block itself. They feature designs originally cut in silhouette, with the details engraved using fine tools. Many are inscribed on both faces. These stamps form the tattooers' 'catalogue of designs', from which pilgrims will have chosen, and their iconography reveals a broad swathe of images linked to the visual culture of pilgrimage, and to the wider tastes of his client base. Their imagery and styles are drawn from a variety of denominational cultures – 'Abyssinian, Syrian, Hebrew, Latin and Slav' – and range from small and simple decorative designs, such as the outline of flowers, through to others which are much more elaborate: one example depicts an assumptive Jesus rising from the arcaded tomb at the Church of the Holy Sepulchre; another stamp, which Razzouk's living relatives estimate is between two and three hundred years old, shows an elaborately dressed St George astride his horse, thrusting a spear through the dragon. Despite being rendered only in stylised outline, the carver has introduced a remarkable amount of detail, energy and potency to the design. The scaly dragon curls and snarls in the face of the saint's thrusting spear, as the steed rears its hooves and appears to flick its mane.

Carswell's book also includes two designs which feature the Jerusalem cross. The first shows a central cross picked out in simple lines and surrounded by four others, encircled by a band comprising three crowns in the top half and a wreath of leaves in the lower half, with the whole design capped by a seven-pointed star. The crowns and star suggest that this is a design for a pilgrim to Bethlehem. The second comprises the outline of a cross surrounded by four smaller crosses also in outline. Again wreathed, this is accentuated by a single crown and the inscription JERUSALEM beneath. This second design is, as Carswell notes, a common design on souvenir medallions sold in the city, where the design is inlaid in mother-of-pearl, making it an obvious choice as a souvenir tattoo design. Intriguingly, during their trial, the tattooing housebreaker in London – Woodward or Williams – showed the judge the 'Mark with which he did it', presumably a wooden design stamp similar to those in (or brought from) Jerusalem itself. The Jerusalem cross had been a common motif in the visual culture of pilgrimage since the seventeenth century, appearing on coins, in coats of arms and stitched onto clothing, forming part of a group of images and symbols emanating from the various religious traditions that hold Jerusalem sacred. Even as late as 1908, anthropologist A. T. Sinclair observed that the acquisition of a Jerusalem Cross tattoo was still common for basically every naval visitor to Jerusalem.

By the conventional reading, the pilgrimage tattoo becomes a spiritual marker of the journey made, a permanent bodily reminder of commitment, sacrifice and deeply held belief. The future king's tattoo is, in this light, a mark of piety, devotion and spiritual engagement. By a different reading, though, the tattooing might be read as a more straightforwardly commercial transaction, as something resembling a tourist souvenir. By the time of Bertie's visit in the mid-nineteenth century, as many pilgrimage accounts attest, Jerusalem had become submerged in base commerce: the sale of trinkets, baubles and tchotchkes to travellers now as much tourists as religious pilgrims. This tension between the spiritual importance of the pilgrimage and its debasement into something resembling 'tourism' had long been a source of contention amongst theologians, but the mass marketing of trinkets at pilgrim sites across the Christian world had been a tradition of such journeys even in the fifteenth century. Some historians even explicitly link the appearance of tattooing at Jerusalem in the late sixteenth century with a move to the promotion of journeys to the city by enterprising, entrepreneurial Franciscans, who considered souvenir tattooing to be part of the growing production of religious memorabilia in the Holy Land.

By the mid-nineteenth century the commercialisation of Jerusalem was in full swing. Even at the Church of the Holy Sepulchre, the site at which Christians believe Christ was crucified by the Romans, our pilgrim visitor Mrs Mott describes 'some grand mart, for the steep stair-like passage, and the quadrangle in front of the church, are crammed with pedlars, and buyers of rosaries, beads, crosses, mother-o'-pearl chasings, stones from the Dead Sea, coffee and sherbet, sweetmeats and snails, silk handkerchiefs, and other trumpery wares'. Tattooing was clearly part of this bazaar. The nineteenth-century French criminologist Alexandre Lacassagne describes how tattooing 'formed a veritable industry for those who sell devotional objects in front of the church', and Edward Hogg, writing as early as 1835, explicitly equates trinkets with tattooing, openly lamenting the poor state of artistic endeavour amongst Jerusalem's vendors:

> The trade of the town is confined to chaplets, crosses, carved shells, models of the sacred places, and mother-of-pearl receptacles for holy water, which, sanctified in the sepulchre, are eagerly sought for, and widely distributed through Catholic Europe. So low, however, is the state of the art, that one individual only, an ingenious and intelligent Jew, can engrave the seal rings so generally worn in the East, while a few native Christians carve rudely in mother-of-pearl, or tattoo the arms of pilgrims, with sacred symbols.

In truth, these kinds of pilgrim tattoos, like their analogues in copper, mother-of-pearl and carved shell, serve both devotional and tourist functions. They are simultaneously a meaningful symbol and an aesthetic trinket, a sign of both spiritual engagement and commercial desire. Journeys to the Holy Land mixed religious obligation with pleasurable social engagement and consumerism, and the material culture of pilgrimage cannot, and should not, be straightforwardly looked at only through one lens or the other.

As with other traditions, we cannot understand pilgrimage tattooing without understanding the surrounding visual and material cultures. It has been the kneejerk instinct of historians and sociologists to interpret tattooing only in relation to itself: as an esoteric practice that exists only in relation to its own narrow subcultural frameworks. Instead – as Bertie's tattoo testifies – tattooing not only reflects its own subcultures, but the wider concerns and visual trends of the mainstream culture of the time and place it was produced.

There is clear continuity between the content and form of pilgrimage tattoos and the designs reproduced on metal, wood and cloth for the same consumers.

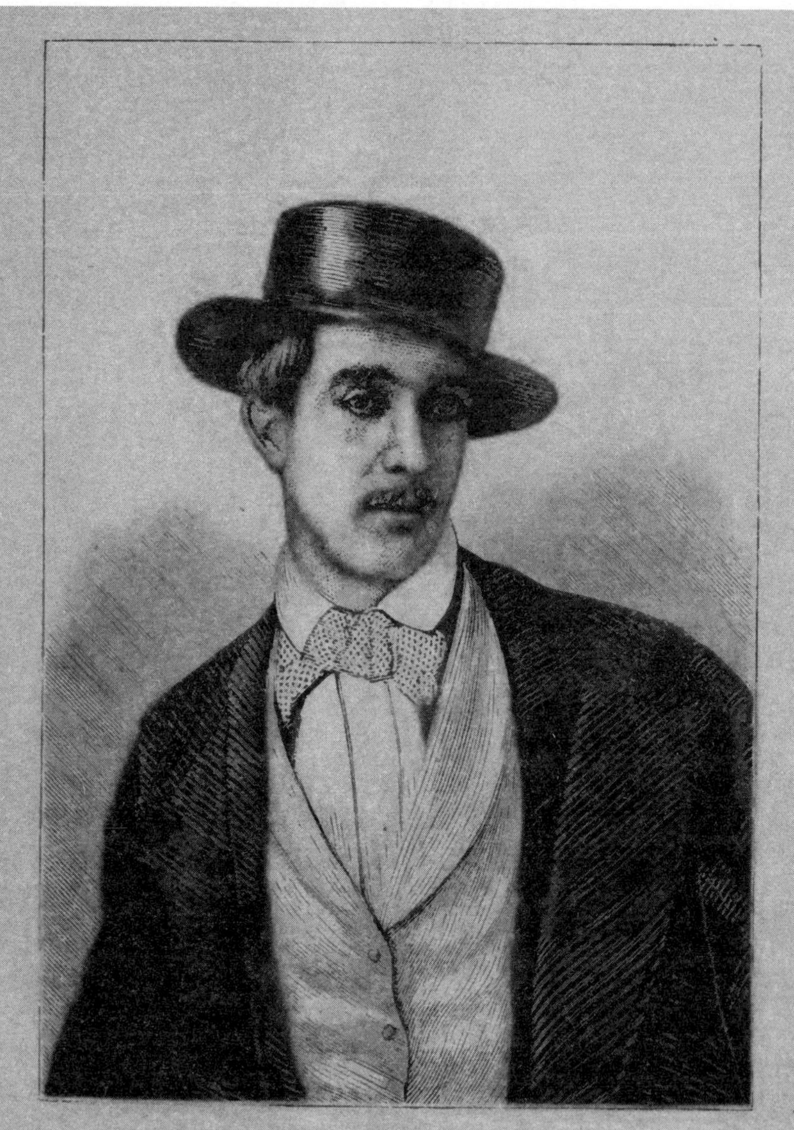

ROGER TICHBORNE (P. 9).

CHAPTER 10

'Do you tattoo your children yet?': Roger Tichborne, 1871

'Then a lot of shillyshally usually followed. Tom for and Dick and Harry against. And then, number one, you came up against the man in possession and had to produce your credentials, like the claimant in the Tichborne case, Roger Charles Tichborne. Bella was the boat's name to the best of his recollection he, the heir, went down in, as the evidence went to show, and there was a tattoo mark too in Indian ink, Lord Bellew, was it? As he might very easily have picked up the details from some pal on board ship . . .'

—James Joyce, *Ulysses*, 1922

'Titchborne is my name
I have been to Deal and Dover
If you saw me in my skin
You would find me tattooed all over'

—'I am the Real Sir Roger', music hall song, c. 1875

Sir John Coleridge was a few days into what would become an epic, twenty-six-day-long opening speech for the defence. The trial had already gripped the country for months. The court in session at Westminster Hall was packed, standing room only, and the trial's every word was serialised over several pages in *The Times* every single day. The entire nation was hooked, and Coleridge, though somewhat long-winded, flaccid in tone and hardly an inveterate showman at the

Left: Roger Tichborne, before his disappearance, illustrated in 1876

bench, was nonetheless relishing his role in the spotlight. With a dramatic flourish, he closed the afternoon's proceedings of 31 January 1872 on a cliff-hanger.

'Well,' he said, 'now I come to what, if I prove it, seems to me conclusive of the case, and I will tell you why. Roger Tichborne was tattooed. He was tattooed largely, but of that tattooing there is not a trace on *this* man.'

He gestured to the corpulent, sweating plaintiff sitting in plain view of the thronging crowd.

'What is more, he swears two or three times over that he that is not and never was tattooed.'

The courtroom, and the public at large, held their breath.

* * *

Coleridge was representing the Tichborne family, who had been sued over a dispute about inheritance. The civil trial was being held in order to discern whether or not the enormous twenty-seven-stone man present in the courtroom was, as he had vociferously claimed, actually Sir Roger Tichborne, rightful heir to the Tichborne baronetcy and the associated large, though by that point rapidly dwindling, family fortune. Roger had disappeared at sea nearly eighteen years earlier in 1854, when a transport ship called the *Bella* had sunk during a storm off the coast of Brazil on its way to Jamaica. He had been on a hunting trip in the Americas and grabbed a berth on the *Bella* as its only passenger to begin his journey home. Six days after it had left port, the ship's lifeboat was found floating bottom up by a passing ship, and no trace of Roger or any of the forty-strong crew had ever been seen since.

Undeterred, however, in a spectacular display of Victorian mourning, his grieving, histrionic mother the Dowager Lady Henriette Tichborne never gave up hope that he would one day be found alive. Rumours had begun to circle shortly after the disappearance of the *Bella* which gave the bereft dowager hope, and she pursued them tirelessly for years, eagerly soliciting information from sailors on shore leave, desperate for any crumb of information. In one story, Roger simply hadn't been aboard the ship as it sunk, due to a mix up with his passport. Perhaps he was still alive and living happily married in

Argentina. In another, it was claimed that a group of survivors had been rescued when a passing ship had come to the stricken vessel's aid, carrying Roger to safety, perhaps to Australia. Henriette simply could not give up hope.

In the aftermath of his disappearance, Roger's younger brother Alfred became the rightful Tichborne heir, ascending to the baronetcy aged fifteen after the death of his father, the elderly Baron Sir James. Roger had long been declared dead, presumed drowned, though Lady Henriette had stubbornly refused to hold a memorial service for him in the family chapel, so convinced was she that he would someday return.

To her horror, almost as soon as he took on the family title, Alfred quickly began to burn through his inheritance at an extravagant rate, buying luxuries including bearskin coats and vast amounts of jewellery, as well as commissioning an opulent luxury yacht, which (he assured his mother) he planned to use to search for his long-lost brother. Bankruptcy loomed, and Henriette became increasingly desperate in her quixotic search, worried that when – when! – Roger returned to claim his rightful position, there would be little of any value left for him.

In desperation, she decided to post adverts in newspapers around the world: 'If anybody can give any clue of Roger Charles Tichborne . . . a handsome reward is promised.'

Her search remained fruitless for two more years, and Alfred continued to fritter away the family wealth. Still singularly driven to find her beloved eldest son, Henriette eventually engaged the services of a 'missing friends' service in Sydney, Australia. Sensing a handsome payout, Mr Cubitt's Missing Friends Office was only too pleased to help and posted a further series of notices in publications across the southern hemisphere on Lady Tichborne's behalf. Tips of varying levels of credibility trickled in, but Cubitt's best lead placed Sir Roger in a colonial militia, fighting the Māori in New Zealand. Astonishingly, though, in late August 1865, a letter finally arrived which claimed that Roger was indeed provably alive and well, against all odds. Miraculously, the letter said, Sir Roger was neither battling Māori nor happily riding horses in Buenos Aires, but instead living in the ramshackle trading town of Wagga Wagga, New South Wales, halfway between Melbourne and Sydney and far off the beaten track.

The letter had come from an old friend of Cubbitt's – a lawyer named William Gibbes, who had met a butcher in Wagga years earlier by the name of Tom Castro. Castro was a notorious gambler and chancer, known for his tall tales of riding llamas in South America and, as he told his drinking mates down the pub, of a long-lost family back in England, rich beyond their wildest dreams. 'One day,' he'd told them, he'd inherit, and would 'own the best butcher's shop in town.' Seeing Cubitt's advert, Gibbes was immediately convinced that Castro had to be Tichborne. Sure, Tom was a little heavier than Roger had been, but twelve years had passed since his disappearance. The fey, effete and idle public schoolboy was now stout, hefty and crude. And yes, Tom was a little rougher round the edges, socially speaking, than they might have expected from an Anglo-French aristocrat, but that's what more than a decade shearing sheep and carving carcasses in the Australian heat will do to even the most refined of men. All Tom's tall tales must have been true after all!

Excitedly, both Gibbes and Cubbitt manoeuvred to bring Roger back to England, each keen to claim their slice of the reward money, and after much chicanery and bluster, on Christmas Day 1866, Sir Roger, once again using his birth name, finally set foot on home soil. He was ready to return to his rightful rank as the eleventh Baronet of Tichborne.

The dowager was predictably ecstatic to learn the news. Alfred had drunk himself to death earlier in the year, leaving the suddenly resurrected Roger as her only remaining son and heir. She was in Paris for the winter, and so Roger headed to see her as soon as he could. They were not reunited until 10 January 1867, as he'd been in a sickbed in the Hotel de Lille, exhausted from his long journey from Australia. Roger had been a sickly child and suffered terribly with asthma throughout his life. The adult Roger smoked incessantly and drank too much, and his fateful trip to the Americas was intended to have been edifying and to save him from his debilitating excesses. Even so his mother was not at all surprised by his condition when they were finally reunited.

'Oh my dear Roger,' she exclaimed. 'Is it you?'

* * *

Clearly, his time in Australia had been unusually rough on him, and the terrible experience of surviving a shipwreck had wrought havoc with his memory. Though bilingual since birth thanks to his Francophone mother, he'd been away so long that he'd forgotten how to speak French. And whilst it was true that Roger was never particularly bright, he'd clearly forgotten an enormous amount of his schooling since the wreck. He could no longer read the Latin in which he'd been drilled. He had no recollection of many details of his youth, did not recognise old schoolfriends from Stonyhurst and could not identify his own father's handwriting. He also struggled to readjust to family life in the fine restaurants of London and the gilded country piles of Hampshire, particularly as he did not, as yet, have easy access to any money, nor every material trapping to which he was now entitled.

Roger and his advisers had also quickly realised that coming back from the dead is rather more bureaucratically complicated than they had initially imagined. Alfred's death had frozen the baronetcy's dwindling estates, which at least saved them from his gambling creditors, but the remaining wealth was, for the moment, inaccessible. Gibbes and Cubbit had not been paid either. To make matters worse, Lady Tichborne, the prime and unshakable supporter of Roger's claim, also passed away in 1868, her own fortunes by then severely thinned. Nevertheless, after her death Roger now stood to inherit the remainder, as well as a number of still fairly healthy trusts and incomes, too. The loss of the vocal and unwavering support of his own mother was a blow, though, because if he could not prove he really was Sir Roger, several Tichborne cousins stood to inherit instead.

Whilst Henriette had been convinced to her own deathbed that her son had returned, and even as some of Sir Roger's memories of his early life returned over the course of lengthy, prompted conversations with some family confidantes, others were immediately suspicious of him. The family solicitor, a cast of old friends and various relatives were staunchly sure that this man, whoever he might be, was not actually the long-lost Sir Roger. To them, as he would become to the baying press, he was simply the 'Claimant', 'a conspirator, a perjurer, a forger, a slanderer and a villain' set to audaciously cheat the Titchborne heirs out of their family fortunes.

The Claimant sued to assert his rights to the Tichborne wealth and titles. The Tichbornes would have to defend themselves, and it was to be left to the courts to decide who this man really was. In an era before fingerprinting or DNA analysis, though, unequivocally proving his identity was going to be a challenge.

Quickly, the case divided public opinion, with supporters on both sides angrily writing letters to the newspapers in order to support their favoured outcome. To many, the Claimant was an obvious and transparent fraud. To others, who formed what became essentially a fan club, he was the victim of a cruel system, set to cheat him out of what was rightfully his. Others, of course, understood quite well that he was chancing his luck, but hoped he'd succeed anyway, getting one over on the pompous aristocracy in the process. Since he was first identified as Roger in Australia more than five years earlier, he and his wife had been living a high life of travel, fine clothes and exquisite food funded by Lady Tichborne or by bank loans, due to be repaid when his inheritance was returned to him. The stakes were high, and not just for the Claimant: rapidly running out of funds to pay for his legal defence, the Claimant supporters had sold bonds – essentially bets on the outcome the trial, with handsome returns when – when! – the Claimant was finally proved to be Sir Roger.

By the time Coleridge came to present his dermatological proof to the contrary, the newspapers had been awash with rumours and titters about the role tattooing might play in this case for months. On the twelfth day of the trial, almost a year earlier, the public had learned that Sir Roger, missing scion to the vast inheritance, may have had tattoo marks on his arms. If that was indeed the case, all the Claimant had to do was roll up his sleeves, and the matter of whether or not he really was Sir Roger would be settled rather quickly indeed.

Early in the trial proceedings, Dr. John Kersley Lipscombe, who had frequently attended the Tichbornes, was called to the witness stand. Lipscombe, told the judge that he remembered Mr Bowker, Lady Tichborne's solicitor, calling at his home. 'I then told him', Lipscombe said, 'of a mark on the arm of Roger Tichborne, with "R. C. T." upon it, and I said to Mr. Bowker that Mr. Roger Tichborne told me that he had got that at school. I remember distinctly seeing someone at Tichborne having a mark on his arm, with a ship or mermaid, or some other device, over it. I said at the time that the person who did it must have been, either a novice or drunk, because the initials were leaning in different ways.'

Pushed during cross-examination, however, Lipscombe conceded that he had perhaps been mistaken in his recollection. When questioned, he remembered only having spoken with a member of the family's household staff and realised that perhaps the tattoo story was about someone other than Roger. Whoever that person was, Lipscombe told the jury, he had explained that the tattoos were done by a schoolmate, but, alas, he could not for the life of him remember who that man was. Moreover, he explained that as the family physician, he had also been able to examine the Claimant himself. In a remarkable plot twist, he revealed that the Claimant had a mark on his arm, 'between elbow and wrist'. 'It looks like the remains of an abscess or boil that had burst and sloughed,' he said. 'A burn or cauterised wound would leave such a mark. There is no other means of getting rid of a tattoo mark excepting by cautery.'

When the Claimant himself took the stand, he was adamant that he had never been tattooed at all. 'I have no tattoo marks about my body,' he grumbled, 'and I was never tattooed by anybody at Stonyhurst or elsewhere.'

It was indeed clear that the man in the dock did not have any tattoos. A conspiracy theory had nevertheless developed on the back of Mr Lipscombe's evidence that the cautery wound on the Claimant's arm was a crude attempt to remove a tattoo which would reveal him not to be Roger, nor even Tom Castro, but a man called 'Long' Arthur Orton, a butcher's son from Wapping who had joined the merchant navy and headed to Australia as a teenager. Orton had become the prime candidate for the Claimant's true identity in several circles, and it was argued that, seeking to hide from an arrest warrant for selling stolen meat, he had taken the name Tom Castro. Orton, witnesses said, was tattooed on his arms with his initials AO, and whilst the Claimant's arms were bare, perhaps that scar revealed an attempt at deception.

To prove their case, then, the Tichborne cousins simply needed to demonstrate to the jury that Roger, a limp young posh boy, had been tattooed 'in the manner of a common sailor'. It was, as one officer of the court had it, rather 'a strange amusement for young Gentlemen of the upper class to tattoo themselves'. Lipscombe's testimony about the tattoos had been unreliable and unconvincing, and so the defence needed to present something far more persuasive.

* * *

On the morning of 1 February 1872, John Coleridge picked up where he had left off.'I repeat to you', he said, 'that whereas the plaintiff was obliged to swear distinctly that he is not and never at any period of his life has been tattooed, Roger Charles Tichborne was beyond all question tattooed in his left arm in the way I will describe. He was tattooed twice in his life, in a separate way by two separate persons . . . Moral demonstration may be strong; physical demonstration must be stronger still. The Tichborne case may be like no other, but if I prove by eight or ten indisputable witnesses that Roger Tichborne was tattooed and bore the marks of this operation the last time he was seen, I do not understand how the plaintiff's case is to survive proof of that description.'

The first witness called to present this supposedly unassailable evidence was Lord Bellew, a schoolfriend of Roger's. To the amazement of the packed courtroom, Bellew was asked to roll up his own sleeves. Doing so, he revealed a spindly blue tattoo of an anchor which, he said, had been tattooed by Roger himself. The two young men had tattooed each other whilst boarding, he said, and the evidence of his own tattooing gave strong credence to the claim that the missing baron bore marks on his arms too. Under examination, Bellew also explained that the idea of tattooing each other came to them because Roger had been tattooed by a sailor on a beach in France during a childhood holiday many years earlier. In their dorms at school, they had fashioned a tattooing tool from three sewing needles lashed onto a handle, and used Indian ink. The resulting designs, Bellew said, were 'of the three cardinal virtues, faith, hope and charity. Faith was represented by a cross, charity by a heart, and hope by an Anchor,' with Roger's initials RCT etched underneath them. In minute detail, he also described how Roger had a small permanent 'splash' of ink on his wrist, the result of an errant poke of the needle. Helpfully, Bellew drew the design to the best of his recollection for the court.

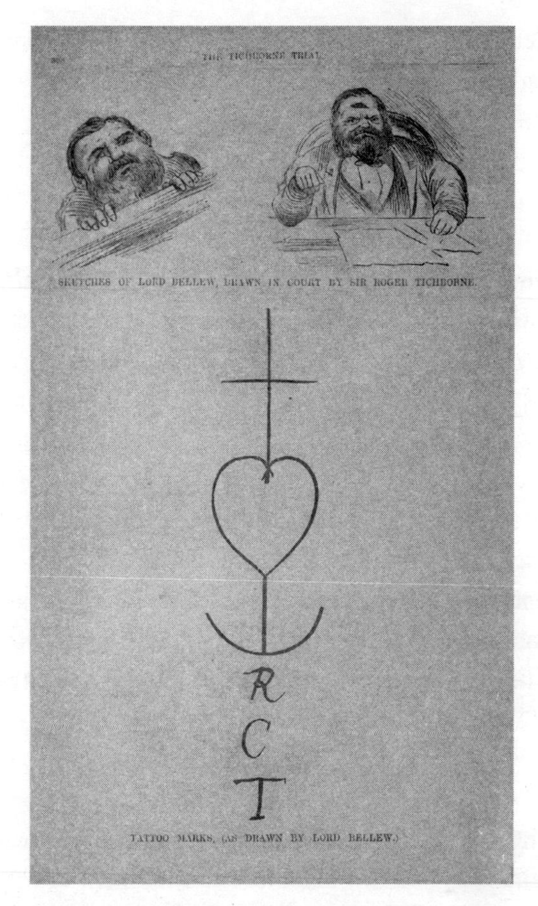

Roger Tichborne's tattoos, according to trial testimony, 1876

In his diary for 21 February, Coleridge smugly noted to himself that following Bellew's tattoo evidence, 'the case could not long survive'. Over the following days, he hammered the story home again and again, presenting a veritable litany of witnesses to Roger's tattooing habits. Roger's aunt explained that she'd first seen Roger's tattoos in 1846. He'd also told her that he'd first been tattooed by a sailor in Brittany whilst on holiday. Corroborating her story, another of Roger's cousins attested that she'd seen them too, as had his French tutor, friends from his regiment in the Army and a raft of chums from Stonyhurst. According to their testimonies, Roger frequently liked to roll up his sleeves to show off the blue-black marks on his arm, and though his mother didn't know about them, he really didn't keep them particularly secret. 'And then I saw those frightful marks, most plainly written on it', a music-hall lyric put it afterwards, 'A heart, and anchor and a cross, were all tattooed upon it.'

This went on for more than a month. By 5 March, an exhausted foreman passed a note to the judge. The jury had heard enough. 'We have now heard the evidence regarding the tattoo marks,' the note read. 'Subject to your lordship's directions and to the hearing of any further evidence that the learned counsel may desire to place before us, I am authorised to state that the jury do not require further evidence.'

With that, the case was over. The Claimant had lost.

* * *

Worse was to come for him. Because he lost the civil trial, indicating that he had lied in court in an attempt to defraud the Tichborne family, he now faced a criminal trial for perjury, with an almost certain outcome. Questions were asked in parliament as to whether it was even worth the government financing another lengthy trial by paying to ship witnesses from South America and Australia, given the irrefutability of the tattooing evidence already presented in the civil case.

The criminal trial was nevertheless undertaken. For the majority of the British public, the conclusion was all but foregone, with the comic magazine *Judy* setting out the final moments as the final scene of a chorus-line script. 'Oh, say I am Sir Roger,' sings the Claimant,

> Ah do! ah do! Oh, say I am Sir Roger.
>
> Jurymen (shaking their heads): Tattoo, tattoo, tattoo!

His supporters, many of whom had directly crowd-funded his case in the hopes of a large payday when he won, were incensed and took to the newspapers to express their utter disbelief at this so-called 'tattoo evidence'. In the manner of a twenty-first-century commenter under a newspaper story online, these Victorian conspiracy theorists argued in letters, broadsides and books that the aristocracy had simply cooked up the tattoo story in order to win the case. 'Begone brave tattoo marks,' said one, 'I do not believe in the Tattoo Business.' 'No tattoo humbug!' Another particularly outraged correspondent to the Tichborne

Subscriber newsletter even signed themselves 'from Guildford who doesn't believe in the tattoo', and yet another asked rhetorically 'who believes in a mother's recognition, but not in the tattoo marks?' The most creative penned rhyming verses taking direct aim at Lord Bellew: 'T stands for Tattoo Marks and Lord Bellew would you doubt it, Thought he'd tell a wapping lie while he was about it.'

The Claimant's defence lawyers bravely argued over the course of more than a year that the whole thing could indeed have been an elaborate conspiracy cooked up by the nefarious Tichborne family, but the criminal trial too ended badly for the Claimant. The jury took only thirty minutes to find the same way the civil one had: the Claimant was not Sir Roger, and had likely been Arthur Orton all along.

* * *

In the wake of the trials and the constant publicity they attracted, interest in tattooing amongst the monied classes rose rapidly. Entrepreneurs sold copies of the drawings of the tattoo marks, and advertised them for sale by mail. *The Saturday Review* suggested that everyone who might feasibly inherit a great estate should take the precaution of getting tattooed. 'Before long,' they said, 'we expect to see an advertisement in all the papers: "Do you tattoo your children yet?" Perhaps having taken this advice, one wealthy young girl who had eloped from England with her boyfriend was tracked down in 1879 by means of an advert placed in the American press which explicitly described her as 'tattooed on the left leg'.

Other newspapers even printed instructions on how to tattoo in the manner of Roger and Lord Bellew, and in the wake of the then-recent opening of Japan after the Meiji Restoration of 1868, English tattooing was compared, rather unfavourably, with the exquisite designs from the Far East. With the social imprimatur of Britain's aristocratic class, the novelty and excitement generated by the Tichborne cases, and the revelation of the fashionable new tattoo styles from abroad, the stage was set for tattooing to move from the vernacular, intimate habit of sailors and schoolboys to become a fully-fledged, legitimate artistic profession.

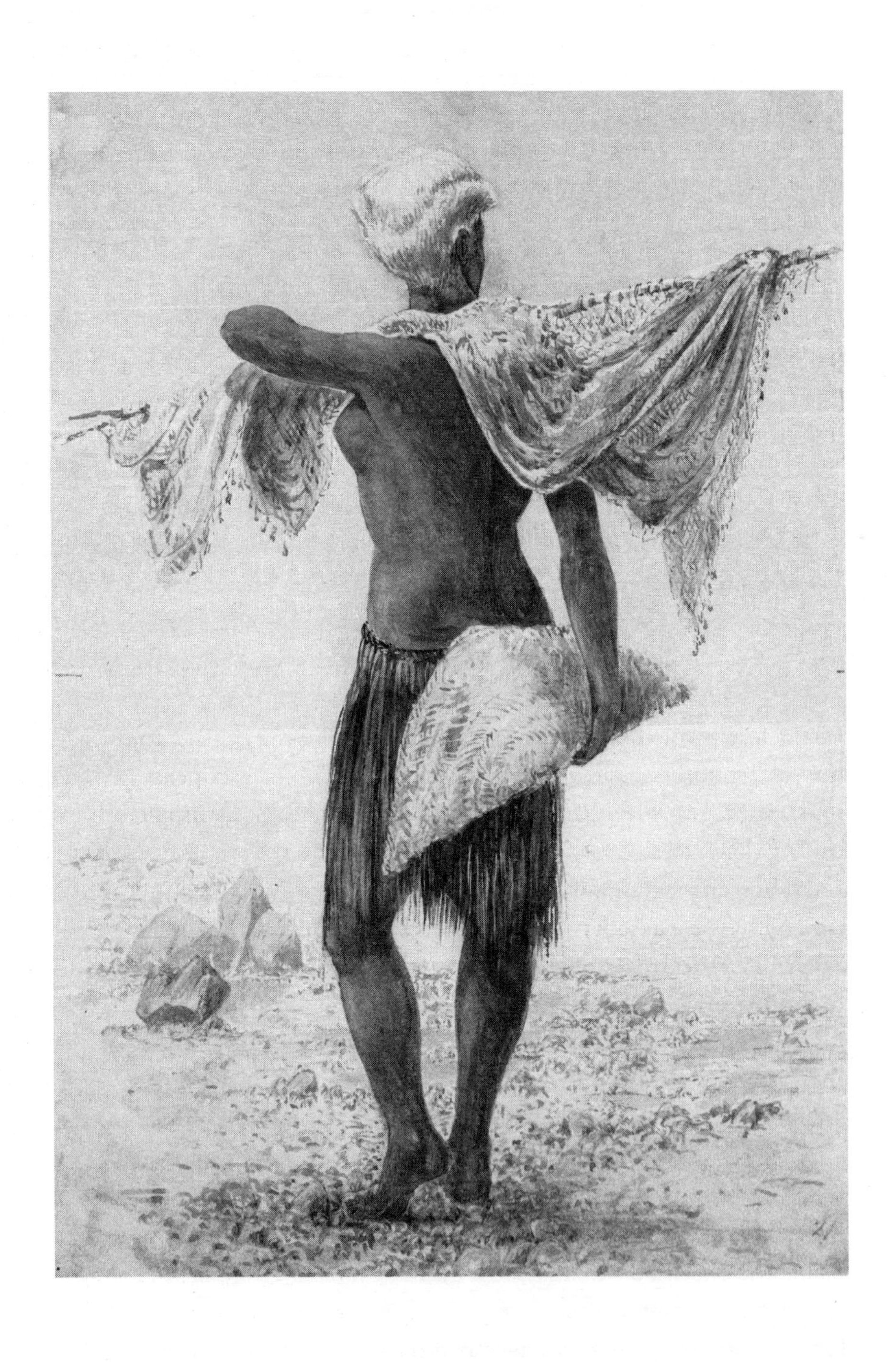

CHAPTER 11

'Some memento of their heart's history': Adi Lebaleba, 1876

> 'I had many lady visitors, all anxious to see my tattoo mark. Little Adi Lebaleba was very jolly, she insisted on my tracing my name on her arm, which was afterwards tattooed, and I returned the compliment by having hers done on my arm.'
>
> —Baron Anatole von Hügel, 29 September 1876

Little Adi giggled. Her friends Viema and Sera had spent the previous afternoon in northern Fiji pricking a young European man to make a *qia* – a blackened tattoo mark in the skin. She was keen to see the results.

Using a traditional tool fashioned from a thorn lashed to a lemon tree twig, the young women had worked together to show their visitor how tattooing was performed. Over the previous few months, they had apparently come to know him well, and they had come to like him. This would be an opportunity not just to help him document their cultural traditions, as they had grown used to doing, but to enable him to actually experience those traditions for himself.

The women had first mixed up a pigment, stirring their spittle with the blackened soot from the underside of their cookpot to form a dark paste. With some evident glee, they dipped the thorn into the paste and sketched out a pattern on his arm, dragging the pigmented

Left: Fijian woman with lime-bleached hair, dressed and equipped for net fishing, likely painted by Arthur J. L. Gordon, 1876. No known image of Adi Lebaleba exists.

tip lightly across his skin to mark out the design. Then, by rapidly tapping the tool with a small mallet, they drove the ink-soaked thorn repeatedly into his arm, pausing periodically to wipe the blood that had begun to pool on the surface. Once the process was complete, forming a blue-black design in the skin, a crowd of other women came to gawp and laugh at the spectacle of this freshly marked white man. As the first rains of the season began to fall lightly, the group drank *yaqona*, a lightly intoxicating drink made from kava root, and whilst the man eagerly made notes, the women sang traditional songs late into the night.

Word had spread quickly of what Viema and Sera had been up to, and the following day several more young women from the village headed to the man's house. Adi was particularly amused. In the excitement, and keen to add to the marks on her own body, she passed him a pen, gesturing that he should write his name on her arm with it. Once he had done so, she insisted that he allow her to sign her name on his arm in return. Over the next hour or so, both signatures were tattooed over, rendering each name in the skin just as permanently as the marks made the day before. She was tattooed with his name, and he was tattooed with hers.

* * *

Anatole von Hügel, the young man in question, was just twenty-two years old. An Austro-British nobleman and ethnographer, he would go on to found the University of Cambridge's Museum of Archaeology & Anthropology. As one of the first Europeans to extensively document Fijian culture, he had become particularly fascinated with tattooing, and devoted much of his energy between 1875 and 1877 to enquiring about the practice as it was variously carried out across the island. He should not have been able to be tattooed, as it was illegal under laws imposed by the colonial occupation. Despite the best efforts of the missionaries to eliminate 'unchristian' tattooing, though, and in the face of ten-shilling fines from the colonial government, it was still a common practice in the inner regions.

Von Hügel's notebooks and sketchbooks of tattooing are extensive, and document tattoo marks almost exclusively on women. In some regions, he observed and depicted facial tattooing on women's cheeks and around their mouths. Elsewhere, he noted marks on arms, upper legs, palms and torsos, forming a symbology linked closely to the flora, fauna and technologies of the island. Some marks, he noted, resembled birds and turtles; others portrayed flowers and trees; and others represented canoes, baskets and water bottles. Some of the marks were apparently medical in nature, and he noted that leprosy sores, for example, would have tattoos around them, in a circle. Others suggested status, or familial or spiritual affiliation. Many seemed to him linked to women's maturation: though women were unwilling to show him directly, he was able to record extensive, intimate stomach and pubic tattooing called *veiqia* through drawings provided to him by female tattooers whose trust he had gained – one of whom he rather unkindly describes as an 'old hag . . . the tattoatic artist of the place'.

The rituals surrounding *veiqia* were shocking to missionaries. The practice results in extensive tattoo marks around the thighs, buttocks and genitals, and was the central component of Fijian girls' puberty rites. It was undertaken in remote locations as part of a complex ceremonial and medicinal process, usually shortly after a girl's first menstruation. The tattooing involved two or three women working together to hold the recipient down, to stretch the skin and to apply the marks. Once the *veiqia* was completed, young women such as Adi, Viema and Sera would wear a skirt, called a *liku,* to hide the tattooing from view and to mark their transition to adulthood.

Though the kinds of tattoos that Europeans acquired from indigenous peoples around the world during the early modern period are diverse, and the circumstances in which they acquired them are not easily summarised, it is generally the case that tattoo encounters like von Hügel's are usually described as moments of cultural appropriation, in which tattooing is an exotic, foreign practice which intrigues the European mind and transforms and besmirches the European body. Foreign recipients of indigenous tattooing throughout the nineteenth century have predominantly been understood as acquisitive and voyeuristic collectors of exotic cultures, much like von Hügel, or celebrated actor Lily Langtree's husband Hugo de Bathe, who was extensively tattooed in Samoa during a hunting and fishing holiday. This understanding has even held when the tattooing has been carried out in Europe by indigenous tattooers, as was the case for German dancer Mademoiselle Heinsel, who was said to have been tattooed in Paris in 1769 by a man called Ahutoru, the first Tahitian to visit Europe. In cases of more extensive tattooing, the acquisition of indigenous cultural marks has often been interpreted as signalling not just a desire to experience a foreign culture, but an explicit decision to try and integrate oneself within it whilst severing any possibility of returning home. Infamous cases of these 'transculturites' include that of John Rutherford, who spun a tall tale of capture and escape to explain the ornate, black facial moko he had acquired whilst living amongst the Māori in New Zealand between 1816 and 1826, and Frenchman Joseph Kabris, who reluctantly returned to Europe from the Marquesas Islands after a decade spent sporting full face and body tattoos in 1804. Both these men's tattoos have been read as attempts to cement their transitions into the new cultures in which they had found themselves.

* * *

In these stories tattooing represents an engagement with newly encountered cultures in only one direction. Whether the recipient is taking tattooing out of its original contexts or using tattooing to take on its contexts for themselves, the practice is by these accounts always 'foreign' to the European body. Since the early twentieth century popular and scholarly accounts have claimed, despite much evidence to the contrary, that tattooing was unknown to Europeans before encounters with Pacific cultures, even though late eighteenth and early nineteenth-century colonial writers knew otherwise. By 1908, though, an American naval report suggested that tattooing had likely originated in the Pacific, and it certainly seems that over the course of the twentieth century, the Western public came to view tattooing as something undeniably foreign to their culture. European colonisers were almost invariably said to be receiving tattooing from the places they explored and conquered, no matter the context.

As we have already seen, many modern iterations of this myth cite Captain Cook's 1769 arrival in Tahiti aboard HMS *Endeavour* as the moment that tattooing was 'discovered', even though tattooing around the Pacific Ocean was first documented by Spanish writers from the early decades of the sixteenth century. After one encounter, as mentioned in the introduction to this book, in 1526, Spanish explorer Alonso de Salazar even named an archipelago in the Western Pacific (possibly in the Philippines or the Caroline Islands) 'Islas de Los Pintados', Islands of the Painted Ones, after the tattooing visible on the native population. Nevertheless, the practice was not extensively reported on – after all, permanent skin-marking was already well known by the Spanish from their conquests in the Americas.

Even in English accounts, officer Samuel Wallis of the *Dolphin* had noted two years before Cook's trip that the men and women of Tahiti were elaborately marked. Wallis was the first European to set foot on Tahitian soil, and wrote that 'it was here a universal custom both for men and women to have the hinder part of their thighs and loins marked very thick with black lines in various forms. These marks were made by striking the teeth of an instrument, somewhat like a comb, just through the skin, and rubbing into the punctures a kind of paste made of soot and oil, which leaves an indelible stain.' During the *Endeavour* voyages, James Cook, his scientific officer Joseph Banks and his draughtsman Sidney Parkinson all wrote extensively about tattoo practices across the Pacific. Parkinson made plentiful drawings of tattooed individuals and their tattoo designs more generally, and both he and Cook's science officer Joseph Banks were tattooed by local artists.

As already discussed in the introduction to this section, the Cook voyages impose a horizon on the history of tattooing in several ways. In a linguistic sense at least, there is no 'tattooing' visible to the English prior to 1769, as there is no single word for it. For historians, it has also been much easier to find evidence of tattooing among Europeans after these moments of Pacific encounter than before it, as the Pacific explorations roughly coincide with the increasingly bureaucratic surveillance of men enlisted into the British fleet, when the Royal Navy and others began to specifically record the 'distinguishing marks' of their men in Description Books. Such official record-keeping leaves abundant traces of tattooing visible in the archival record where previously there were none.

The colonial projects of the eighteenth and nineteenth centuries, such as von Hügel's, which perceived white European culture as 'more advanced' than those encountered elsewhere, were some of the earliest examples of scientific racism. For example, Henry Balfour, the founding ethnographic curator of the Pitt Rivers Museum, thought that tattooing indicated how far along an evolutionary timeline a particular culture was. The cultures he thought more 'primitive' had crude, black patterns tattooed. Those he thought more 'advanced' used more complex, pictorial designs. European culture, at the apparent pinnacle of this timeline, had no tattoos at all. This misconception, which runs historically parallel with coordinated legal, religious and educational programmes to stamp out traditional tattooing in the Americas and across much of the Pacific, has entrenched the perception of tattooing as alien and exotic to Western culture.

* * *

In the light of this, it makes sense to think again about the tattoo that von Hügel received in Fiji. And even more sense to revisit Adi Lebaleba's tattoo – Anatole von Hügel's name permanently inscribed on her arm. The act of tattooing an intimate partner's name on oneself had apparently become fairly pervasive in Fiji as European colonists taught Fijians writing. As one ethnographer explained at the turn of the twentieth century, 'there are comparatively few who do not carry some memento of their heart's history thus ineffaceably recorded'. Missionaries were reportedly horrified by this habit, not simply because they disliked tattooing, but also because such marks made plain that their puritanical attempts to enforce a Christian sense of monogamy were frequently unsuccessful. Permanently marking the names of lovers as part of what one writer dismissively called a 'fickle' romantic culture was, by this token, 'inconvenient'. For decades prior to von Hügel's visit, travellers to Fiji had also recorded rare tattoos on indigenous men which were not part of any local tradition. In one example, such marks were said to include roughly drawn images of animals on their arm or chest, 'put on by some white, rather than by themselves'. Elsewhere in the Pacific, in Hawaii, depictions from 1819 by French artist and explorer Jacques Arago show a high-ranking man named Aniheneho sporting tattoos of goats, a species then only recently introduced by colonists, integrated seamlessly alongside his other traditional marks.

Through dating of tool artefacts, tattooing in the Pacific can currently be dated back to at least 700 BCE. Scientists have recently discovered tattooing tools in Tonga from 2,700 years ago, the needles of which were fashioned from bones which likely came from humans. Instinctively, then, these adaptations of local tattoo styles after colonial encounters might be understood as moments where traditional practices such as *qia* expanded during the colonial period to include European writing and symbols. If you think that tattooing is simply a Pacific practice, you can only really make sense of the Fijian men tattooed with animal designs as another awkward moment of cultural appropriation. If you believe that tattooing was unknown in Europe, then these examples might suggest that European sailors had learnt tattooing in the Pacific, adapted the techniques to produce designs from their own visual culture, and then carried out the techniques they had been taught in order to tattoo indigenous men they met. Von Hügel's name inscribed on Little Adi's arm is, by this account, still a foreign phenomenon to the Baron, even as it absorbs European characteristics.

Nevertheless, during the nineteenth century, it is clear that many sailors and explorers understood the antiquity and continuity of the practice rather differently. London's *Literary Gazette* wrote as early as 1819 that 'the European seamen also, particularly in the Northern kingdoms and the British Islands, have from time immemorial marked themselves with a kind of tattooing, by pricking on their arms, legs and sometimes on other parts of their bodies, single figures, for instance, the cross, letters, or names'. By 1880, the *Graphic* wrote about tattooing as an 'Ancient Custom' that rivalled (and was not predated by) South Sea tattooing. Furthermore, in perhaps the most amusing example, four years before Baron von Hügel's tattoo, the American tattoo artist Martin Hildebrandt joked that as tattooing was so prevalent amongst the sailors who made up much of his clientele, perhaps it had actually been brought to the Pacific *by* Cook or other European explorers, rather than the other way round.

This clearly isn't the case, of course, but if we look closely at a longer history of tattooing before and after the Pacific encounters, the story becomes rather more complicated. We can, for example, compare Adi and Anatole's intimate inscription of each other's names with records of 'Indian Ink' and 'gunpowder' marks in references to tattoos made in colonial gazettes of the late eighteenth century. To pick again from amongst many possible examples from the colonial gazettes in Virginia mentioned earlier, one records the likeness of one Bartholomew Savage, an Irish carpenter. Savage was an indentured servant, and in 1761 he was on the run from his master, who offered a reward for his capture. Savage could be identified not only by the fact he was missing three fingers, but by the letters marked in Indian ink just above his wrist. In a Pennsylvania gazette from 1752, we can read about James Smith, a runaway English shoemaker, known by the letters I.P.W.H etched in gunpowder on his arm. In an even earlier Virginian example, from 1738, a more pictorial tattoo tradition is also revealed: a Richard Kibble has 'several marks made . . . particularly one on his breast being the figures of a woman and a cherry tree'. Far from being a practice that European sailors learnt from specialists in the Pacific, tattooing was clearly present both long before and immediately prior to the Pacific missions of the late 1760s. Even though missionaries clearly worried about fickle Fijians tattooing themselves with the names of their boyfriends and girlfriends, by the time of von Hügel's visit the English press had been reporting on adolescents and adults marking themselves with the names of their 'fancy men and women' for some decades. Adi's tattoo, in this light, is not an adaptation of a Fijian tradition, but the acquisition of an English one.

One other example of this phenomenon further illustrates the point. In 1847, Henry Byam Martin, an officer on board HMS *Grampus,* sketched a portrait of a Tahitian woman who had been tattooed across her face with the word 'MURDERER', written prominently in large, upper-case letters. The brutal proclamation was written upside down, indicating that the tattooer had worked with her head between her knees, as someone else restrained her. Martin reports that the woman had killed her husband 'under circumstances of great atrocity', and that a missionary, John Williams, had interfered with the local custom of putting her to death by suggesting that she instead be prominently tattooed with the stigmatising indication of her crime.

It is perhaps difficult to understand that any missionary would condone this act, given that tattooing was banned on religious grounds in Tahiti, as it had been elsewhere in the Pacific, and that Williams himself had even written some of the laws. Why would a Christian missionary, apparently opposed to tattooing as a fundamentally pagan practice, sanction punitive tattooing as an act of apparent mercy? Of course, this punitive tattoo was well within the standard mode of punishment for the English legal system. Though this horrific tattoo was carried out in Tahiti, it wasn't a 'pagan' Tahitian tattoo, but a thoroughly European one, hardly out of character with the great antiquity of facial tattooing for stigmatising purposes in Christian cultures discussed on pp. 41–42, which was still permitted under British law as a punishment for military deserters at the time.

The cultural mega-myths of colonisation in European understanding rest on countless examples of ahistorical and ultimately racist misconceptions which see European culture as separate from and/or superior to the cultures of the places they colonised. Colonial missionaries sought to stamp out Fijian tattooing due to its significance within traditional belief systems, and of course one of the reasons von Hügel was so keen to document tattooing was that it was rapidly being driven towards extinction. Von Hügel's account ended up in Cambridge, and the tools with which he was tattooed (and, one suspects, with which Adi was tattooed too) are now kept permanently alongside them. For many visitors to the museum, these may symbolise the instruments of a strange and exotic practice. As anthropological museums such as von Hügel's in Cambridge, Balfour's in Oxford and countless others across Europe and America filled their storehouses through trade, purchase, plunder and theft over the nineteenth century, tattooing became just one part of a taxonomy of otherness, increasingly indicative of European cultural superiority and dominance. But perhaps for Little Adi Lebaleba, these tools, and that name on her arm, were indicative of something else entirely: that these Europeans had more in common with her than they could have imagined.

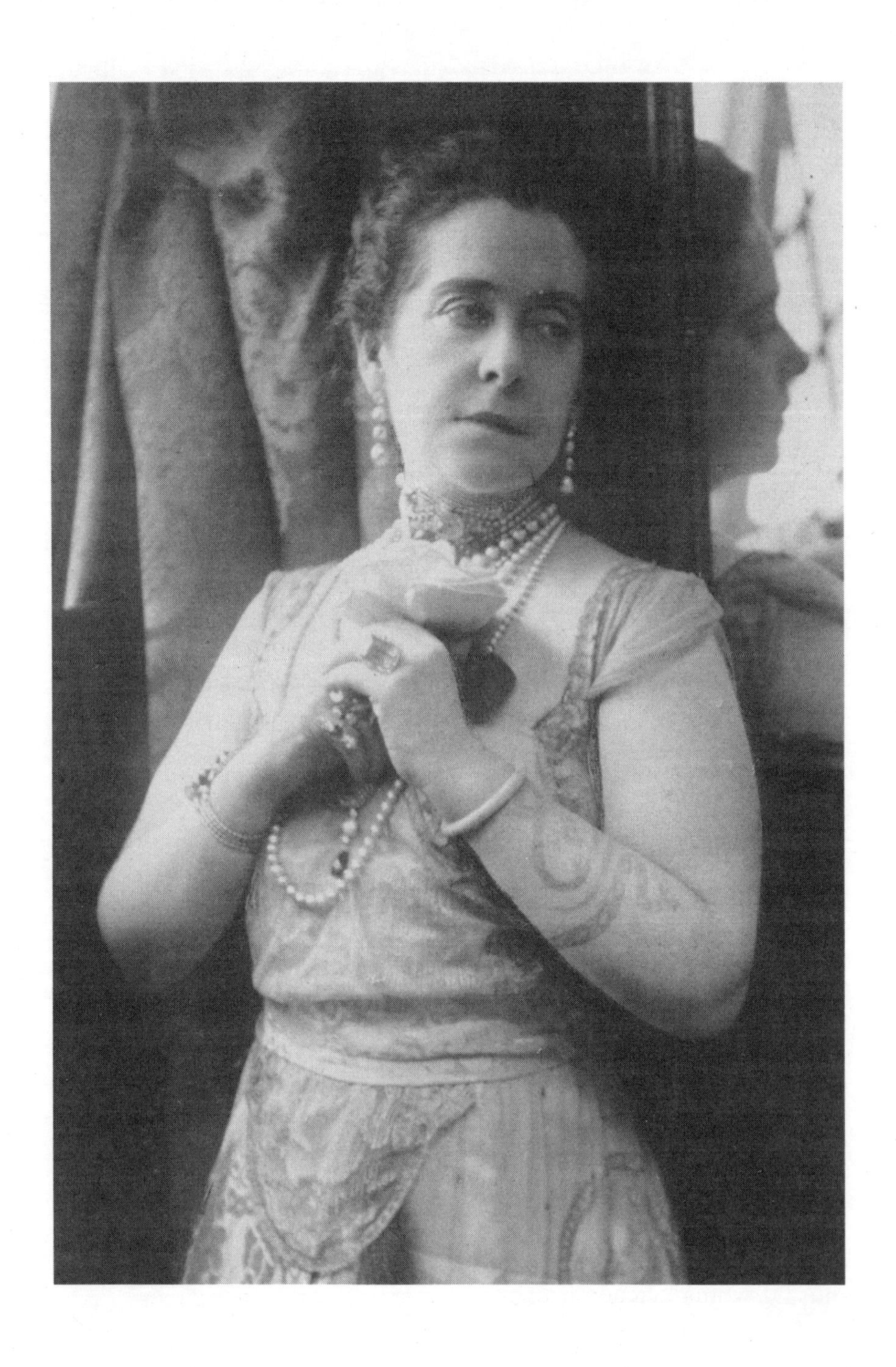

CHAPTER 12

'Elegant specimen of chromatic needlework': Aimee Crocker, 1900

'Come good Horitoyo, decorate my rosy-tinted skin,
With devices fin de siecle – just the finest of the fin!
Place a lizard on my forehead, and about my neck a rope,
With the rhapsody "Good Morning!", Have you used Plum's Soap?

Oh good Horitoyo, make me out a martyr to the fad,
And a walking ad department. Won't the untattooed be mad,
When I glide across the ballroom with my haughty nose turned up,
And the legend on my shoulder, "Lost a White Bull Pup?"

Oh good Horitoyo, truly I am overwhelmed to think,
When my name is full of glory and my hide is full of ink,
How the jealous ones will envy as I pass them by in state,
Bearing on my nose the legend, "Jones, he pays the Freight!"

Bring your needles Horitoyo! You will find a martyr here,
Longing to be decorated like a Texas steer!
And the low born ones of earth shall read with many eerie thrills,
On my epidermis, eulogies of Paine's Pink Pills.'

—'The Tattooing Fad', *LA Times*, 23 December 1900

It was a rather unusual request, but then Aimee Crocker was an unusual woman. Known to many as the 'Queen of Bohemia', and

Left: Aimee Crocker, photographed by Jacob Schloss, *circa* 1885

an inveterate and decadent light at the heart of New York's social scene, she was the very definition of an eccentric millionaire. To the *Philadelphia Enquirer*, she was a 'millionairess, an aesthete, a genius at bizarre and extravagant entertainment, a citizeness of many lands, a dabbler in art and the occult, a seeker after weird adventure'. Her father had amassed an incredible fortune after investing in railroads, and on his death she inherited something close to a quarter of a billion dollars in twenty-first-century terms. In the 1890s, she was earning $100,000 a year. With such vast wealth, Aimee was free to indulge every instinct of her curious, bold, passionate and flamboyant character. In that spirit, the 36-year-old heiress dispatched one of her servants from her lavishly appointed property on West Thirty-Fifth Street in Manhattan into the city to summon the best Japanese tattoo artist then working in New York. Only the best would do. As one newspaper put it, 'When society wants anything at all, it wants to be the best of its kind; and when society wants to be tattooed, it demands the best tattooer the world has to offer, no matter from what distance he has to be imported.'

The best tattooer in question was a master of his art named Yoshisuke Kudo, using the professional moniker Hori Toyo. Forty years old and short of stature, he was a gentle, refined man, fluent in English, willing and able to tattoo both Japanese and Western designs with elegance and skill. By most accounts, he was quiet as he worked, and discreet to a fault. He always travelled with a small black bag containing his tattooing needles, and a book filled to bursting with designs of every size and price, from small pictures of frogs, mice and locusts to vast scenes of eagles and snakes battling to the mortal death. For the more cautious clients, he was also sure to bring with him more traditional Western tattoos – crossed flags, wreaths, entwined hearts – even as he attempted to steer people towards more ambitious and artistic designs. Despite the opinion of the sneering poem in the *LA Times*, he was not in the habit of inscribing his clients with commercial advertisements, as if they were human billboards, though it does seem to have been the case that once word spread of his talents, his tattooing served as an advertisement for his extraordinary work.

The son of a vet, Toyo claimed to have trained as a tattooer in Japan, and had come to the United States alongside his young English bride Annie. His trip to America was announced in the newspapers, and he arrived to great fanfare and excitement. Prior to arriving in America, Toyo had been leaving his delicately wrought marks on the bodies of wealthy clients across Europe, including in the fashionable centres of Paris and London. There, he had boasted (probably untruthfully) of tattooing a pantheon of prominent clients including the Duke of Marlborough, Prince Waldemar of Denmark, King Oscar of Sweden, Grand Duke Constantine of Russia and Prince Henry of Prussia, as well as many female clients including prominent suffragette Lady Montagu. A design of a crawling newt had been particularly popular in Paris; in London, many of his clients had been tattooed with snakes. In at least one advert, he had also offered to teach his trade to others.

This status was something of a recent turn of events. Just a few years previously, Toyo had been so impoverished that he had been ejected from a Liverpool boarding house and was forced to spend a few months living in a workhouse under the anglicised and far less exotic name 'Peter'. By the time Aimee called upon him in March 1899, though, a craze for Japanese tattooing in Europe and America had allowed him to earn both a comfortable living and a global reputation. In New York, he was employed at both a prominent tattoo studio off the Bowery, and more salubriously in an atelier installed on the fourth floor of Vantine's Oriental Department Store on Broadway. The going rate for Japanese tattooing in New York, *Vogue* said, was $5–$10 a session. (At about $325 in 2021 dollars, this suggests that high-end tattoo pricing has, inflation notwithstanding, remained rather stable over the intervening century or so!)

His technique was familiar – one journalist observed that 'after shaving the flesh bare with a razor the design is outlined with a small brush made of the moustache hairs of a mouse, then the pigment is pricked in, and when all is done the part is washed with salt and water. There is a slight soreness for a while and the skin peels off around the incisions.' He tattooed in a range of brilliant and proprietary pigments, guaranteed to stay bright in the skin for twelve years. Toyo had quickly adapted his Japanese methods to include the faster and more efficient electric tattoo machine which had recently been patented by his host in New York, Samuel O'Reilly, who tattooed on Chatham Square. He was busy, drawing in throngs of clients in the wake of a large advert which had been placed prominently in the *New York Times*. Above enticing descriptions of Oriental nougat, crystallised ginger and a wide variety of tea, bargain deals on imported carpets and silks, and the availability of special Japanese porcelain eggs for Easter, the advert proclaimed the presence of 'the world renowned Japanese tattooer, who will receive and execute all commissions. Hori Toyo has successfully tattooed over fifty thousand people, Royalty amongst them.'

At Aimee's home, Toyo spent an afternoon inscribing several designs on her arms, including a fearsome dragon's head in red, green, blue and black. That was, perhaps, shocking enough amongst the smart New York social set. Most scandalous of all, however, was the tattoo of a hissing snake on her arm, its sinewy body curled into a monogram of the letters 'J. G.'. In the long tradition of lovers being marked with each other's initials, 'J. G.' signified the name of her new boyfriend, a lowly English ragtime songwriter called Jackson Gouraud. At the time, however, Aimee was still married to her second husband, naval commodore and amateur opera singer Henry Gillig. Toyo, ever the artist, added a beetle and a demon's mask to Aimee's arm during the same sitting. The uniquely delicious tale of gossipy infidelity and exotic tattooing was splashed across the tabloids, with a beautiful coda: the following day, Gouraud had Toyo over to his place to mark Aimee's initials on him in the same style. Far from subtle signs of love that could be discreetly hidden under jewellery or by long dresses, Aimee's tattoos were large, visible and appropriately shocking in both form and content.

By 1899 Aimee was already something of connoisseur of tattooing. She had spent a large period of her life travelling in the Far East and the Pacific, and after being divorced from her first husband and losing custody of her daughter, she set about exploring the world with abandon. She had spent time in a Far Eastern harem, survived abduction in the jungles of Borneo and taken lovers everywhere from Hawaii to Hong Kong. A few years before summoning Toyo, she was travelling in Yokohama, Japan, with her husband Gillig, and records that they had met the man who was then the most famous tattoo artist in the world: Hori Chiyo, the son of a samurai. In contrast to the demure Toyo, Chiyo was a flamboyant gambler, lothario and raconteur. It's unclear if Aimee was tattooed in Japan on this visit, but Chiyo clearly made a vivid impression on her, and her autobiography devotes a short chapter to his exploits, including the particularly brazen seduction of one of his European client's wives, whose portrait he had been employed to tattoo.

* * *

The colourful tattooing of woodblock designs in Japan was not particularly old at the time of Aimee's visit, but the practice was sufficiently exotic and unusual to Western eyes that it had already come to symbolise the fundamental strangeness of the culture. Tattooing in general does have a long history in Japan, both as part of the ancient cultural practices of indigenous Ainu and Okinawan communities and as punishments in Imperial Japan dating back to at least the fifth century CE, but the recognisably decorative tattooing that so captivated Western visitors such as Aimee only blossomed in the late eighteenth and early nineteenth centuries, and was largely obscured from the wider world by Japan's self-enforced isolation. The country had been a feudal military state for centuries and was all but closed to the Western world for more than two hundred years. Few Westerners were able to visit, and few trade goods left the country. Under threat of invasion by the United States in 1853, a new government came to power in a period known as the Meiji Restoration, and quickly decided that it was better to change and survive than refuse and be invaded and destroyed. Very rapidly, Japan sought to present itself to the world as a modern nation state, and in the process many old customs and habits were outlawed. Tattooing was made illegal as early as 1872.

As discussed in the introduction to this part, the Meiji Restoration ignited a trading boom. Japanese goods flooded the European market for the first time, and popular taste for all things Oriental took hold across the visual and decorative arts, with everything from ceramics to stockings taking on a Japonesque mood over the 1870s and 1880s. Though the government desperately wanted to appear modern to European and American eyes, it was old Japan that so thrilled foreigners. By the early 1890s, though, it was becoming harder and harder for wealthy travellers to find authentic Japanese antiques, as the best examples had already long been exported, and as such, the best chance of acquiring an 'authentic' piece of old Japan was to get tattooed. Against that backdrop, Chiyo worked out of a curio shop in Yokohama owned by English immigrants Arthur & Bond, with tattooing just another of the commodity arts on sale to the intrigued tourist. Chiyo's services were advertised alongside those for ornaments and *objets* to serve the latest fashions (as would Toyo's be at Vantine's). Though Arthur & Bond's silverware and cloisonné had been mass-produced for the export market, visitors could be assured that Chiyo's art was the genuine article.

Because tattooing Japanese nationals had been made illegal, Japanese tattooers had to find a wider clientele. Some, like Toyo, simply left Japan. Records attest to Japanese tattooers working in places including Singapore, Hong Kong and Malta, for example. Others, like Chiyo, adapted, and made explicit efforts to market themselves to the wealthy tourists now flocking to Yokohama and Tokyo. Over the latter decade of the nineteenth century, Chiyo had forged a worldwide reputation on the basis of a perhaps fraudulent claim to have tattooed the future English King George V and George's late brother, Prince Albert Victor. The princes had famously been tattooed in Yokohama in 1881, as George attests in his own journal, but Chiyo would seem to have been too young to have been the artist responsible. Chiyo's fame meant that several English-language guidebooks to Japan made extensive mention of his beautiful tattooing, though Japanese sources are more circumspect about his workmanship. It seems likely that he was more famous than he was talented. Nevertheless, he left a deep impression on English and American travellers.

Even if Chiyo wasn't the artist responsible, it is definitely the case that Prince George, along with many other members of the British and European aristocracy, were tattooed whilst in Japan. Moneyed American travellers were also good customers, and Chiyo tattooed noted travellers including Charles, the son of the poet Henry Longfellow, and ethnographer William Henry Furness. Furness even boasts in his own book about his research in Borneo: showing Chiyo's 'handiwork' to people he encountered in the jungles, they could scarcely believe that the flamboyant images on Furness's back were made in the same way as the black marks on their own bodies. In America, Britain, France and beyond, stories filled the papers of dukes rolling up their sleeves to reveal dragons and snakes, of New York Racquet Club members having their club emblems tattooed on them, and of young women enduring the needle to acquire decorative designs on their shoulders, wrists and ankles. As travellers returned to Europe and America with Japanese tattoos during the 1880s, demand back home grew as people sought to copy the latest royal fashion. It is arguably the emergence of an upper-middle-class customer base that propelled the spread of a professional tattoo industry in England and the United States, making it financially viable to run a permanent business in major cities, tattooing customers for cash.

* * *

As tattoo artists competed for the cream of the client base, competition emerged amongst artists abroad to present themselves as orientally authentic as possible. Even the most established of salty old American tattooers sought to ally themselves with Japan somehow, as it was through their association with the East that they could attract the most prestigious customers. The boldest of these claims was perhaps that made by the very first full-time professional tattooer in North America, Martin Hildebrandt. Hildebrandt had learned to tattoo in the Navy in the 1840s, and is first visible as a professional when he was listed as working part-time from a saloon in New York's docklands around 1859. He later claimed to have been undertaking tattooing as his 'full time profession' from about 1866. Though as yet unconfirmed, in later interviews Hildebrandt boasted of having served aboard one of the ships in the US Navy's gunboat diplomacy fleet which first threatened Japan in 1853, after two and a half centuries of isolation. He said there was no other sailor in this squadron who could tattoo as well as he could.

It is in this same context that Samuel O'Reilly decided to invite Toyo to New York, just as London tattooer Tom Riley had hosted Toyo in London. Toyo moved from New York to San Francisco, delighting local customers and celebrity clients such as actress Helen

Redmond in the cosmopolitan cities, and terrifying more conservative columnists in places like Alabama, who hoped that the decadent tattooing fad of the coasts would not take hold in their more reserved corners of the country. Aimee's exploits were likely the cause of some of the consternation, particularly as she kept unashamedly getting tattooed, providing the tabloids with plenty of gossip fodder. In 1901, she appeared on the front page of the New York tabloids in full colour, being tattooed again by Samuel O'Reilly, and for years the press delighted in regaling their readers with each new addition to her body. Alongside Jackson's serpentine initials, she apparently added more beetles, birds and demons, and proudly showed them off in portrait photographs throughout her life. In one, she is dripping in pearls and jewels. Her dress is a gorgeous silk, and from her wrist, a group of snakes twist their way up her arm.

Late in life, Aimee married again. At the age of sixty, she wed a Russian count, and of course that allowed the press to dub her the 'Tattooed Countess', an 'elegant specimen of chromatic needlework', her leg wrapped in yet another snake tattoo, and her back sporting a butterfly. One report speculated that these particular images were designed to bring her luck, and she was so taken with the motif of a snake that she commissioned a jeweller to make her a bejewelled bronze serpent, sparking a craze across New York for snake-shaped paperweights, pen racks and cigarette cases. Through the detailed lens of her life story, though, another explanation presents itself for the snake tattoos on her arms, around her waist and coiling up her leg.

In her autobiography, *And I'd Do It Again,* snakes are a recurrent leitmotif in her life, usually doubly emblematic of female sexuality and Aimee's suspicion of other women. In India, harem girls played a trick on her, releasing a defanged cobra into her sleeping quarters. 'The practical joke, with its rather mean twist,' she wrote, 'will serve to illustrate for you the jealousy and suspicion which reigned in that colony of women.' Later, she witnessed a dancing girl encoiled by a python during an erotically charged snake dance, where the girl allowed the animal to asphyxiate her into a state of ecstasy. When spectators rushed to save her, she screamed at them, protesting their interruption of her reverie. Back in New York, a friend brought a boa constrictor named Kaa to Aimee's house. One night, the snake crawled into her bed, and she describes its cool, muscular body slithering over her. 'He rubbed close to my body. He gave me a strange tickling sensation that was, I confess, very enjoyable . . . I could feel the vast power of him. I have never felt so helpless nor so overpowered in my life . . . It was like being in the strong embrace of a man.' She spent the night with Kaa wrapped around her body, and in the morning she lifted him up and carried him downstairs. The snake coiled itself around Aimee's waist, and as she emerged for breakfast carrying this enormous reptile, another one of her houseguests expressed shock, and then quickly jealousy.

Aimee did not, by her own admission, really understand other women, nor did she like them much. She much preferred the company of men. 'Women have always been a mystery to me, a woman,' she writes at one point. Elsewhere, she pondered 'What is there about women that is so perverse, so incomprehensible? . . . Personally, I do not like women very much, but they are curious to watch.' Aimee, with her tattooed body crawling with snakes, was certainly just that.

PART FOUR

TATTOOING IN THE EARLY TWENTIETH CENTURY

Life

1950
NUMBER

PRICE 10 CENTS
Vol. 64, No. 1676. December 10, 1914

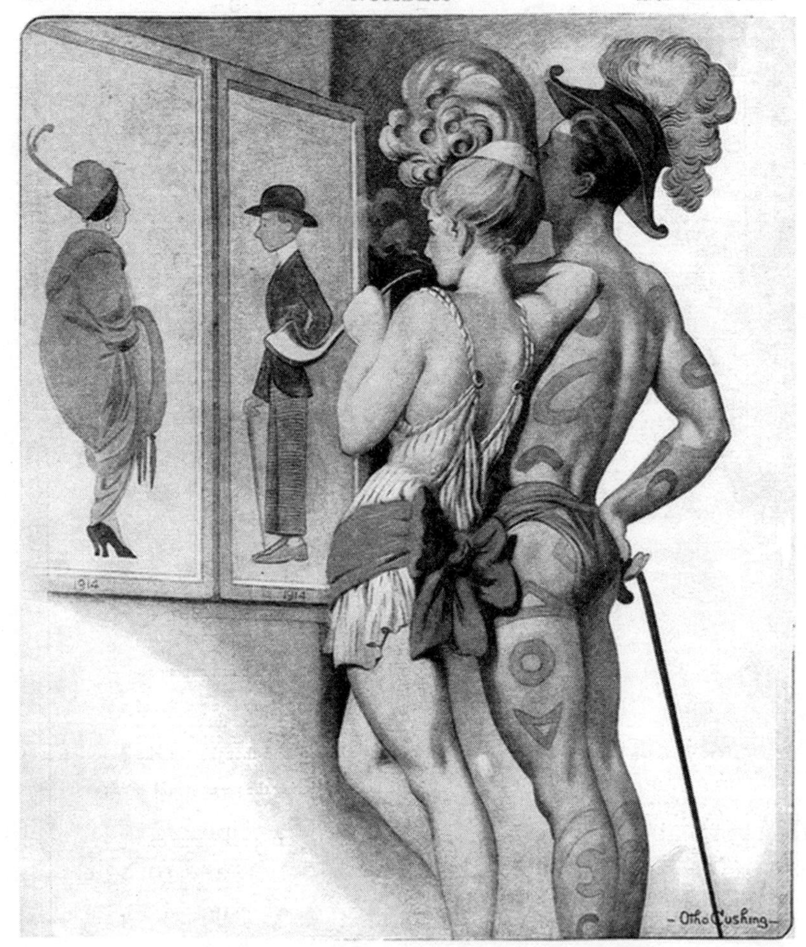

"WEREN'T THEY FUNNY?"

TATTOOING IN THE EARLY TWENTIETH CENTURY: 'A THING OF BEAUTY AND A JOY FOREVER'

'O Fashion! You are very frivolous; you have caused many complaints against the most beautiful half of the human race! But you have not come to this, and I believe you will not be permitted to come to it.'

—Cesare Lombroso, 'The Savage Origin of Tattooing' (1896)

'Gentleman, Interested in Tattooing and Largely Covered, would like to hear from other enthusiasts to compare notes.'

—*Punch*, 11 February 1920

In 1914, *Life* magazine devoted its mid-December issue to imagining what life would be like several decades into the future, in 1950. Europe was erupting into war, and *Life*'s editors, writers and illustrators – already anxious about a world order on the precipice of collapse after decades of rapid industrialisation, urbanisation and social change – used the issue to satirise and discuss a range of issues of contemporary concern to its readers.

Cartoons depict visions of the coming mid-century. Few of them are particularly optimistic views of the future, from the artists' points of view, at least. In one, captioned 'After the War is Over', a bandaged, broken embodiment of the globe holds out a tattered, empty cap, panning

Left: 'Weren't They Funny?', *Life* cover illustration by Otho Cushing, 10 December, 1914

for loose change. In another, 'The Horse Show of 1950', the horses are all dead. In others, the president is female, feminists have literally kicked men off the face of the earth, boys are unemployed because every business in town is only hiring girls, men are pushing baby buggies, brides will soon have beards, and a besuited woman strides about on business holding a portable, wireless telephone. In *Life's* future, the cars are faster, and the kings and kaisers are all out of work.

On the cover is the image that sums up the magazine's attitude to the coming century. A young couple in 1950 are visiting an art gallery. They huddle together to get a better look at two paintings on the wall. The pictures are two separate full-length portraits, one of a woman, the other of a man. With austere decorum, they are separated from one another by the heavy frames encasing each image, each engraved '1914'. Both subjects are smartly dressed, he in a business suit and bowler hat; her in a long, formal coat, fur hat and heels. In stark contrast, the couple from 1950 are pressed together tightly, unrestrained by any social norms against public displays of affection. The young woman hangs louchely and seductively on her partner's shoulder. She is smoking a pipe, and dressed in a tiny slip dress which reveals her arms, back and legs up to the near top of her thighs. He, bizarrely, carries a cane, wears a plumed military hat and, frankly, not much else. Aside from a small pair of underpants, his body is entirely uncovered, save for the large abstract, geometric tattoo designs that are scattered over his legs, arms and torso.

'Weren't they funny?' the woman exclaims.

* * *

As the nineteenth century ticked over into the twentieth, tattooing had begun to seep into mainstream culture in the Western world, and a conservative older generation were increasingly shocked by it. By 1898, French newspapers were already depicting tattooing as a decadent teenage craze, imagining wayward girls pairing smoking and gambling with afternoon tattoo sessions in the park, and in 1904 a salacious novel called *The Deranged People of Paris* invited its readers to imagine something they'd never seen before: 'tattooed women'.

By the time of this *Life* cover, drawn by the artist Otho Cushing, the aristocrats and kings whose money and patronage had driven the establishment of the professional tattoo industries in the English-speaking world had begun to lose interest, and, like all cultural trends, a wave of middle-class imitators had adopted the fashion instead. For the first time, in the 1910s, tattooing had become a bona fide youth culture craze in Britain and America. And for pearl-clutching moral guardians, it heralded a kind of moral decay, a collapse of gender norms and social codes, redolent of frivolity, licentiousness and barbarism.

To many who so eagerly embraced tattooing in those years, that was rather the point.

* * *

Up to and through the First World War into the 1920s and 1930s, tattooing diffused into every social stratum, and by examining its uptake, we glean a fresh perspective on the arrival of the modern era. The coming chapters present the complex face of modern tattooing in the first half of the twentieth century, as it emerged from an early professional period characterised by the polar perceptions of princes and performers to become a more quotidian presence in urban life. A close look at tattooing in this period provides a stark set of illustrations into the effects of war, economic turbulence, and the quickening pace of industrial and social change on issues such as childhood, gender roles and expectations, and the crumbling foundations of empires. Cushing was astonishingly prescient, really, and the future he envisioned of scantily clad women and handsome tattooed men rupturing the social order did play out repeatedly.

Many of the cultural, political and technological anxieties of the early twentieth century are ultimately discernible in the discourse around tattooing. As discussed in the previous chapter, it was the opening of Japan in 1853 that prompted the growth of professional tattooing in North America, Great Britain, Western Europe and even in places like Hong Kong and Australia. The trend for all things Japanese in the latter decades of the nineteenth century made it financially viable to operate permanent tattooing business in ports and major cities, to meet the increasing demand of moneyed customers, which was fuelled by the social authorisation afforded by the patronage of royals, socialites and clubmen.

Professional tattoo studios began to be established in Britain in the 1880s, and quickly there were opportunities for a huge variety of tattooers to make a living. During that decade, there were several high-end tattoo studios in London, as well as a market catering to visitors to the vaudeville shows who might like to be tattooed. There is also evidence of diversity in the industry. In 1880, in the very earliest days of professional tattooing in Britain, a tattooer born in the West Indies, Thomas Chapman, is recorded as plying his trade at Liverpool docks.

By just 1897, though tattooing was already becoming too passé for some. That year the London illustrated magazine *The Sketch* asked tattoo artist Sutherland Macdonald if he thought that tattooing was becoming too trendy. 'Numbers of people got tattooed,' MacDonald opined, 'but whether the number was greater one year, as compared with the previous year, who could tell?' . . . 'He did not want to see the thing become quite common,' the article continued. 'What was common was apt to be regarded as vulgar. Meantime, the artistic tattooist found his clients among the best people.'

MacDonald's hope of keeping tattooing as a high-class practice is interesting, given that he ultimately failed to do so. The timeline of his career begins with the rise of tattooing as a legitimate and almost respectable profession, and ends with his death shortly before the imagined horrors of *Life's* vision of 1950 had fully come to pass.

He had been an Army telegraph engineer, chiropodist and bath-house manager before taking up tattooing professionally, eventually becoming the most prominent early pioneer of the industry in Britain. He worked in the basement of the Jermyn Street Hammam, Turkish Baths situated just south of Piccadilly, in a high-class part of town. As such, MacDonald was the first tattoo artist who was visibly working from a permanent premises in London, and claimed to have coined the term 'tattooist' – a contraction of 'tattoo artist' – to distinguish his practice from that of a mere 'tattooer', which he felt associated his profession too closely with the workaday business of a plumber or a bricklayer. The term had been used infrequently prior to his adoption of it, but it certainly took on a new cachet in the professional era. The

Post Office Directory for London in 1894 – the *Yellow Pages* of its day – actually created the category of 'Tattooist' specifically for him, a category under which he was the only entry for four years, and he was the first Englishman to hold a patent for an Electric Tattoo Machine, awarded in 1894.

Tattooing, he explained to one interviewer, usually lasted between one and six hours, with one piece having taken over twenty-two hours to complete. He would charge four or five shillings for small pieces, and as much as £20 for extensive ones – the equivalent of about two to three months' wages for an artisanal tradesman (carpenter, shipwright) of the time. Word of his skills spread internationally and barely three years after having set himself up, an article on his work appeared in the *Boston Daily Globe* in 1892, asserting that through his efforts tattooing has been 'elevated to a place among the arts' and a 'great fad', with a later article praising him as 'the most artistic tattooer in the world', noting his 'exquisite colouring and softest gradations of tint'.

He pioneered permanent makeup, tattooing rouge into cheeks. He developed techniques for tattoo removal, effacing marks from the hands of a waiter who could not find work because of them. He also catered to a diverse clientele of both genders and a range of pockets, particularly at the upper end of the market. 'I charge pretty high,' he claimed, 'but my customers can afford it.' He made innovative developments in pigments, too, creating new coloured inks from soluble minerals, using ultramarine for blues, burnt sienna for browns, cuttlefish-derived Indian ink for blacks, cinnabar (obtained from mercury ore) for reds and a secret recipe of his own devising for green ink, derived from a green stone. Only a good, non-toxic yellow eluded him. After testing a particular formula on himself in the search for a decent yellow ink, he was forced to cut chunks of skin out of his arm to alleviate the toxic reaction it.

As was the fashion, he was careful with hygiene, creating 'the most perfect system of disinfecting that the most careful medical practitioner could wish for, as he fully realizes the mischief that may be caused by the use of needles which are not properly disinfected on one person after the other, as many have found out to their cost abroad'. He also developed a process to help ease his customers' pain, using cocaine injections at the tattoo site to act as an anaesthetic. As one customer reported,

> this proved to be the most painful part of the operation, as every minute line in the drawing had to be separately injected with the drug on the same principle that doctors inject morphine. The entire quantity of cocaine used was not over two grains. But it was visible enough to produce that dazed and pleasant sensation which accompanies the after-effects of all strong opiates. Of course the action of the needle after this was painless. In fact, Mr. MacDonald implied that after all it was not really necessary to use cocaine, because the pricking was almost as slight as the sensations of an electric shock.

From the outset, he boasted of an upper-class clientele including earls, ladies and regimental officers, several noblemen and 'a countess or two', though he was always coy about who, precisely, they might be. Conveniently, MacDonald's society clients always demanded secrecy, discretion and anonymity, so he could make claims such as 'Of course I am not at liberty to give you the names, because the majority of them are done secretly. One of the cleverest things I have done lately was to tattoo a little red imp on the ankle of a celebrated society woman' with impunity.

* * *

There is also a remarkable illustration of just how surprisingly present tattooing became in the early twentieth century in my own family history. My great-grandmother, Ethelwynne Darby, was born in 1884 in Ramsgate, Kent, to an unremarkable family. Her father, Samson, was a labourer. By my dad's account, she was something of an austere woman, serious, conservative and stolid. I never met her, as she died nearly a decade before I was born. I don't even remember seeing a photograph of her until very recently. Growing up, though, one story about her resonated so deeply with me that it is still the most striking thing I relate to her memory: Ethelwynne had a tattoo. Inscribed into her left wrist – my grandmother told me – in thick, poorly rendered, spidery black lines, were her initials, ED.

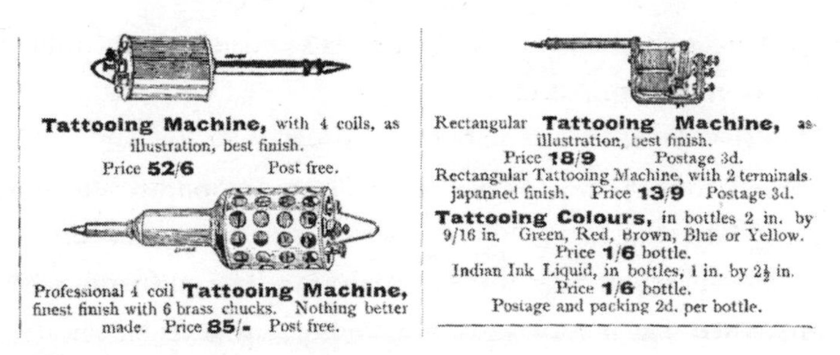

Advertisement from the Gamages catalogue, London, 1911

The story, to the best of my recollection, went as follows. Sometime around the turn of the century, when she was in her late teens, Ethelwynne's younger brother Albert had come home one day with a tattoo machine he had bought or acquired somehow. Seeking a willing victim, he asked his sister if she would let him try the machine out on her. She agreed, on the understanding that whatever he was going to draw on her, he would promise that it would wash off with some soap and water. Bert assured her that the marks would be temporary and proceeded to etch his sister's initials quickly into her wrist using the kit he had bought, leaving a mark that would stay with her for the remaining seventy-odd years of her life, which she resolutely kept covered up, even in the oppressive heat of the Australian summers she would experience in her adopted homeland. She hated those black lines on her arm, and her daughter's hearthside retelling of her tale was intended to warn me off ever making the same mistake.

Until very recently, I had no idea where my great-uncle Bert, as a boy of about sixteen in 1904, might have acquired a tattoo machine, but perhaps the contents of dusty old department store catalogues provide a suggestion. Several editions of the annual 'Gamages of Holborn' catalogue reveal that – for a time – tattooing equipment was available over the counter or by mail from one of London's most popular stores, listed alongside magnets, hobbyist electrical toys, humorous light-up ears and theatrical electric eyes. The equipment came in two finishes ('best' and 'japanned'), for eighteen shillings and nine pence, with green, red, blue, brown, yellow and black (Indian) ink available for one shilling and sixpence. The machine itself, of which several have survived in private hands, is basic and yet fully functional: the familiar design of two coils mounted onto a steel frame power a sprung armature bar which moves a needle rapidly up and down inside a tube as the current alternates.

In one of the earliest of these catalogues, tattooing machines are 'electrical novelties', featured with other gags and gimmicks. In the next, on page 173, they are displayed alongside a mixture of hobbyist electricals, with the introduction of professional accessories, including a walnut foot pedal. In another, later edition, tattoo machines are such unremarkable products amongst their wider offerings that they get mentioned in the page heading as part of a presumably recognisable category: 'Tattooing Machines, Telephones, etc.'

I cannot, of course, prove that it was with a Gamages machine that my great-grandmother was tattooed, but what this remarkable slip of paper proves is that, at least for a moment, tattooing equipment was available on a London high street, sitting uncontroversially alongside toys, games and gags, and available to anyone with a few bob. It is certain that these machines were sold, and that they (in amateur, playful hands) left brightly coloured marks on bodies like Ethelwynne's, which will have lasted many decades afterwards.

* * *

By the 1930s, as he approached retirement, it is clear that MacDonald's business was waning, and that the tattoo boom amongst upper-class people that had propelled his career had fizzled out almost entirely. He was simply old-fashioned, and the young, hip crowd were getting tattooed elsewhere. The London press printed picture after picture of young women with pretty butterflies tattooed on their shoulders, and squealed about new vogues in tattooing, fashions for having film stars' portraits, and a 'new craze' beyond tattooing's typical demographics. But MacDonald couldn't capitalise on any of it. He had at some point been shunted from the large basement of the hammam to a tiny shed perched on its roof. In articles in the American press he bemoaned the fact that his client base had 'fallen off considerably' and that his 'art is on the wane now'. In a letter to a friend dated 13 October 1931, he complained that he had given up even bothering to go into his studio as walk-in trade was so rare.

In the United States, an older generation of artists did nevertheless remain particularly obsessed with Japanese tattooing. Whilst visiting Chicago in 1928 to give a lecture, Japanese pathologist Dr Masaichi Fukushi had a bag containing the preserved tattooed skins of several Japanese men stolen from his hotel room, most likely by a local tattooer enamoured by the designs. In order to try and preserve some of the history of Japanese tattooing which by the 1920s was literally dying out, Fukushi had decided to undertake a collecting programme to preserve tattooed skins post-mortem for the collection at the Nippon Medical School in Tokyo. He ultimately acquired several thousand specimens, many of which were donated by wearers who had been members of the Tattoo League of Japan. After a demonstration at the Art Institute, a tattoo artist had asked Fuskushi to sell him a specimen, which he refused. The following day, the bag had vanished, and despite a euphemistic advert offering a generous reward in the *Chicago Tribune* for the return of 'Japanese tattooing articles, valuable manuscripts, lantern slides and scientific photographs, no questions asked', the bag, and the tattooed skins it contained, were never seen again.

Yet despite Japanese tattooing remaining desirable amongst some old-timers, younger clients in the States were, like those in London, looking for fresher designs. Two years before Fukushi visited Chicago, a tattoo artist from Brooklyn, one Professor Sharkey, told *Vanity Fair* that tattooing was by then exactly as vulgar as MacDonald had feared it might become. Sharkey had been tattooing for forty years and had come to 'mourn the practical side of the art, whose memory lingers fondly over the days when tattooing was a thing of beauty and a joy forever'. 'Times ain't what they was,' he told the reporter. He had made a lifetime speciality of tattooing exquisite Oriental designs – real works of art – on discerning clients. Now, as tattooing was to be 'found beneath many a tailored shirt', he was reduced to tattooing pictures of diving girls, Kewpie dolls, and Venus rising from the sea. 'Now in my day,' he sighed, 'they wanted dragons.'

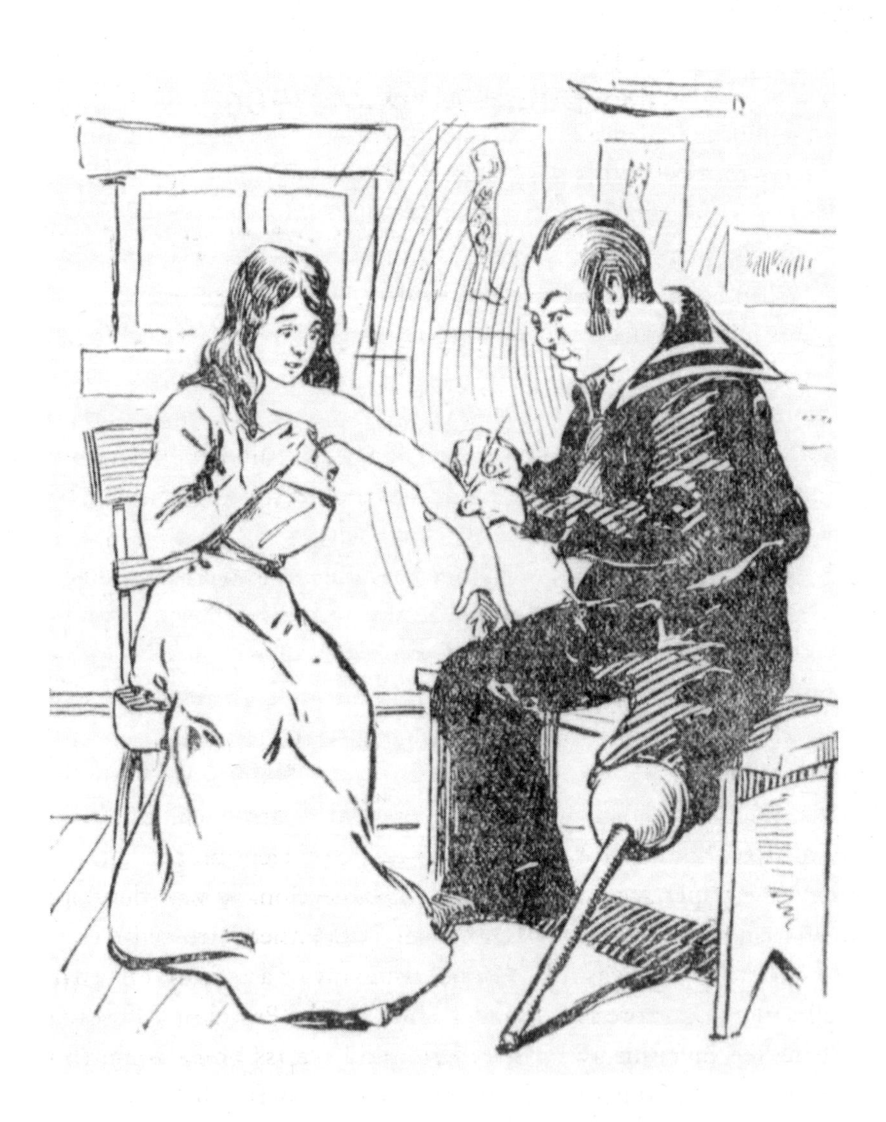

CHAPTER 13

'I just love sailor boys': Madeline Altman, 1906

> 'When he found Madeline, Agent King noticed that her left arm was much swollen and wrapped in a bandage. He asked her what the trouble was.
>
> "Why, don't you know?", asked Madeline, shifting her gum from right to left sides. "I'm having New York Pete tattoo me arms and chest."'
>
> —*Detroit Free Press*, 15 September 1906

Gum-chewing teenager Madeline Altman was hauled before the Brooklyn police courts on 14 September 1906. She had been picked up on the Bowery, the notorious street in Manhattan packed with beer halls, flophouses, brothels, pawn shops and theatres, which had long served as a hub of vice, gambling and booze. Described in one prurient newspaper account as 'pretty and exceptionally well-developed for her age', Madeline was a sassy, smart-mouthed, streetwise young girl of fifteen who was found in the company of a couple of ne'er-do-well sailors on shore leave from a stint aboard President Roosevelt's yacht. She had run away from her middle-class home some three weeks earlier, and her parents were desperate to find her.

When agents from New York's Society for the Prevention of Cruelty to Children (NYSPCC) picked her up, a search found her pockets

Left: 'Latest Fad of Gotham's Smart Set', sensationalist account of a trend for tattooing among young girls, 1901. No known image of Madeline Altman exists.

stuffed full to bursting with photographs of amorous Navy men, and scores of love letters. Most strikingly, her left arm was swollen, and wrapped in a cloth bandage.

Peeling away the sodden cloth revealed a freshly tattooed design of a sailor holding an American flag proudly inscribed into her young skin. Above his head, was a heart, starkly inked in red. Further inspection showed that she had clearly spent much of her time on the run in tattoo studios: as well as the flag-waving seaman, her back was covered with a large battleship, both her arms were tattooed from elbow to wrist with daggers and other naval designs, and on her chest, not yet healed, was another warship and an eagle. Proudly, she also sported a self-portrait of sorts – a girl dressed in sailor togs alongside her own initials, M. A.

In Madeline's plight, age-old worries about the licentiousness of sailors, the sexual immorality of young women, the strict policing of gender norms and the vulnerability of children (especially girls) intersect, and the New York press were predictably captivated by her story for some days. Several takes on the tale emerge in the newspaper coverage, each revealing a different mode of moral panic amongst America's chattering classes. In particular, Madeline's use of tattoos to attract the attentions of sailors predominates. It's unclear in the various tellings if she got tattooed in order to meet sailors, or if her tattoos were the after-effects of a series of particularly rambunctious encounters, though in one interview she does claim that she hoped her new designs would help her garner some attention. 'All the girls are getting it done,' she told the *New York Times* reporter. 'It's getting so the sailors won't look at you if you ain't got some tattoos on you!'

Another angle on the story is Madeline's refusal to conform to the expectations placed on girls and young women at the time. In some reports, Madeline is said to have been using tattooing in a vain attempt to go undercover as a boy, so as to be able to enlist in the Navy. She was not just using tattoos to attract the amorous advances of the handsome sailor boys, it seemed, but actively trying to become one of them. Even in the court hearing, she was wearing a sailor's cap perched on her head, and had her sleeves rolled up, showing off her tattoos. And as she left court, she turned to the assembled reporters and exclaimed 'Ah, I wish I was a boy! If I was, I bet your boots

I'd be enlisted in the Navy. But the sailors are alright, they are. I just love sailor boys.'

By contrast, The *Brooklyn Daily Eagle* painted the story as a cautionary tale of a fashionable fad gone too far.

> 'MANIA TO BE TATTOOED MAY COST MADELINE DEAR', the headline screamed. Brooklyn Girl Who Ran Away From Home, Found in a Shocking Condition. BLOOD POISONING MAY ENSUE. The Girl Found Covered with the Showy Emblems Sought After by Sailors.

Her right arm, tattooed with anchors, a torpedo boat and a lighthouse, was apparently in such bad condition that a doctor testified to her need for urgent, hospital attention. In the pages of the *Standard Union*, she was portrayed sympathetically as a vulnerable juvenile victim of three predatory tattooists, all of whom were charged with impairing the health of a child and had apparently faced numerous prior complaints of, as the *Union* put it, 'disfiguring children'.

* * *

The tattooing of children in the United States had clearly been going on for some time – perhaps even as long as tattooing had been a recognisable profession in America. In a museum store in Scotland, there survives a particularly vivid illustration of this phenomenon in the form of four large pieces of preserved skin from a young Irish American man, acquired in 1896. Each piece, taken from his back and front, is completely covered in red and black nautical and patriotic designs, including a ship, a liberty bell, and a portrait of George Washington, alongside a copy of a cherub from Raphael's Sistine Chapel Madonna. The man, who died at the age of twenty-nine, had, according to a contemporaneous report by curious surgeons, 'been operated on by his brother when a boy from four to seven years of age, and the process of tattooing had occupied nearly three years. The whole surface of the skin except the face, hands, soles of feet, and front of pelvis was covered with the most artistically executed designs in red and black, in which several Irish and American

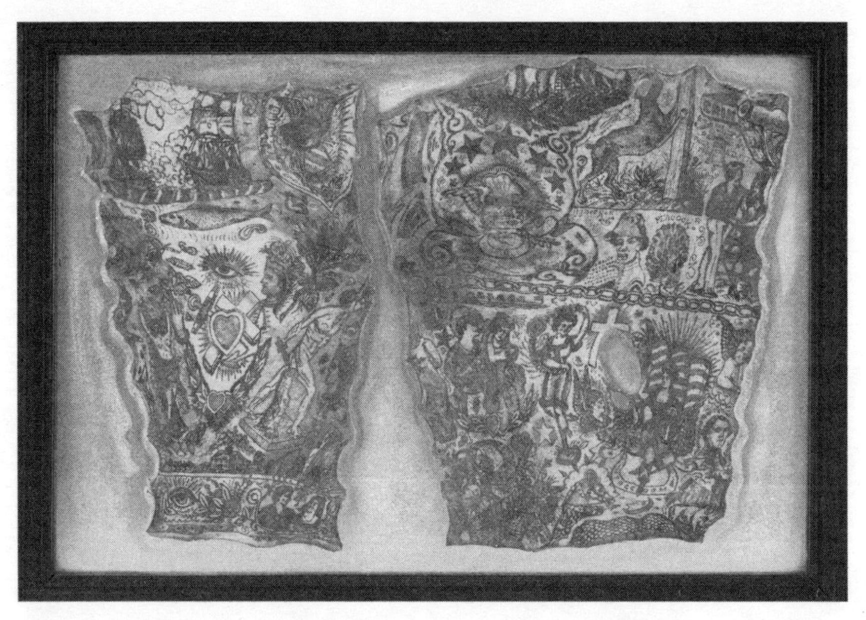

Preserved tattooed skin, Anatomical Museum, University of Edinburgh, acquired 1896

emblems were introduced'. If the reported dates are correct, this child began to be tattooed in the early 1870s, coinciding with the moment German immigrant Martin Hildebrandt started to appear regularly in the New York press as the first recognisably full-time professional tattooer in the Western world.

By the time of Madeline's adventure, eradicating the tattooing of minors in New York had already been something of an obsession of the NYSPCC for many years. Also known as The Children's Society, the organisation had been founded in 1874 at a time when the welfare of America's children was far from most legislators' minds. They worked on a number of fronts to safeguard New York's youth, including running a shelter for vulnerable children; serving as lobbyists for new laws and protections; and eventually working as an extension of the city's legal apparatus to bring prosecutions against those who put children in harm's way. They quickly became a real presence in the city, striving to protect children who had been neglected or abandoned, to save young girls from sex work and to push for new laws on a spectrum of issues relating to juvenile welfare, including child labour, the sale of alcohol and tobacco to minors, and the delivery of pornographic or otherwise obscene material by messenger boys. As their director proudly announced in 1902: 'No pains and no money were spared in collecting evidence and prosecuting those shown to be offenders against the physical and moral being of these children.'

Tattooing represented both a physical and a moral offence. As in Madeline's case, at least in the public imagination it entailed risks of syphilitic infection, and signalled a particularly reckless form of dissolute behaviour. It also involved interaction with so-called 'Jackies' – the libidinous, drunken sailors of the American Navy, as legendarily soaked in rum and sodomy as seafarers had been for generations. And so when the children of reputable parents got tattooed, the Society got involved. As early as 1898, a case extraordinarily similar to Madeline's reached the courts, after an officer of the Society tracked down another wandering fifteen-year-old girl, named Hannah, to an appropriately disreputable hostelry on the Bowery. 'The young girl,' the state records attest, had been known as 'ungovernable and wayward, and keeping the company of depraved persons.' She had, the records go on, furthermore been to subjected to 'a sad story of precocious depravity'. When they found her drinking with a group of sailors on shore leave, Hannah was nattily dressed in a sailor's uniform. Like Madeline, 'her arms and breast were extensively tattooed'.

Tattooing minors was not specifically illegal, but the Society had ensured that rules against endangering children were on the books in New York, and they were drafted broadly enough to put the tattooing of juveniles over the edge of acceptability as far as the law was concerned. In 1902, a Bowery tattooer named Charlie Wagner had narrowly avoided punishment after extensively tattooing a young Jewish boy with designs including a crucifix and the head of Christ. That year, there had been such a craze for tattooing amongst the children of New York's Lower East Side that one school reported that 'a dozen little boys and several little girls appeared with beetles, shrimps, lobsters and butterflies crawling over their faces'.

The same NYSPCC agent who tracked down Madeline, Agent King, found that Wagner and another tattooer had been responsible. In an echo that further lends credence to the tale of the Irish American boy tattooed by his brother, Wagner and his accomplice were apparently practising their skills on children so as to be able to work more skilfully on their adult customers. Despite the expert testimony of a rival tattooer, Elmer Getchell, who had argued that true professionals would not stoop to tattooing children who lacked the capacity to wisely choose a design that would be on their bodies for life, Wagner pleaded ignorance of both the law and Jewish customs, and was issued with a stern warning. However, it seems he did not heed the warning seriously enough, and in 1906 was sentenced to twenty days' imprisonment for tattooing an eleven-year-old boy, just two months before Madeline's case was brought to court.

The three tattoo artists accused of 'disfiguring' Madeline also worked at various shops in and around the Bowery. William R. Davis worked out of the back of a saloon on the Bowery itself. He claimed to have tattooed so many young girls in recent weeks that he could not specifically remember Madeline. Peter Farley – 'Tattoo Pete', who also went by 'New York Pete' – tattooed at 5 Chatham Square at the southern end of the Bowery, and Samuel O'Reilly, at the time of his arrest, was working down the street on Chatham Square at number 11. On the basis of Madeline's testimony and the inarguable, permanent evidence on her arms, each man was charged with endangering the health, life or morals of a minor.

As discussed in the previous chapter, O'Reilly in particular is not just some backroom scratcher, but an important, pivotal figure in the history of American tattooing, having held the first patent in the world for an electric tattooing machine. It was he who hosted Hori Toyo in New York, and his time working at both number 5 and number 11 Chatham Square is rightly spoken of as a halcyon moment for early American tattooing. He is regarded as one of the founding fathers of the modern tattoo industry. But his role in this debacle clearly illustrates just how common the tattooing of minors had become in New York around the turn of the century, no matter what Elmer Getchell had testified in court a few years earlier. Getchell had himself tattooed at 11 Chatham Square, and it is worth noting that he had been in a bitter public feud with O'Reilly over rival claims to the invention of the tattoo machine in the late 1880s. Given that Wagner, against whom Getchell had testified, was O'Reilly's pupil, one has to take his claims of professional superiority with at least a small pinch of salt. Despite

Getchell's assessment of Wagner's abilities, following his incarceration Charlie also went on to become one of the most feted tattoo artists in the pantheon of early twentieth-century American tattooing.

* * *

The judge at the hearing against the three men in Madeline's case asserted that the court was determined to 'put a stop to this heinous practice of disfiguring young girls'. Davis and Farley each served ten days in the Tombs jail. O'Reilly escaped imprisonment, paying a $25 fine. As for Madeline, following her tattooers' convictions, she was sent to an infamous Protestant correctional institution called the House of Mercy to be 'reformed'. As the decision was handed down, she wept openly, begging the judge that she be allowed to stay with her mother. Her father Jacob, though, was persuaded by the judge's order, hoping it would finally cure her of her 'sea-madness' once and for all.

The House of Mercy was described in a contemporaneous report on the sex trade in New York as a 'preventative institution', tasked with taking 'girls, some of them very young girls, who are subject to bad influences, who are incorrigible, or who for various reasons find difficulty in their home life'. Given the moral climate of the time, such incorrigibility was often extraordinarily minor by modern standards, and resulted in the incarceration of young girls for transgressions as minor as underage drinking and dancing. It was a large, imposing building of austere grey stone, separated from the city by tangles of trees. It had the air more of a prison than an institution of care. Rooms and windows were barred by iron gratings. The recreation yard, open to girls who had behaved appropriately once they arrived, was surrounded by an imposing 15-foot fence, and the entire building was guarded from visitors by tall railings and a heavy wooden door.

In 1910, it provided a home to 107 young women, including twenty-three girls found to have been sex-working. As part of a wider network of religious and secular missions in New York at the time, the House's work mirrored the NYSPCC's care for the physical and moral health of young women, 'raising the tone of conversation in places where girls assemble and work. Lectures on sex hygiene are given, wholesome recreation is encouraged, and higher ideals of life cultivated.' And yet, as had been the case with such institutions elsewhere, these well-meaning intentions often collided with a culture of mismanagement, neglect and cruelty.

What precisely happened to Madeline at the House of Mercy is not known. It is unlikely, though, that her time there was a happy one. Decades of reports detail miserable conditions, including the humiliation of girls by nuns at the House in 1895. Annie Sigalove, who had been picked up at a dance hall in Coney Island aged eighteen and sent to the House for three years, spoke of abuse, the withdrawal of food and having had her head shaved, as well as having been banned from contacting her parents. The usefulness of head-shaving as a disciplinary tool was boasted about by the sisters, one of whom once told a reporter that 'we find the girls do not like to lose their hair, and that the fear of having it cut off tends to make them obedient'. Gagging, too, was routine. In November 1907, during or only shortly after Madeline's period of incarceration, a teacher called Josephine Hall shot herself in the head in her quarters, having been 'despondent of late'. Miss Hall left a letter addressed to the diocese, apparently intended to be mailed after her death. In the summer of 1905, one year before Madeline arrived, Isabel Cowan, a teenager of the same age was picked up by the Society after having absconded from custody. She had been sleeping rough in Central Park, malnourished, dishevelled and surviving only on the discarded food scraps left by picnickers. She told a judge that she'd rather live in the park than at the House of Mercy.

In 1915, resident girls started a riot in protest at the poor conditions and the execrable quality and quantity of food. By 1920, the House had closed amid further reports of shackling and under-feeding, and in 1933, as it was about to be pulled down, a *New Yorker* writer documented chilling graffiti scrawled on its walls, including 'I wish I was dead', 'God help me to get out of here', and 'I was put in this House of Mercy for nothing'.

* * *

As for Madeline, after release from the grim horrors of the House of Mercy, her life did take on some form of normalcy, albeit briefly.

In 1908, she married Frederick Perry Dickinson Jr., the eldest son of an influential and wealthy Texas family involved in metal smelting. In what might have been a happy ending to this tale, Fred was indeed a sailor boy – a naval reserve who served stints in the yards at Virginia and Brooklyn, perhaps alongside Madeline's brother Herman, who had also gone to sea and with whom Madeline and Fred had lived shortly after their marriage. They were together for more than a decade until at least 1920, when the federal census records the young couple as living with Fred's well-to-do parents in El Paso.

By late 1922, however, Fred was dating another woman, and by 1923 he had married her. Unlike his marriage to Madeline, which had gone unremarked in the gossipy society pages of the local newspapers, which frequently reported on even the simple gatherings of the 'pioneer residents' who made up the Dickinson family, Fred's marriage to his new wife Vera was hailed as a great occasion on the front pages. No mention was ever made of his previous wife.

In a final ignominy for Madeline's dreams of everlasting love with a dashing sailor, Fred went on to a decade-long career in the Navy, and was ultimately buried at Fort Bliss, El Paso's military cemetery. He died relatively young, aged just forty-nine, infected with syphilis.

There seems to be no clear trace of our Madeline Altman, or Madeline Dickinson, in either New York or El Paso records thereafter. Whatever her fate, it seems that she was never fully embraced into the Dickinson family's gilded life. It seems wayward, tattooed tough kid Madeline Altman just wasn't a neat fit in the drawing rooms of 1920s Texas, and that her sailor boy didn't love her as much as she did him.

Perhaps the 'mania to be tattooed' did finally cost her dear in the end.

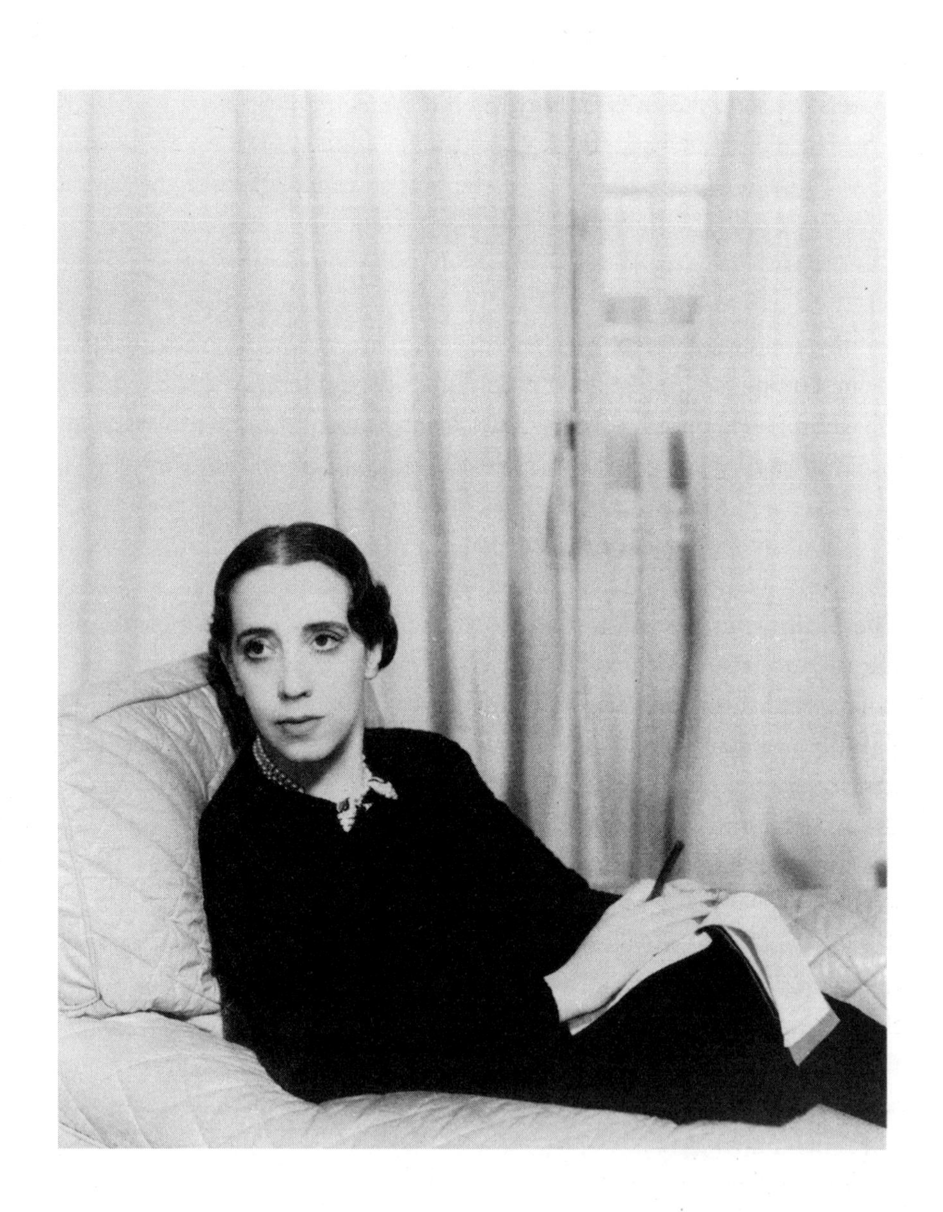

CHAPTER 14

'Tattooing is in Fashion': Elsa Schiaparelli, 1929

> 'I've simply got to tell you about the latest mode in bathing dresses in Europe . . . The shortest cut tunics are adorned with huge embroidered initials or designs similar to sailor's tattooing.'
>
> —*The Bunbury Herald and Blackwood Express*, SW Australia, 5 July 1929

The bathing suits were a sensation. Nautical fashions had been all the rage that summer, and plenty of other designers had produced ranges with nods and winks to life at sea. It was Elsa Schiaparelli, though, who had made the ultimate statement of sailor chic. For her summer collection in 1929, she sent models down runways in Paris, Barcelona and Seville in daring flesh-coloured, hand-knitted costumes, each embroidered all over with dark blue tattoo motifs. Much like the real thing, these stitched tattoo designs were crudely drawn, and haphazardly placed. But these were not merely elaborate imitations. Schiap – as her friends called her – proudly boasted that the designs were resolutely authentic. She had collected them from tattoo artists in Marseilles and Le Havre, she said, having 'combed the sailor quarters for samples copied faithfully from the manly chests of French mariners'.

The daring sartorial experiment barely caused a ripple in the cool, authoritative pages of American *Vogue*. In their dispatch from the Paris shows, these risqué nude swimming costumes were

Left: Fashion designer Elsa Schiaparelli, 1934

described matter-of-factly. 'Bathing suits', it was calmly reported, 'are hand-knit in a SUNBURN shade, with tattoo designs knitted in black.' Nothing much shocked the New York office. Their French counterparts were, by contrast, disgusted – not by the fact the designs were tattooed, of course, but simply that they were gaudy and discordant. How gauche! In more mainstream publications, however, far from the characteristic ennui of the fashion world, the tattooed swimsuits caused a rather more appreciative commotion.

In London, the *Daily Telegraph* raved at the 'delicately defined designs knitted in blue navy wool'. The *New York Times* marvelled at patterns including mermaids, sirens and pierced hearts. The provincial newspapers of Virginia noted snakes coiling on figure-hugging suits. Schiaparelli was 'clever', and she was 'ingenious'. As far away as Australia, fashion reporters shivering in the southern hemisphere winter wrote breathlessly and incredulously about 'amusing' costumes which would 'imitate the tattooing on sailors. There will be arrow pierced hearts with mottoes.' For the runway, some were adorned with the slogan 'Till Death', others 'He's my Man', or the dual-purpose 'Ever True to Mary', a slogan which is respectfully religious or romantically committed depending on your point of view. For discerning clients, however, the choice was limitless. As the suits were made to order, customers could choose their own unique patterns, exactly as they would have been able to do in a tattoo studio.

The effect was striking, and salacious. Any woman wearing these swimsuits would appear almost nude, their fashionably tanned flesh blending in with the beige wool, giving the effect that their own bodies had been covered in inky blue icons. The hyper-masculine associations of tattooing were particularly perfect, too, as androgyny and boyishness had become *de rigueur*. These suits had all the roguish romance and cultural transgression of real tattooing, but none of the risk of infection or – worse – being stuck with a tattoo after it had become unfashionable! As part of a whole ensemble, the analogy with bare skin was even clearer: Schiap had designed the tattooed swimsuits as only the first layer of a 'lizarding suit' which would allow a smooth transition from town to beach, and back again, without fear of offending delicate local sensibilities with the sight of semi-nudity.

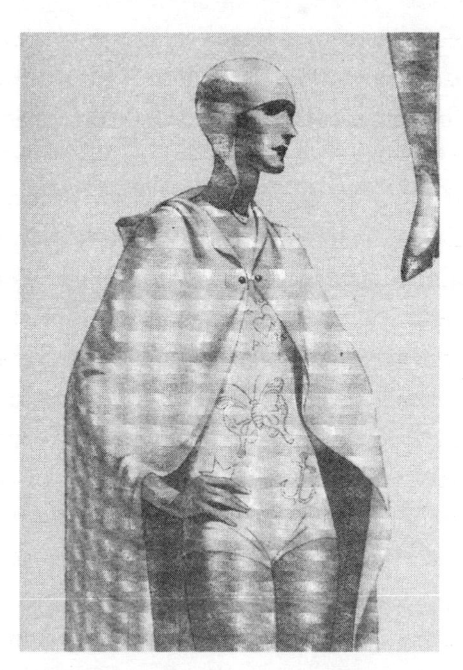

Schiaparelli's summer collection, illustrated in *Delineator* magazine, 1929

Over the fleshly bathing costume, some of her models wore yellow linen pinafores and matching yellow coats, with pockets picked out in bright orange and with lining to match. Others covered up with short black skirts and white tops for a chicer look. With their suggestively tattooed swimsuits concealed, fashionable young women could head straight from the pool to the Ritz, as long Parisian days turned into longer Parisian evenings.

* * *

Born in Italy to a bookishly academic family, Elsa Schiaparelli had studied philosophy at university in Rome. After she spent a brief stint writing salacious poetry, her scandalised father had dispatched her to a convent, which did little to quench her appetite for the world. From Italy, on her way to London in search of adventure, she stopped for a week in Paris – at the time, the veritable centre of the world. In the aftermath of the First World War, Paris had become the beating heart of the avant-garde, with modernist artists, writers, jazz musicians and designers mixing and meeting in the city's infamous cafés and bars. It was also a place where young women could be confident, expressive and free. The place captivated her. It was noisy, filthy, sexy and inspiring. 'This', she exclaimed to herself, 'is where I am going to live.'

By her 1929 summer show, she had only been working as a designer for a few years, having arrived back in Paris from New York in the aftermath of a disastrous marriage – single, cosmopolitan and liberated. The heady atmosphere of the French capital had inspired her to experiment with her own clothing in the surrealist spirit of the age, and she quickly amassed a long list of customers seeking to buy copies of the audacious knitted sweaters she had initially commissioned from Armenian women living in Paris.

On the face of it, Elsa was perhaps an unlikely woman to change the face of fashion so monumentally. She had no training in dressmaking. She could not cut a pattern, nor construct a garment. Though a visionary designer of knitwear, she could not knit, and found the process of turning balls of wool into coherent sheaths of fabric an unfathomable mystery throughout her career. But she was blessed with a visionary zeal, a head full of ideas and a pocketbook full of contacts which traced a transatlantic network of Dada and Surrealist artists and tastemakers and put her at the centre of the Parisian beau monde. Most importantly for her clothing career, however, she had a *philosophy* about clothes.

The intellectual clarity of her designs was born of a moment of absurdity, confusion and disgust. Schiap described how the transformational moment on her path to being a fashion designer had occurred at a nudist colony in Italy. There, she told a journalist later in life, 'we arrived in bathing suits and felt immediately overdressed'. In a town full of naked people, from the portly mayor to the hairdressers and the waitresses at lunch, she realised simultaneously both the power of clothing and of the body, the all-important frame upon which her creations would hang. Dresses that were never worn were lifeless, inanimate, useless. Bodies without clothes were strange, fleshy and often ugly. Yet combined, bodies in clothes that respected their lines could be *magnificent*.

Though she had incorporated tattoo motifs into some of her earliest sweaters, the tattooed bathing suits feel like a particularly powerful distillation of this idea. Trompe l'oeil tattoo designs allowed her to make the line between clothed and nude as permeable as possible: at the beach, in their temporary tattoos, Schiaparelli's customers could be slightly more than naked, but only marginally less than dressed. Their bodies were on display in all their sensuousness, but their clothing could communicate something beyond the blank, lumpen frames underneath.

* * *

With changing times had come changing hemlines. More and more skin was being revealed as French women and the women of the world who emulated them gained economic and social confidence through First World War and into the roaring twenties. As the decade progressed, consumerist and reactionary fads for 'health' and 'fitness' propelled trends for tanned skin and activewear which could be worn during sport and exercise. Bathing suits in particular were becoming skimpier and skimpier each year, and designers and their eager clients pushed hard against entrenched ideas about women's bodies which had insisted they be kept covered up. As one fashion writer at the time put it, as bathing suits had increased in meaning, they had decreased in size.

Several anthropologists in the early decades of the twentieth century believed that clothing was a cultural evolution from tattooing, and that, in line with prevailing racial theories, extensive tattooing waned in popularity as cultures became more clothed (an obviously absurd theory given many of the examples already discussed). Making the same visibility error as the Italian criminologist Cesare Lombroso, one German tattoo historian, Wilhelm Joest, claimed that 'the less a man clothes himself, the more he tattoos his skin; and the more he clothes himself, the less he tattoos'. Hermann Heinrich Ploss and Max Bartels, two pioneering German gynaecologists, agreed, writing that 'the original meaning of tattooing is to be found in the endeavour to cover nakedness'. And so as more and more skin was revealed, French humourists were already posting scornful cartoons, perhaps only half-mockingly, predicting that bathing suits were becoming so skimpy that if the trend continued, they would soon themselves be painted or even tattooed on.

Such was the moral panic about the visibility of female flesh that the idea of women having designs applied directly to the skin was a common refrain, though of course the imaginative drawings of women who might have done so provided a useful excuse to draw all-but-naked young women in the pages of your otherwise rather austere and sensible periodical. In 1913, *La Vie Parisienne* dedicated a whole illustrated page to what they suspected may become the fashion for decorated thighs, calves and ankles, featuring speculative designs for 'lovers' and 'generals' wives' poking out from under ruched petticoats, but by the early 1920s, at least some young women had taken the joke and turned it into reality, with daring designs drawn on bare legs, backs and even, in one photo in *Petit Journal* from 1922, on the face. 'Bad taste!' the headline scoffed, claiming that this 'trend' had arrived from America, leaving young French girls with strange icons plastered on their cheeks.

Of course, where newly bared skin provided fresh canvases for painting and tattooing, the revelation of previously hidden parts of the body in public also allowed tattooing acquired in previous decades to finally be seen beyond intimate moments. For much of the history of modern tattooing in Europe, it was invisible under clothing, particularly amongst more salubrious and conservative patrons, allowing a stubborn misconception to develop that in earlier generations the middle and upper classes were hardly tattooed at all. As such, with the trend for womenswear that exposed growing inches of bare flesh with each passing season, tattooing had become a visible fashion fad in Europe and America for the first time, reflecting on the body all that was trendy in textiles.

Even the ancient Greeks had noted a continuity between designs on skin and designs on clothing, with representations of Thracian women on pottery often suggesting aesthetic similarities between their exotic tattooing and the designs on their robes, but before Schiap's swimsuits, this connection had never been expressed so explicitly in modern fashion. Though celebrated Japanese tattoo artists had received a great reception in Paris, New York and London in the late nineteenth and early twentieth century, for the most part their creations were rarely on public view. Women who had been tattooed in earlier decades largely obscured their designs under long skirts and demure jackets.

In the late nineteenth century, stockings and gloves were often decorated with orientalist patterns, allowing women to wear a suggestive echo of Japanese tattoos without having to actually undergo the procedure. Anthroplogists such as Eton College's Wilfred Mark Webb noted the similarities more overtly than fashion writers did: 'In many cases the stockings are dark in colour, and the effect of tattooing is produced without the preliminary pain and inconvenience,' he wrote in 1907. Even in gloves, he went on, 'as in that of stockings and other garments, we meet with the modern tendency towards transparency. Often also the patterns are dependent upon the skin showing through, and we are once more reminded of tattooing.' Some adventurous ladies even played with this equivalence directly, asking their tattooers to deliberately suggest hosiery in their tattoo designs. Social commentator René Schwaebele had remarked in 1904 that in addition to a single continuous design tattooed across the backs of two young women living on the Rue de la Pompe, he'd seen a fancy libertine deceptively tattooed with a pair of stockings 'so delicately executed that they imitated embroidered silk!'

Rumours swirled in the international gossip columns about what exactly the most fashionable of French women were hiding under their dresses, and the side streets of Montmartre had even briefly been the European destination of choice for female travellers seeking intimate nipple piercings which only their husbands might ever see, but these were always beyond the gaze of mainstream culture. By the 1920s, visible shoulders, arms and ankles were providing public canvases for new tattooing crazes.

Tattooing had particularly captured the imagination of the artistic circles in which Schiap moved. Tattooing in France had clearly become a signifier of youthful rebellion much earlier than elsewhere in Europe. In the late nineteenth century, at the same time as British papers were describing the sophisticated tattoo habits of lords and aristocrats, in Paris the stories were scandalised tales of gambling, smoking and tattooed young women led astray by modernity.

In this new fashionable, youthful age, flamboyant Japanese painter Tsuguharu Foujita had tattooed several French women in the late 1920s after moving to Europe to study art, and many of them had proudly flaunted his work during their trips to the beach. Foujita's paramour, the artists' model Lucie 'Youki' Badoul, had a mermaid tattooed on her leg, and the same image served as the bookplate inserted into volumes of her personal library. Not wishing to be outdone, her future husband Robert Desnos, the seminal Surrealist poet, had opted for a dramatic scene of a bear on its hind legs.

Following Schiap's lead, other designers produced pieces adorned with tattoo designs over the following seasons. *Marie Claire* magazine, for example, dedicated a whole-page feature to tattoo-themed knitwear in 1938, and Schiaparelli herself returned periodically over her career to tattoo designs to decorate sweaters and skirts. The advertising for her 1930s fragrance 'Sleeping' featured the name of the perfume tattooed onto the muscle-bound arm of a sailor embracing a serene mermaid, and as late as 1959 Schiaparelli was designing stockings that gave the effect of a floral motif tattooed on the wearer's calves.

* * *

Various designers would continue to appropriate tattoo designs over the following decades, though rarely with the full-bodied commitment to authenticity that defined Schiaparelli's innovations. Edward Stevenson dressed Ginger Rogers in a tattoo-esque top in 1938; Gloria Swanson appeared in a remarkable tattoo-motif sweater in publicity stills for her 1941 film *Father Takes a Wife;* LA darling Suse produced a line of dresses embellished with large, pierced hearts in the late 1950s; Issey Miyake presented a printed dress with Japanese designs in 1971; and Sinead O'Connor wore a leather jacket by John Richmond which was painted in traditional tattoo designs in 1989. Perhaps no one did more than Jean-Paul Gaultier to make tattooing a centrepiece of their design language. When he sent tattooed models down his Paris catwalks throughout the 1990s, applying appropriated tattoo designs to sheer tops, bodysuits and leggings, *Vogue's* March 1994 issue told its readers that tattoos 'are the ultimate in individualised body enhancement, but for the uninitiated or faint of heart, Jean-Paul Gaultier's tattoo patterned T-shirts . . . are the perfect alternative'. Tattoos featured in his adverts and on his product packaging, and the tattooed sailor has become his avatar in the fashion world, instantly recognisable as a symbol of sex, transgression and salty romanticism.

In the 1990s, bringing tattoos to the runway was still edgy, shocking and scandalous. The fashion world had forgotten that Elsa Schiaparelli had already done it thirty years before Gaultier was even born.

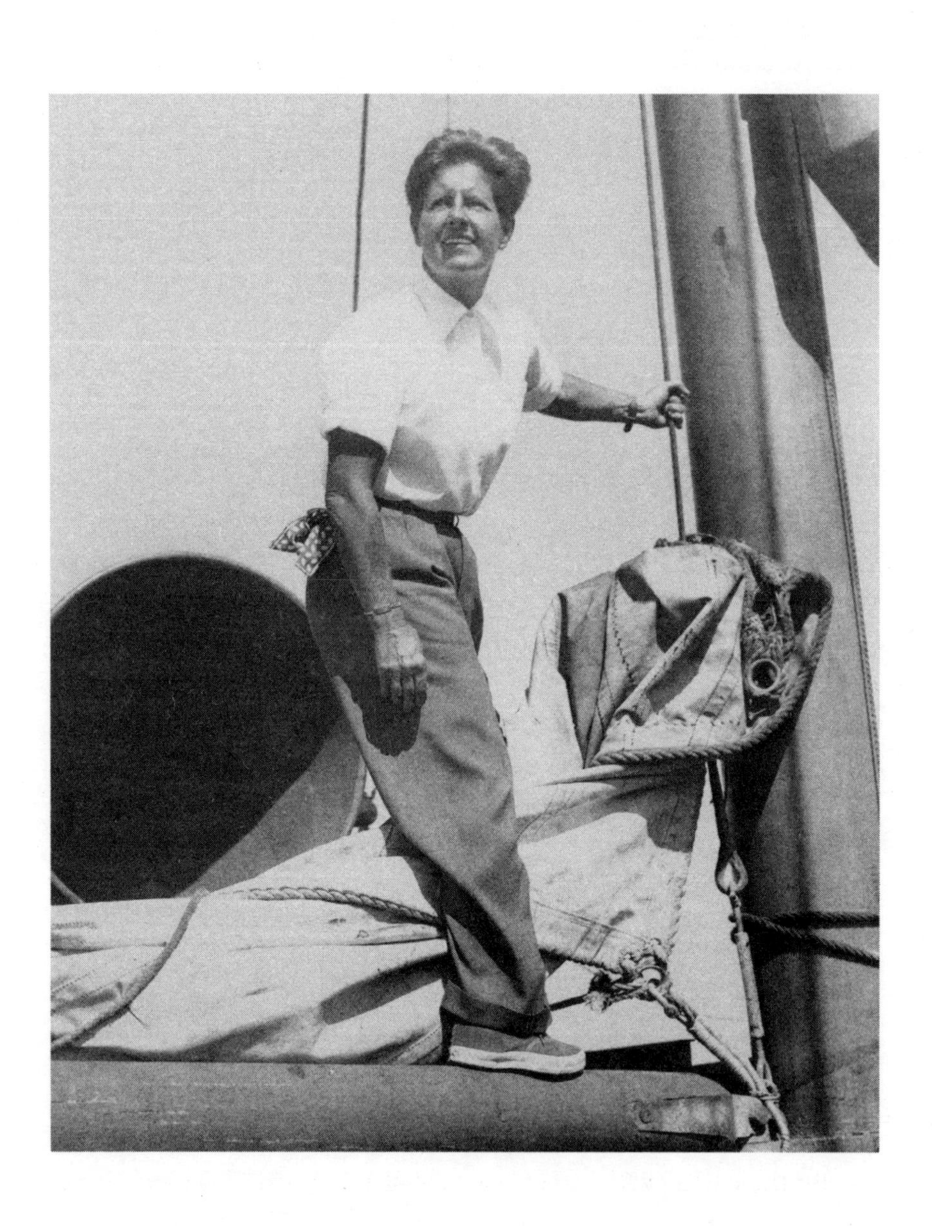

CHAPTER 15

'Hurt like fun': Joe Carstairs, c. 1925

'Betty substituted a skirt for her favourite slacks and added a tie to her ensemble. The bright tattoo marks on her left arm – a star and a seahorse – were discreetly covered by the sleeve on an expensive coat.'

—*The American Weekly*, 4 May 1947

Joe Carstairs told anyone who asked that she was 'never a little girl'. She had 'come out of the womb queer'.

American newspapers would often call her 'Betty', a name she hated. Born Marion Barbara Carstairs in February 1900, her family briefly called her 'Tuffy', a name she chose for herself in 1905, after having been thrown from a camel at London Zoo. It was an awakening. A new beginning. From that moment on, she forged a life and an identity that were entirely unshackled from the normative expectations placed upon her. As her biographer put it, 'she took a name that assigned her to no one sex or time, marked her only with her resilience. To start her life story with this mock death and birth was to erase the first few troubled years of her existence, undo the bonds of parentage and gender, and claim the power of self-creation.'

By the early 1920s, for reasons that remain somewhat unclear, she was Joe to all who knew her well. Through her transgression of gender norms and her open sexual and romantic relationships

Left: Joe Carstairs on the rigging of her yacht, *Sonia 2*, 1944

with women, Joe has become an icon of queer history, championed as a paragon of visible, proud lesbianism from a time before homosexuality was prominently celebrated in the public sphere. But her life story isn't one that easily generalises to wider lesbian experiences or to modern categories of self-identity or sexuality. In fact, we may speculate that had she lived in later decades, she may have identified as a transgender man. Modern labels for gender identity and sexuality map imperfectly onto the past, though, and it is generally inappropriate to ascribe contemporary labels to historical figures who did not use them themselves. Despite adopting a male name, taking on a normatively masculine gender presentation in her haircut, clothing choices and behaviours, and despite living a specifically, self-descriptively masculine life, she, her biographer and her friends refer to her using female pronouns. I will continue to do so here.

Joe's ability to carve her own route through the social constraints of the early twentieth century was no doubt eased, even if only a little, by her vast wealth and social privilege. Eccentricity and antisocial behaviour of the moneyed classes was enabled, tolerated and even celebrated in a way that it would never have been for anyone of a lower socioeconomic echelon. She was born in London to her American mother, Evelyn. Her father Albert, a captain in the Royal Irish Rifles, was entirely absent during her infancy, and she would later claim not even to know his name. And though emotionally complex, her early life was not one of privation. Joe's grandfather was an oil magnate called Jabez Bostwick, a man who worked as treasurer to John D. Rockefeller at Standard Oil during the rapid boom of the industrial revolution. Jabez died before Joe was born, but through him Joe would eventually inherit an almost unimaginably vast fortune. After splitting from Albert, Evelyn was a lady-in-waiting to Queen Alexandra, but went on to a turbulent life, remarrying twice and becoming enamoured with alcohol and heroin. Young Joe did not have a good relationship with her first stepfather and her step-siblings, and was ultimately sent off to an American boarding school, aged eleven.

* * *

From her youth, Joe was obsessed with 'boyishness'. She was not butch in the contemporary understanding of that term – she did not consider herself 'a stomper' – but she was certainly deliberately masculine in her appearance and obsessed with creating an image of herself in line with all the trappings of the idealised modern man, performing masculinity through the tropes of the 1920s. Several writers have speculated that openly embracing masculinity was a way to project confidence, stability and power. From childhood, she wore boys' clothes, and whilst driving ambulances in Paris during the First World War, she would pilfer items of uniform from men serving at the front. There, too, she developed a love for engines and speed which would define her life. After the war, she refused to go quietly into domestic life, and worked as a driver in Ireland for the British Army.

Astonishingly, her mother's fourth husband, Serge Voronoff, attempted to transplant monkey testicles, or 'testicular pulp', into humans as a rejuvenating technology, perhaps cementing in Joe's mind a link between bodily masculinity and youthful vigour. She exercised religiously, building a muscular, lithe physique. She obsessively chewed gum. She had, one reporter wrote, 'a man's spirit, viewpoint and force'. She smoked cigarettes, cigars and pipes from childhood, primarily for the transgressive aesthetic. She wore fashionable, loose-cut suits from Savile Row, and cropped her hair short. She occasionally took on disguises as tradesmen, going unnoticed backstage at theatres, and later in life she occasionally took to wearing a false moustache. Making glorious and reckless use of her fortune, she established her reputation in a hypermasculine world as one of the greatest and most daring powerboat racers in the world, one of a group of three speed-obsessed pilots who called themselves the 'Hell Divers'. She drank. She was promiscuous, seducing Marlene Dietrich, Tallulah Bankhead and Oscar Wilde's niece Dolly, amongst others. And as a huge proportion of articles throughout her lifetime delighted in mentioning, she was tattooed.

* * *

Joe once turned up to meet Marlene Dietrich and the American singer Grace Moore for a formal dinner at a fancy restaurant. She was wearing a stereotypically male tuxedo. Horrified, her companions sent her back to her hotel to get changed into an acceptably feminine evening dress. When she returned, the fashionable sleeveless gown revealed that her arms were covered in tattoo designs. Dietrich, shocked for perhaps one of the only times in her adult life, sent Joe away again to change back into the tuxedo.

Although tattooed women were not strictly shocking by the 1920s, it was Joe's choices of design and their placement which were most scandalous to British and American audiences. She was frequently unfavourably compared with tattooed contemporaries in high society; whilst debutante gals with blue forget-me-nots on their ankles were hailed as pretty trendsetters, one report cautioned its readers not to 'go as far as Betty Carstairs, who has tattoo things on a forearm'. Unlike Aimee Crocker's delicate, elaborate and expensive bohemian tattoos of the early twentieth century, and unlike the dainty trompe-l'oeil designs that echoed silk stockings embroidered with flowers and butterflies, Joe's tattoos were hard, manly sailor marks. As the century had progressed, the thin, careful work of English and Japanese tattooers had given way to a new fashion for graphic tattoos that were inscribed in thick, bold outlines and filled in with flat planes of colour.

Joe's tattoos would come to encapsulate her masculine self-fashioning in the public imagination. Her 'strong, tattooed arms, gripping the wheel' and her 'not exactly delicate epidermis' became a frequent trope of reporting over the course of her powerboat career, and in many iconic photographs of Joe, her tattoos are unashamedly visible. She spent her life aboard boats, and lived on – indeed, eventually owned – an island in the Caribbean, necessitating rolled-up sleeves to make the hot weather bearable. 'On her arms', the *Press and Sun Bulletin* wrote in 1930, 'are tattooed in blue and red designs dear to sailors these hundred years. Arms that are strong, roughened by sea, wind and water – arms that match the doggedness of her chin, the coldness of her eyes (that is belied by their twinkle), the heavy boots, sailorman trousers, white cap, and inveterate cigarette.' On her left arm she sported amongst other designs a dragon and a star; on her right, a monkey sitting under a palm tree. Over the years, newspapers reported other tattoos across her legs and chest, too. Her first, she said, 'hurt like fun', and she had been 'awfully scratched'. But by the time she realised how much pain the procedure was causing, the tattooer had already completed the dragon's tail. 'I had to carry on. I couldn't go through life with just a tail on my arm.'

Most reports put this first tattoo experience in Hawaii, in the immediate aftermath of her mother's death in 1924 when Joe finally inherited her full fortune. Details of the procedure and location are vague, but being tattooed there makes for the perfect creation story for a swarthy sailor design with impeccably macho pedigree. As all archetypal sailors must be, she was drunk at the time.

Honolulu has become an almost legendary location in American tattoo history in particular, as it was home to the pioneering tattooer Norman 'Sailor Jerry' Collins for his career through the Second World War, and has also for decades been the retirement home and publishing hub of Don Ed Hardy, father of postwar tattooing in the West. Back in the 1920s, when Joe was first tattooed there, it was a thronging hub of naval activity, as it had been since April 1917 when the United States joined the First World War.

Honolulu became a wildly profitable city for tattooers during the war, hosting two Army bases, an Air Force base, and a strategically important Naval base. Wars are good for tattoo artists in many ways, particularly in the ports, as sailors who cannot take much with them in their kitbags, and who risk losing what they do carry at sea, have often turned to tattooing to take some memento of home with them as they travel. Tattooing also enabled sailors to collect souvenirs of the exotic places to which they'd travelled, to inscribe their allegiance to crew and country, and to connect themselves to traditions of tattooing at sea, which span several centuries.

The main tattoo shop in the city had been opened downtown by a Philippines native called Domingo Galang in 1916, and had rapidly expanded, eventually hosting a team of artists to keep up with demand which ebbed only a little after the war ended. We cannot be sure, but it seems likely Joe was one of the eager customers at either Galang's shop, or one of the establishments set up by Galang's successors after he died in 1926.

In 1932, when Sailor Jerry was already working at Galang's nephew's shop, Joe and her tanned girlfriend at the time were spotted in Honolulu, a pair of glamorous, openly queer tattooed women walking along the beach, turning heads and setting tongues flapping as they passed by. 'Betty Carstairs, famous as a motorboat speedster . . . is a young woman of striking appearance,' the papers crowed. 'Striking' is a word frequently used to describe Joe by writers who could find no other adjective to apply to her subversive self-presentation. Occasionally, a writer would reach for 'pretty', perhaps as a barb but more likely purely out of convention, but 'striking' conjures both Joe's playful use of fashion and polite society's utter lack of a useful framework to make sense of a cross-dressing, openly gay, multimillionaire, tax-avoiding female powerboat racer. 'Her hair is shingled like a boy', (of course!), 'bronzed skin and quite a few tattoo emblems on her arms and back.' Fittingly, her mysterious girlfriend had a scorpion tattooed on her shoulder.

* * *

In 1923, just as Joe was beginning her tattoo collection, a book by the German anthropologists Mathilde and Mathias Vaerting was published in its English translation.

The text, called *The Dominant Sex* in English but whose original title in German was best translated as *Feminine Particularities in the Men's State and Masculine Peculiarities in the Women's State*, purported to offer 'a study in the sociology of sex differentiation', drawing upon the best insights of the contemporary social and evolutionary sciences to formally understand why men and women were, by their account, seemingly so fundamentally different. The Vaertings had become fascinated by the implications of the kind of monkey-testicle transplant experiments that Joe's stepfather had been pioneering just a few years earlier. If implanting male monkey testicles into humans really did lead to vigour, strength, mental acuity and hairiness – all 'masculine' qualities – they reasoned that not only was there a fundamental biological essence separating men from women, this essence could also be changed through scientific means. It was not immutable. Moreover, this basic, hormonal basis to sex difference was therefore something quite distinct from the social categories of 'man' and 'woman', which were determined by their relationships to dominant cultural norms at particular places and times in history and not by some unchangable fact of biological embodiment.

The book's fundamental thesis was extraordinarily progressive for the period. The goal of its analysis was to distinguish a narrow set of inherent, 'congenital' features of gender difference from those more common ones which are culturally determined and passed from generation to generation. The Vaertings argued that 'what we call masculine qualities today are merely the qualities of a dominant sex; and that what we call feminine qualities are merely the qualities of the subordinate sex'. In a society run by women, those qualities would reverse. In a culture where women are dominant, the argument goes, 'femininity' would map to things that in the West have long been thought of as quintessentially masculine, such as acuity, strength and bravery.

As the tabloid responses to Joe's tattooed arms showed, tattooing in the modern West has long been understood as a fundamentally masculine trait. In fact, even in 2022, *The Times* published an opinion column which asserts that a supposed increase in the numbers of tattooed women in modern Britain is indicative not of a masculinised culture, where young women are corrupted by manly things, but instead further proof that Western culture is now *so* irretrievably feminised that even tattoos are no longer sufficient for sex differentiation. 'In a feminised culture where masculine characteristics are held to be an affront to civilisation,' the column squealed, 'tattoos have become vogueish unisex adornments.'

In *The Dominant Sex,* the Vaertings devote a substantial part of a chapter to trying to explain the masculine associations of tattooing.

Their theory suggests that cultural habits are considered 'male' or 'female' depending on which sex is considered dominant in a given culture. The subordinate sex, they say, is the one that is wooed, explaining why in our patriarchal society women are so interested in clothes, makeup and hairstyling. Most importantly, members of the subordinate sex do not usually work outside the home, and thus have more time and inclination to beautify themselves. 'We may presume that the inclination towards self-adornment displayed by members of the subordinate sex, and the tendency of members of the dominant sex to dispense with ornaments and to wear drab clothing are both intimately connected with the sexual division of labour. Those who belong to the sex which works in the home have more time and opportunity for self-adornment than those who belong to the sex which works away from home. The arts of the toilet become a pastime.'

Men's hairstyles in patriarchal societies, they point out, are 'ugly but convenient'. 'Convenience is the decisive factor for one whose long hours of work make timesaving of the utmost importance. The desire to save time is the probable explanation of the fact that the men of States in which the rule of their sex is unchallenged usually let their beards grow.' The masculine association of tattoos, too, is thus explainable with reference to work. Men, apparently, simply do not have the time to put makeup on every day, as they are so busy working and ruling and being clever and strong. A tattoo, by contrast, is done once, and then it need not be done again. Very efficient. As proof of their theory that tattooing is a practice of the dominant sex, the Vaertings cite ancient Egypt – for them, a paradigmatically woman-dominant culture – where tattooing was seemingly a predominantly female trait.

This explanation seems rather implausible to a present-day reader, and of course the reasons tattooing is thought of as manly are much more complex, multivalent and varied than this straightforward analysis suggests. Nevertheless, the fundamental idea here is basically correct: our cultural associations of tattooing, and the gendered implications of those associations, are obviously produced by social expectations of how men and women should behave, how they should dress and how they are understood to relate to others. Moreover, not only are those associations produced by cultural forces, they actually produce and reinforce them in turn.

* * *

As part of the same zeitgeist, Joe had a similar curiosity about the social construction of sex and gender differences to the Vaertings. She was drawn to tattooing, and particularly to martial, military tattooing – precisely because of its cultural associations with masculinity. Tattooing became part of her transgressive toolkit, and as sailor tattooing was so fundamentally masculine in the cultural imagination, its masculinity would help her present and produce her own.

In the twentieth and early twenty-first centuries, tattooing as a tool for navigating, producing and signalling gender identity continues to appear in many narratives of trans men and women, both in those written by themselves, and in the notes and opinions of physicians, psychologists and therapists who seek to support or simply to study trans lives. For those in the latter category, tattooed trans women were often written about extraordinarily cruelly by those whom they approached for help because their tattooed bodies meant that they could never be conventionally feminine. The *American Journal of Psychotherapy* mentioned a case report in 1953 of a trans woman who was so keen to hide her desire to transition from those close to her that she overemphasised her masculinity by having her entire body tattooed, and in 1974 a pamphlet published by a religious support group for trans people interviewed a 'professional in transexual therapy' who admitted that he refused to help a trans woman with her transition because her tattoos meant that she 'would have made a most unconvincing woman'. Likely driven by these cultural and clinical resistances to squaring tattooing with femininity, trans women also wrote to community magazines for advice on if and how they might get their tattoos removed. In 1981, one trans woman wrote woefully that unless she could get her youthful tattoo removed, she would be unable to wear a sleeveless dress or a sheer top.

For trans men, by contrast, as was the case for Joe, the cultural associations of tattooing with masculinity can serve a useful role in navigating, presenting and creating a traditionally 'masculine' appearance. In 1990, a magazine for trans men called *Rites of Passage* featured a bearded, tattooed guy on the cover, his tight vest revealing huge, tattooed muscular arms. Modern social science research has found that trans men often discuss their tattoos as ways through which they have been able to 'reclaim' their bodies, something that is also visible in their own writing. A recent collection of essays called *Gender Euphoria* collects stories of transitions, and tattoos are frequently cited as a key part of the process, particularly by trans men and by transmasculine non-binary people. In their contribution, Halo Jedha Dawn, a queer non-binary writer from London, explains that they cannot currently take testosterone. Instead, they say 'there are other ways to queer my presentation. I'm planning tattoo sleeves emphasising my baby-boosted biceps. With inked arms and a shaved head I'll give off strong butch vibes.' Echoing Joe, an interviewee called Emmett Nahil also points out that 'the aesthetics and presentation of having tattoos bring gender home. They act as an anchor to my skin, holding me down and protecting my insides when the entirety of my body simultaneously feels like too much and not enough.' There's a more practical use, too: 'As it turns out, tattoos also help convince your doctor that you have a good enough pain tolerance to self-inject hormones.'

* * *

As Joe Carstairs aged, the presentational masculinity of her tattoos never dwindled. In a picture of her aged sixty, she is standing at a pool table in front of a wall covered in hunting and fishing trophies. She faces the camera square on, her hand in her pocket and her sleeves rolled up. Just as reporters often remarked about her in the 1930s, she could never get her hand in her pocket far enough to hide that dragon on her forearm, and here, forty years or so after that drunken session in Honolulu, it remains indelible. As her biographer wrote, she delighted in subverting people's expectations right to the end. 'She would stride into a room full of strangers, her skin tough and tanned, her hair cropped and white, and comment loudly on it being "fuck-awful cold", before rolling up her sleeves to reveal her wrinkled tattoos.'

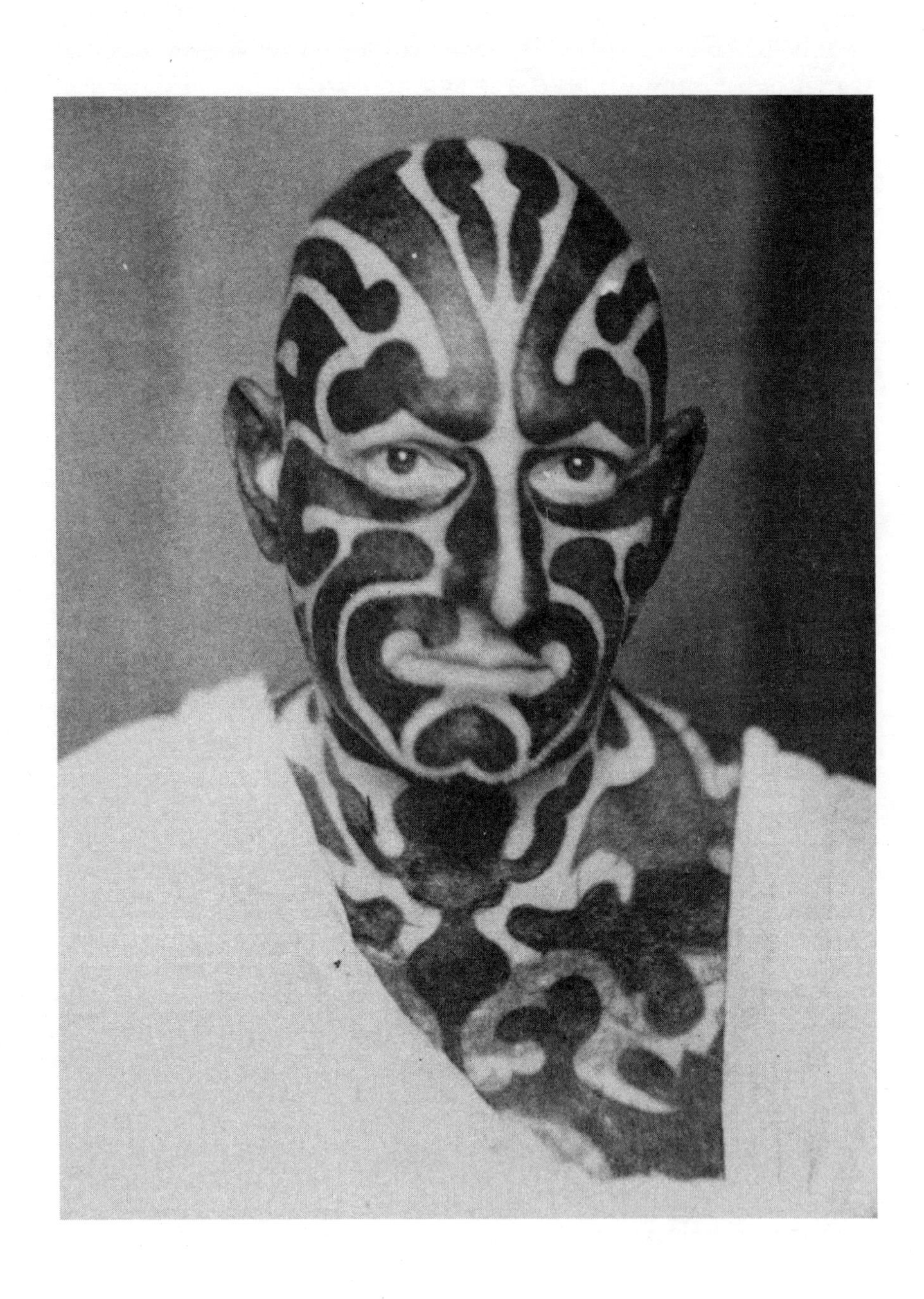

CHAPTER 16

'Blue all over': Horace Ridler, 1934

'NOW OMI IS PRESENTED TO THE WORLD! PART MAN! PART MONSTER! ONCE HANDSOME, NOW GROTESQUE! STILL A CHARMING PERSONALITY WITH A GENTLE ENGLISH VOICE. FOR EVER – AMAZING! THRILLING!! AND UNFORGETTABLE!'

—Advertising postcard, c. 1939

Over the course of two days in May 1934, tattooist George Burchett received two handwritten letters. Taken together, they amounted to a contract for what would become the defining commission of his tattooing career.

24 May 1934

Dear Mr Burchett,

This letter is to confirm my desire that you should completely tattoo me all over, including head, face and hands. My wife, Gladys J. Ridler, signifies her agreement with this by adding her signature with mine.

Yours sincerely,

H. Ridler. G. J. Ridler.

Left: Horace Ridler, the Great Omi, 1934

26 May 1934

Dear Mr Burchett,

In consideration of you agreeing to tattoo my head, face, shoulders, hands and arms to elbow, feet and legs to just above the knees, and outline on the remainder of body, I agree to pay you the sum of one hundred pounds (£100) paid by instalments beginning from the time I start public exhibitions. I agree to take on the treatment at my own risk.

H. Ridler.

More than a year later, though Burchett had by then spent hundreds of hours tattooing him, Ridler had still not settled his bill. Writing to London from France that his attempt to earn money as a performing tattooed man had to that point been a colossal failure, he presented George with a litany of excuses for his late payment including gas poisoning caused by close proximity to circus lions, flu, the language barrier in rural France, a dodgy agent promoting him not as a tattooed man but as a literal human-animal hybrid, rent arrears, overpriced ferry tickets, a surfeit of tattooed attractions and the upcoming stresses of Christmas.

Burchett was presumably not surprised. He had long since taken to referring to Horace as 'The Great Omi', a stage name derived from an ancient imperial Japanese political title that was both usefully reminiscent of Capitan Cook's Raiatean translator Omai, and an appropriate, exasperated pun: Great! Owe Me!

* * *

In contrast to his later penury, Horace Leonard Ridler's early life was one of relative affluence. He was born in Clapham in south London on 26 March 1882. His father William, 'of Devonshire stock', was a bookseller and antiquarian of considerable means, as the family were able to send Horace to a private school in Kempston, Bedfordshire. As a boy, he was tutored by his father's groom, a man named Joe Green, who had worked as a clown at the famous London

Aquarium, and who taught young Horace to trick-ride horses, to somersault and to act.

After leaving school in 1901, Horace was given a large allowance to embark on a grand tour, allowing him to travel idly to exotic destinations across Europe and North Africa on a gap year of sorts before taking up a commission in the British Army. At this time, Burchett remembered, 'he was a handsome, upstanding, regular Army officer, and from all reports a thoroughly pleasant, clean-limbed young man with a particular weakness for horses, foreign travel, and any bizarre tribal customs which he happened to come upon during his wanderings'.

Horace reportedly enjoyed his time in the military, and began earning promotions up the ranks, but his life was to take a defining turn. In 1904, William died, leaving his youngest son to inherit a large fortune. But in a forlorn attempt to keep up appearances with his aristocratic pals in the officer corps, Horace spent most of it in a whirlwind of misbehaviour and frivolity, and was ultimately ejected from his commission under a cloud. Unemployed, with no skills other than soldiering, he drifted aimlessly from role to role, watching what remained of his bank balance slowly trickling away.

In 1914, at the outbreak of war, he was welcomed back into the Army, rising to the rank of Acting Major in the machine gun squadron of the Westminster Dragoons, a mounted cavalry unit that saw action at the Western Front and in the Egyptian deserts, but at the war's end, he was back where he'd been before it started – aimless, jobless, and perilously short of cash. He invested his war pension in a chicken farm, which promptly failed, and he was absolutely unqualified for any white-collar work whatsoever. All he really had to offer the world was his boyhood showmanship, but even the circuses weren't particularly interested in him and his rudimentary, unrefined skills.

Horace urgently needed an act. A gimmick. Perhaps remembering a show he'd seen on his travels, or recalling a lesson from the clown who'd taught him to perform as a boy, he decided that he'd copy the heavily tattooed attractions who'd performed at the Westminster Royal Aquarium when he'd been just a child.

* * *

Over the preceding centuries, theatrical performances of and by tattooed people in Europe and North America generally took two forms. The first were the grotesque spectacles of the tattooed captives brought to Europe from the Pacific and the Americas in past centuries to serve in what often amounted to little more than human zoos. As we have seen in previous chapters, this kind of voyeuristic spectacle dates back to the sixteenth century. The second were performances by Europeans who had returned home and claimed to have been tattooed during their travels abroad.

Perhaps the most famous of these was John Rutherford, the self-proclaimed 'White Chief' who spent ten years living amongst Māori people as part of the Ngāpuhi tribe between 1816 and 1826. In his performances, Rutherford claimed to have been captured during a skirmish, and told an increasingly vivid and implausible story that a group of warriors had stormed the ship, killed and eaten seven of his crewmates and then dragged the survivors away to their village. There, he was apparently held down and forcibly tattooed in the local style all over his body, including his face. (The book of his adventures claimed, of course, that 'while I was undergoing this operation, although the pain was most acute, I never either moved or uttered a sound; but my comrades moaned dreadfully'.) Over the following months, the remaining Englishmen died, leaving him as the sole survivor. For the next decade, he said, he survived amongst the Māori, earning the trust of his captors, before finally escaping on a visiting British ship.

Very little of Rutherford's account can be corroborated, including whether the ship he claimed to be aboard ever even visited New Zealand, and the book he wrote about his adventures is filled with absurdly salacious details of things such as cannibalism which have no basis in fact. Instead, it seems more plausible that he was a deserter who decided to acquire facial tattoos to better fit in with the cultural context in which he found himself, or to avoid detection should any of his paymasters come looking for him, or both. In any event, Māori facial tattooing, moko, is a high social honour, and there is no reason why Māori would forcibly tattoo anyone with such important designs. Whatever the truth of the matter, Rutherford's performances once he was back in England established a particular kind of typology which would frequently be replicated.

In the modern era, tattooed men and women had performed in London since at least the 1870s, a generation after Rutherford's return and more than a decade before Horace Ridler was born. These performances became a staple of the various public shows on offer at the Westminster Royal Aquarium shortly after it had opened in 1876, as despite an initial intention to run the space as a place of scientific learning and cultural entertainment, its owners quickly realised that keeping fish was both more expensive and more complicated than they had imagined. To pay the bills, they started using the vast water tanks to stage spectacular re-enactments of famous naval battles in miniature, and hired vaudeville and music hall acts, comics, burlesque performers, clowns and medical quacks to fill the stalls instead. As business boomed, the aquarium acquired a rather insalubrious reputation as a place for a pretty wild night out, and it became somewhere that sex-working women could attract clients.

Against this cacophonous, bacchanalian backdrop, tattooed performers initially revivified and parodied the kinds of spectacular storytelling about far-off lands and violent, savage natives of Rutherford's era. This kind of performance added a particularly salacious and anthropological edge to the already Orientalist and colonialist tone of many of the magic, sideshow and musical acts on the bill. Of these tattooed headliners, a Greek-Albanian man, Captain George Costentenus, was the earliest and most important, performing in London, America and across Europe throughout the 1880s and 1890s.

Costentenus was covered in elaborate and exquisitely rendered tattoos of animals including elephants, monkeys and birds. His act involved regaling the crowd with a story of how he had been captured by Tartars in China and tattooed all over his body in spectacular fashion. In some versions, the tattoos were a punishment for participating in an illegal gold-mining expedition, in others for fomenting a rebellion of mineworkers against their overseers. The story of his tattooing also shifted frequently in its precise details over the course of his career, but he usually explained that he had been tattooed slowly and tortuously over a period of more than three months, before staging a daring escape and embarking on an arduous return voyage back to Europe. As with Rutherford, most of these details are implausible

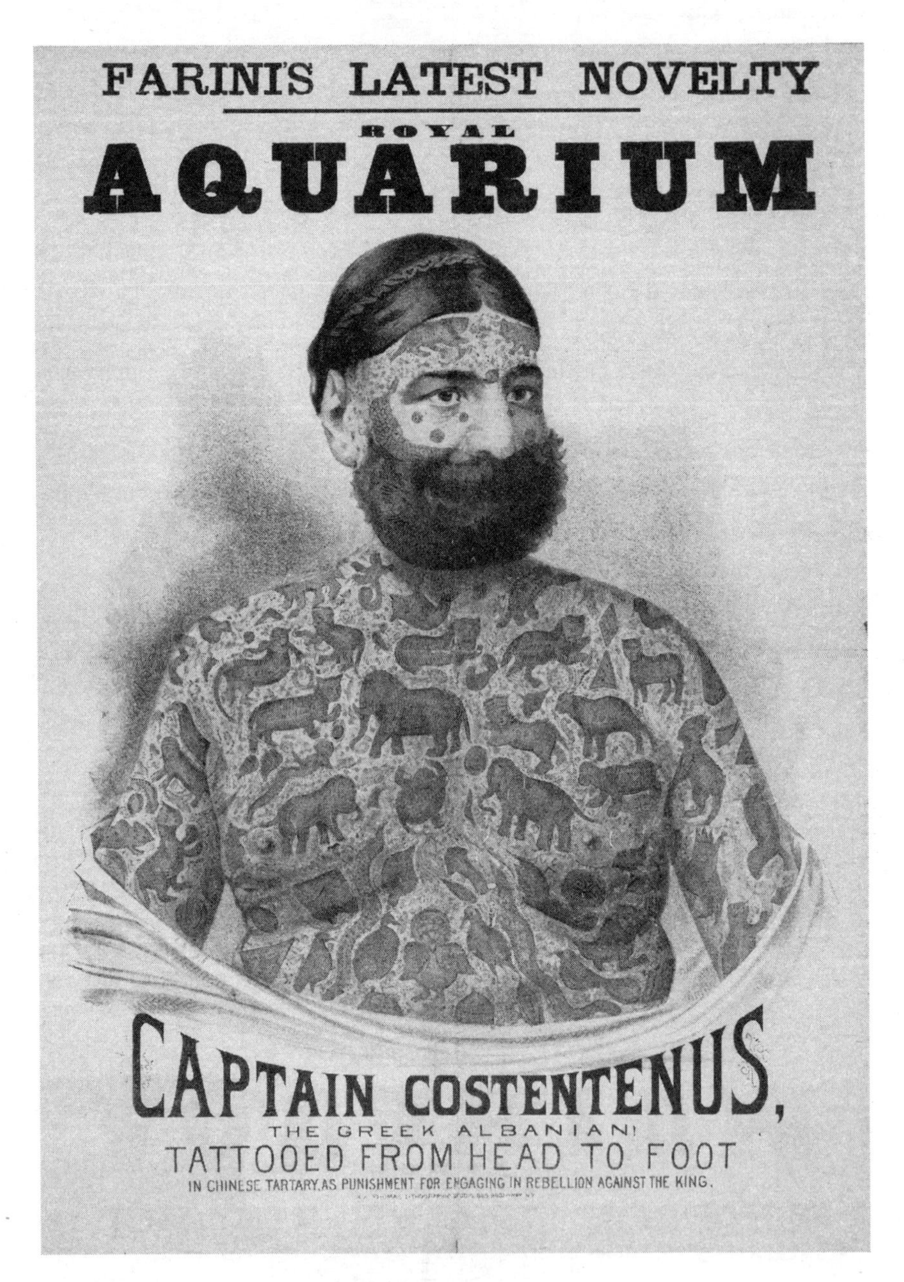

Captain Costentenus, colour lithograph, *circa* 1900

or obviously fantastical, though his tattoos did appear to be authentic Burmese designs to experts who examined him.

As tattooing became increasingly popular in London following the opening of Japan and the revelation of the royal family's own tattoo habits, the tattooed performers at the aquarium moved away from regaling visitors with fanciful accounts like Costentenus', and began staging live exhibitions of tattooers' best work. Tattooed ladies were very popular indeed, as their shows offered a plausible excuse for appearing on a public stage with rather less clothing than was usually acceptable in Edwardian Britain.

Right up until its closure in 1903, its stage played host to visiting tattoo acts such as Frank and Emma De Burgh, a fantastically tattooed American couple who had been worked on by Samuel O'Reilly in New York, as well as home-grown acts including Flo Riley, the 'Living Gallery of Japanese Art', who served as a walking advertisement for her husband Tom's business. An American tattooer called Professor Williams had begun some years earlier not just to exhibit himself as a tattooed man, but to offer patrons the chance to be tattooed themselves, and the Aquarium quickly earned a reputation as one of the best places in London to get tattooed as well as simply see tattoos on other people. Tattooing visitors to the Aquarium was so profitable, in fact, that Tom Riley and a rival tattoo artist called Alfred South almost came to blows over control of the lucrative tattooing pitch inside the premises, and a full-blown fight was only averted when the venue's high-dive act stepped in to mediate.

* * *

A rare photograph of Ridler before he acquired his facial tattoos shows that his first attempt to work as a tattooed performing man was based on a rather conventional and by then pretty old-fashioned body suit of conventional Western tattoo designs. He was first tattooed by Burchett in 1927, and from him he acquired tattoos across his back, chest, arms and legs, but it obviously wasn't making much of an impact, even when paired with a pseudo-oriental turban of sorts to evoke some sense of exoticism. 'He was a tall, well-built man,' Burchett remembered, 'with a handsome face. He was cultured,

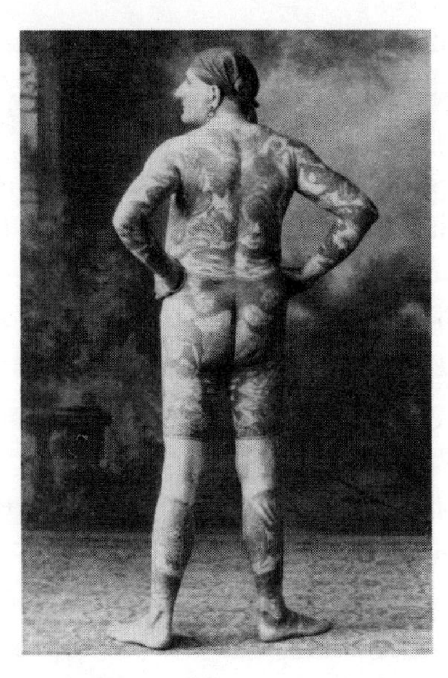

Horace Ridler before 1934, from photo-collage owned by Dora Maar

and obviously of good education. He wished to become one of the great human oddities.' His tattoos were not entirely uninteresting, as evidenced by the fact that Dora Maar, the French surrealist artist, photographer and model and muse to Pablo Picasso, was sufficiently intrigued by the picture that she bought a negative of it from Burchett whilst she was in London. But by the 1920s, this kind of Japonesque tattooing had fallen somewhat from fashion, and had certainly ceased to carry much novelty with the paying public. As a slightly overweight former public schoolboy in his forties, the sight of his half-naked body was also not particularly titillating to the masses, tattoos or no tattoos.

Desperately looking for an edge, Horace thought he'd try and become a performer of the kind Rutherford and Costentenus had been over the previous century, but without any of the complexity and cost of actually having to get captured by some so-called savage tribe. Burchett explained that Horace himself created the symmetrical design of thick, wide stripes which would be tattooed on his face, reminiscent of some exotic land, but not actually a specific copy of any indigenous tattoo style anywhere in the world. The process was arduous and painful, particularly where Burchett needed to properly disguise some of Horace's existing tattoos under the new designs.

Old George remembered it taking 150 hours in total, in three sittings a week, though Omi's stage show stretched the tale to thousands of hours.

The result was strange enough, but Burchett was expressly concerned about sending Horace home after a session with the project still unfinished. Though the final sight confused and delighted people for the rest of his life, those few months where half his face was tattooed and the other half still gloriously unblemished must really have been quite baffling to anyone who saw him. He enjoyed the attention, admitting to vanity and narcissism, but the inescapable curiosity quickly became exhausting. Even though in several interviews Omi expressed hope that answering the common questions once, in print, would save him having to answer them several times per day in person, the bafflement never truly subsided.

In 1948, Omi gave an interview to his hometown's paper, while 'resting from the hurly-burly of show-business in a secluded avenue in Hove'. Even though it was by then more than a decade since he had first had his face so thoroughly tattooed, people were still consistently astonished at the sight of him. The interviewer describes him as literal nightmare fuel, the human equivalent of too much cheese before bedtime. Perhaps a frustrated arts writer, the author conjures an unrestrained description of Omi's visage as if he were reviewing a modernist sculpture in the cultural pages.

> Omi is blue all over, a deep cobalt shade varied on his body with some fancy shaded patterning but quite unrelieved until you get to his hands and neck. From there, the design is of an emphatic and startling kind that Picasso would not be ashamed of, and which inspires less sensitive small boys to begin experimenting on themselves with ink and indelible pencil. The livid markings on Omi's face and head – he is shaved quite bald – follow a rigorously symmetrical pattern, the ears themselves being a deep plain blue and frequently ornamented with a kind of monster earring – an ivory dagger five inches long, which is inserted through a hole he has specially pierced in the lobes.

It is of great credit to both Burchett and Omi that their collaborative work of art still had so much power to delight and confuse onlookers, and given Dora Maar's interest in Omi's old tattoos, this evocation of Picasso's imagined opinion is amusing indeed.

* * *

After the disastrous first French tour, Horace – or now, I suppose, properly the Great Omi – was running out of ideas, and of money. In one last desperate bid to properly excite interest in his freakshow performances, he asked a veterinarian to pierce his nose through the septum, and to help him stretch his earlobe piercings in the manner customary amongst Kenyan Masai. He had a dentist sharpen his teeth into animalistic fangs, and he enlisted his wife Gladys to be his compère in a double act, dubbing her Omette. He wore gaudy costumes of gold silk and sequins, and grew his fingernails long. The grandiloquent critic explained that these were 'over two inches long and lacquered blood red like the talons of a prehistoric monster'.

Almost instantly, Omi's fortunes were transformed. There really was an audience willing to pay good money to see and hear from a man who had willingly broken with every social nicety. 'Marvels of nature' such as bearded ladies and people with dwarfism were interesting enough, but a self-made freak?! People didn't understand why anyone would do that to themselves, and they flocked to find out more. Omi and Omette wowed crowds in London and Manchester, and were invited in 1939 to perform at the World's Fair in New York, followed by a twenty-six-week residency at Ripley's *Believe it or Not! Odditorium* on Broadway.

As war had broken out in Europe while they were in the United States, they were unable to return to England, instead seizing the opportunity to tour with Ripley's, and with the circus Ringling Bros. and Barnum & Bailey. The pair also crossed into Canada frequently over the following years, and performed at sideshows and fairs in Ottowa and Vancouver, where the act was specifically marketed to curious and incredulous children. Omi's incredible appearance drew headlines across the world, and he earned sobriquets including 'The Zebra Man' and 'The Ninth Wonder of the World'. 'Look kids!', his ad for Happyland Fair shouted, 'Great Omi! The strangest man in the world! Bring your parents too!'

* * *

By the 1950s, Omi had retired. He and Omette bought a modest caravan on a site in a small village in Sussex, and lived out their retirement in an odd kind of obscurity, given that his identity was painted indelibly on his face. Occasionally, newspaper photographers would show up to take a picture of this increasingly elderly man vainly trying to disguise himself with a hat and scarf as he popped to the shops for a pint of milk or a loaf of bread, but the locals took him to heart, and both Horace and Gladys remain fondly remembered, even forty years after their deaths. Horace passed away in the autumn of 1965, and Gladys four years later.

In some senses, though, perhaps Horace had died the day Burchett finished grinding out those black shapes on his tired, swollen face. Omi rarely gave his real name out in public, even though it was hard to keep it totally a secret when former members of his platoon turned up to see Omi and were surprised to see their old commanding officer up there on stage, still recognisable despite the tattoos, piercings and sharpened teeth. As one writer put it in 1935, 'To live, he died. Yes, his old self, his own name he put behind him. He became an oddity. Nature could not help him in this respect, so he turned to the skill of the tattooist and to the shutting away of the past, added the obliteration of his appearance. Courage? Verily, yes. Brave as he was in his military carer, Omi showed an even greater degree of courage in doing what he eventually did. And Omette, his wife? Perhaps even greater.'

Even formal authorities had trouble trying to make sense of his identity. On one official document, a dumbstruck official filled in the 'complexion' box for Ridler not as 'white' but as 'tattooed'. Most strikingly, at the Buffalo border crossing between the United States and Canada in 1940, an official on the American side filed a separate index card for the Ridlers' arrival, presumably to help any future border guard avoid the confusion he'd just gone through. In the appropriate boxes, in handwriting that suggests even in its penmanship some degree of puzzlement: 'FAMILY NAME: GREAT. GIVEN NAMES: OMI, THE.'

PART FIVE

TATTOOING TOWARDS THE MILLENNIUM

North Korean marines stationed at Wonsan have marks tattooed on the back of both the right and left hands of officers and men. The right hand has the mark of an anchor and the Korean characters meaning "navy." The left hand bears the motto "struggle for the unification of the fatherland" with the date 1950.1.1. The tattoos are to prevent officers and men from deserting, since the chance of recognition is great, and to facilitate the identification of bodies.

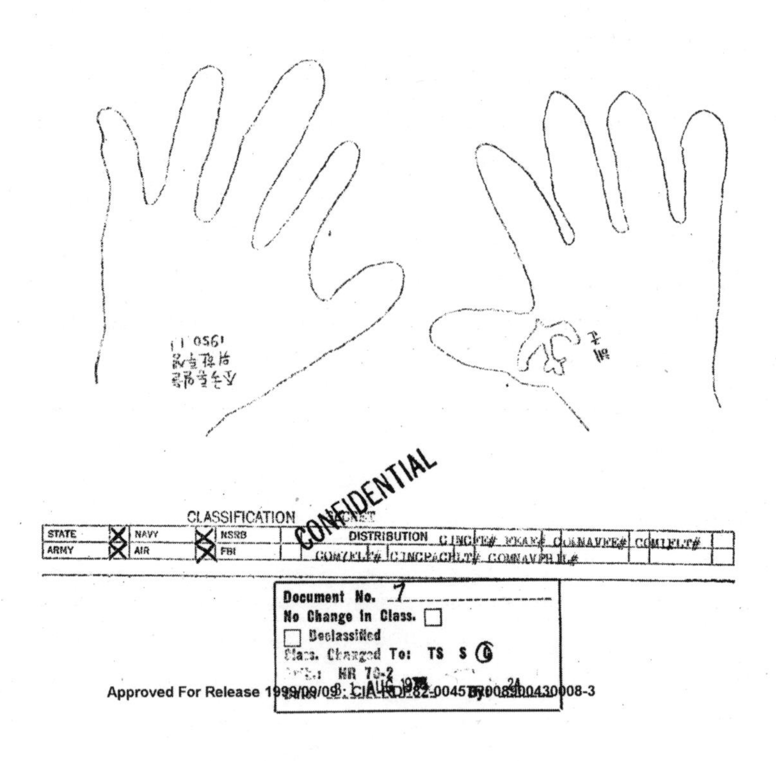

CLASSIFICATION ~~SECRET~~ CONFIDENTIAL

STATE	X	NAVY	X	NSRB		DISTRIBUTION	CINCFE#	FEAF#	COMNAVFE#	COMTFLT#	
ARMY	X	AIR	X	FBI		COM7FLT#	CINCPACFLT#	COMNAVPHIL#			

Document No. 7
No Change In Class. ☐
☐ Declassified
Class. Changed To: TS S (C)
Auth.: HR 70-2
Date: 1 AUG 1978 By: 024

TATTOOING TOWARDS THE MILLENNIUM: 'AN IN-AND-OUT BUSINESS'

> 'The practitioners of the prickly arts – the tattoo Tintorettos and Toulouse-Lautrecs of Lower Burnside Street – have closed their studios and faded . . . Tattooing, inherently an in-and-out business, has been having its ups and downs since at least 1300 BC, when the Egyptians got decorated before they got mummified.'
>
> —Harold Hughes, *The Oregonian*, 15 June 1955

> 'Necrophilia, narcissism, sex, superstition or swank – anthropologists can take their pick of the timeless motives which keep this weird private art alive.'
>
> —*The Economist*, 28 December 1963

In 1937, tattooing was mainstream enough that American newspapers and tattoo artists encouraged people to get tattooed with their social security numbers, lest they forget them. As the Second World War began, just as was the case during the First World War, enlisted men flocked to have permanent memories of home inscribed onto their bodies, and to acquire icons and symbols through which they could signal their affiliations to their countries, their regiments and their friends. Those left at home also used tattoos to affirm permanent connections and commitments to lovers and children sent abroad, or to memorialise them if they did not return home. In 1943,

Left: Declassified CIA report depicting North Korean marine identification marks, 23 October 1951

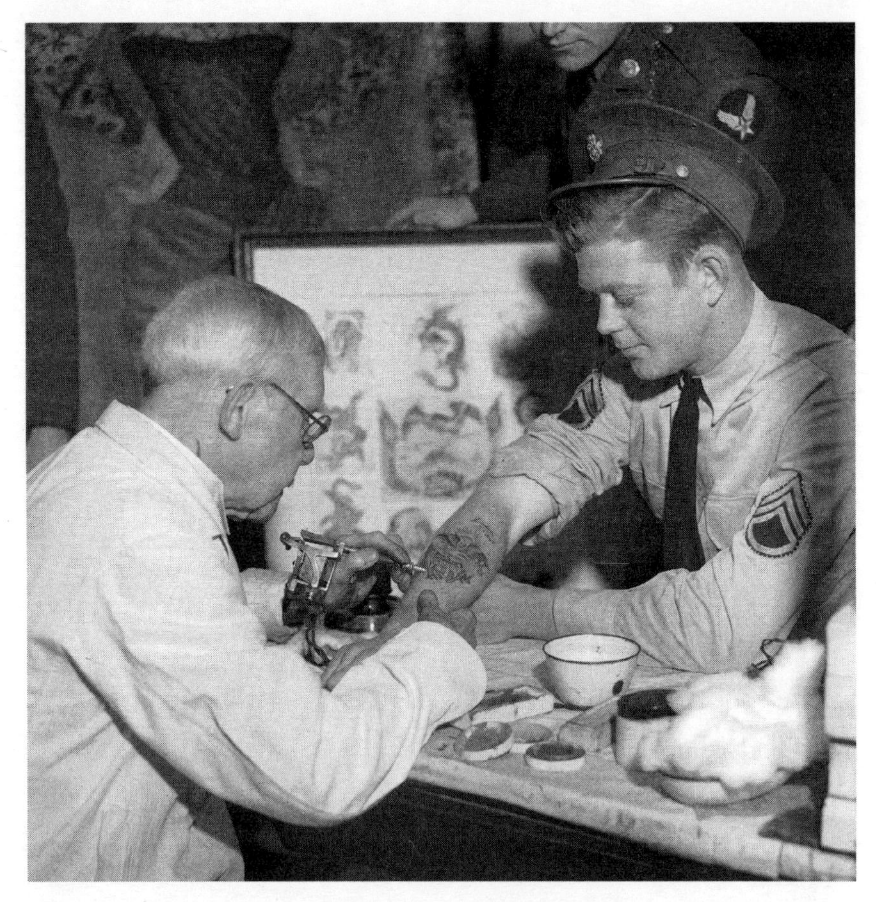

Soldier being tattooed by George Burchett, London, 1943

Illustrated magazine in London reported that 'thousands of people come in to have their identity numbers or their blood groups imprinted indelibly on them . . . Many of them want their badges on their arms. Some ask for Winston Churchill's head on the body of a bulldog. Others want the swastika with a dagger through it. But the old favourites, where love and luck intermingle, are still the favourites.'

Elsewhere in the world, ancient tattoo traditions in Southeast Asia, including in Borneo, Cambodia, Laos and Myanmar, where tattooing had been undertaken for centuries as a spiritually protective practice, took on new resonances during the armed conflicts of the 1940s. Across the region, sacred tattooing from a number of cultural traditions has been understood to offer the wearer strength, vitality and magical protection. As warfare became militarised, the extent and power of the protection expanded, so that some wearers even believed themselves to be protected from bullets. One elderly tattooer from Borneo, for example, explained late in life that his tattoos had protected him from Japanese machine-gun fire during skirmishes in the Second World War, telling an anthropologist that 'they just went around me and I was never wounded'. These beliefs also persisted in the following decades, as many Cambodian veterans who fought the Khmer Rouge in the 1970s and 1980s also describe how their Buddhist tattoos protected them from landmines, with one crediting his tattoos for the fact that the two (two!) landmines he had stepped on in his life had both fizzled and failed to detonate, and that he had once emerged unscathed from a night-time ambush. As long as the wearers remained moral and religiously observant, they believed the tattoos would work. 'During the war,' he told a journalist in 2009, 'we believed in the magic. We knew a lot, including magic that prevents you from being tied up or hurt by torture.'

After the war, though, attitudes against tattooing in the Western world hardened as tastes again changed. Though many tattooed men had returned home, only the tattoos on those whose arms

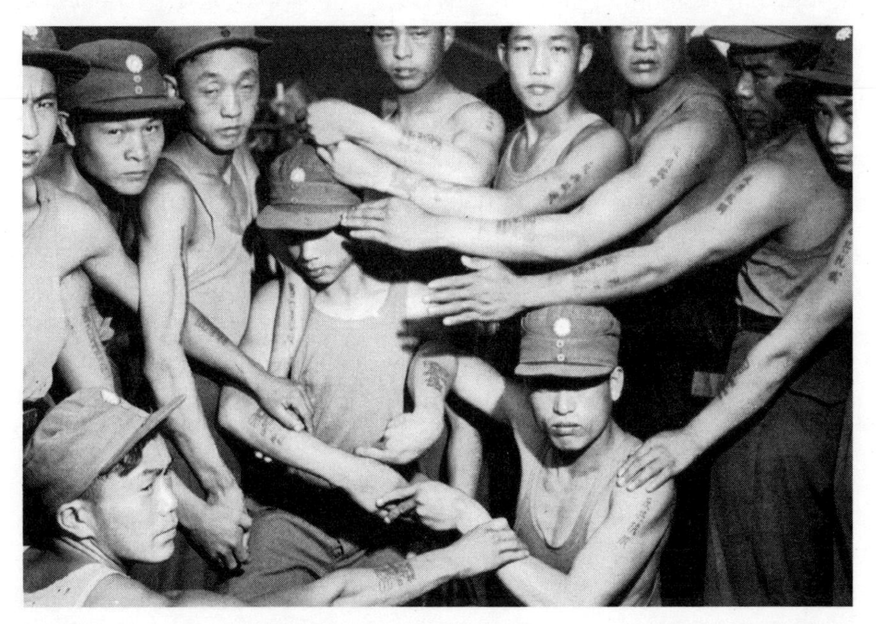

Prisoners of war with tattooed anticommunist slogans on their forearms, Korea, 18 July 1952

were regularly on display were usually seen, leading to a perception that tattooing was something unique to the labouring classes. Tattooed bank managers, whose sleeves were never rolled up at work, remained invisible.

Images of the tattoos that were forcibly carried out on victims of the Holocaust who had been imprisoned and murdered at Auschwitz were particularly striking, reinforcing the idea that tattooing was a stigmatising practice. Similarly, during the Korean War, a CIA report noted that North Korean conscripts wore mandatory tattoos to signal their allegiance to communism: 'The right hand has the mark of an anchor and the Korean characters meaning "navy". The left hand bears the motto "struggle for the unification of the fatherland" with the date 1950.1.1. The tattoos are to prevent officers and men from deserting, since the chance of recognition is great, and to facilitate the identification of bodies.' And on the other side of the same conflict, many Chinese and North Korean prisoners of war in Taiwan and South Korea were forcibly tattooed with anti-communist slogans (though many also apparently chose these tattoos willingly in order to signal their loyalty to the anti-communist cause). And, more broadly, as time moved on, tattooing again simply waned in popularity, particularly as post-war fashions in art and design discarded decoration and chintz in favour of modern, sleek minimalism.

By 1955, Portland, the major seaboard city on the West Coast of the United States, did not even have any tattoo studios, the last one having closed early that year. 'Tattooing', *The Oregonian* told its readers with a wry pun on the action of a tattoo machine, is 'inherently an in-and-out business.'

But all was about to change. Tattooing returned to prominence from this juncture, when the practice was experiencing its lowest ebb for almost a century, to the turn of the millennium, when, again, it had become so unthreatening to mainstream sensibilities that a tattoo studio opened in London's esteemed department store, Selfridges. By 2003, the *Financial Times* remarked, 'tattooing, once the exclusive but downmarket domain of sailors, soldiers and bikers, is to become a permanent feature at the favourite haunt of London's fashionistas'.

* * *

Having been born into this moment of tattooing's nadir, the baby-boomer generation have stereotypically been sceptical of tattooing. They were born after the fashions for grand and ornate Oriental tattooing had faded from memory, and they were raised in an era that celebrated a set of aesthetics that did not easily accommodate tattooing's ornamental results. Because so many of the tattoos young people in the 1950s and 1960s saw were on men and women who had been marked during the war, the association of tattooing with sailors and soldiers which returned with gusto over the post-war decades makes complete sense, even if, as ever, it was an association which was hardly grounded in a nuanced engagement with the truth. What's more, during their childhood, tattooing had been increasingly regulated – it was banned on under-18s in Britain in 1969, after a decade of reports about wayward schoolchildren who had spent their pocket money at the local tattoo shops, and the conviction of at least one tattoo artist for the crime of assault following his work on teenagers. In 1961, tattooing had been made *completely* illegal in New York City, the wellspring of the professional Western tattoo industry, following a hepatitis outbreak, and it would remain banned there for almost forty years, until 1997. A similar outright ban was enacted in Massachusetts the following year. In Europe, Denmark banned facial and hand tattooing in 1966, legislation which technically remains in force today. Across the Eastern Bloc, professional tattooing was also completely banned in many countries, including Russia, where restrictions were only lifted after the fall of the Iron Curtain. In general, the 1950s and 1960s were a period characterised by a suspicion of and aversion to tattooing.

Nevertheless, throughout these same decades, tattoo artists continued to advocate for themselves and their customers to be taken seriously, and the media frequently reported on just how surprisingly trendy and popular tattooing was. In 1950, the *Hull Daily Mail* was receiving letters from young tattooed women who had been born in the 1930s, angry at being tarnished by the reputations of drunken sailors, given that there was 'all the difference between some of the crude, inartistic designs plastered about the arms of men we have seen (probably done under the influence of drink) and a small, neat design on the shoulder where it can only be seen under a transparent dress'.

And by 1965, the American press were again reporting that 'that most intimate art form – tattooing, or the old skin game – still flourishes in Britain'.

* * *

Even though many of the most common myths about tattooing were perpetuated by those who grew up in an era when tattooing was stigmatised, and when a huge amount of visible tattooing was demographically restricted to servicemen, tattooing's transformation in the last decades of the twentieth century was of course also undertaken by baby boomers.

Academic writing about tattooing's resurgence over this period conventionally places the so-called 'renaissance' of tattooing in the 1970s. In that decade, youthful celebrities such as Janis Joplin were prominently flaunting their tattoos, and tattooing was slowly beginning to be acknowledged by the mainstream institutions of the art world. In New York, despite (or perhaps because?) tattooing had been recently banned there, the Museum of American Folk Art put on an exhibition of tattoo history in 1971. In London, British tattooing pioneer Les Skuse staged a temporary exhibition of contemporary tattooing, including live tattooed models, at the Camden Arts Centre in 1974, and was also invited to give guest lectures at the art school in Bristol. Skuse's tattooing also featured alongside other contemporaries as part of an exhibition of historical art and design called *Vanity* at Brighton Museum in 1972. It is also in the 1970s that a prominent new generation of tattoo artists who had been trained at art schools burst into the public consciousness, including such luminaries as Ed Hardy, and publications such as Hardy's *Tattootime* reignited interest in tattoo history. But as has become a stubbornly recurrent theme in this book, this so-called 'renaissance' in the 1970s was not as disconnected from the past as that phrase suggests. In Britain, the media were already reporting on tattooing's artistic rebirth almost twenty years earlier, when TV magazine programme *This Week* ran a segment called 'The Renaissance of Tattooing'. The segment visited both George Burchett's son Leslie, tattooing on Waterloo Road after his father's recent death, and a young artist with a gold tooth called

Cash Cooper, a man who would go on to be a legend of the tattoo industry in the following decades. At Cooper's studio, though the surviving footage is frustratingly mute, the customers are, predictably, a pair of young women. In terms of a presence in the art world, an oil painting over which George Burchett had painted tattoo designs – the image Brighton's *Vanity* exhibition picked for the cover of its catalogue – had already appeared in seminal folk-art exhibition *Black Eyes and Lemonade* at the Whitechapel Gallery in 1951. And Skuse had been playing his part too, starting the Bristol Tattoo Club in 1953 in order to establish a global network of tattoo artists who were willing to keep the profession alive.

It is professional tattoo artists, of whom Skuse and Hardy are but two of the most vocal out of thousands, to whom we must hand the credit for the diversity and impact of tattooing today. There was no 'renaissance', no clear moment where tattooing's present was ultimately ruptured from its past. There was no moment when tattooing had disappeared, and thus no way it could ever really reappear. Throughout the whole period, influential artists always shared knowledge, encouraged their fellow artists to improve, and became visible and eloquent ambassadors for tattooing and its history in the media and to governments. They traded designs, equipment and treasured historical ephemera with tattoo artists in every corner of world, visited far-flung tattoo studios to exchange ideas, and encouraged their customers to get tattooed with an infinite and experimental range of designs which drew upon tattooing's rich history in innovative ways. They improved techniques and tools, and they nurtured new generations of younger tattooers, who themselves have continued to pass the torch onwards.

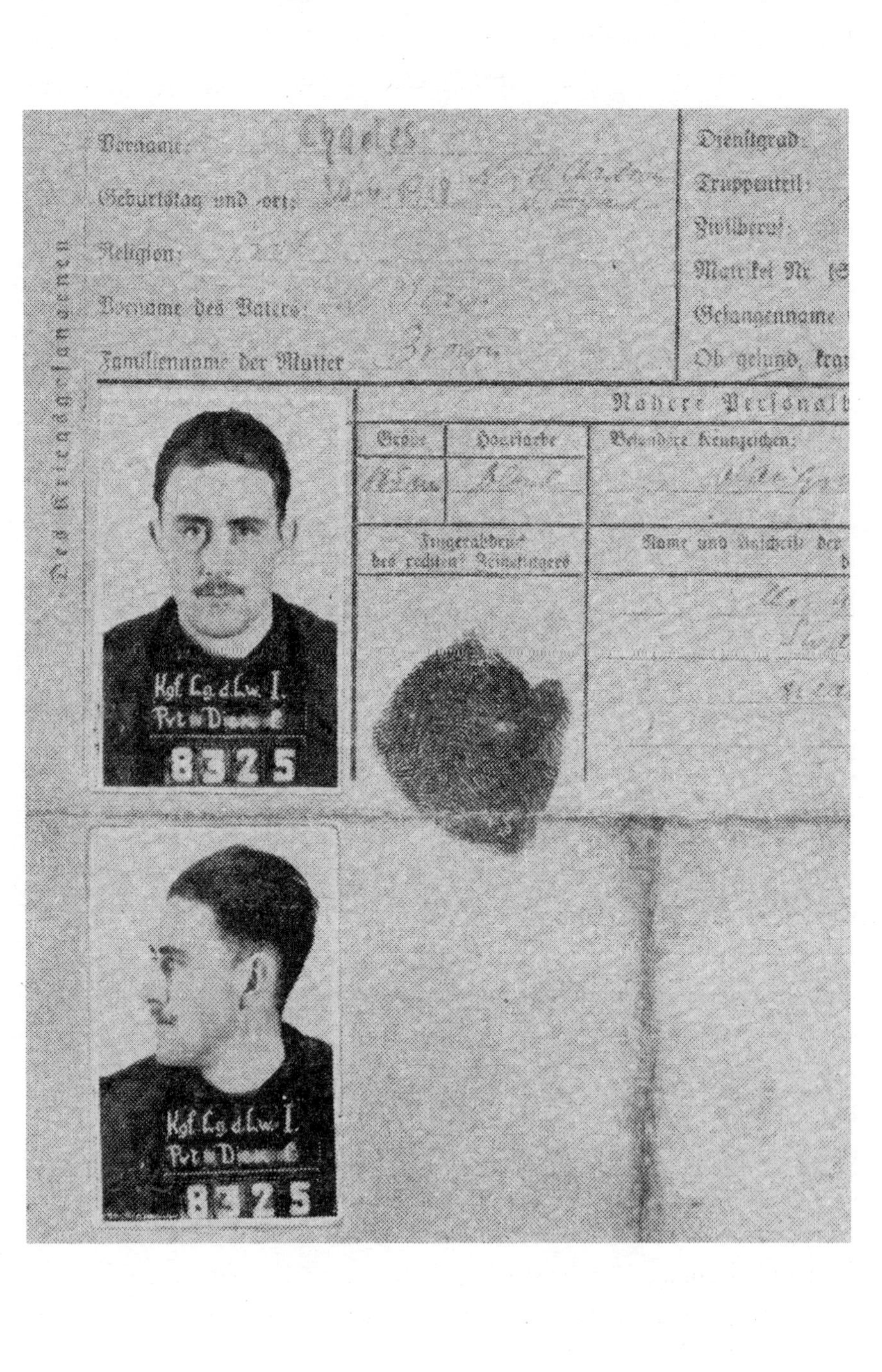
Des Kriegsgefangenen

Vorname:

Geburtstag und -ort:

Religion:

Vorname des Vaters:

Familienname der Mutter

Dienstgrad:

Truppenteil:

Zivilberuf:

Matrikel Nr.

Gefangennahme

Ob gesund, kra

Nähere Personalb

Größe	Haarfarbe	Besondere Kennzeichen:

Fingerabdruck des rechten Zeigefingers	Name und Anschrift der

CHAPTER 17

'The songs of my heart': Charlie Dick, 1941

> 'Girls tattooed us because we lost our names the minute we arrived. Everyone was called out by their tattooed number. My mother was such an aesthete that she checked out each girl to see who gave the neatest tattoo. I never saw a nicer tattoo, if you can call it nice.'
>
> —Susan Eisdorfer Beer, Auschwitz survivor

> 'Throughout my experience as a tattooist, I had never worked so deeply as I did on that German, and throughout my experience, I had never known a client so unflinching.'
>
> —Charlie Dick, *POW: True Prison Camp Horrors*, 1958

On Christmas Day 1941, the Kommandant – a 'gigantic German with the flabby red face of a swine and the voice of a Devil' – had nearly kicked Charlie Dick to death. That morning, the Nazi officer had overseen the brutal beatings of men and women who lived opposite the prisoner of war camp at Grudziądz in occupied Poland. Charlie and his fellow prisoners had loudly protested the horrific spectacle from their windows. As punishment for their impudence, the Kommandant decreed that the inmates be served a dinner of thin gruel instead of a proper festive meal.

In his hunger, Charlie decided to sneak back into the cookhouse later that evening, to try and grab a further desperate scraping of soup

Left: Charlie Dick, identity document from Nazi POW camp in Poland, 1940

from the boiler. After several hours of waiting in the freezing cold, Charlie barely heard the cookhouse door as it clicked open behind him. The Kommandant caught Charlie unawares, clattering him with a punch from behind and then raining a torrent of hard blows with his boots on his victim's stomach. Fortunately, when the officer drew his pistol, it misfired and jammed.

To Charlie's surprise, the Kommandant asked to be tattooed just a few weeks after the incident. 'My mind was not yet free of bitterness against him,' he later reminisced, 'for my own body was still discoloured by the wild tattoo he had beat upon me with his heavy boots.' Nevertheless, he realised that the request would present a unique opportunity. 'I would put this monster in hospital for many days to come, and at the same time expose him to his superiors as a tattooed man. Here was revenge but this revenge would be as bitter as it was possible to make.'

Greedily, the Kommandant asked Charlie for five designs: oak leaves surrounding a swastika, a Virgin Mary, a horse standing rampant on its hind legs, a heart with his wife's name across it, and a large eagle with particularly savage eyes. The fee would be a mess-tin full of black minced horsemeat, a true feast. Charlie hurried to his bunk to collect his tools, discarding his usual fastidiousness for cleanliness and care. He grabbed the rustiest, most pitted needles he could find amongst those he had discarded after previous tattooing sessions, and steeled himself for a 'long, tedious and tiring night'.

* * *

Charlie had been captured at Dunkirk in 1940 and found himself imprisoned in a Nazi prisoner of war camp in Poland at an outpost north of Stalag XXA at Toruń. It was hell. The prisoners were malnourished, frequently sick with dysentery and exhausted, as they had been put to work digging roads. The guards were cruel, stupid and capricious. The camp itself was infested with rats, fleas and lice, and it was bitingly cold. Amongst the misery and deprivation, though, the men held there were able to steel their spirits through friendship, camaraderie and art. 'Poets began to write,' Charlie wrote, 'artists to paint, singers to sing'. Charlie himself frequently wrote pages and pages of lyrical verse, fantasising about bumper ration packs, reminiscing about the Northumberland landscapes where he'd grown up, and longing tenderly for his wife Wynne back home. These, he said, were the songs of his heart, 'conceived as my body grew weak and gaunt behind the rusting wires of a German cage'.

In addition to his talents for poetry, he was also a skilled draughtsman, having studied art at school and, at the encouragement of his parents, taken a correspondence course from the British and Dominions School of Art. While imprisoned, he sketched intimate, kindly scenes of camp life, decorated the walls of the cookhouse with patriotic murals (much to the Germans' ire), and also painted a commissioned portrait of an earlier Kommandant which earned him a tin of minced meat and a supply of brushes and inks.

His greatest artistic outlet, though, was tattooing. As a child, he had become fascinated by the tattoos he saw poking out from under his uncles' shirtsleeves. Indeed, it was getting his first tattoo, aged just fourteen, that had been the catalyst for him to become so interested in art in the first place. In a bustling fairground tent, roundabouts whirling just outside, oil-lamp fumes, carbolic antiseptic and cigarette smoke thickening the air, he had been tattooed with a swallow, propelling him into the trade that he would make his career.

As soon as he enlisted in the Army in 1939, Charlie began to carve out a reputation as a barrack-room tattoo artist, often called upon by his mates to fix the poor work they'd been subjected to by the old-timer in town. With money scarce, he took payment in cigarettes and beer, and was forced by circumstance to tattoo by hand with the needles from his kitbag lashed to a meat skewer. He couldn't get hold of coloured ink – so all his early work was in black which quickly settled to that familiar, smudged blue. There was plenty of work for him, though, because the old guy had done so many botch jobs. He was so heavy-handed that to lessen the pain, soldiers had to ensure they were sufficiently drunk before sitting in his chair to be subjected to his enormous machine, which, as Charlie described it, had 'the flash of a welding nozzle and the kick of a road drill'.

When he was captured, Charlie was quick to set up a studio of sorts in the dormitory, turning his own top bunk into a rickety platform for tattooing – a tiny, confined space six feet six inches long by three feet wide. It was a scene that became common across the network of POW camps, with amateur tattooists marking their fellow prisoners with symbols of home and of hope. (In at least one case, this backfired. An escapee from a camp in Italy had 'Rule Britannia' indelibly tattooed across his chest, meaning that his attempt to pretend to be German didn't evade discovery by the authorities for long!) Even at Grudziądz, Charlie initially had some competition – a ventriloquist called (rather implausibly) Blood, who would undercut Charlie's prices. Blood was soon forced out of business, however, as all his tattoos became infected, earning him the extended sobriquet 'Blood Poisoning' amongst his fellow captives.

Having cornered the market, Charlie drew up flash sheets of a couple of hundred designs, and estimated that he had tattooed hundreds of men during his internment, fully half the camp. Because he still could not obtain coloured ink, and because it was Blood's experiments with unsafe coloured pigments that had likely caused the infections, he further promised that every tattoo he executed came with the assurance that he would colour them in when he made it back home. (Only one fellow POW ultimately took him up on the offer, returning to get the piece finished at Charlie's north-eastern tattoo studio some twenty-one years later.) And without access to cash, he advertised a price list which offered to trade tattoos for rations:

> Name – 3 cigarettes
> Name with Scroll – 10 cigarettes
> Swallow – 15 cigarettes
> Eagle & Snake – 1 Loaf of Ration Bread
> Chest Piece – 1 oz pack of tobacco + half a loaf of ration bread
> Back piece – 2 loaves, 50 cigarettes.

Most of his work was at the cheaper end of this menu, though he did once earn the fat commission of 4 oz of good tobacco and a full loaf to complete a back piece which had been started in India, but left unfinished. The customer told him that the tattoo artist had been shot dead by a sniper in the middle of the process. Charlie later found out from the guy's mate that he'd actually been kicked out of the studio with a half-finished piece for drunkenly vomiting on the tattooist's floor.

* * *

Most German officers were deeply opposed to tattooing, particularly where designs celebrated any of the nations with whom Germany was at war. At Wallenstein, one unfortunate Scouse POW, Ginger Conley, faced a court-martial for gleefully disrobing in front of a guard to reveal a portrait of Churchill tattooed on his chest, and a scene of Churchill boxing Hitler to the ground on his arm. But even those without obviously anti-Nazi tattooing were usually looked upon with suspicion and disgust.

The racialised criminological theories of Cesare Lombroso and his followers had embedded a strong sense in the intellectual echelons of German society that tattooing inevitably correlated with savagery and crime, and that any German who was tattooed was thus to be regarded with suspicion. Charlie was once berated by an SS officer who caught sight of the British lion tattooed on his chest, only to have a Wehrmacht guard leap to his defence. The guard rolled up his shirtsleeves to reveal a cornucopia of designs of his own, as if to demonstrate to his senior officer that tattoos were nothing to fear, but the SS man turned his ire on his fellow countryman. 'You have degraded German culture!' he screamed. 'The Führer forbids it strongly. Only the sub-normal are tattooed! It is debased! It is the lowest art form! You are not a true German! You are a lust begotten bastard, bred in some Western seaport!'

In the same pseudo-intellectual tradition, the camp physician at Buchenwald, Dr Eric Wagner, undertook a systematic record-keeping project of the tattoos of the men and women brought there. His project proposed to further the study of what he called 'the tattooing question', seeking to discover links between the captive's character and racial background, and the design, location on the body and circumstances of acquisition of their tattoos. Inmates' tattoos at Buchenwald were recorded from 1938 onwards, and he was perversely excited by the opportunity to use the imprisoned to test Lombroso's theories. The demographic make-up of the camp would allow him access to a study cohort which included criminals and non-criminals alike.

Though he was obviously impressed by particularly aesthetically ambitious tattoos, Wagner's study is run through with a tone of incredulity. Predictably, he finds himself unable to adequately replicate Lombroso's findings as to a strong statistical link between tattooing and crime, instead discovering a class-based connection, with tattoos predominant amongst lower-class individuals. Amongst Jewish detainees, for whom tattooing was rare, those who were tattooed before being brought to the camp were primarily unskilled workers and artisans who had been in the military or in gaol. Wagner describes, again with some tone of incredulity, that amongst the small number of tattooed Jewish people at Buchenwald, 'primitive images were rare, yet even numerous well-executed illustrations indicative of a certain taste could be found which were moreover often done in bi- or multi-coloured fashion'. Many Jewish people believe that tattooing is religiously forbidden, and Wagner even cites one Jewish man who explained that he had been tattooed to fit in with his friends, even though he knew it was against his faith.

Wagner's colleague at Buchenwald, the camp overseer and war criminal Ilse Koch, was accused of keeping dead detainees' tattoos and turning them into macabre objects, including most infamously a lampshade. Rumours were rife throughout the camp that tattooed prisoners were being specifically killed to harvest their tattoos, and one spectacularly tattooed Frenchman was said to have 'disappeared' suddenly, before his memorable snake and tall ship tattoos appeared in the camp pathology lab. Koch has been held up as a uniquely evil perpetrator of such horrific crimes, but on the matter of tattoo collection, at least, she is far from alone.

Through the late nineteenth and early twentieth century, it was morbidly routine for pathologists and anatomists around the world to collect and preserve tattoo specimens from dead bodies, usually without the prior consent of the people from whom they were collected, and many medical museums around the world have several examples in their storerooms. Particularly as the kind of pseudoscientific connections between tattooing and character took root across Europe, such collecting became part of the investigatory process for scientists such as Wagner. As such, at Buchenwald, the preparation of tattoo specimens seems to have been a relatively routine part of the post-mortem process against the backdrop of an intellectual interest in tattooing in Wagner's team, even after Koch's departure. In 1944, for example, three years after she had moved to a camp at Majdanek, a telex to Buchenwald from a central SS medical facility specifically requested that 142 tattooed specimens be sent from Buchenwald's lab as soon as possible. One of the inmates forced to work as a medical technician at the camp, Werner B, testified that he had been tasked by a Dr Müller to create the lampshade by covering a wire frame with tattooed skin. None of the inmates questioned were able to link the creation of the lamp with Koch. At Koch's trial, the charge of making objects from tattooed skin was dropped due to a lack of evidence as to her involvement.

Wagner's written account of his project discusses the history of forced tattooing for identification purposes, but his thesis does not make any mention of the systematic, dehumanising tattooing of numbers on prisoners which was being undertaken at Auschwitz, some of whom would have later been transferred to Buchenwald. At Auschwitz, detainees fit to work were forcibly tattooed on arrival from May 1940 onwards, as a stigmatising means of record-keeping. Sewing numbers onto clothing had proved impractical as mortality rates soared and uniforms were recycled from the dead. Many of those carrying out the tattooing were women, and several survivors, including Susan Eisdorfer Beer, quoted at the beginning of the chapter, latterly reported a darkly unsettling hope, of sorts, that their number would be tattooed competently and clearly, so it wouldn't look so bad. The most moving of these accounts was given by Edgar Krasa, who was deported to Auschwitz in the autumn of 1944. 'Three people were doing the tattooing,' he said. 'I was at the edge of my life, or edge of death, or whatever they called it in Auschwitz. In the nicest way, I went to see who did it. That was because I had seen inmates with irregular tattoo numbers. Some numbers were big, others small, some sideways. I wanted to have it done neatly. My number was 11636.' Years later, Krasa told his son that the number was his telephone number, in order to spare the boy from learning of the horrors of the Holocaust at such a young age.

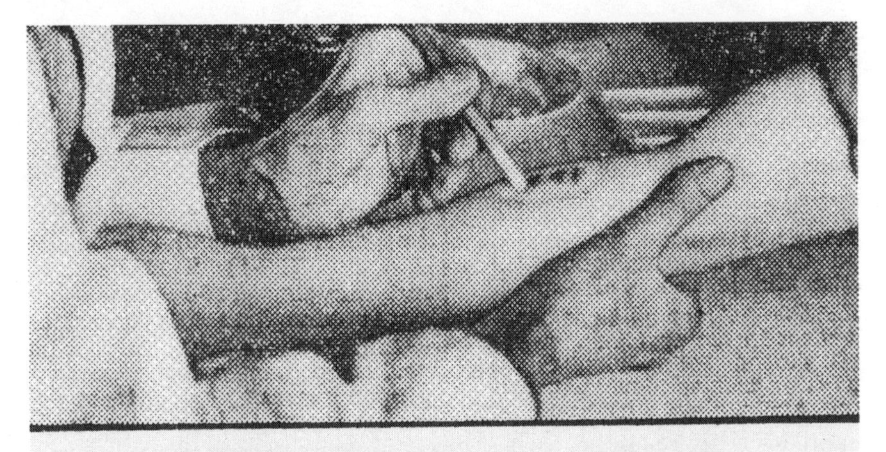

TATTOOIST BURCHETT removes the Nazi brand.

George Burchett removes a Nazi brand, 1948

In many testimonies from survivors, these spindly black numbers are frequently mentioned as a visible, physical manifestation of their pain and loss. Joyce Wagner, for example, the sole survivor from a family of eleven people, wrote: 'On my left forearm, in black ink, is my number 57779, with an upside down triangle underneath, representing a Jew. From that day on we had no names, only our numbers. The tattoo is so ugly, and since they put it on me, I cannot look at it. It always reminds me of the horrible place called Auschwitz and the loss of my whole family. I seldom wear a short-sleeved blouse.' Because of this, after the war, many tattoo artists offered to cover up or attempt to remove camp numbers – in London, for example, George Burchett removed a number from a Slovakian woman who had settled in Wembley, refusing to take payment for the job.

Tattoo removal had also been undertaken during Nazi rule, as many sailors sought to efface their tattoo marks in the light of changing cultural attitudes. Tattoo removal tonics and techniques had been experimented with since the late nineteenth century, but rarely with much success. In the 1930s, however, Hamburg tattoo pioneer Christian Warlich developed a tincture of mineral acid and acetone which could successfully remove tattoos cleanly. The formula could be painted on the skin, covered by a bandage, and then, after an appropriate period of time, the top layers of skin could simply be peeled away, allowing the tattoos to be removed whole. The procedure was so non-destructive to the tattoo image that the resulting skin sample could be preserved, with the tattoo appearing exactly as it did when on the body. Warlich would not share his precise recipe, and insisted that the local university hospital refer any patients wanting their tattoos removed to him, as he was unwilling to divulge its ingredients to the medical staff there. He kept it so closely guarded that it wasn't written down anywhere in his voluminous archives, and was thought lost with him when he passed away in 1964.

Recently, however, a document surfaced in the Hamburg State Archive which showed that the authorities had forced Warlich to hand over his recipe in 1935, following an infection in one of his customers after the procedure. Historians and chemists recreated the formula from the document Warlich had submitted almost a century earlier, and proved, through tests on pigskin, that it worked exactly as Warlich had boasted.

* * *

Though tattooing was severely restricted in the German Army during the Second World War, an exception to this general disdain was the routine tattooing of blood-type markers on members of the Waffen SS. Enlistees would be marked under their armpits by a medical doctor shortly after their initial enrolment. In theory, this was intended to permit rapid battlefield transfusion, but it had an unintended upside for the Allied forces as it made members of the SS, the military arm of the Nazi Party and the men most complicit in carrying out the Nazi project of industrialised murder, rather easy to identify after the war. Most famously, Adolf Eichmann, the major architect of the Holocaust, was unmasked in part due to the faint presence of a partially removed tattoo of the letter 'A' under his armpit. He had attempted to convince his Israeli captors in Argentina that his name was Ricardo Klement. The tattoo firmly proved otherwise, even though he had tried to burn it away with the end of a lit cigarette.

In contrast, it was the absence of a tattoo that allowed Josef Mengele, the sadistic physician of Auschwitz, to evade detection. In discharging German prisoners of war, the US Army inspected everyone for an SS tattoo first, before any other checks. In fact, inside the American POW camps, SS members routinely tried to remove their tattoos before they were discovered. Mengele, though, had joined the SS before the war, and thus before the routine marking of blood types, and so when he was initially held by the Americans, he was able to pass as a humble rank-and-file officer.

At the Nuremberg Trials, the American Medical Association called Dr Andrew Conway Ivy from the University of Illinois as an expert witness to comment on the human experiments carried out by Nazi physicians during the war. Inspired by details of the SS blood-typing tattoos, he went on to develop a Cold War programme to tattoo Americans with their blood types, believing such marks would be a useful tool in the aftermath of a Russian nuclear attack. Ivy arranged for a thousand people to be marked with their blood group at the Chicago Summer Fair in 1950. The scheme was rolled out across more states, becoming known as 'Operation Tat-Type', and by 1953 Illinois, Indiana, Massachusetts and Utah all had state-wide plans. In Indiana, the programme was even carried out in schools, with every child expected to be typed and tattooed. Like the SS tattoos which had inspired them, these would be tattooed under the left armpit, a location chosen, apparently, because it is the region of the body least likely to be seriously burned or slashed by flying debris.

* * *

The camp Kommandant, for all his brutality and fanaticism, was clearly unperturbed by the potential opprobrium or punishment he might face for being so heavily tattooed by Charlie. In fact, it seems he positively, masochistically relished the entire experience. 'I took full advantage of his ignorance,' Charlie said, and began work upon him without delay, 'driving into his flabby arm the rusty needles with sadistic resolve and cleaning them deep within his soup-nourished flesh.' As the night dragged on, he ground his needles into the man harder and harder, but the Kommandant sat unflinching, sedated by his sadism and, Charlie surmised, a wicked cocaine habit. 'He was unmoved, even thrilled . . . Could I not tattoo deeper? It would make them the best tattoos throughout the length and breadth of the Fatherland. With renewed vigour I worked upon his arm till the blood flowed from his finger tips and drenched the knees of my trousers.'

By the early hours of the morning, Charlie could barely see his work through bloodshot eyes and a thick, crusted black film of ink and blood. Three broken needles remained lodged in the man's arm, though he apparently barely noticed, let alone cared. The Kommandant urged Charlie on, and on, but eventually, exhausted, the poor tattooist collapsed into his lice-ridden bed, unable to incise a single line more. As he drifted to sleep, he happily imagined the man standing before a medical officer in the coming days, his arms swollen and infected.

Incredibly, the next time Charlie saw the man, he was brisk and alert. And that same evening, he called for Charlie again – his arms were not swollen at all, and the tattoos had healed perfectly. He wanted more. Charlie made his excuses – he had damaged his hand earlier in the day on a coal-wagon, and would not tattoo such an important and prestigious customer unless he could be sure of doing his very best work.

The Kommandant agreed to postpone until Charlie had recovered, but he never saw the man again. Rumours swirled the camp that he had been dispatched to the Russian Front as punishment, a remarkably severe consequence for a senior officer.

Charlie, for his part, returned to his career as a tattooist after the war, working in the northeast of England into the 1970s. In the 1980s, he told a tattoo magazine that an old solider in his company had once told him, 'Charlie, always remember this: The best people are tattooed.' I suspect the Kommandant would have been considered an exception.

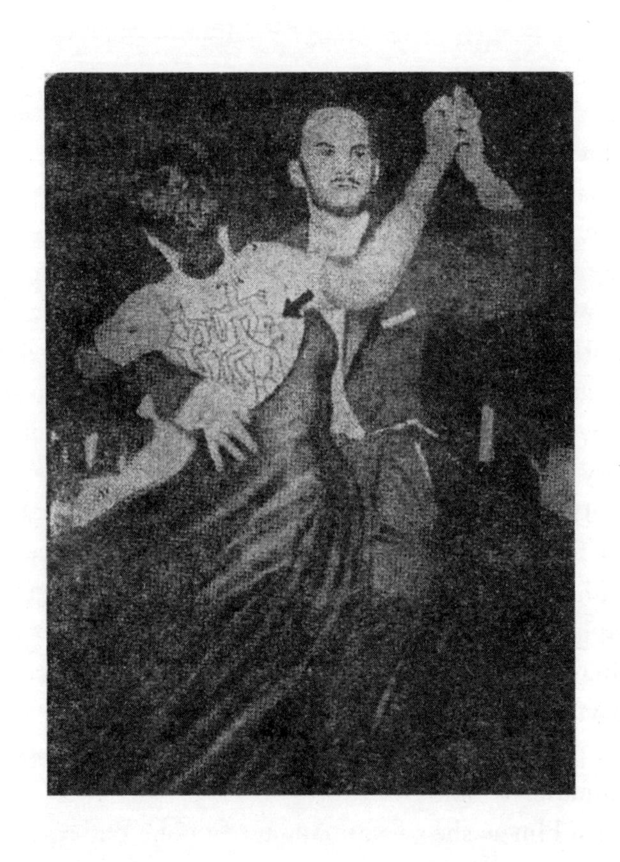

CHAPTER 18

An Artistic Hammer and Sickle: Anita Alores, 1953

'We all know that art is not truth. Art is a lie that makes us realise truth, at least the truth that is given us to understand.'

—Pablo Picasso, *The Arts Magazine,* May 1923

Unlike the other stories in this book, this one is not centred on a tattoo. Instead, this is a story about a story about a tattoo. To be even more precise, it's a conspiracy theory about a story about a tattoo.

The story goes like this.

In June 1953, the Cold War was gathering pace. In the months immediately following Joseph Stalin's death, Anita Alores, the wife of an extraordinarily wealthy and influential Argentinian beef magnate, was photographed at a glamorous party in Buenos Aires hosted by President Juan Perón. Clad in a figure-hugging Dior gown, the picture shows Mrs Alores dancing an energetic tango with her husband, their bodies pressed passionately together. In archetypal style, each of them dramatically holds one arm aloft. His other arm clutches her tightly against him as she swishes her head to one side. On her back, revealed by the plunging cut of her dress, is a large tattoo depicting the crude outlines of two animalistic figures and, most shockingly of all, a clearly rendered hammer and sickle, the instantly recognisable symbol of international communism.

The political fallout of this revelation – that an ardent communist sympathiser was so close to the heart of a regime friendly to the

Left: 'Anita Alores' dancing the tango with her husband as illustrated in *Free Nation*, 1953

United States – was swift. The tattoo sparked a major political scandal and diplomatic incident. Perón's Secretary of State, Señor Filaz, was reported to have reacted in horror when he spotted the symbol. America's ambassador to Argentina had also been present at the banquet, and had quickly sent notice back to Washington. Senator Joe McCarthy, infamous scourge of communist sympathisers in America, took to the airwaves, incensed, and ordered that a large import of Argentinian beef from Alores' husband's company immediately be cancelled.

The twist in the tale is that Mrs Alores was not, in fact, a tattooed red under the bed, but the victim of a cruel trick played by the most famous artist of the twentieth century: Pablo Picasso. At a hastily organised press conference, Alores pleaded with the world's assembled press to forgive her. Far from asking to be permanently marked as a dissident communist, she had actually chosen to seek out a tattoo from Picasso on the recommendation of an influential art critic. The critic had mentioned in his weekly column in *Le Figaro* that the hottest clubs in Paris were full of fashionable women sporting designs tattooed on them by Picasso himself. 'It is fun', the article claimed, 'to wear a work of art by a great master artist on your shoulder or back.' Picasso had taken up tattooing a few months earlier, having realised that it would enable him to produce unique works of great artistic beauty and novelty for wealthy art collectors, which could never be stolen, as works in museums might be. Alores claimed to have paid Picasso the enormous sum of three million francs to produce a large tattoo on her back, simply hoping to appear particularly avant-garde and à la mode when back home in Argentina. Picasso, who had joined the French Communist Party in 1944, had apparently snuck in the hammer and sickle without Alores noticing and against her will.

The story was published in the Icelandic weekly newspaper *Frjáls þjóð*, the *Free Nation*, in May 1954, almost exactly one year after the incident was said to have occurred. That month had seen the French Army humiliated by communist government troops in North Vietnam, and American-backed forces defeating communist guerrilla rebels in the Philippines and embarking on the overthrow of democratic socialists in Guatemala, sparking a Marxist insurgency. It is a long piece, coming in at nearly a thousand words, and it presents a compelling and almost comedic tale of tense Cold War foreign relations and international trade, wrapped in a prurient and surprising tale of tattooing and high art.

Tattooing is used in the narrative in a way that is now familiar: to provide a contested account of its bearer's true beliefs. The mark on the skin is understood, at least at first glance, to signify some inalienable truth about the wearer's deepest ideological commitments. Yet despite being replete with detail, and accompanied by a photo of the Alores strutting their tattooed tango, the story appears to be a complete and utter fiction. Though the article's Icelandic author claimed to have based it on a story originating from a Swedish newspaper, the source periodical named did not exist. Though there are papers called the *Gothenburg Post* and the *Evening Paper* published in Stockholm, and there is an *Evening Post* published in Norway, there is no paper called the *Gothenburg Evening Post*, from where the story was said to have been lifted.

The article attributes the belief that Picasso had begun to tattoo to a column in *Le Figaro* by Daniel Kahnweiler, Picasso's biographer. If such an article had been written, Kahnweiler would have been a likely candidate to have written it, but he did not write any articles for *Le Figaro* in 1953 or 1954 at all. Furthermore, the *Free Nation* story claims that news of the scandal had first been broken by Paris broadsheet *France Soir* three weeks after the event, on 20 June 1953. No such story was published. The entire tale seems only to have made it into print in Iceland. It wasn't picked up by the press in France, the US or elsewhere, and though it has occasionally been mentioned in Scandinavian newspapers in subsequent decades, it has not even been noticed, let alone verified, by any of Picasso's biographers.

Most of the details of the story crumble in the face of even gentle examination. None of the central facts are verifiable, and many are certainly false. There's no mention in congressional records or in American newspapers of the dramatic press conference, nor of Joe McCarthy's beef boycott. 'Filaz', Perón's named Secretary of State, is a fiction, and doesn't appear elsewhere in the historical record. There's no mention of the incident in surviving diplomatic cables written by Albert Nufer, the then US ambassador to Argentina. Most damningly of all, Anita Alores and her unnamed husband don't seem to have actually existed.

And so the story evaporates into the thin air of history. Maybe we could just leave it there. Picasso wasn't a tattoo artist. Perhaps it was simply a tall tale told to amuse or bemuse the readers of a small Icelandic newspaper some seventy years ago. An absurd, fluffy concoction to provoke chuckles over breakfast in Reykjavik as the Cold War rumbled on in the background. Nevertheless, within the tale lurk so many details that are sufficiently close to real events that it is remarkably plausible, both to the contemporaneous Icelandic audience and to anyone encountering it in the twenty-first century. And even once we've discarded every detail, one fascinating question remains: as the story wasn't true, why was it published at all?

* * *

Picking at the threads of this deftly woven story reveals a great deal about the political machinations of Cold War Europe, and Picasso's imaginary tattooing career becomes a lens through which much deeper currents of mid-century ideologies are communicated. The *Free Nation* was not a newspaper prone to satire or comedy, and the article is not written in a tone that suggests absurd humour. Its editorial line was primarily anti-American, and it positioned itself as the voice of principled, nationalist opposition against the contentious encroachment of American influence in the country, particularly as US forces remained stationed in Reykjavik and assumed responsibility for Iceland's defence. Interestingly, though, it was also vocally anti-Soviet, and harshly critical of Icelandic political parties who pledged fealty to Russian communism.

In this context, a story that simultaneously makes the United States look paranoid and petty, and also manages to turn ideological communism into a punchline feels editorially appropriate. Citations to familiar and influential authorities such as *France Soir* and *Le Figaro,* and the use of well-known names such as McCarthy, Kahnweiler and Perón, anchor the story firmly in a kind of reality, and it would have been difficult, if not impossible, for average readers to verify the minute details at the time.

There is, however, much more detail in the story than one might expect of a piece intended to be an open and transparent gag. Most strikingly, there's the image. The article was indeed published alongside a photograph of a tango-dancing couple. The woman, whose face is not visible, does appear to have a design drawn on her back. On close inspection, the hammer and sickle is discernible, but the expanse of her bare back is not taken up by a crude sketch scribbled on the negative by a jocular Icelandic journalist who was hoping simply to give a visual impression of the kind of tattoo one imagines Picasso might have done. Instead, the design is a close replica of a 1946 triptych mural by Picasso in Antibes called 'Satyr, Faun and Centaur with a Trident'. The contentious hammer and sickle, by contrast, is tucked away at the edge of the composition. It's an extraordinarily literate quotation of Picasso's work, but not quite recognisable enough to a lay audience to quickly read as a joke. It's just a little too subtle to really work as a gag image.

By the 1950s, tattooing in France (as elsewhere in Western Europe) had fallen from grace amongst the upper echelons. Nevertheless, a tastefully rendered shoulder tattoo would not have been out of place in high-end Parisian circles before the Second World War. Some of those tattoos might even have been political: a wannabe nude dancer in the burlesque revues reportedly had to abandon her career plans after it proved impossible to remove a hammer and sickle that she had tattooed on her left breast in 1936, following a dalliance with a communist politician. It is also true that Picasso and his circle certainly did have at least a passing interest in tattoos, even if there's no good evidence he actually performed any himself: in 1968, for example, he sketched an elaborately tattooed woman picnicking with a bearded man.

Secondly, though Anita Alores appears to be an Icelandic invention, in real life Picasso *was* patronised by a politically influential, ideologically outrageous, artistically inclined Argentinian beef magnate and his extravagant wife. In the mid-1940s, Picasso, alongside Henri Matisse, had been commissioned by a couple called Marcelo and Hortensia Anchorena to produce art for their fashionable Parisian apartment. The Anchorenas were major figures economically and politically in the relationship between Argentina and

Europe, and persistent rumours suggest that Marcelo had played a key part in the diplomatic efforts involved in bringing Argentina over to the side of the Allies in the latter years of the war. The couple were famed in Paris for their ration-busting parties. Like the fictional Anita, Hortensia was indeed a great aesthete, art collector and trendsetter. Such was her influence that Eva Perón was even said to have copied Hortensia's haircut.

The political details underpinning the story are also rooted in reality. There was deep concern within the US security services regarding Picasso's political sympathies. He was perhaps the most internationally famous member of the French Communist Party, and had generously donated to them for more than a decade by the time the story was published. The idea of Picasso inserting communist propaganda into his art – even when carried out on skin – is certainly plausible, given that he had painted a controversial portrait of Joseph Stalin in March 1953, shortly before Señorita Alores was supposedly tattooed. Picasso is reported to have marked 1953 as the moment in which he became disillusioned with politics in the wake of criticism he received for his depiction of Stalin.

Though he painted a door for the Anchorenas apartment, Picasso openly despised them, even whilst quaffing their champagne. Far from being crypto-communists, Marcelo apparently kept a portrait of Adolf Hitler in his library, and admiringly brought out his copy of *Mein Kampf* at dinner. In the context of that detail specifically, which seems not to have been mentioned prominently in the Icelandic press, the idea of Picasso taking out ideological revenge on his fascist-sympathising patrons is compelling.

The spectre of communist incursion into the Argentinian government which plays a role in the narrative thrust of the story is also visible in the historical record. The commitment of President Perón and supporters to the capitalist cause was certainly a subject of great anxiety in America throughout 1953 and 1954, both publicly and privately. After secret meetings with Perón, American ambassadors did frequently report their concerns about named communist sympathisers within the Argentinian government back to President Eisenhower, and did genuinely fear that so-called 'crypto-communists' posed a particularly grave threat to the stability of US-Argentine relations. The Argentinian press was nowhere near as close to the United States' ideological position as Perón's government was, and newspapers frequently ran articles sympathetic to Soviet communism, despite censorship by Perón and private outrage by Ambassador Nufer and Eisenhower's Secretary of State John Foster Dulles.

At the level of macropolitics, the story also encapsulates much of the global mood of the period. Early in May 1954, the Soviet Union had invited Latin American envoys to Moscow to discuss increasing trade, and had explicitly signed a new trade deal with Argentina which hinged on the importation of Argentine beef into Russia. The previous year, Perón's policies had dramatically reduced the global supply of Argentinian beef and the amount exported into the United States. And just a week after the *Free Nation* published their story about Picasso's tattooing, the *New York Times* splashed a report about the Soviet Union's cultural cold war across Europe and Latin America, where they had sponsored chess tournaments, ballets, scientific collaborations and sporting tournaments in countries including both Iceland and Argentina.

Perhaps this really is just a comedic satire of the machinations of international agricultural trade. But if this is all simply a politically-inflected joke by someone at *Free Nation* or by someone providing information to them, it is a remarkably subtle one, which weaves the esoteric details of global beef trade, the Parisian art scene, the reputations of Francophile Argentinian art collectors and the political machinations of the Perón government into a vivid tale of Picasso working as a tattooer.

My best guess as to the genesis of this absurd but oddly plausible story is that it is the product of a propaganda campaign either by the editorial team at *Free Nation*, or by security forces in the United States. Every single detail, though few of them are true, resonates with political and ideological anxieties of the precise moment of the story's publication. Every single detail is just about close enough to real events, even where those events were unlikely to have been uppermost in Icelandic readers' minds at the time.

Declassified archival material from the American intelligence and diplomatic services shed light on one possible explanation. Perón had told Ambassador Nufer in February 1953 that he had evidence of CIA-backed propaganda campaigns working to undermine him elsewhere in Latin America. CIA documents from the period show that there was genuine fear in Washington that Icelandic communists could capitalise upon widespread anti-American sentiment to push the country leftwards.

In March 1954, the Operations Coordinating Board, which lead the United States' covert operations under President Eisenhower, was briefing on euphemistically-titled 'cultural activities' to be undertaken in Iceland. The OCB's Executive Officer Elmer Staats noted in a secret memo that 'increased communist activities and problems relating to the American military program in Iceland led the OCB to foster a renewed emphasis on increasing American prestige in Iceland. The OCB undertook the development of a coordinated action program to accomplish political effects and to improve the climate of opinion.' In the same month, the CIA also compiled an extensive, secret report on how best to encourage Icelanders to read US-friendly literature and not communist texts in translation. And just a week before the story in *Free Nation* was published, the CIA penned a secret cable exclaiming that ongoing negotiations about the presence of American troops in Reykjavik could plausibly and imminently lead to the fall of the US-friendly government.

If taken as fact, some readers of the story might have concluded on the basis of Señorita Alores' implausible denials that tales of communist sympathisers in the halls of the Argentinian government were as well founded as President Eisenhower feared. Even as it pokes fun at American overreaction, on this reading, the story does still serve a dominant American political narrative about covert communist infiltration within governments allied to the West, and highlights the cultural threat posed by artists who were sympathetic to Soviet communism. And as the CIA understood in July 1954, Iceland, like Argentina, was heavily reliant on foreign exports, with huge amounts of fish being sold to both the United States and the USSR. In that context, the fabricated retaliation taken by the US against Argentina in response to communist tendencies in government could serve as a warning to any Icelanders tempted by communism.

This is a conspiracy theory, of course. There's no direct evidence that this tale was the result of an active propaganda operation. There are alternative explanations, and it is also possible to read the story as one hostile to the US, given that it hinges on a hysterical overreaction by Joe McCarthy. The story was published during the Army-McCarthy hearings which were being broadcast on American television, revealing the heights of his zealotry to an increasingly sceptical public. Nevertheless, the fact that this inscrutably strange tattoo story appeared in the middle of a diplomatic crisis during an active propaganda campaign does further reveal just how embedded tattoo history is with the wider tribulations of human lives.

* * *

The Icelandic article has a coda. It tells another story, that of Iris Joan Hunter. Hunter was a wealthy art collector who had fallen on hard times, consumed by a debilitating and ruinous cocaine addiction. After her premature death, there was nothing left for her heirs to sell. On her body, though, was a tattoo by Picasso – her last remaining asset. Her heirs tried to broker the sale of the tattoo to Alfred Barr, the Director of the Museum of Modern Art, but were prevented from doing so by angry government officials and interfering religious clerics. Word got back to Picasso, and he was so incensed that for the next several weeks, he did nothing but feverishly tattoo women.

Prompted by Kahnweiler, Picasso decided to organise a public art show of his tattoo works. For two nights a week, these living canvases stood behind a cardboard wall, anonymous and invisible to gallery-goers save for their tattooed extremities pushed through strategically placed holes. These women were, like Alores and Hunter, well-bred society women, and a Paris newspaper began to offer prizes to any of their readers who could identify them. This sweepstake motivated visitors to take knitting needles to the exhibition with which to poke the models, hoping to somehow identify them from their cries, and scissors with which to enlarge the holes to allow more of a peek at just who was lurking just out of sight. Which famous ladies were secretly hiding such exquisite works of art under their clothing?

Like the rest of the story, neither Iris Joan Hunter's death, MoMA's attempted acquisition of her tattoo, nor the riotous live exhibition in Paris have any basis in fact. The story of Hunter's tattoo being sold to a museum mirrors the plot of Roald Dahl's macabre short story *Skin,* which had been published two years earlier. In that tale, another real-life Parisian artist, Chaim Soutine, is said to have tattooed a masterpiece on the back of a doomed collector who was so down on his luck that he sought to sell it to wealthy collectors. The story of Picasso's Paris exhibition is simply a vivid new twist on century-old tabloid traditions of telling titillating, though often unverifiable or outright false, rumours about which celebrities sported what tattoo designs under their clothes.

What ties these final stories together with Alores' is an idea that art is the direct communication of ideas. In these marks, ideas become material. But rather than simply reading tattoos as physical representations of their owner's deepest thoughts, all three stories actually describe how tattooing renders visible the relationship between the customer, the artist and the ideological contexts in which the tattoo is produced.

For Iris Joan Hunter and the Parisian fashionistas, ascribing their tattoos to Picasso allows us to understand that tattoos are in many ways just like other art forms. Their meanings come, at least in part, from the artist making them, not simply from the client's own desires. And for our fictional crypto-communist heroine, Anita Alores, as the client she has no ideological input into the tattoo's meaning whatsoever. Instead, the tattoo on her body is indicative of her artist's deeply held convictions.

In this bizarre article, amongst the weeds of its inscrutable origin story, is once again the idea that though we might always want to ask a tattooed person what their tattoo means, the answer will always be partial. Context, and the intentions of the tattooer, will always complicate any ability to understand a tattoo as a piece of straightforward communication.

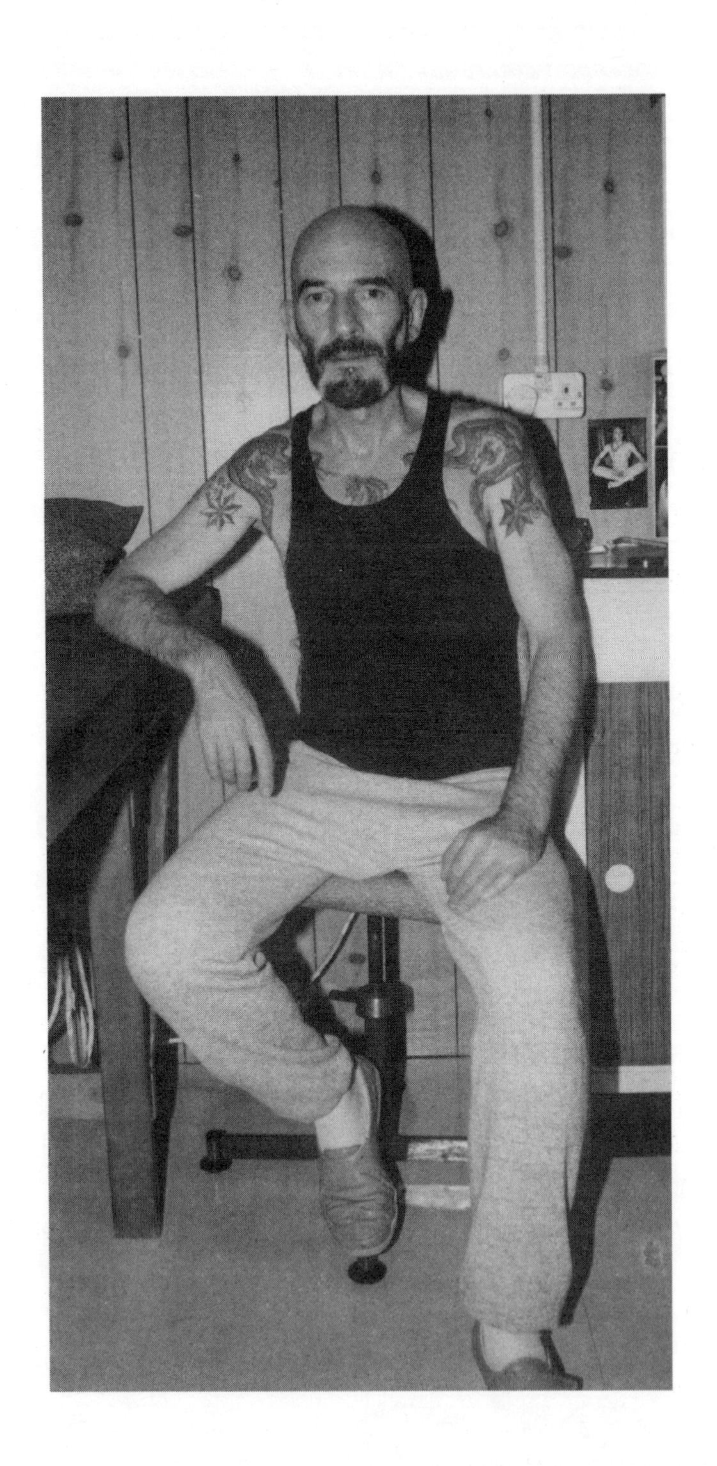

CHAPTER 19

'A bit more on his arse': Alan Oversby, 1988

'Hi, Alan? It's Dave here. Yeah, I just picked a guy up over in Earl's Court. I reckon he could do with a few piercings.

Yeah? Yeah? Can you do it now?

OK, fine.

Yeah, yeah . . . Yeah.

I want his tits, and, err. If you can do a couple on his balls? Yeah, that would be really good. And I want to tattoo him a bit more. He's got a few, but he could do with a bit more on his arse.'

—Dave Gregory, *Moths to a Flame* (dir. Roger Earl), 1988

This call takes place twenty-four minutes into a gay porn film called *Moths to a Flame*. Dave, a handsome, moustachioed, leather-clad man has just given oral sex to a man named Ken, restrained him with cuffs and slowly and deliberately shaved his genitals.

Seconds later, the scene cuts to the two men, now both fully dressed in full biker leathers and sunglasses. They are boarding a District Line train to Earl's Court, a remarkably suburban setting for a hardcore sex film.

Before they can reach their final destination, a title card jarringly

Left: Mr Sebastian in his Mount Pleasant studio, early 1990s

interrupts the narrative. 'From the beginning of time,' it states in heavy white characters crawling upwards over a black background, 'civilizations have used body piercing to adorn their bodies and to give them status not only in the sight of God, but also in the sight of men.'

It's rare that porn movies include text better suited to an anthropology lecture, but *Moths to a Flame* is not quite – or perhaps, not simply – a porno. Billed in its opening sequence as 'a psychological study of sado-masochistic relationships between adult men' and an educational production for safe S&M sex 'in lieu of the current health crisis', the film lays a thin veneer of pseudo-academic discourse over what is basically an hour and a half of beautifully shot sadomasochistic gay sex scenes featuring what one contemporaneous review called 'a variety of punishments, restraints, and yes, love'.

When Dave and Ken finally arrive, Alan is already naked. A distorted, rhythmic voice pulsates and echoes over a discordant ambient soundtrack. The camera pans slowly down his body from his collarbones to his knees, lingering on the extensive blue tattoos which coil across his torso. His testicles are encircled by a heavy metal collar, and he sports elaborate jewellery through piercings in his nipples, navel and penis.

With no introduction, the piercing of Ken begins in stark, graphic close-up. Alan slowly and deliberately pushes a needle through the man's nipple first. Dave holds his hand over Ken's mouth, as if to stifle a scream. Ken simply moans, in pleasure more than anguish. Another piercing follows, this time through his navel. Alan leans over his body, whilst Dave, still head-to-toe in leather, watches on attentively. Again, Ken groans. A third piercing, the needle pushed through the thin skin under Ken's testicles, between his legs. A fourth, at the base of his penis. A fifth, under its head. A sixth, a so-called 'Prince Albert', is pierced through his urethra to hold a ring.

Throughout, the camera holds its gaze fixed as Alan's needles puncture the young man's flesh. He winces in pain. But Alan isn't finished yet. It's time for the tattooing to start.

* * *

Alan Oversby is better known by his professional pseudonym, Mr Sebastian, a name he had taken from the third century martyr, frequently depicted in art as a beautiful young man pierced through with arrows. Alan was born in Liverpool in 1933 and was first pierced by fellow field hands while he was working on a sugar plantation whilst travelling in Guyana in the 1950s. He had become fascinated by the fact that many of them had their nipples pierced through with gold rings, and after a drunken evening fuelled by rum, he had persuaded one of them to insert a simple gold ring into one of his.

Back in Britain, he worked as an art teacher. He also began to get tattooed, acquiring work from the most celebrated tattooers in England at the time, including George Burchett's son Leslie on Waterloo Road, and Bill Skuse in Aldershot. He appears in the press first as a client of London tattoo stalwart George Bone in the mid-1970s, presented simply as a middle-class professional, a cameo in the article to illustrate the now-familiar refrain that tattooing had earned some middle-class credentials. 'He is a teacher,' the article tells us, 'and as such one of the professional minority who frequents tattoo shops.'

> 'I thought about it all very carefully before I began. If you don't you end up looking a mess.' Alan is tattooed solidly from the tops of his arms down the front of his body to his legs with the designs placed in such a way that he can wear a short-sleeved, open-necked shirt without any of them being visible. This is not to avoid incurring opposition in the school where he teaches, but 'to make sure my mother doesn't find out. She would be terribly upset if she knew about it.'

In the privacy of his own home, inspired by anthropological photography and some photos of pierced men which he'd seen on the walls of Burchett's tattoo studio, he had also continued to experiment with piercing himself and his lovers. Over a period of a few years, he learnt to pierce other people by iterating and perfecting techniques through trial and error, and through conversations with medically trained friends. Though he enjoyed having piercings, by his own account the act of piercing others was 'not in the least bit erotic', given how closely he needed to focus on the procedure at hand. Instead, his motivation in learning to pierce was primarily one of self-preservation: by the early 1970s, body art had become an integral part of the subcultural S&M corners of the British, American and European gay scenes of the period, and needle-play and body piercing had become a regular feature of the underground orgies he was frequenting around the UK. Despite its increasing popularity, knowledge was scarce and there was little care taken to pierce safely, cleanly and carefully.

In the early 1970s, wanting to learn how to tattoo, Alan made contact with a group of gay tattooists in the United States, including Cliff Raven, Sid Diller and Dave Slack. In the years after the Stonewall riots and against the backdrop of an increasingly confident gay rights movement in America, tattooing's popularity in gay culture had become ever more visible. On their invitation, Alan used a period of leave from his teaching job, financed in part by a recent pay-rise, to travel across the Atlantic in order to learn from them in person. Quickly, they entrusted him with tattooing their clients. (In a later interview, Alan reasoned that they likely imagined they'd be able to fix any mistakes he made.)

In the same underground S&M circles in the United States, Alan encountered Doug Molloy and Jim Ward, the two men who would go on to found the world's first professional body piercing studio, Gauntlet in San Francisco in 1975. Doug and Jim were part of California's subcultural S&M scene, and had themselves become fascinated by piercings in the context of orgies and parties. Doug, who had recently published his book *Adventures of a Piercing Freak*, was happy to share his knowledge and experience with Alan, and Alan's experiments were inspiring to Doug in return. Doug, independently wealthy, also funded much of Alan's early career. They also struck a chord with Jim, who had no piercings at all when he first met Alan but who would later go onto interview him for his nascent magazine, *Piercing Fans International Quarterly*. 'Between us talking about it,' Alan said, 'and pooling what experience we had, we worked out the best way of doing it.'

From these networks and contacts, Alan began to further improve his techniques, and would set himself up as a professional tattoo artist and body piercer in London shortly after returning. The collaboration between Alan, Jim and Doug became a lifelong friendship, and it is undoubtable that from these subcultural survival strategies, the three men kickstarted the modern body piercing industry. Doug's *Adventures*, with an additional postscript on the erotic potential of tattooing, went on to be sold as a pamphlet entitled *The Art of Pierced Penises and Decorative Tattoos*, with Alan's pierced cock and pubic wing tattoos serving as the cover image.

* * *

In terms of his tattooing career, it was Cliff Raven who made the strongest impression on Alan. He was a kindred spirit, as one of the few tattoo artists of the period who (like Alan) had studied Fine Art at university. Though facing frequent homophobia from the deeply conservative tattoo industry, Raven built a career first in Chicago and then in various locations in Los Angeles and San Francisco, publicising himself throughout his career with explicitly homoerotic advertisements, whilst also earning a strong straight client base on the basis of his extraordinarily beautiful and ambitious tattooing.

Raven, in turn, had been tutored by Phil Sparrow, a pseudonymous tattooer called Samuel Steward, who was himself a bona fide intellectual. Steward began to tattoo in the summer breaks between terms at De Paul University in Chicago, where he was a professor of English Literature. He had been drawn to tattooing in the early 1950s by an increasing dislike of his students, who he thought were growing 'duller and more stupid year by year', and through a prolific sexual attraction to military men, whom he found increasingly difficult to pick up in bars as he got older. 'I wanted freedom,' he wrote in his autobiography, 'a grand new way to feast the eyes on male beauty, that one could now touch the skin which you could only look at in the classroom – the arms, the legs, the chest – and there was no one to raise an eyebrow, and even that you could in the right instances take a young man to the cot in the back room.' His studio spaces were such notorious cruising grounds – one reputedly featured a glory hole cut in its bathroom door – that he ultimately had to ban men from the shop who weren't there to get tattooed.

As an academic, Steward also treated tattooing as something of a research project, both artistically and sociologically. On the artistic side, he devoured books on the history of Japanese tattooing, to which he introduced Raven and a young tattoo fan and art student called Ed Hardy who had sought him out based on his artistic reputation and not his sexuality. Steward had moved from Chicago to the Bay Area in California, and Hardy made a pilgrimage to his shop in 1966, becoming a regular visitor, soaking up knowledge about Asian art and scepticism of academia. Hardy would eventually drop out of art school to become a tattoo artist, initially working for Steward before going on to become perhaps the most famous and influential tattooer of the latter decades of the twentieth century. Hardy, with Raven, reintroduced Japanese tattooing into the American mainstream, published historically researched tattoo journals and pushed tattooing around the world to new levels of ambition and visibility from the 1970s onwards. Without Hardy, and without his encounter with Steward, modern tattooing would look very different indeed.

On the sociological side, Steward kept meticulous records of his clients and what he inferred were their motivations for being tattooed. He was a key confidante and source for Alfred Kinsey's research project into human sexuality in the 1950s, and explained to Kinsey that the desire to be tattooed was overwhelmingly a sexual one: of his list of thirty-two distinct motivations for tattoos, twenty-five were sexual in nature. Nevertheless, on reflection, he also noted that 'generalizations about tattoos are extremely dangerous and unreliable. Your reaction to a tattoo is established only by the fashion in which your own emotions and observations, your backgrounds and personality are fused together.' Steward would also go on to write an academic book on tattooing called *Bad Boys and Tough Tattoos*, codifying these arguments, though they seem more indicative of his own appetites and predilections than any truly generalisable theory.

Whilst not all of his clients were gay, Steward's career intersects with the increasing interest in the S&M gay leather scenes from the late 1950s, and he describes a great number of his gay clients seeking him out to tattoo particularly macho designs on them. Steward also describes how many clients sought him out specifically because he was known for being willing to tattoo genitalia. 'Tattooing is merely the last of the unchanged folk arts, a highly lucrative calling for the exceptional practitioners, and the most superb substitute for cruising that has ever been invented,' he explained. 'If you become a tattoo artist, you will never have to go searching into the bars and baths again, for then you will find, as I did, that all the beauties will come looking for you.'

As such, one suspects that the sexual nature of his clients' motivations may well have been skewed by the particularly high percentage of sexually motivated customers specifically seeking him out. Apparently several were so turned on by the act of being tattooed that they would come to him to be run over with a tattoo machine without the use of ink, bringing them to orgasm.

Alan had similar clients, as is perhaps obvious given his appearance in *Moths to a Flame*. His portfolio includes a large number of pictures of tattooed penises and anuses, including one tattooed with an image of a group-sex scene, and the middle entirely tattooed black. On the back, he wrote ruefully that 'I wouldn't have done all the black filling in – but he wanted it! He also once confessed that the most unusual tattoo he was ever asked to perform was on the inside of a man's urethra, which had been opened through a process of subincision.

He did not share these clients' enthusiasms for pain, though, and as with piercing, he did not admit to deriving sexual pleasure from the process nor from tattoos *per se*. Another of his portfolio photographs, depicting a penis fully tattooed all over with a design of flames, is captioned 'This kind of total coverage of a man's genitals camouflages his equipment, which to me is rather a pity.' 'Some people find practically anybody who has tattoos or piercings madly attractive,' he told Jim Ward. 'But I don't.' 'I just knew for many years that I liked tattoos,' he told another interviewer, 'and I wanted a tattoo. Who knows whether it has sexual connotations. Who knows whether it's vanity?'

* * *

Tattooing became a core component of certain gay subcultures from the 1950s through into the 1990s, notably as part of the kind of performative hypermasculinity which would come to define a subsection of gay style. The 'rough trade tough' developed into a recognisable trope in both American and European gay subcultures, and tattooing frequently featured in the erotic art of the movement, including in the work of canonical gay artists such as Robert Mapplethorpe and Tom of Finland. The roughness was not entirely performative: in London, Greville Hallam was tragically murdered by two men whom he had picked up at the Golden Lion pub in Soho, specifically described in court as a place where 'men, large and tattooed and fairly tough in appearance' could be met.

The fashion iconographies of the hyper-masculine skinhead movement of the 1980s were also taken up by young gay men and lesbians. 'Gay skins' became a recognisable typology in gay bars and in the pages of gay magazines, where hard-as-nails, working-class male sex workers with shaved heads and facial tattoos carved a particular niche. Alan didn't tattoo faces (there were other, more predatory tattooers who would), but many of his portfolio pictures do include images of men who at least gesture towards the familiar skinhead tropes.

Troublingly, though only a fraction of the skinhead movement was racist, skinhead fashion quickly became closely associated with white nationalist and neo-Nazi politics. As such, the adoption of similar styles amongst a proportion of London's gay community in the 1980s has often been thought of as a parodic or even Freudian response to the martial masculinity of the period. Some psychotherapists even rationalised it as an over-correction by self-loathing, effeminate gay men who were seeking to re-assert their masculinity.

Whilst gay skins claimed they could spot each other easily and instantly, the reverse wasn't obviously the case, as white nationalist music fanzines were frequently filled with letters bemoaning how frustrating and embarrassing it had become now that their fascist fashions had become so associated with homosexuality. Nevertheless, this story is complicated. Some of the fascist skinheads also happened to be gay. Some of the gay skinheads also happened to be fascist.

The American Nazi Party advertised for a while in the pages of leather S&M magazine *Drummer*, for example, and in the UK, National Front organiser and scene luminary Nicky Crane was outed in 1992 by *The Sun* in a clumsy, homophobic headline which read 'Nazi Nick is a Panzi'. Crane, his body covered in far-right political tattoos, had been quietly working as a doorman at gay bars in Soho. In 1993, a Black man was attacked at a gay skinhead club called the London Apprentice, and though the club organisers accused interlopers, it seems plausible that the assailants weren't only in the club to cause trouble.

* * *

This kind of violence of gay men against each other became part of an increasingly fever-pitch narrative about just how dangerous homosexuality was, both to gay men themselves, and to the wider community. Sadomasochists were particularly vilified, as their sexual desires were framed as dangerous and perverse even by other, more mainstream parts of the gay rights movement. A sadomaoschist called John Hudspith was kicked to death on Hampstead Heath by men he had asked to beat him as part of a sex game, and a suite of murders of gay men in London went unsolved. The AIDS crisis was rapidly worsening, casting gay men as a biological risk to all around them and thus the bloody results of S&M play were increasingly stigmatised. Gay, necrophiliac serial killer Dennis Nilsen, who found victims by preying on vulnerable young men, claimed that he did not know the name of one of the men he confessed to have killed, but recalled only that he was a skinhead who had a tattoo around his neck reading 'Cut Here'. And to top it all, the Metropolitan Police's Vice Squad were absurdly convinced that there was a spate of Satanic ritual murders taking place undetected in suburban homes, and that gay sadomasochists were the ringleaders.

Against this frenetic, paranoid backdrop, Alan was arrested around the time that *Moths* was filmed, as part of a series of police raids called Operation Spanner, which targeted gay sadomasochists around the United Kingdom for alleged harm inflicted during sexual activities involving piercing, whipping and other sadomasochistic sex acts. Despite his professed lack of interest in piercing as a sexual act for himself, the act of piercing in the context of sexual activity did lead to his arrest. In 1990 Alan was charged and convicted of the crime of grievous bodily harm, the same charge that would apply if an injury was inflicted during a violent assault. Even though all parties involved fully consented to everything that occurred, and despite none of the men involved having sustained any injury at all, the courts decided that consent was no defence to the charges.

Alan was ultimately given a suspended sentence, though many of his co-accused in the case, which became known as *R v Brown*, were not so fortunate, serving time in prison. As a result of the rulings, the Law Commission of the United Kingdom proposed a review of the law on consent, reasoning partly on the basis of Alan's conviction that it was manifestly absurd that someone could potentially go to prison for carrying out a body piercing at night on their boyfriend, but operate a lawful tattooing business by day. The law made a number of rather arbitrary exceptions where it *was* indeed possible to consent to injury, including sports, circumcision, circus performances and, yes, tattooing, and ultimately, though the review was not enacted, it did clarify that tattooing and body piercings were unambiguously legal so long as they were 'carried out for decorative or cosmetic purposes, and not for sexual gratification'.

* * *

The tattoo industry, of course, was not immune to the cultural paranoia around homosexuality. Most visibly, as tattooing was growing in popularity in the gay scene at the same time as the AIDS crisis was worsening, and in the grip of the profound fear of the disease bred by a deeply reactionary culture, the tattoo industry found itself divided over how it could respond to the reality of a virus that was transmitted in blood. Tattooing's sole business, after all, is breaking the skin.

'Tattooing needles draw the blood of customers,' one tattooer told *The Sun*, apparently on the basis of medical opinion, 'and there is a chance of my pricking myself with the needle and the blood becoming intermingled.' Some of the older guard, scared, confused and deeply conservative, tried more vocally to ban gay men from their shops, declaring in ranting oratories to their local newspapers that 'gays and drug addicts' were henceforth prohibited. Publications in which tattooers shared their views amongst themselves were more candid, frequently acknowledging, though not precisely endorsing, vicious, cruel homophobia of the basest kind. Amid a volley of slurs, British tattoo trade magazine *Tattoo Buzz* identified a 'camp (?)' of its readership who had written in to say that they 'would not touch a homosexual with a disposable tattoo machine, whilst dressed in a suit of armour'. Other correspondents found the moral and literal panic absurd. The editor of *Tattoo Buzz* mockingly pointed out the absurdity of any proposed ban in practice. It was obviously impossible to tell if someone was gay simply by sight, there was no obvious way to respond if a gay client simply lied about their orientation when asked, and of course, what were gay tattooists supposed to do? Moreover, the precious, homophobic readers were reminded, wasn't tattooing meant to be a little dangerous? So, the editor wrote:

'Life's a risk we gladly take, and there's more fun to be had in fuggy, shabby tattoo shops around the world that do not look like a stainless steel morgue or a dentist's characterless studio. A puritanism has developed in this business, which holds its hands up in horror at anything deemed by some to be unhygienic, or too-oo risky. Personally, I hope I shall never fear a Tattoo Parlour, Shop, Grott, Studio, Clinic, Surgery, Tabernacle or what-ever. Nor either, the tattooist, who might not fit the image of a top notch surgeon, which ever way he/she is inclined. Soon, the customers will require a medical and a trip through sheep dip before entering the operational area. We will need a trained, sterile nurse to pick them up and hand us the instruments – and then, I will go back to catering, and poison them.'

In the United States, conservative commentator William F. Buckley grotesquely called in the *New York Times* for HIV+ men to be 'tattooed on the upper forearm, to warn common needle users, and on the buttocks, to prevent the victimisation of other homosexuals', a policy for which upwards of 20 per cent of Americans professed support.

It is certainly possible, in theory, to transmit HIV through tattooing if needles are shared between clients. But this simply does not occur in professional tattoo settings. There are precisely zero publicly reported cases of HIV in the known history of the virus that can definitively be attributed to tattooing. According to a 2021 review article, there have only ever been three reported cases of transmission of the HIV virus even *associated* with tattooing. Two of those cases occurred in prison, with already at-risk men explaining at the time of their diagnoses that they had shared tattooing needles with other inmates. The third is the case of a woman from Vietnam who had been tattooed at home by an unlicensed beauty therapist. Nevertheless, as knowledge about the virus' modes of transmission increased, the tattoo world responded professionally and systematically, introducing single-use disposable gloves and increasing the industry-wide vigilance. Industry spokespeople such as Lal Hardy and Lionel Titchener were loud advocates for improved hygiene and for measures to be taken against unlicensed 'scratchers' who tattooed recklessly from their homes without taking proper precautions over sterility and cross-contamination.

* * *

So it is perhaps no surprise to learn that the tattooing scene in *Moths to a Flame* takes place in Mr Sebastian's studio – because he needed it filmed there and not in a dungeon or private residence. 'He insisted,' the director Roger Earl told *Drummer* magazine. 'See, I wanted to shoot it somewhere else, in kind of a scene thing, but he said, "In my studio I know there can never be an infection, and for sanitary reasons I will not do this outside the studio." The minute he told me that, I said, "There's no more discussion. You're absolutely right."'

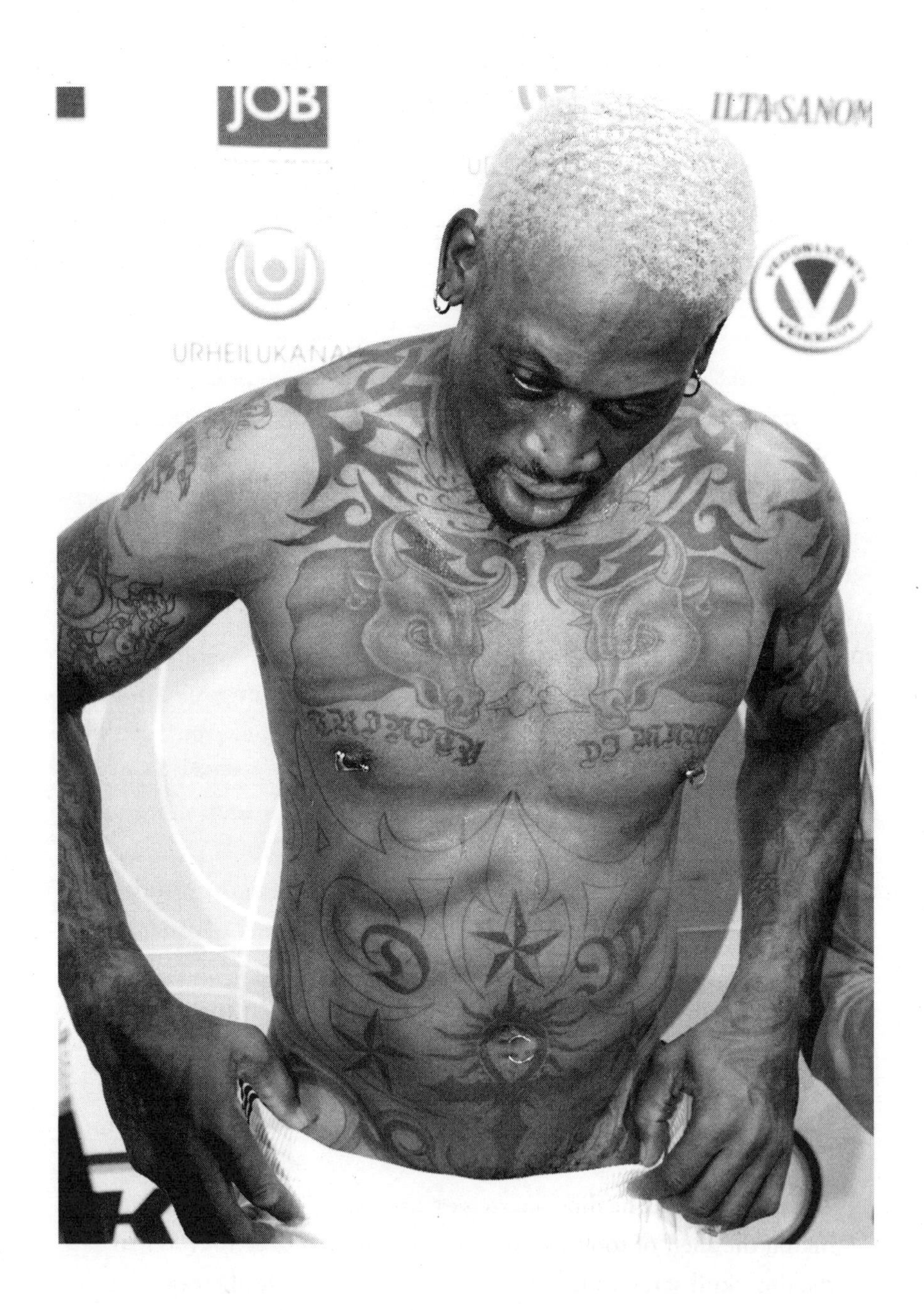
JOB
ILTASANOM
URHEILUKANA

CHAPTER 20

'Pain doesn't scare me': Dennis Rodman, 1994

> 'It was time to show them I was a normal person. Or at least as normal as a six-foot-eight, pierced, tattooed, blond-haired Black man can be.'
>
> —Dennis Rodman, *I Should be Dead by Now*, 2006

Sports journalists don't often interview major-league athletes at tattoo studios. At least, they didn't before Scott Raab accompanied basketball legend Dennis Rodman into Trilogy Tattoos in the winter of 1994.

Trilogy, in Dallas, Texas, usually locked its doors at midnight, but Rodman was still in the chair long past closing. Late-night revellers, drag queens and drunks pressed their faces to the glass as they stumbled past the shopfront, jostling to catch sight of Rodman hunched over a backrest at the far end of the shop.

Erik ground an astrological symbol into the nape of Rodman's neck, the second tattoo he'd added that week. 'Erik finishes a long, ravishing stroke,' Raab wrote in his feature for *GQ* magazine, 'withdraws the needle and dabs at Rodman's pinkened sweat with the towel in his other hand.' He added:

> Then, once more, he dips the stinger into a small cup of blue-black ink on the shelf of tools behind him. As he turns back to Rodman, the tiny skull screwed into the top of his spinning needle begins to buzz, jaws dancing, chattering noiselessly under the machine's drone

Left: Dennis Rodman playing in the Finnish Basketball League, Helsinki, 2005

and the Pearl Jam thrumming out of the shop's speakers. Jabbing into Rodman's skin, he begins to draw.

* * *

In one of his autobiographies, Rodman claims to have received his first tattoo after he joined the San Antonio Spurs in October 1993. His tattooed arms were actually first revealed whilst he was in his last months at the Detroit Pistons. *The Washington Post* reported in December of 1992 that 'in previous seasons, Rodman had a fondness for carving words or symbols into his hair; this year, there's a series of tattoos running down his arm'. Images of him in a Pistons jersey show that he'd had a cross and a Harley Davidson motorcycle etched into his right bicep during the latter half of that year. (So much, I suppose, for tattoos straightforwardly being diaries of our lives).

Even before transmogrifying into the transgressive, salacious cultural icon he would eventually become, though, Rodman had been making an impact for years. He had struggled to stand out whilst playing sports at school, but hit a growth spurt in his late teens and almost instantly became a dominating force on the basketball court. After an impressive stint in college (athletically speaking, at least), he was drafted to the Pistons in 1986 with a burgeoning reputation as an outstanding defensive small forward, and quickly earned a reputation as a standout in the league, winning Defensive Player of the Year by 1989. And yet whilst he was physically fit, he had always struggled with mental health issues, and by his own account, 'even though I had money, fame, and two championship rings, I was still too scared to let loose and live the way my heart was telling me to'.

In the aftermath of his childhood basketball coach's death, and in the midst of a tumultuous break-up from the mother of his beloved daughter, Alexis, Rodman found himself sitting in the seat of his car in the parking lot outside the Pistons' home stadium in Auburn Hills one summer night in 1993. With a gun in his hand, he considered pulling the trigger. Instead, he made a different decision. Rather than die that night, he'd live his authentic self on his own terms.

Though he'd been toying with his appearance for a year or so, and acquired some small tattoos, he resolved to stop holding himself back. No more pretence. No more conforming to expectation. No more shame. 'The crazy guy you see now,' he later confessed, 'with the multi-coloured hair and the tattoos and the nose rings and the woman's wardrobe and the all-night parties is not an act. But the real me.'

* * *

Beauty, fashion, gender and diet are things over which each individual nominally has some control. But our choices in these areas are never free from circumstance, nor from external influence. More profoundly, the embodied categorisations of race, age and disability constrain, privilege and determine the ways in which our identities and our bodies relate to one another. It is thus no surprise that the way human beings present their bodies to others is a fundamental channel through which we signal our adhesion or deviation from the expectations placed upon us by the time and places in which we find ourselves. Resisting the social moulds that shape our self-presentations can be a powerful tool.

Selfhood is a creative process. We are all always navigating and inventing ourselves, but in circumstances where we are most acutely constrained by norms and expectations, the drive to express ourselves often builds. But as we have seen in this book, tattooing in the West is paradoxical when it comes to individuality, as acts of tattooing produce a kind of individuality which also, almost inevitably, ends up allying the tattooed person with some subcultural group or other. This is certainly the way tattoos function in places like prisons, public schools and military forces, where individuality is so harshly constrained by discipline and uniform, and where group solidarity against those in power is so comforting and necessary.

In a similar way, professional sportspeople, and particularly those who play team sports, have to navigate complex tensions between their individuality, their relationship with their team-mates, and the institutional forces of their clubs, their leagues and their fanbases. Professional sportspeople, like public schoolboys and so many prisoners, soldiers and sailors, are almost always young, and discovering the contours of their identities politically, sexually, emotionally and aesthetically.

All these threads intertwine. On the one hand, you're a cog in a machine, part of the team, striving for shared success. You wear a uniform, and your will is subservient to that of the coaches and owners. Teamwork, as they say, makes the dream work. It's worth acknowledging that historically sports culture has been notoriously conservative, long riven with overt and pervasive cultures of racism and homophobia, further constraining the spaces in which self-discovery can occur.

On the other hand, you are, like your peers, also a young adult who is just trying to figure out who you are, and who you want to become. You have loyalties to your teammates, and to the club, but those loyalties do not always align, and frequently, a group of players will find themselves antagonistically sparring as individuals against one another, or as a unit against their bosses and even their own fans.

In the highest echelons of mainstream sport, all this navigation happens under the intense scrutiny of the public eye, inflating and crushing your ego with the rhythms of a season. Sportspeople – and given the cultural dominance of men's team sports, predominately sports*men* – are thus in a difficult bind when it comes to self-presentation. Even where they want to find a streak of individuality, they must usually do so within unimpeachable boundaries of cultural expectation.

Under these circumstances, it is no wonder that so many professional athletes have made so many discordant fashion choices over the decades. If you spend your teenage years training for athletic success, eschewing many of the spaces in which most young people are able to experiment with their appearance, and you suddenly find yourself being thrust into the public eye while earning too much money, it will be difficult to hit the sartorial mark every time. Even if you do, the burden is then increased, as you're a fashion icon now too, not just a sports star, with all the added scrutiny that imprimatur carries with it.

* * *

Rodman's embrace of his authentic self seemed to largely avoid these pitfalls. Unlike his peers, he wasn't trying to be fashionable and failing. Quite the contrary. His proudly queer experimentation with gender-fluid clothing, his bright hair, his piercings and his tattoos were so radical and so discordant with the rest of his cultural context that he was operating in an entirely different sartorial universe from basically everyone else around him. Plenty of teammates, fans and admirers followed Rodman's cue and embraced tattooing, but no one was really copying Rodman. To do so would have been impossible.

Raab, the writer from *GQ*, was more directly inspired by Rodman to get tattooed than by the culture at large. As part of his feature interview, and to get as close to his subject as possible, he was tattooed at Trilogy that day too, acquiring his magazine's logo on his wrist and the caricatured Chief Wahoo logo of the now-renamed Cleveland Indians baseball team on his upper arm. The resulting article is typical of so much men's magazine writing of the time – hyper-masculine, performatively misogynistic and desperately run through with the familiar sad tone of a man who once clearly fancied himself as a progressive, transgressive outsider but who over the decades has grown suspicious of the young. His questioning is more pruriently focussed on Rodman's sex life than his basketball career. Embarrassingly, Raab reports his opening question as 'What's Madonna like in bed?' Even the decision to follow Rodman to the tattoo shop in the first place feels, by the author's own admission, like a rather pathetic move to ingratiate himself with someone much younger, fitter, more attractive and more interesting than himself.

Raab had been tattooed more than twenty years before, high on quaaludes in late-hippie California, but clearly hated the process, describing the pain in agonising detail. He also admitted to being suspicious of tattooed people – 'I think we can adopt one general rule about persons who have undergone extensive tattooing,' he asserts. 'They're extremely hurt about something, and they're taking it out on themselves.'

Though this perhaps reveals more about Raab than Rodman, other critics would also read Rodman's appearance in the same way, interpreting his brightly coloured hair, his tattoos and his body piercings as outward manifestations of his mental trauma. One hundred years on from Lombroso, and the same tropes played out, with his interior state supposedly discernible from, and caused by, some defect or other in his character. 'Rodman has a problem,' *The Washington Post* declared. 'It doesn't take Freud to determine that Rodman, who has pierced, tattooed, and dyed himself beyond recognition, is a self-destructive man who is still in search of love.'

* * *

Whatever his more conservative critics thought of them, Rodman's tattoos did come to define him in the public imagination for the rest of his career. Tattoos were unusual in mainstream cultures in the West anyway, but they were particularly rare in sports and almost unheard of in African American communities, though he clearly opened the floodgates for many who followed him. Newspaper reports about his antics on and off the court almost always referred to them, and in interviews and public writings he returns to them frequently as indicators of his constant feelings of friction against the expectations placed upon him. By crafting his appearance, Rodman was able to be a true individual in a deeply conservative culture.

Rodman's tattoos were so iconic, and so cool, that in late 1996 the clothing manufacturer Fanatix started selling long-sleeve T-shirts printed with exact copies of them, matched on the shirts to the real locations on Rodman's body. Actually, they weren't quite exact – the bootlegger, a man named Micky Goldschmidt, was embarrassed enough by what he was doing to not directly copy the portrait tattoo of Rodman's infant daughter, instead replacing it with a picture of his own nephew. Fearing a lawsuit from the motorcycle manufacturer, he also decided to change Rodman's early Harley-Davidson tattoo to read 'Harley Devotion'. What Goldschmidt didn't reckon with was Rodman taking legal action against him.

Fantatix had sold several thousand shirts through independent boutiques and by hustling outside game venues, all without permissions from either Rodman or his tattoo artists. Goldschmidt reasoned, perhaps not illogically, that Dennis Rodman didn't have permission from Harley-Davidson to reproduce the image on his body either, and that tattooing could not reasonably be covered by copyright law in any straightforward way. If anything, he told *Rolling Stone,* surely it's the tattoo artists, and not Rodman, who would have grounds to sue him?

Rodman's lawyers disagreed. They filed suit in New Jersey for $1m in damages for (amongst other things) trademark violations, misappropriation of publicity rights and copyright infringement. In court, they reasoned that Rodman had been actively involved in the design and placement of each one of his tattoos, and that he therefore had some authorial stake in their creation. Legally speaking, his lawyers argued, his tattoos were commissioned or even perhaps collaborative works of art, and Rodman had the right to be identified as their creator. Moreover, Rodman had official licensing and appearance deals with sports manufacturers, and these tattoos constituted part of his 'likeness'.

Goldschmidt was just twenty-five years old at the time. Though he'd sold a lot of shirts, he certainly didn't have a million dollars. He also couldn't really afford to take on a legal team hired by one of the wealthiest athletes in the country. Faced with an impossible battle, he conceded, settling out of court for an undisclosed sum. The shirts are now collectors' items, still changing hands for hundreds of dollars on online auction sites.

In the following years, the precise legal status of tattoos in relation to copyright law remained formally undecided in the United States, though most legal scholars agree that by any reasonable standard, tattoos are works covered by the intersecting copyrights of both the person on whose body they appear, and of the artist who tattooed them. Depending on the degree of collaboration, the authorial rights over any individual tattoo lie with a combination of the artist of the design on paper, the tattoo artist who inscribed it on the body and the customer who commissioned and paid for it.

Several cases have reached the courts, the most high-profile of which have also all featured prominent African American sportsmen. In every case, the infringing defendants have settled out of court, indicating that their lawyers ultimately reasoned that they were likely to lose at trial. In 2011, Warner Brothers films settled out of court with the Missouri-based tattooer who designed and executed Mike

Tyson's iconic facial tattoo, after they had included it in a scene in the film *The Hangover Part II* without permission. The artist who tattooed Rodman's fellow NBA star Rasheed Wallace also scored an out-of-court settlement in 2005, after the tattoos he had drawn and applied were animated as part of a Nike shoes TV commercial in which Wallace prominently featured.

These cases all hinge on a tattoo being reproduced in a different medium. The inverse case, where an owner of a particular piece of intellectual property might object to their image being used as the basis for a tattoo, has also not been formally tested in court. Nevertheless, as I write this chapter in the autumn of 2021, photographer Jeffrey Sedlik is suing the celebrity tattoo artist Kat von D for having tattooed a copy of a photo he took of jazz musician Miles Davis back in 1989. It seems plausible that by any strict reading of international copyright law, inscribing an image for which you have not sought permission could be a breach of the original creator's copyright. The case is ongoing, though it is also likely to end in an out-of-court settlement.

This case does however pose one final question on this issue. Where books or artworks are found to be in breach of copyright laws, the courts can rule (in addition to monetary damages) that infringing works be removed from sale or display, and any future distribution be prohibited. Books can be pulped. Films can be banned from being screened. In fact, fear of having *The Hangover Part II* pulled from cinemas was one of the reasons cited for Warner Brothers settling their case with Tyson's tattooer so quickly. But how could any such order apply to cases where the tattoo itself was the infringing artwork?

Tattooing is a fundamentally acquisitive medium, with source images from other media often appropriated as the basis for designs. From the earliest days of professional tattooing in Europe and America, tattooers copied and collected print sources. Even so, tattoo artists often bemoan others stealing their designs, and some of the most prominent distributors of commercial flash sheets would reputedly include deliberate mistakes in their line drawings in order to trip up anyone who had copied their work without paying them a fee. It seems impossible, though, to apply a 'cease and desist' order to a completed tattoo. Could a court order that a tattoo be removed, or covered up?

Could someone be ordered not to show their tattoo to anyone? How could such an order even be enforced?

In 2007, an activist called Rich from the advocacy group *New Freedom* decided to use this gap in the law to test a different piece of United States intellectual property law, the Digital Millennium Copyright Act, or DMCA. Rich went to a tattoo studio in Boston and asked them to tattoo a string of hexadecimal numbers on his chest. No one holds the copyright to any string of numbers, of course, but the particular 128-bit string that Rich chose was the cryptographic key needed to decrypt and copy Blu-Ray DVDs. Once hackers had reverse-engineered this numeric key, it circulated rapidly online.

The DMCA makes circumventing digital copy protection a crime, and criminalises the act of helping others to circumvent such protection, too. The Motion Picture Association of America and their technology partnership AACS LA argued that the number was a tool for piracy and copyright infringement, and thus its distribution amounted to aiding and abetting the theft of intellectual property through the provision of circumvention methods.

Attempts to suppress the circulation of the code caused it, counterproductively, to spread even more fervently. The AACS did announce that they were planning to deploy 'legal and technical' tools to subdue its distribution online, but ultimately lost out simply to the sheer quixotic nature of any such endeavour. Given that the code was already so widely available as to make any attempts at censoring it entirely pointless, Rich was never at any real risk of being sued, but the incorporation of the infringing content into a tattoo provided an interesting new angle to the philosophical and political discussions around free speech, intellectual property and individual rights in the face of corporate power. As Rich reasoned, even if AACS LA had been somehow successful in banning websites from distributing the code online, there seems to be no obvious, ethical legal means through which someone might be compelled to remove a tattoo.

* * *

In Rodman's wake, professional sport is now awash with tattooed professionals. The NBA, who were initially so horrified by Rodman's metamorphosis, now celebrate his tattooed legacy. A huge proportion of NBA players are now very heavily tattooed indeed, and it is undoubtable that subsequent generations of basketball fans were inspired by Rodman's tattoos to get their own.

Perhaps Rodman's greatest impact was in transforming the way tattooers and their clients thought about tattoos on Black skin. Darker skin can be difficult to tattoo for those unfamiliar with it, sometimes scarring, for example, and it takes experience and care to work with coloured inks in Black skin to ensure they look good when healed. Many tattooers would turn Black customers away, telling them that it wasn't even possible to produce a good tattoo on people with dark skin tones. What Rodman and his contemporary tattooed Black celebrities proved to the conservative tattoo industry, however, was that it was possible to tattoo Black bodies and that the excuses which Black customers so often heard from tattooers were just that – excuses.

It goes without saying that Black Americans, and other Americans of colour, had been part of the tattoo industry as customers and professionals for decades. Jacci Gresham is credited as the first professional Black tattooer in the United States, beginning her career in New Orleans in the 1970s after shifting from her planned path of architecture. But as Roni Zulu explained in a 2012 documentary called *Color Outside the Lines,* the tattoo industry was so overwhelmingly white that it was extraordinarily difficult through the 1980s and right into the 1990s to get an apprenticeship to learn tattooing as a Black artist, even in the liberal environs of Los Angeles. After Rodman's very public embrace of tattooing, though, things began to change, and African American celebrities' tattoos began to be celebrated and imitated. *Ebony* magazine reported in 1998 that as well as Rodman, stars such as Janet Jackson, Halle Berry, Prince, Sean 'Puffy' Combs and Lenny Kravitz were also pioneering trend for tattoos in Black communities.

There is now a vibrant, visible and hugely influential African American tattoo community. Rodman's profoundly individualistic decision to untether himself from the strictures of social expectation paradoxically created the circumstances that propelled tattooing on and by communities of African Americans into the global spotlight.

As Raab put it in his article, 'his tattoo is done at last, and Dennis Rodman is ready to dance'.

TATTOOING AS ANCIENT AS TIME, AS MODERN AS TOMORROW

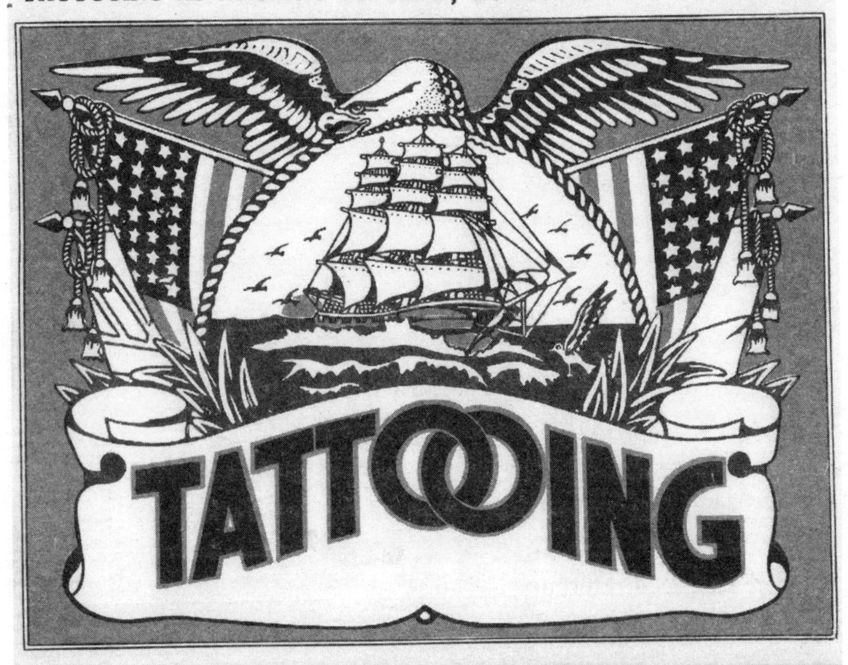

CONCLUSION

AS ANCIENT AS TIME, AS MODERN AS TOMORROW

> 'They get their particular interest tattooed on them, and so they're enthusiastic about it. Hell! They're getting it indelibly etched on their body for the rest of their life, and they're willing to tell you about it. So, you're working with people who are on an upswing instead of a down-swing. It's a pleasant profession.'
>
> —Lyle Tuttle, 1990

There is a famous, though oft misinterpreted, quip made by Chinese Premier Zhou Enlai about the interpretation and impact of historical events. When asked by Henry Kissinger in the early 1970s about what he thought the influence of the French Revolution had been, he replied dryly that it was 'too early to tell'. This answer was interpreted as a reference to the revolution of 1789, and in that light his aside has been read as a wry comment on events of the distant past. He was, however, alluding to a thwarted revolution which had taken place only four years previously: the *évenements* of the general strikes of 1968, which had almost, but not quite, seen the overthrow of the French state.

Similarly, the threads that connect ancient tattooing to the present day run back centuries. In the three decades since Dennis Rodman's tattooing captured the public imagination, the practice has continued to increase in popularity and visibility in the Western

Left: Advertisement for Zeis Studios Professional Tattoo Outfit, Rockford, Illinois, 1930–40s

world. And with it, the narrative cliché that – for real, this time! – tattooing has finally become common cultural currency. But perhaps, like the impact of both French Revolutions, it is still too early to properly assess the influence that relatively recent developments in tattoo culture have had.

* * *

Over the course of the twentieth century, modern, Western tattooing has continued to expand, and is frequently said to be moving towards mass cultural acceptance. As in the first half of the century, every decade since the 1950s has again been hailed as a 'new dawn', when tattoos finally broke free from their associations with sailors and entered the bona fide cultural mainstream. In the 1960s, we learned from an *Associated Press* writer in London that 'about every three years, a tattooing craze seems to break out in this country', and that 'as long as there's an England, there'll be tattooing it appears, what with kings and ladies, viscounts and housewives, typists and even babies patronizing the art'.

In the 1970s, customers of tattoo legend Lyle Tuttle in California were 'no Tugboat Annies, nor women who work for Barnum & Bailey. One tattooed lady is an attorney, another a banker, a third a writer and the fourth, a mother of three.' In 1984, *City Life* magazine in London reminded its readers that 'all sorts of people are doing it – lecturers, housewives, skinheads, architects, pop stars and sailors; the old and the young, all classes and sexes', and scolded them that 'if the very word "tattoo" makes you think of a) servicemen, b) Victorian freakshows, c) sleazy pornography, d) the Exotic East, or e) hepatitis, you are out of date.'

After the boom in tattooing's pop cultural visibility in the 1990s, its palette of designs exploded in unfathomable ways. Post-Rodman, it really did feel as though any misunderstanding of tattooing's maritime past would surely now recede in our collective memories. In a particularly illustrative example of this transition, supermodel Kate Moss was tattooed by British painter Lucian Freud in 2002. It transpired that, before becoming one of the most important British painters of the late twentieth century, Freud had learned to tattoo whilst in the Navy, and inked a pair of swallows on Moss's lower back as a token of friendship. In Moss's swallows, naval tattooing, in the hands of a great fine artist and on the body of an iconic supermodel, *became* the fashion, once again.

By 2003, tattooing was such an unthreatening commercial proposition that a tattoo studio opened in Selfridges, London's high-end department store (though, unlike Gamages a century earlier, they weren't selling tattoo machines to the general public). But since then, the same clichés have frequently resurfaced, and still – still! – the idea that tattooing has only just emerged from a salty past has persisted. A decade after the Selfridges studio had lit up the headlines, the *Guardian* exclaimed in 2011 that 'tattoos conquer modern art as needles and ink replace brushes. Once the mark of sailors and bikers, body art is now sought after by the fashion hungry', following its claim a year earlier that 'one fifth of British adults are now "inked"', and asking its readers 'why the artform of sailors, bikers and assorted deviants became mainstream?'

* * *

I recently spoke to a journalist at the BBC. He wanted, of course, to ask me why tattooing was so fashionable and so mainstream now. Wasn't it just for sailors and criminals when he had been young, in the 1990s? How interesting that this moment, which seems to me to be such an important, final breakwater for tattooing's entry into popular culture, was remembered by someone a decade younger than me as a period of deviance and outsider culture.

So is there a way to finally make sense of this paradox, where tattooing is always new, and where its present is always newly severed from its past? Perhaps.

In the third decade of the third millennium, tattooing is undeniably more visible, more widespread, more popular and more culturally acceptable in the West than ever before. Polling company Harris Interactive estimated in 2016 that 30 per cent of Americans are tattooed, up from 20 per cent in 2012, and 16 per cent in 2003. Facial tattooing, once taboo even within the tattoo industry, is increasingly common in various subgenres of rap music and across mainstream music, too. There are tattooed armpits in skin-cream commercials. A few years ago, I saw an advert for tattoo healing balm in the cinema, aired before a *Star Trek* movie. In 2021, the British Post Office released a leaflet which featured a wholesome father on the cover, cradling his young child. Unlike such images in decades past, the man's arm was covered in a full sleeve tattoo of a burning church, presumably deemed sufficiently inoffensive to inform pensioners about the price of stamps.

Attitudes are softening elsewhere in the world, too. In 2013, Vladimir Franz, a university academic and composer from the Czech Republic whose whole face is tattooed, achieved 6 per cent of the vote in his country's presidential election. The first international tattoo convention in China was held in 2015, something that would have been unthinkable a decade earlier. In Japan, though tattooing remains taboo in many contexts and had been threatened with a blanket ban, a long fight in the Supreme Court during 2020 ruled definitively that tattooing could continue. The same year, in Aotearoa /New Zealand, tattooed politician Nanaia Mahuta, who wears traditional Māori moko on her lips and chin, was made foreign minister. And in Canada, Prime Minister Justin Trudeau has a large Haida eagle design tattooed on his upper arm.

But as ubiquitous as tattooing is undoubtedly becoming, tabloid websites continue to feature sneering, negative tattoo stories almost every single day. During March 2022, a non-exhaustive list of website headlines in just *one* major daily newspaper in Britain includes 'I was temporarily blinded and scarred by freckle tattoo'; 'British model and tattoo addict got more than 150 tattoos in just 6 years'; 'Woman told her forehead tattoo looks like beautiful boobs, now she can't unsee it'; 'I got a tattoo tribute to my beloved dog – it's the worst £95 I've ever spent'; 'Woman left red-faced after discovering hidden code in her pineapple tattoo'; and 'Woman endured high level of pain after getting black tattoo covering whole arm'. That last story was taken from TikTok, where it amassed five million views.

In each of those stories, tattooing is an object of ridicule, curiosity, disgust or shame. Tattoos are so commonplace that they can generate daily headlines, but still so strange, and so associated with recklessness, drunkenness and masochism, that those headlines are overwhelmingly ones of mockery and contempt. Just as in every previous decade since the birth of professional tattooing, there remains a constituency of people who want to be tattooed, and a larger, more stubborn population of people who simply don't understand why anyone would choose to permanently mark their bodies.

The reasons the headlines from 2022 and 1922 and 1872 are so similar in their astonishment about tattooing's presumably recent emergence from the shadows is that the people writing them really are surprised. No matter how popular tattooing becomes, to get one, you have to sit still, be touched by a stranger, endure a good deal of pain and discomfort, and be left with a permanent mark on your body. There have been some recent innovations: attempts to build tattooing robots; QR code-based tattoos and designs that connect to augmented reality software; and now, in 2022, some tattoo artists are even minting non-fungible tokens of their designs on the blockchain. But as more and more people get tattooed, many people in Western nations will continue to find them deeply strange, as they continue to transgress basic cultural norms.

Rather than showing that tattooing has finally entered the mainstream, then, headlines that persistently repeat the claim that tattooing is now socially acceptable show the precise opposite. It never will be. Not totally. We've been hearing for more than a century that tattooing has left its maritime stigmas behind, and yet, that chorus continues. I am resigned to the fact that even after writing this book, I will still be cataloguing examples of tattooing's 'recent' emergence from the subcultural penumbras for the rest of my career.

Because the truth is, tattooing is old and new at the same time. The designs on any tattooed body are always of a particular moment, and each tattoo tells us something particular about its moment of creation. But fundamentally, tattooing has not changed much in thousands of years, and the last truly transformative technological advance happened in the nineteenth century, when the electric tattoo machine was invented.

As the early twentieth century tattoo equipment supplier Milton Zeis once said, tattooing is 'as ancient as time, as modern as tomorrow'.

NOTES

Introduction: 'Tattooing our Skins and Calling it Painting' 1

p. 2 **Tattooing is a medium, not a phenomenon:** Matt Lodder, 'A Medium, Not a Phenomenon: An Argument for an Art-Historical Approach to Western Tattooing' in *Tattooed Bodies: Theorizing Body Inscription Across Disciplines and Cultures*, James Martell and Erik Larsen (eds), (London: Palgrave Macmilllan, 2022), 13–42.

p. 3 **Elizabeth Arden published a long advertorial:** 'The Skin should be Soothed', *Ladies' Home Journal*, May 1930, 128.

p. 3–4 **once confined to rough sorts such as navvies, convicts or soldiers:** Melanie Phillips, 'Seeing tattoos makes me feel physically sick', *The Times,* 8 Feb. 2022.

p. 4 **one theory about the derivation of the European name 'Arapaho':** Hugh Lennox Scott, 'The Early History and the Names of the Arapaho', *American Anthropologist* 9, No. 3 (July–Sept., 1907), 545–560. Loretta Fowler, *The Arapaho* (New York: Chelsea House Publishers, 1989).

p. 4 **stories from seventh-century China:** Carrie E. Reed, 'Tattoo in Early China', *Journal of the American Oriental Society* 120, No. 3 (July–Sept. 2000), 360–376. Benjamin B. Olshin, *The Mysteries of the Marco Polo Maps* (Chicago: University of Chicago Press, 2014), 104.

p. 4 **this is where they have sent us, this land of tattooed people:** *Three Hundred Poems of the T'ang Dynasty*, trans. Yu-pai T'ao (Taiwan: Hsin-lu, 1964), 97.

p. 4 **Spanish colonial explorer Alonso de Salazar dubbed a group of islands in the Western Pacific 'Islas de Los Pintados':** Ione Stuessy Wright, *Voyages of Alvaro de Saavedra Cerón, 1527–1529* (Coral Gables, FL: University of Miami Press, 1951), 58. Francis X. Hezel, *The First Taint of Civilization: A History of the Caroline and Marshall Islands in Pre-Colonial Days, 1521–1885* (Honolulu, HI: University of Hawaii Press, 1983), 16.

p. 4 **Many English-language scholars used to believe**: see, for example, 'Embassy of Vietnam in the United States', *Viet-Nam Bulletin*, Vol. III, No. 1

(1–7 Sept. 1968). Walter J. Sheldon, *Tigers in the Rice: The Story of Vietnam from Ancient Past to Uncertain Future* (UK: Crowell-Collier Press, 1969).

p. 4 **today the consensus is that it was named after a particularly revered species of wading bird:** Dieu Thi Nguyen, 'A Mythographical Journey to Modernity: The Textual and Symbolic Transformations of the Hùng Kings Founding Myths', *Journal of Southeast Asian Studies* 44, No. 2 (2013), 315–337. L. Shelton Woods *Vietnam: A Global Studies Handbook* (UK: ABC-CLIO, 2002).

p. 4 **it has been suggested by linguistic scholars that the very name 'Britain':** John T. Koch, 'Celts, Britons and Gaels', *Transactions of the Honourable Society of Cymmrodorion* 9 (2003), 41–56; Koch is cautious about the hypothesis that the Welsh root is a reference to tattooing, noting for example that *prydydd*, a 'maker of forms', is actually an elite poet, not a tattoo artist. See also Bernhard Maier, *Dictionary of Celtic Religion and Culture*, trans. Cyril Edwards (Woodbridge: Boydell Press, 1997), 230; A.L.F. Rivet and C. Smith, *The Place Names of Roman Britain* (London: Batsford, 1979), 281.

PART ONE: TATTOOS FROM THE ANCIENT WORLD: LANDS OF PAINTED PEOPLE 7

p. 9 **Current estimates place:** L. Wadley, 'What Stimulated Rapid, Cumulative Innovation After 100,000 Years Ago?', *Journal of Archaeological Method and Theory 28* (2021), 120–141.

p. 9 **Some paleoanthropologists**: J. Joordens, F. d'Errico, F. Wesselingh, et al., 'Homo erectus at Trinil on Java used shells for tool production and engraving', *Nature* 518 (2015), 228–231.

p. 9 **consistent symbolic behaviour was present in modern humans from about forty-five thousand years ago:** S.M. Bello, 'Boning up on Neanderthal art', *Nature, Ecology & Evolution* 5 (2021), 1201–1202. Adam Powell, Stephen Shennan and Mark G. Thomas, 'Late Pleistocene Demography and the Appearance of Modern Human Behavior', *Science* 324 (2009), 1298–1301.

p. 9 **The best current evidence suggests a longer pre-history of tattooing in the Eastern and Southern continents than in Europe:** Luc Renaut, 'What to make of the Prehistory of tattooing in Europe?' in Lars Krutak and Aaron Deter-Wolf (eds), *Ancient Ink* (Seattle, WA: University of Washington Press, 2017).

p. 10 **Tattoos last, as one tattoo artist once put it, 'for life, plus six months':** Samuel Steward, *Bad Boys and Tough Tattoos* (New York: Harrington Park Press, 1990), 164.

p. 11 **In surviving histories:** this argument is drawn primarily from Richard Dibbon-Smith, 'The Pictish Tattoo: Origins of a Myth' in *New Ideas about the Past: Seven Essays in Cultural History* (n.d), https://www.academia.edu/9800078/The_Pictish_Tattoo_Origins_of_a_Myth. See also Martin T. Dinter and Astrid Khoo, 'If "Skin were Parchment": Tattoos in Antiquity', in *Tattoo Histories,* edited by Sinah Theres Kloß (New York: Routledge, 2020); Charles W. Macquarie, 'Insular Celtic Tattooing: History, Myth and Metaphor' in Jane Caplan (ed.), *Written on the Body* (London: Reaktion, 2000).

p. 12 **Though based on little primary evidence, these classical sources became the foundational descriptions of ancient Britons in the early modern imagination:** Stuart Piggott, *Ancient Britons and the Antiquarian Imagination* (London: Thames and Hudson, 1989), 62–63, 74–84.

p. 12 **William of Malmesbury remarks:** 'Angli ... puncturatis stigmatiem insignitii', William of Malmesbury, *Gesta Regum Anglorum,* Book III, trans. Thomas Duffus Hardy (London: Samuel Bentley, 1839).

p. 12 **Ranulf Higden wrote:** Ranulf Higden and John Trevisa, *Here endeth the discripcion of Britayne ...* (Westminster: William Caxton, 1480). Early English Books Online Text Creation Partnership, 2011. http://name.umdl.umich.edu/A68181.0001.001

p. 12 **several archaeologists have argued**: Gillian Carr, 'Woad, Tattooing and Identity in Later Iron Age and Early Roman Britain', *Oxford Journal of Archaeology* 24, No. 3 (2005), 273–292.

p. 13 **In a 1991 study:** F.B. Pyatt et al., 'Non Isatis Sed Vitrum Or, the Colour of Lindow Man', *Oxford Journal of Archaeology* 10, No. 1 (1991), 61–73.

p. 13 **Other sources suggest:** B.W. Cunliffe, *Fifth Report on the Excavations of the Roman Fort at Richborough, Kent* (Oxford: Society of Antiquaries of London. Research Committee, 1968), 105.

p. 13 **In 1990, two young postgraduate students from Germany:** Wijnand van der Sanden and Sabine Eisenbeiss, 'Imaginary People: Alfred Dieck and the Bog Bodies of Northwest Europe', *Sonderdruck aus Archäologisches Korrespondenzblatt (Römisch-Germanischen Zentralmuseum Mainz)* 36, No. 1 (2006). Luc Renaut, 'Marquage Corporel et Signation Religieuse dans L'Antiquité' (PhD diss., École Pratique des Hautes Études, 2004).

p. 14 **indigenous American tattooing dates to at least a thousand years earlier:** Aaron Deter-Wolf, Tanya M. Peres and Steven Karacic, 'Ancient Native American bone tattooing tools and pigments: Evidence from central Tennessee', *JASREP* 37 (2021), 103002. See also Andrew Gillreath-Brown, Aaron Deter-Wolf, Karen R. Adams, Valerie Lynch-Holm, Samantha Fulgham, Shannon Tushingham, William D. Lipe and R.G. Matson, 'Redefining the age of tattooing in western North America: A 2000-year-old artifact from Utah', *JASREP 24* (2019), 1064–1075; Aaron Deter-Wolf and Tanya M. Peres, 'Flint, Bone, and Thorns: Using Ethnohistorical Data, Experimental Archaeology, and Microscopy to Examine Ancient Tattooing in Eastern North America' in Philippe Della Casa and Constanze Witt (eds), 'Tattoos and Body Modifications in Antiquity', Proceedings of the sessions at the EAA annual meetings in The Hague and Oslo, 2010/11, *Zurich Studies in Archaeology*, Vol. 9 (2013), 35–45.

Chapter 1: Crosses and Dashes 17

p. 17 **5,300 years ago:** Aaron Deter-Wolf, Benoît Robitaille, Lars Krutak and Sébastien Galliot, 'The world's oldest tattoos', *JASREP* 5 (2016), 19–24. Adrian C. Williams, Howell G.M. Edwards and Brian W. Barry, 'The ' Iceman': molecular structure of 5200-year-old skin characterised by Raman spectroscopy and electron microscopy', *Biochimica et Biophysics Acta* 1246 (1995), 98–105

p. 17 **he had carried:** A. van Loon, 'Early Alpine industry' *Nature* 392 (1998), 221. See also Lawrence Barfield, 'The Iceman Reviewed', *Antiquity* 68, No. 258 (1994), 10–26; James H. Dickson, Klaus Oeggl and Linda L. Handley, 'The Iceman Reconsidered', *Scientific American* 288, No. 5 (2003), 70–79

p. 17 **His body has revealed:** Klaus Oeggl, Werner Kofler, Alexandra Schmidl, James H. Dickson, Eduard Egarter-Vigl and Othmar Gaber, 'The reconstruction of the last itinerary of "Ötzi", the Neolithic Iceman, by pollen analyses from sequentially sampled gut extracts', *Quaternary Science Reviews* 26 Nos. 7–8 (2007), 853–861. See also K. Oeggl, W. Kofler and A. Schmidl, 'New aspects to the diet of the Neolithic Tyrolean Iceman "Ötzi"', *Journal of Biological Research - Bollettino Della Società Italiana Di Biologia Sperimentale* 80, No. 1 (2005); R. Goedecker-Ciolek, ,'Zur Herstellungstechnik von Kleidung und Aüstrustungsgegenständen' in M. Egg, R. Goedecker-Ciolek, W. Groenman-van Waateringe and K. Spindler (eds), *Die Gletschermumie vom Ende der Steinzeit aus den Ötztaler Alpen* (Mainz: Jahrbuch des Römisch-Germanischen Zentralmuseums, 2003), 100–113; W. Kutschera and R. Werner, Ötzi, the prehistoric Iceman', *Nucl Instrum Methods Phys Res B* 164–165 (2000), 12–22.

p. 18 **Ötzi has sixty-one discrete lines tattooed on him:** Marco Samadelli, Marcello Melis, Matteo Miccoli, Eduard Egarter Vigl and Albert R. Zink, 'Complete mapping of the tattoos of the 5300-year-old Tyrolean Iceman', *Journal of Cultural Heritage* 16, No. 5 (2015), 753–758.

p. 18 **Close spectrographic analysis:** M.A. Pabst, I. Letofsky-Papst, E. Bock, M. Moser, L. Dorfer, E. Egarter-Vigl and F. Hofer, 'The tattoos of the Tyrolean Iceman: a light microscopical, ultrastructural and element analytical study', *Journal of Archaeological Science* 36 (2009), 2335–2341.

p. 19 **Tattoos remain permanently:** Michelle D. Miranda, *Forensic Analysis of Tattoos and Tattoo Inks* (Boca Raton, LA: CRC Press, 2015).

p. 19 **If the ink is deposited too deeply:** Ian Eames, 'Effect of Aging on Tattoos', *Mathematics Today,* April 2011, 90–92.

p 20 **evidence of degenerative joint conditions:** Albert Zink, Marco Samadelli, Paul Gostner and Dario Piombino-Mascali, 'Possible evidence for care and treatment in the Tyrolean Iceman', *International Journal of Paleopathology,* 25 (2019), 110–111. See also Luc Renaut, 'Les tatouages d'Ötzi et la petite chirurgie traditionnelle', *L'Anthropologie*, 108, Issue 1 (2004), 69–105 ; Dario Piombino-Mascali and Lars Krutak, 'Therapeutic Tattoos and Ancient Mummies: The Case of the Iceman' in S. Sheridan and L. Gregoricka (eds), *Purposeful Pain. Bioarchaeology and Social Theory* (Cham: Springer, 2020); L. Dorfer, M. Moser, F. Bahr, K. Spindler, E. Egarter-Vigl, S. Giullén, G. Dohr and T. Kenner, 'A medical report from the stone age?', *Lancet* 354 (1999), 1023–1025; Lars Krutak, 'The Power to Cure: A Brief History of Therapeutic Tattooing' in Della Casa and Constanze Witt (eds), *Tattoos and Body Modifications in Antiquity* (2013), 27–34.

p. 21 **Wilson Dyson Hambly wrote:** W.D. Hambly, *The History of Tattooing and its Significance* (London: H.F & G. Witherby, 1925).

p. 22 **sites from the so-called 'Catacomb Culture' of the Russian Bronze Age:** Natalia I. Shishlina, E.V. Belkevich and A.N. Usachuk, 'Bronze Age Tattoos: Sympathetic Magic or Decoration?' in Della Casa & Constanze Witt (eds), *Tattoos and Body Modiications in Antiquity* (2013), 67–74.

p. 22 **In the southern stretches of Europe:** Renaut, 'What to make of the Prehistory of tattooing in Europe?' in Lars Krutak and Aaron Deter-Wolf (eds), *Ancient Ink* (Seattle, WA: University of Washington Press, 2017).

p. 22 **Bone needles from archaeological sites in Romania:** Petar N. Zidarov, 'The Antiquity of Tattooing in Southeastern Europe' in Lars Krutak and Aaron Deter-Wolf (eds), *Ancient Ink* (Seattle, WA: University of Washington Press, 2017). Petar N. Zidarov, 'Tattooing in the Balkan Copper Age: Bone needles and mineral pigments from Pietrele, Romania', *Saxa Loquuntur: Essays in Honour of Nikolay Sirakov on his 65th Birthday* (Sofia, Bulgaria: Avalon, 2009), 327–330.

Chapter 2: Raging Bull 25

p. 25 **I saw lying in the grave:** E.A. Wallis Budge, *By Nile and Tigris, a narrative of journeys in Egypt and Mesopotamia on behalf of the British museum between the years 1886 and 1913* (London: J. Murray, 1920).

p. 25 **It was only in 2014:** Renée Friedman, Daniel Antoine, Sahra Talamo, Paula J. Reimer, John H. Taylor, Barbara Wills and Marcello A. Mannino, 'Natural mummies from Predynastic Egypt reveal the world's earliest figural tattoos', *Journal of Archaeological Science* 92 (2018), 116–125. See also Renée Friedman, 'New Tattoos from Ancient Egypt: Defining Marks of Culture' in Lars Krutak and Aaron Deter-Wolf (eds), *Ancient Ink* (Seattle, WA: University of Washington Press, 2017); Daniel Antoine and Janet Ambers, 'The Scientific Analysis of Human Remains from the British Museum Collection Research Potential and Examples from the Nile Valley' in Alexandra Fletcher, Daniel Antoine and J.D. Hill, *Regarding the Dead: Human Remains in the British Museum* (London: The British Museum, 2014), 20–30.

p. 26 **By 2017, only about thirty tattooed Egyptian and Nubian mummies had been identified:** Aaron Deter-Wolf, *Tattooed Human Mummies Database* Version 5.0 [data file] Figshare. (2022) http:/dx.doi.org/10.6084/m9.figshare.5738439

p. 26 **though bound bunches of copper needles have been documented in several grave sites:** Geoffrey J. Tassie, 'Identifying the Practice of Tattooing in Ancient Egypt and Nubia', *Papers from the Institute of Archaeology* 14 (2003), 85–101.

p. 27 **the designs are familiar motifs within the wider visual cultures of the period:** Stan Hendrickx, Heiko Riemer, Frank Förster and John C. Darnell, 'Late Predynastic/Early Dynastic rock art scenes of Barbary sheep hunting in Egypt's Western Desert' in Heiko Riemer, Frank Förster, Michael Herb and Nadja Pöllath (eds), *Desert Animals in the Eastern Sahara* (Cologne: Heinrich-Bärth-Institut, 2009), 189–244. Stan Hendrickx, 'Hunting and social complexity in Predynastic Egypt', *Bulletin des Séances Mededelingen der Zittingen* 57 (2011), 237–263

p. 29 **Heinrich Wölfflin once remarked:** Heinrich Wölfflin, *Prolegomena zu einer Psychologie der Architektur* (Munich: C. Wolf & Sohn, 1886). See also J. Gantner (ed.), *Kleine Schriften* (Basel: Schwabe, 1946), 45; Frederic J. Schwartz, 'Cathedrals and Shoes: Concepts of Style in Wölfflin and Adorno', *New German Critique*, No. 76 (Winter, 1999), 3–48.

p. 29 **In 1891, for example, the mummified, bandaged body of woman named Amunet was discovered:** Daniel Fouquet, 'Le Tatouage Medicale en Egypte dans l'Antiquite et a l'Epoque

Actuelle', *Archives d'Anthropologie Criminelle*, Tome 13 (1898), 271. Robert Bianchi, 'Tattooing and Skin Painting in the Ancient Nile Valley' in T. Celenko (ed.), *Egypt in Africa*, (Indianapolis: Indianapolis University Press, 1996), 81.

p. 29 **her role was interpreted by archaeologists:** Joann Fletcher, 'Marks of Distinction: The Tattooed Mummies of Ancient Egypt', *Nile Offerings* 1 (Sept. 1997).

p. 30 **Scholars concluded:** Ellen F. Morris, 'Paddle Dolls and Performance', *Journal of the American Research Center in Egypt*, Vol. 47 (2011), 71–103. L. Keimer, *Remarques sur le Tatouage dans L'Égypte Ancienne* (Paris: L'Institut Français d'Archéologie Orientale, 1948), 97.

p. 30 **In 2014, archaeologists were examining:** Anne Austin, 'Tattooing in Ancient Egypt', *American Research Center in Egypt,* https://www.arce.org/resource/tattooing-ancient-egypt. Anne Austin and Cédric Gobeil, 'Embodying the Divine: A Tattooed Female Mummy from Deir el-Medina', *Bulletin de L'Institut français d'archéologie orientale* 116 (2016), 23–46.

p. 32 **Tattooing is not necessarily directly indicative of a particular profession, however:** Luc Renaut, 'Tattooed Women from Nubia and Egypt: A Reappraisal', *Flesh and Bones: The Individual and His Body in the Ancient Mediterranean Basin,* in Alice Mouton (ed.), *Semitica & Classical Supplementa* 2 (Turnhout: Brepols, 2020) 67–87.

Chapter 3: 'Call for the revolt of Ionia' 35

p. 35 **Histiaeus had been a trusted confidante:** The primary sources for the narrative of this chapter come from the following classical texts: Herodotus, *Histories* V; Polyaenus *Stratagems* I; Aneas Tacticus *Siege Defence* XXXI; Aulus Gellius *Attic Nights* XVII. The following secondary sources have also been referred to in preparing the background narrative: J.A.S. Evans, 'Histiaeus and Aristagoras: Notes on the Ionian Revolt', *The American Journal of Philology*, Vol. 84, No. 2 (Apr. 1963), 113–128; A. Blamire, 'Herodotus and Histiaeus', *The Classical Quarterly*, Vol. 9, No. 2 (Nov. 1959), 142–154; J. Neville, 'Was there an Ionian Revolt?', *The Classical Quarterly*, Vol. 29, No. 2 (1979), 268–275; Truesdell S. Brown, 'Aeneas Tacticus, Herodotus and the Ionian Revolt', *Historia: Zeitschrift für Alte Geschichte* (4th Qtr. 1981), 385–393; Pericles B. Georges, 'Persian Ionia under Darius: The

Revolt Reconsidered', *Historia: Zeitschrift für Alte Geschichte* (1st Qtr. 2000), 1–39.

p. 35 **the Greeks did not have any tradition of mainstream tattooing:** C.P. Jones, 'Stigma: Tattooing and Branding in Graeco-Roman Antiquity', *The Journal of Roman Studies*, Vol. 77 (1987), 139–155. See also C.P. Jones, 'Stigma and Tattoo', in Jane Caplan (ed.), *Written on the Body* (London: Reaktion, 2000); Martin T. Dinter and Astrid Khoo, 'If "Skin were Parchment": Tattoos in Antiquity', in *Tattoo Histories*, ed. by Sinah Theres Kloß (New York: Routledge, 2020).

p. 37 **Persian monarchs had built the world's first transcontinental postal system:** Richard R. John, 'Postal Systems', *International Encyclopaedia of the Social & Behavioural Sciences*, Vol. 18 (2nd ed. Elsevier, 2015).

p. 38 **Histieaus noticed that the boy's eyes were red and swollen:** this detail is specific to Aulus Gellius (XVII 9). On shaving, see Jerry Toner, 'Barbers, Barbershops and Searching for Roman Popular Culture', *Papers of the British School at Rome*, 83 (2015), 91–109.

p. 38 **eye diseases were thought to be caused by build-ups of fluids:** G. Papadopoulos et. al., 'Treatment of Eye Diseases in the Hippocratic Era', *Hellenic Journal of Surgery,* 90:3 (2018), 143–145.

p. 38 **Those diseases that drugs do not cure, the knife cures:** Hippocrates *Aphorisms* VII.87.

p. 39 **story about a duplicitous spy:** 'Le Rire de la Sémaine', *Le Rire,* 23 Dec. 1911; 'The Unusual Stratagem of Lieutenant Schorveder', *The Washington Post,* 21 Jan. 1912; 'Les Modes Improbables', *Le Journal*, 5 Feb. 1912; 'Plan of the Fort', *Daily Mail*, 13 Feb. 1912; 'Theft of Fortress Plans', *Bunbury Herald*, 4 July 1912; 'Beautiful Women Spies', *Fort Wayne Sentinel*, 11 Sept. 1915; 'The Love Tricks of a Woman Spy', *Indianapolis Star*, 10 Feb. 1918.

p. 40 **Elaborate tattooing was practised by many neighbouring tribes ... depicted on Greek vases:** Owen Rees, 'Incompatible Inking Ideologies in the Ancient Greek World' in *Tattoo Histories*, edited by S.T. Kloß and E.R. Dodds, *The Greeks and the Irrational* (Berkley: University of California Press, 1959), 163 fn 43 & 44.

p. 40 **Thracians, it is as an adornment for girls to be tattooed:** from the *Dossoi Logoi*. T.M. Robinson (ed.), *Contrasting Arguments: An Edition of the* Dissoi Logoi (London: Arno Press, 1979). On the reception of these classical sources in England, see 'Curiosities of Naval Literature: Tattooing', *Colburn's United Service Magazine*, August 1864, 495–507.

p. 41 **Stop me, I'm a runaway!:** Aeschines II.79 in Ferdinand Schultz, *Aeschinis Orationes* (Lipsiae: B.G. Teubneri, 1865).

p. 41 **less of a face than a narrative:** *Dissoi Logoi* IV.46 (as cited in C.P. Jones, 'Stigma' (1987). See also the story of Bion of Borysthenes in Diogenes Laertius, *Lives of Eminent Philosophers* IV.7. I am grateful to Luc Renaut for this and the previous source.

p. 42 **tattooing was a commonly codified consequence of law-breaking:** W. Mark Gustafson, 'Inscripta in Fronte: Penal Tattooing in Late Antiquity', *Classical Antiquity*, Vol. 16, No. 1 (Apr. 1997), 79–105.

p. 42 **with the point of a needle, or [they] opened it with a razor:** John Baptista Porta, *Natural Magick,* Book 16 (London: John Wright, 1669), 349.

p. 42 **the marking of men who had fled their enlistments to the British army:** Richard L. Blanco, 'Attempts to Abolish Branding and Flogging in the Army of Victorian England before 1881', *Journal of the Society for Army Historical Research*, Vol. 46, No. 187 (Autumn 1968), 137–145.

p. 42 **a teenage girl:** UN Economic & Social Council Commission on Human Rights, Fifty-second session (Item 9 (a) of the provisional agenda), 'Report on the mission to the Democratic People's Republic of Korea, the Republic of Korea and Japan on the issue of military sexual slavery in wartime'. E/CN.4/1996/53/Add.1, 4 January 1996, para 54.

p. 42 **During the Korean War:** Charles S. Young, *Name, Rank and Serial Number* (Oxford: Oxford University Press, 2014). See also Monica Kim, *The Interrogation Rooms of the Korean War: The Untold History* (Princeton, NJ: Princeton University Press, 2019); Young-sil Park, 'Efforts by the Republic of China Government to Convert Chinese Communist Prisoners of War during the Korean War', *Korea Journal*, Vol. 60, No. 2 (Summer 2020), 75–97.

p. 42 **classical writers describe recipes and tinctures:** Owen Rees, 'Incompatible Inking Ideologies in the Ancient Greek World' in S.T. Kloß (ed.), *Tattoo Histories*. E.R. Dodds, *The Greeks and the Irrational* (Berkley: University of California Press, 1959).

p. 43 **a man named Pandarus:** as relayed from primary sources in C.P. Jones 'Stigma' (1987)

See also Ulrike Landfester, *Stichworte: Tätowierung und europäische Schriftkultur* (Berlin: Matthes & Seitz, 2012). For an alternative interpretation of this story which reads the marks not as tattoos but as a medical skin condition, see Clarisse Prêtre and Charlier Philippe, 'Stigmata et grammata dans les récits de guérisons miraculeuses d'Épidaure. Une nouvelle analyse sémantique et Clinique', *Bulletin de correspondance hellénique*, Vol. 138, Livraison 1 (2014), 185–199.

Chapter 4: A Lady's Tattoos 45

p. 45 **In the crook of the Lady's knee:** Natalya Polosmak, 'A Mummy Unearthed from the Pastures of Heaven', *National Geographic*, Oct. 1994.

p. 45 **The skin bears an ancestral imprintation:** Kim Trainor, *Ledi* (Toronto: Book*hug , 2018).

p. 45 **already riddled with cancer:** A.Y. Letyagin, A.A. Savelov and N.V. Polosmak, 'High Field Magnetic Resonance Imaging of a Mummy from Ak-Alakha-3 Mound 1, Ukok Plateau, Gorny Altai: Findings and Interpretations', *Archaeology, Ethnology and Anthropology of Eurasia*, Vol. 42, No. 4 (2014), 83–91.

p. 45 **a bone-shattering fall:** V.I. Molodin and N.V Polosmak, 'A multidisciplinary approach to the study of archaeological complexes with mummified objects'. *Her. Russ. Acad. Sci.* 86, 111–117 (2016).

p. 45 **her grave:** N. Polosmak, 'The Ak-Alakh "Frozen Grave" Barrow',

Ancient Civilizations, Vol. 1, No. 3. (1994). N. Polosmak, 'The Burial of a Noble Pazyryk Woman', *Ancient Civilizations,* Vol. 5, No. 2. (1998).

p. 46 **a shamanic, soothsaying or ritual role:** S. Pankova, 'Identifications of Iron Age Tattoos from the Altai-Sayan Mountains in Russia' in Lars Krutak and Deter Wolf (eds), *Ancient* Ink (Seattle, WA: University of Washington Press, 2017). Zaur Hasanov, 'A Method for Determining the Practice of Shamanism in Archeological Cultures', *Anthropology & Archaeology of Eurasia*, Vol. 55, No. 3–4 (2016).

p. 46 **The Pazyryk buried their noble dead with coriander fruits:** Sergei Rudenko, *Frozen Tombs of Siberia*, trans. Mark Thompson (Berkeley, CA: University of California Press, 1970).

p. 47 **she saw that the shoulder bore a tattoo:** N. Polosmak, 'Tattoos in the Pazyryk world', *Archaeology, Ethnology & Anthropology of Eurasia*, Vol. 4, No. 4. (2000), 95–102.

p. 48 **The Pazyryks were from the Altai Mountains of southern Siberia:** St John Simpson and Svetlana Pankova (eds), *Scythians: Warriors of Ancient Siberia* [ex. cat] (London: British Museum, 2017).

p. 48 **Hippocrates ... wrote:** Hippocrates, *Air, Waters & Places* XX

p. 48 **Pomponius Mela wrote:** Pomponius Mela. *Cohorographia* II.2.20.

p. 48 **inspired ... Greek legends about the mythical Amazons:** Adrienne Mayor, *The Amazons* (Princeton, NJ: Princeton University Press, 2014). See also H.A. Shapiro, 'Amazons, Thracians and Scythians', *Greek, Roman & Byzantine Studies,* Vol. 24, No. 2 (1983); V.I. Guliaev, 'Amazons in the Scythia: New finds at the Middle Don, Southern Russia', *World Archaeology*, 35:1 (2003), 112–125.

p. 48 **the remains of seven Pazyryk mummies have been found:** Karina Iwe, 'Tattoos from Mummies of the Pazyryk Culture' in Philippe Della Casa and Constanze Witt (eds), 'Tattoos and Body Modifications in Antiquity', Proceedings of the sessions at the EAA annual meetings in The Hague and Oslo, 2010/11, *Zurich Studies in Archaeology*, Vol. 9 (2013). See also L.L Barkova and S.V. Pankova, 'Tattooed Mummies from the Large Pazyryk Mounds: New Findings', *Archaeology, Ethnology & Anthropology of Eurasia* Vol. 2, No. 22 (2005); Guilio Maresca, 'Archaeological evidence for tattooing from the Eurasian steppes in the Iron Age: Some remarks' in E. Scarpanti (ed.), Mantua Humanistic Studies VI (Mantova: Universitas Studiorum, 2019).

p. 50 **Pazyryk tattooing is intimately intertwined with the wider visual cultures from which it emerges:** Trudy S. Kawami, 'Greek Art and the Finds at Pazyryk', *Notes in the History of Art* 10 (1991), 16–19. I.V. Trishina, 'Multifigured Compositions in the Art of the Pazyryk Culture', *Anthropology & Archaeology of Eurasia*, 43:4 (2005), 19–48.

p. 50 **Even the tattoos of apparently mystical beasts:** Gala Argent, 'Inked: Human-Horse Apprenticeship, Tattoos, and Time in the Pazyryk World', *Society & Animals* 21 (2013), 178–193.

p. 51 **creative contact with the East:** see also V.S. Slavinsky et. al, '*Trichuris* *trichiura* in the mummified remains of southern Siberian nomads', *Antiquity* Volume 92, Issue 362 (2018), 410–420.

p. 52 **presumed tattooing tools:** Leonid Yablonsky, 'The Discovery of a Sarmatian Tattoo Toolkit in Russia' in Lars Krutak and Aaron Deter-Wolf (eds), *Ancient Ink* (Seattle, WA: University of Washington Press, 2017).

p. 53 **increasingly acrimonious arguments about her identity:** Gertjan Plets, 'Exceptions to Authoritarianism? Variegated sovereignty and ethno-nationalism in a Siberian resource frontier', *Post-Soviet Affairs*, 35:4 (2019), 308–322.

p. 53 **Russian scientists ... argued on the basis of DNA analysis:** Plets, above, summarises this evidence. For discussions of the wider programme see also A.S. Pilipenko, R.O. Trapezov and N.V Polosmak, 'A Paleogenetic Study of Pazyryk People Buried at Ak-Alakha-1, The Altai Mountains', *Archaeology Ethnology & Anthropology of Eurasia* 43/4 (2015), 144–150 and Martina Unterländer et al., 'Ancestry and demography and descendants of Iron Age nomads of the Eurasian Steppe', *Nature Communications* 8:14615 (2017).

p. 54 **banning of future excavations of funerary sites:** Junhi Han, 'Impact of the Climate Change on the Frozen Tombs in the Altai Mountains' in Christoph Macat, John Ziesemer and Michael Petzet (eds), *Heritage at Risk: ICOMOS World Report 2006/2007* (Berlin: Hendrik Bäßler Verlag, 2008–10).

PART TWO: TATTOOS IN THE EARLY MODERN WORLD: 'A THING OF BEAUTY AND A JOY FOREVER' 55

p. 57 **Both sexes paint their bodys, tattow:** Cpt. W.J.L. Wharton (ed.), *Captain Cook's Journal during his First Voyage Round the World made in HMS Bark 'Endeavour' 1768–71* (London: Elliot Stock, 1893), 93.

p. 57 **The European seamen ... have from time immemorial marked themselves:** 'Tattooing', *The Literary Gazette*, 20 Feb. 1819, 126.

p. 57 **a letter written by English novelist Fanny Burney:** 'tattoo, v.2'. OED Online, June 2022, Oxford University Press, https://www.oed.com/view/Entry/198125 (accessed 2 Aug. 2022). Annie Raines Ellis (ed.), *The Early Journals and Letters of Fanny Burney,* Vol. I (London: George Bell & Sons, 1889), 325. Burney to Crisp, 1 Dec. 1774, Barrett Collection, Vol. V, ff. 138, Egerton MS 3694, British Library. Facsimile of original manuscript kindly provided to me by Stewart Cooke at the Burney Centre, McGill University.

p.57 **Omai was feted in London:** Eric H. McCormick, *Omai: Pacific Envoy* (Auckland, NZ: Auckland University Press, 1977). Apyrexia, 'Genuine Account of Omiah, Native of Otaheite ... ', *Wonderful Magazine*, Vol II, 1794, 148.

p. 58 **'tattoo' had existed in English since at least 1644:** per OED. T.C. Hine, 'Col. Hutchinson's Orders' in *Nottingham: its castle: a military fortress, a royal palace, a ducal mansion, a blackened ruin, a museum and gallery of art* (London: Hamilton, Adams, 1876), App. §8. An 1851 Tahitian–English dictionary cites '*tatau, s.* the marks or points on the human skin; not *tattoo* as it has been called'. John Davies, *A Tahitian and English Dictionary* (Tahiti: Missionary Society Press, 1851), 258.

p. 58 **It has often been suggested:** see, for example, Nicholas Thomas, Anna Cole and Bronwen Douglas, *Tattoo: Bodies, Art & Exchange in the Pacific and the West* (London: Reaktion, 2005). For a summary of such cases and a full account of the 'Cook Myth', see Anna Felicity Friedman Herhily, 'Tattooed transculturites: Western expatriates among Amerindian and Pacific Islander societies, 1500–1900', (PhD diss., University of Chicago, 2012).

p. 58 **US Navy Surgeon A. Farenholt wrote:** A. Farenholt, 'Tattooing in the Navy, as shown by the records of the USS Independence', *United States Naval Medical Bulletin, January 1908* (Washington: Government Printing Office, 1908), 37. Hanns Ebensten, *Pierced Hearts and True Love* (London: Derek Verschoyle, 1953).

p. 58 ***Newsweek* wrote:** Douglas Davis, 'Pins and Needles', *Newsweek* (13 Dec. 1971).

p. 59 **documented, in Europe:** Elizabeth Gansen helpfully suggests (personal correspondence, 2021) that it is important to note that many of the Spanish sources documenting tattooing in the Americas and elsewhere were not published contemporaneously, further exacerbating the erosion of cultural knowledge. For example, Gonzalo Fernández de Oviedo's *Historia general y natural* (1535) was not fully published until the nineteenth century (Madrid: Real Academia de la Historia, 1851).

p.59 **foundling children:** Diana Bullen Presciutti, 'Signs of Belonging: Identifying Foundlings and Orphans in Early Modern Europe' in Nicholas Terpstra (ed.), *Common Children and the Common Good: Locating Foundlings in the Early Modern World* (Florence: Villa I Tatti and Instituto degli Innocenti, 2022). Presciutti cites Biblioteca Apostolica Vaticana, CVL, 5521, fol. 6/39v. Claudio Schiavoni, 'Il problema del baliatico nel brefotrofio dell'Archiospedale di Santo Spirito in Saxia di Roma tra '500 ed '800' in *Trovatelli e balie in Italia: secc. XVI– XIX Atti del Convegno Infanzia abbandonata e baliatico in Italia, secc. XVI–XIX* (Bari, 20–21 Maggio 1993), Giovanna Da Molin (ed.), (Bari: Cacucci, 1994), 93–95; 107, n. 122. Duccio Balestracci and Gabriella Piccini, 'L'ospedale e la città' in *Lo spedale di Santa Maria della Scala in Siena: Vicenda di una committenza artistica*, Daniela Gallavotti Cavallero (ed.), (Pisa: Pacini, 1985), 35. Casimira Grandi, 'P come Pietà: I segni corporei dell'identità istituzionale sugli esposti di Santa Maria della Pietà di Venezia (secoli XVII–XIX)' in *'Benedetto chi ti porta, maledetto chi ti manda': L'infanzia abbandonata nel Triveneto (secoli XV–XIX),* Casimira Grandi (ed.), (Treviso: Edizioni Fondazione Benetton Studi Ricerche/Canova, 1997), 245.

p. 59 **an English anthropologist recorded:** John George Keysler, *Travels through Germany, Bohemia, Hungary, Switzerland, Italy and Lorrain* (London: A. Linde, 1756), 46.

p. 60 **John Abbot:** 'Leeds, Jan 14. 1769', *Virginia Gazette (Rind)* (Williamsburg, 26 Jan. 1769).

p. 60 **John Kent:** *Maryland Gazette* (Annapolis, 12 Oct. 1748).

p. 60 **John Headford:** 'Clarks County in Maryland, July 2nd 1739', *Virginia Gazette (Parks)* (Williamsburg, 13 July 1739).

p. 60 **Francis Power:** *Pennsylvania Gazette* (Philadelphia, 14 Aug. 1766).

p. 61 **a rose and lemon seller named Lorenzo:** Tribunal de La Inquisición de Sevilla (España) 'Lorenzo, N.' (1743), ES.28079.AHN/1.1.11.6.1.9// INQUISICIÓN, 3733, Exp.343, Archivo Histórico Nacional, Madrid. Original research on this manuscript by Dr Francois Soyer; @FJSoyer '1/ Stories from the Archives of the Spanish #Inquisition: Tattoos can be controversial but Lorenzo, a rose and lemon seller in Seville, had a #tattoo that attracted the unwelcome interest of the Inquisition in 1743.' 6 Nov. 2018. https://twitter.com/FJSoyer/status/1059761377961697282

Chapter 5: 'Serve the nation with utmost loyalty' 65

p. 65 **'I raise the embroidery needle':** Liangqing Zhu, 'Duo Qiukui chuanqi' in Du Yingtao and Yu Yun (eds), *Collected Drama and Songs on the Yue Fei Story* (Yue Fei gushi xiqu shuochang ji), (Shanghai: Shanghai guji, 1985), 7–56. Cited in Daphne P. Lei, 'The Blood-Stained Text in Translation: Tattooing, Bodily Writing, and Performance of Chinese Virtue', *Anthropological Quarterly* 82, No. 1 (2009), 99–127. The overarching narrative of Yue Fei's story as relayed in this chapter is largely adapted from Lei's account of the story and its historiography.

p. 66 **made into plays**: A helpful list is collated on Wikipedia. See 'Cultural depictions of Yue Fei', *Wikipedia, The Free Encyclopedia,* https://en.wikipedia.org/w/index.php?title=Cultural_depictions_of_Yue_Fei&oldid=1058644516 (accessed 8 Aug. 2022).

p. 66 **proud nationalism**: Sunny Han Han, *Literature Journals in the War of Resistance against Japanese Aggression in China (1931–1938)* (Singapore: Springer Nature, 2018), §4.2, 120 fn. 4. Marc Andre Matten, 'The Worship of General Yue Fei and His Problematic Creation as a National Hero in Twentieth Century China', *Frontiers of History in China* 6, 1 (2011): 74–94.

p. 67 **arrested by a political rival named Qin Hui:** Daphne P. Lei renders Qin Hui as 'Qin Kuai'. Huang Donglan, 'Shrines of Yue Fei: Spaces for Creation of Public Memory', *Chinese Sociology & Anthropology*, 37:2–3 (2005), 74–112.

p.67 **poisoned, stabbed or strangled:** see, for example, John E. Willis Jr, *Mountain of Fame: Portraits in Chinese History* (Princeton, NJ: Princeton University Press, 2012), 179.

p. 67 **Yue's decision to renounce a pirate chief:** Cai Qian, *General Yue Fei*, trans. Honorable Sir T.L. Yang (Hong Kong: Joint Publishing (H.K.) Co., Ltd, 1995).

p. 68 **Since the 1950s**: Nimrod Branovitch, 'Others No More: The Changing Representation of Non-Han Peoples in Chinese History Textbooks, 1951–2003', *Journal of Asian Studies*, 69:1 (Feb. 2010), 85–122. Gareth Davey and Xiang Zhao, 'Tattoos, Modernisation and the Nation-State: Dai Lue Bodies as Parchments for Symbolic Narratives of the Self and Chinese Society', *Asia-Pacific Journal of Anthropology* (2019).

p. 68 **tattooing seems to have been fairly common in the Han military**: Carrie E. Reed, 'Tattoo in Early China', *Journal of the American Oriental*

Society 120 (3) (2000), 360–376. Carrie E. Reed, 'Early Chinese Tattoo', *Sino-Platonic Papers* 103 (June 2000).

p. 68 **tattooing was a useful shorthand to demarcate social deviance and foreignness:** see Reed, above, and Sean Marsh, 'Clothes make the man: Body Culture and Ethnic Boundaries on the Lingnan Frontier in the Southern Song' in Victor H. Mair and Liam C. Kelley (eds), *Imperial China and its Southern Neighbours* (Singapore: ISEAS Publishing, 2015), 80–110.

p. 69 **later ethnography begins to be more specific:** Ben Kiernan, *Viet Nam* (Oxford: Oxford University Press, 2017). Lars Krutak, *Tattooing Arts of Tribal Women* (London: Bennett & Bloom, 2007).

p. 69 **Polo describes:** quotes from Polo's *Travels* here taken primarily from L.F. Benedetto, *The Travels of Marco Polo*, trans. Aldo Ricci (London: George Routledge & Sons, 1931). Accounts of tattooing vary across manuscript editions of *Travels*; see, for example, J. Homer Herriott, 'The "Lost" Toledo Manuscript of Marco Polo', *Speculum* 12:4 (Oct. 1937). See also Arthur Christopher Moule and Paul Pelliot, *Marco Polo. The Description of the World* (London: George Routledge & Sons, 1938); Nigel Cliff's modern critical edition, *Marco Polo, The Travels*, trans. N. Cliff (London: Penguin Classics, 2015). On the historicity of Polo's voyage to China see Stephen Haw, *Marco Polo's China* (Oxford: Routledge, 2006).

p. 70 **Tattooing is ... central to the folk history of Vietnam:** Nguyen, 'A Mythographical Journey', *Journal of Southeast Asian Studies* 44, No. 2 (2013), 315–337. See also L. Shelton Woods *Vietnam: A Global Studies Handbook* (UK: ABC-CLIO, 2002); Kiernan, *Viet Nam* (Oxford: Oxford University Press, 2017).

p.70 **the first English translation of Polo's *Travels*:** trans. John Frampton, *The Most Noble and Famous Travels of Marcus Paulus ...* (London: Ralph Newbery, 1579).

p. 71 **ink crimes**: Reed, 'Tattoo in Early China' and Reed, 'Early Chinese Tattoo' (see above).

p. 72 **The pigment ... may have been made from a mixture of a peacock's gallbladder and verdigris:** Rebecca Shuang Fu and Xiang Wan, 'The Peacock's Gallbladder: An Example of Tibetan Influence in Late Imperial China' in Mair and Kelley (eds), *Imperial China and its Southern Neighbours*, 268–289.

p. 72 **Lady Deng**: Reed, 'Tattoo in Early China' (see above).

Chapter 6: Facial Tattooing on the Unknown Shore 75

For this and the following chapter, I am deeply indebted to anthropologist and traditional Inuit tattoo artist Maya Sialuk Jacobsen. In late 2021, Jacobsen orally shared with me at length some of her as-yet-unpublished indigenous and scholarly knowledge on the histories of tattooing in the Arctic, and on wider Inuit practices and beliefs. She also kindly read late drafts of these two chapters. Where specific claims regarding Inuit tattooing are made here without citation to a published source, I learned them from Jacobsen. For more on Jacobsen and her work, see Krista Langlois, 'Ancestral Ink', *New York*

Times, 6 July 2021, Section D, 1. Thanks are also due to Caroline Pennock, who shared thoughts with me from her forthcoming book about indigenous Americans in Europe, *On Savage Shores* (London: Orion, 2023).

p. 75 **hee found men of blacke hayre:** William Camden, *The True and Royall History of the Famous Emppresse Elizabeth ...* (London: Benjamin Fisher, 1625), 365.

p.75 **Arnaq's real name has been lost to written history:** Arnaq's narrative is relayed in William C. Sturtevant and David Beers Quinn, 'This new prey: Eskimos in Europe in 1567, 1576 and 1577' in Christian F. Feest (ed.), *Indians & Europe* (Lincoln, NB: University of Nebraska Press, 1989), 61–140. See also Neil Cheshire, Tony Waldron, Alison Quinn and David Quinn, 'Frobisher's Eskimos in England', *Archivaria* 10 (Summer 1980), and in Alden T. Vaughan, *Transatlantic Encounters: American Indians in Britain, 1500–1776* (New York: Cambridge University Press, 2006).

p. 75 **Like all Inuit women from her community**: see, for example, Lars Krutak, *Tattoo Traditions of Native North America* (Arnhem, NL: Stichting LM, 2014). Krutak's work is an invaluable source, particularly as it collates a great deal of secondary sources, though Jacobsen is critical of some of Krutak's analysis regarding the meanings and social significances of variolus tattoo practices.

p.75 **under the command of Martin Frobisher:** for an account of Frobisher, see James McDermott, *Martin Frobisher: Elizabethan Privateer* (New Haven, CT: Yale University Press, 2001). Frobisher's voyages are chronicled in George Best (ed. Vilhjalmur Stefansson), *The three voyages of Martin Frobisher in search of a passage to Cathay and India by the north-west, A.D. 1576–8* (London: Argonaut Press, 1938).

p.76 **'They bee like Tartars':** Christopher Hall, 'The first Voyage of M. Martine Frobisher, to the Northwest, for the search of the straight or passage to China, written by Christopher Hall, Master in the Gabriel, and made in the yeere of our Lord 1576' in Richard Hakluyt, *The Principal Navigations, Voyages, Traffiques, and Discoveries of the English Nation,* Vol. VII (Glasgow: James MacLehose & Sons, 1904), 209.

p. 78 **another Inuit woman had been abducted and brought to Europe:** William Sturtevant, Mattheus Francker and Hans Wolf Glaser, 'The First Inuit Depiction by Europeans', *Études/Inuit/Studies* 4, no. 1/2 (1980), 47–49.

p. 78 **Columbus first observed body decorations on San Salvador:** Antoinette B. Wallace, 'Native American Tattooing in the Protohistoric Southeast' in Aaron Deter-Wolf and Carol Diaz-Granados (eds), *Drawing with Great Needles* (Austin, TX: University of Texas Press, 2013), 4. Though Wallace cites the entry for 13 Oct., it appears the correct date is the 11th. Oliver Dunn and James Kelley Jr (eds), *The Diario of Christopher Columbus's First Voyage to America 1492–1493* (Norman, OK: University of Oklahoma Press, 1989); see Thursday 11 Oct., 1492, 67.

p. 78 **Diego Álvarez Chanca ... wrote:** Diego Álvarez Chanca, 'A Letter addressed to the Chapter of Seville ... ' in R.H. Major (ed.), *Select Letters of Christopher Columbus* (London: The Haluyt Society, 1847), 36.

p.79 **Michele da Cuneo, described:** Michele de Cueno 'Lettra, Savona 15–28 ottobre 1495' In Guglielmo Berchet (ed.) *Fonti Italiane per la Storia della Scoperta del Nuovo Mundo*, [Raccolta di documenti e studi pubblicati dalla R. Commissionie Colombiana] (Roma: Ministero della Pubblica Istruzone, 1898), Parte III, Vol. III, 101 para. 30. Some scholars have interpreted the Italian '*atartato*' (literally 'like the Tartars') to mean 'tattooed', though this is too speculative, in my view. See also Kathleen Deagan and José Maria Cruxent *Columbus's Outpost among the Taínos* (New Haven, CT: Yale University Press, 2002), 28.

p. 79 **Ten Taíno people who were kidnapped during this voyage:** Alden T. Vaughan, *Transatlantic Encounters: American Indians in Britain, 1500–1776* (New York: Cambridge University Press, 2006). 12.

p. 79 **men who 'have their face marked with great signs':** Pietro Pasqualigo, 'Letter to the Segneury of Venice, October 18th 1501' in Clements R. Markham (ed.), *The Journal of Christopher Columbus* (London: Hakluyt Society, 1893), 235.

p. 79 **'seven savage men':** Robert Gaugin, *Les grande chroniques* (Paris, 1514). See also Vincent Masse, 'Les "sept hommes sauvages" de 1509' in Andreas Motsch and Grégoire Holtz (eds), *Éditer La Nouvelle France* (Laval: Presses de L'Université Laval, 2011); Vincent Masse, 'Newness and Discovery in Early Modern France' in James Dougal Fleming (ed.) *The Invention of Discovery, 1500–1700* (London: Routledge, 2011), 167–179.

p. 79 **tattooing on the North American continent dates back over five thousand years:** Aaron Deter-Wolf, Tanya M. Peres and Steven Karacic, 'Ancient Native American bone tattooing tools and pigments: Evidence from central Tennessee', *JASREP* 37 (2021), 103002.

p. 79 **In the Arctic … tattooing is at least 3,500 years old:** Lars Krutak, 'Sacrificing the Sacred' in Aaron Deter-Wolf and Lars Krutak (eds), *Ancient Ink* (Seattle, WA: University of Washington Press, 2017). See also James W. VanStone and Charles V. Lucier, 'An early archaeological example of tattooing from northwestern Alaska', *Fieldiana Anthropology*, Vol. 66, No. 1 (1974).

p. 80 **Inuit cosmology does not recognise 'gods':** Brigitte Sonne, *Worldviews of the Greenlanders* (Fairbanks, AK: University of Alaska Press, 2017), 157.

p. 80 **Colonial writing frequently understands its application as a 'fertility rite':** Lars Krutak, *Tattoo Traditions of Native North America* (Arnhem, NL: Stichting LM, 2014), 22.

p. 80 **gender is not strictly bound to biology or physiology:** Sonne, *Worldviews*, 240. See also Richard G. Condon and Pamela R. Stern, 'Gender-Role Preference, Gender Identity, and Gender Socialization among Contemporary Inuit Youth', *Ethos* 21, No. 4 (1993), 384–416; B.S. d'Anglure, 'The 'Third Gender' of the Inuit', *Diogenes* 208 (2005), 134–144; Meghan Whalley, 'Exploring Potential Archaeological Expressions of Nonbinary Gender in Pre-Contact Inuit Contexts', *Études Inuit Studies*, Vol. 42, Nos 1–2 (2018), 269–289.

p. 80 **Dionyse Settle ... noted:** Dionyse Settle, *A true reporte of the laste voyage into the west and northwest regions, &c. 1577* (London: Henrie Middleton, 1577).

p. 80 **The first myth concerns tattooing on the face**: the details of these myths were related to me by Maya Sialuk Jacobsen. See also Meghan Walley, *Incorporating Nonbinary Gender into Inuit Archaeology: Oral Testimony and Material Inroads* (London: Routledge, 2020), 114; Mariah Carillo, *Transformative Skin: The Ongoing Legacy of Inuit and Yupik Women's Tattoo.* (PhD diss., University of New Mexico, 2014).

p. 81 **'she seized an ember and ran beyond the earth':** Lucien M. Turner, from an 1887 manuscript held at the Smithsonian in Washington D.C, cited in Lars Krutak, *Tattoo Traditions of Native North America* (Arnhem, NL: Stichting LM, 2014), 22.

p. 81 **Some ethnographers have analogised breath:** Daniel Merkur, 'Breath-Soul and Wind Owner: The Many and the One in Inuit Religion', *American Indian Quarterly* 7, No. 3 (1983), 23–39.

p. 82 **Sea Woman:** Birgitte Sonne, *Worldviews of the Greenlanders* (Fairbanks, AK: University of Alaska Press, 2017), 41, Chapter 2. See also Sonne, 'The Acculturative Role of Sea Woman', *Meddr Grønland, Man & Soc.*13, 1990; Jarich Oosten and Frédéric Laugrand, 'Representing the "Sea Woman"', *Religion & the Arts* 13 (2009), 477–495.

p. 83 **All three were drawn and painted:** Sam Smiles, 'John White and British Antiquity' in Kim Sloan (ed.) *European Visions: American Voices* (London: British Museum, 2009). See also William C. Sturtevant, 'Ethnographic Details in the American Drawings of John White, 1577–1590', *Ethnohistory* 12, No. 1 (1965), 54–63; Kim Sloan (ed.), *A New World: England's First View of America* (Chapel Hill, NC: University of North Carolina Press, 2007).

p. 83 **falsely believed that the Inuit were cannibals and literal devils**: Hakluyt, *The Principal Navigations, Voyages, Traffiques, and Discoveries of the English Nation,* Vol. VII (Glasgow: James MacLehose & Sons, 1904). See also *The three voyages of Martin Frobisher in search of a passage to Cathay and India by the north-west, A.D. 1576–8* (ed. Vilhjalmur Stefansson), (London: Argonaut Press, 1938), Vol II, 17; Renara Wasserman, *Exotic Nations* (Ithaca, NY: Cornell University Press, 1994), 60.

p. 83 **ethnographically connected to Europeans:** Joel Konrad, '"Barbarous Gallants": Fashion, Morality and the Marked Body in English Culture, 1590–1660', *Fashion Theory*, Vol. 15, Issue 1 (2011), 29–48. Stuart Pigott, *Ancient Britons and the Antiquarian Imagination* (London: Thames & Hudson, 1989), 85.

p.84 **'small needle points and the juices squeezed from grasses':** 'minutis opifex punctus, expressos nativi graminis succos includit'. William Camden, *Britannia siue Florentissimorum regnorum* (London: George Bishop, 1594), 60.

p. 84 **'the Inhabitants of the great Bretannie':** Thomas Hariot, *America. A briefe and true report of the new found land of Virginia, of the commodities and of the nature and manners of the naturall inhabitants* (Frankfurt am Main: Sigismundi Feirabendii, 1590).

p. 84 **copied his depictions from those painted from life:** Nicole Blackwood, 'Meta Incognita. Some hypotheses on Cornelis Ketel's lost English and Inuit portraits', *Netherlands Yearbook for History of Art*, Vol. 66, Issue 1 (2006), 28–53.

Chapter 7: Kakiuineq Hiding in Plain Sight: Mikak, 1768 119

As well as Maya Sialuik Jacobsen, cited above, I am also grateful to Marianne Stopp (Parks Canada) and Hans Rollmann (Memorial University) for their assistance in navigating the details of Mikak's story and its surrounding context, and to Neal Jeffares (Dictionary of Pastellists) and Gemma Haigh (Guildford Borough Council Heritage Services) for help making sense of Russell's pictures of Mikak and their confusing provenances.

p. 87 **'Her face and hands, with tattoo rich':** 'A Lady' (attr. Mary Lyon), *A Peep at the Esquimaux, or Scenes on the Ice* (London: H.R. Thomas, 1825).

p. 87 **The first ever Royal Academy Summer Exhibition:** *The Exhibition of the Royal Academy MDCCLXIX* [ex. cat] (London: William Bunce, 1769), 12n. 98

p. 87 **She was brought to England:** the story of Mikak's life, her capture and time in England are summarised in Marianne Stopp, 'Eighteenth Century Labrador Inuit in England', *Arctic* 62, No. 1. (March 2009), 45–64. See also Marianne Stopp, *The Life Story of the Inuit Woman Mikak*. Final Report submitted to Nunatsiavut Gov't., Nain, NL (2007) and J. Garth Taylor, 'The Two Worlds of Mikak', *The Beaver* (Winter 1983 and Spring 1984).

p. 88 **Many who reported on her visit:** see, for example, *The Kentish Gazette* No. 53, 18–21 Jan. 1769.

p. 88 **presented to the Queen:** *Bath Chronicle*, 26 Jan.1769 (Williamsburg Gazette, Virginia, 30 March 1769).

p. 88 **Russell's portrait**: Hans-Windekilde Jannasch, 'Reunion with Mikak', *Canadian Geographical Journal*, Sept. 1958. There are three versions of the picture, and many scholarly and art-world sources confuse them for one another. One, the oil painting exhibited at the Royal Academy, is kept at the Institute of Social and Cultural Anthropology at University of Göttingen. The second, a studio riccordo, is now housed at the Guildford House Gallery, owned by Guildford Borough Council. Erroneous details of the Guildford picture's provenance, which confuse that version with the original, are in A. Fuller, 'Esquimaux in England', *The Sunday Times*, 28 July 1957, 4, and in Sotheby's sale catalogue from 12 Nov. 1997, filed in John Russell's folio at the Witt Library, Courtauld Institute of Art. The third is (likely) an engraving, reproduced in Francis Henry Webb, *Catalogue of the works of John* Russell, Vol. II, *c.* 1910 (National Art Library, Victoria and Albert Museum IV.RC.D.8). It was perhaps commissioned by Blumenbach, who indicated to Joseph Banks a desire to have one made. See F.W.P. Dougherty, (ed.) Norbert Klatt, *The Correspondence of Johann Friedrich Blumenbach* (Göttingen: Norbert Klatt, 2012), Vol. IV, Letter 869, 347; its current whereabouts are unknown. Russell also produced a far less flattering pencil sketch featuring

Mikak, included in a sketchbook at Birmingham Museums and Art Gallery. A further contemporaneous portrait of Mikak by Katherine Read (Society of Artists, *A Catalogue* … (London: William Bunce, 1769), no. 146), is lost.

p. 88 **'I had the Esquimaux Indian woman to sit for me':** John Russell, *Diaries, 1766–1802*, Vol. III. 11 Dec. 1768–2 April 1770 (National Art Library, Victoria and Albert Museum 86, ff.40).

p. 88 **a bloody skirmish:** anonymous, *The Moravians in Labrador* (Edinburgh: J. Ritchie, 1833), 75. See also Hans Rollmann, 'English–Inuit hostilities at Cape Charles (Labrador) in 1767', *Études/Inuit/Studies*, Vol. 39, No. 1, Les Inuit au Labrador eridional /The Inuit in southern Labrador (2015), 189–199; Hans Rollmann, '"So fond of the pleasure to shoot": The Sale of Firearms to Inuit on Labrador's North Coast in the Late Eighteenth Century', *Newfoundland and Labrador Studies* 26, 1 (2011), 1719–1726.

p. 89 **the British were keen to once again exert territorial and economic power:** Gerald M. Sider, *Skin for Skin: Death and Life for Inuit and Innu* (New Haven, CT: Duke University Press, 2014), 46.

p. 89 **According to missionary records:** Hans Rollmann, 'English–Inuit hostilities' collects and translates the Missionary records. Palliser's 'official narrative' is told in Hugh Palliser, *Letter to Lord Hillsborough*, 20 Oct. 1768 [letter], CO 194/12, 53; Kew, UK National Archives. Ship's captain Nicholas Darby recounted his version in *Petition of Nicholas Darby praying relief with respect to his losses in endeavouring to establish a fishery on the Labrador Coast to the Kings Most Excellent Majesty in Council*, 6 March 1769, Privy Council 1/3183, Kew, UK National Archives and *The Particulars of the Case of Nicholas Darby, Merchant*, CO 5/114, Kew, UK National Archives.

p. 89 **'fair trade'**: John Horsnaill, 'An account of the voyage of the four missionaries …' in Anne M. Lysaght (ed.) *Joseph Banks in Newfoundland and Labrador 1766* (Berkeley, CA: University of California Press, 1971), 207–212. See also Joseph Irving, *Masters Logs 1772*, ADM 52/ 1387, HMS *Otter* Master's Logs 1768–1773, Log Book no. 9, Kew, UK National Archives; William Whiteley, 'Governor Hugh Palliser and the Newfoundland and Labrador Fishery, 1764–1768', *Canadian Historical Review*, Vol. 1, Issue 2 (June, 1969), 141–163.

p. 90 **Palliser happily reported:** Palliser, *Letter to Lord Hillsborough* 20 Oct. 1768.

p. 90 **she did not fully trust … her captors:** J. Garth Taylor, 'The Two Worlds of Mikak', *The Beaver* (Winter 1983), 8.

p. 90 **young orphan boy called Karpik:** Hans Rollmann, 'Karpik (*c* .1754–1769) *First Fruit* among the Inuit of Labrador' in Claudia Mai (ed.) *250 Jahre Unitätsarchiv – Beiträge der Jubiläumstagung vom 28. Bis 29 Juni 2014* (Herrnhut: Herrnhuter Verlag, 2017) .

p. 90 **she was also said to have already begun to become interested in Christian theology:** James Hutton recounts, for example, that Mikak had memorised a prayer, see Daniel Benham, *Memoirs of James Hutton*

(London: Hamilton, Adams Co., 1856), 448. Missionary accounts from the first encounter with Mikak to her death recount her interest in Christian thought, though of course these claims ventriloquise her, and so must be treated with scepticism.

p. 90 **One account describes her admonishing Lucas:** *Auszug aus Br. Jens Havens Aufsaz von seiner recognoscirungs Reise u[nd] Aufenthalt unter den Eskimoern in Terra Labrador von Ao. 1770 bis 1784, Erster Theil*, 6–33; R15.K.a.5.4., Unity Archives Herrnhut. A scan of this document was kindly provided to me by Hans Rollmann.

p. 90 **confused by English dining habits:** *Caledonian Mercury*, 10 Aug. 1774. *Salisbury Journal*, 23 Jan. 1769. F. D. Cartwright (ed.), *Life and Correspondence of Major Cartwright*, Vol. I (London: Henry Colburn, 1826), 41. Iris Rhodes claims that Mikak's presence 'caused a traffic jam' of onlookers outside Russell's studio, but this cannot be corroborated in contemporary sources. It is likely sourced from A. Fuller, 'Esquimaux in England', *The Sunday Times*, 28 July 1957, 4. See also Iris Rhodes, *John Russell RA* (Guildford: Guildford Borough Council, 1986).

p. 90 **'there is so much to be said ':** Charles Henry Parry, *A Memoir of the Revd. Joshua Parry* (London: Hamilton Adams, 1872), 302. Ann Savours, 'Early Eskimo visitors to Britain', *Geographical Magazine*, Vol. 36, Issue 6, 336–343.

p. 91 **double-poke method:** Maya Sialuk Jacobsen derived this method after examining a hafted copper awl at the National Museum of Denmark. A similar tool is pictured in Jens Peder Hart Hansen, *Qilakitsoq: De grønlandske mumier fra 1400-tallet* (Greenland: Grønlands landsmuseum, 1985). Aaron Deter-Wolf shared these findings on Instagram; @archaeologyink 9 August 2021. https://www.instagram.com/p/CSWiwPUKJJQ/

p. 91 **account ... of Captain George Francis Lyon:** G.F. Lyon, *The Private Journal of Captain G. F. Lyon* (London: John Murray, 1824), 121.

p. 92 **kakiuineq:** Michael Fortecue, Steven Jacobsen and Lawrence Kaplan, *Comparative Eskimo Dictionary* (Fairbanks, AK: University of Alaska, 1994), 152. There is no OED entry for *kakeen*. See also 'Additional Particulars respecting the late Arctic Voyage', *Lady's Magazine* (June 1824), 297.

p. 92 **Georges de Buffon:** Georges de Buffon, *Histoire Naturelle*, Vol. III, (2nd edition. Paris: Imprimerie Royale, 1750), 376.

p. 92 **'have a thread blackened with soot drawn betwixt the skin of their chin':** David Crantz, *The History of Greenland*, Vol. I (London: Bretheren's Society, 1767), 138.

p. 92 **two tattooed Choctaw and Creek 'Princes':** Lars Krutak, *Tattoo Traditions of Native North America* (Arnhem, NL: Stichting LM, 2014), 200. Alden T. Vaughan, *Transatlantic Encounters: American Indians in Britain, 1500–1776* (New York: Cambridge University Press, 2006).

p. 92 **'Four Kings'**: anonymous, *The Four Kings of Canada* (London: John Baker, 1710). See also Lars Krutak, 'America's Tattooed Indian Kings', *Skin and Ink Magazine* (June 2005), 18–21; Kevin R. Muller 'From Palace to Longhouse: Portraits of the Four Indian Kings in a Transatlantic Context', *American Art*, Vol. 22, Issue 3 (2008), 26–49; Eric Hinderaker, 'The 'Four Indian Kings' and the Imaginative Construction of the First British Empire', *The William and Mary Quarterly* 53, No. 3 (1996), 487–526. Vaughn, *Transatlantic Encounters* (see above).

p. 92 **Overhill Cherokee:** Duane H. King (ed.), *The Memoirs of Lt. Henry Timberlake* (Cherokee, NC: Museum of the Cherokee Indian Press, 2007).

p. 93 **he renamed her Nutarrak:** Marianne Stopp, 'Eighteenth Century Labrador Inuit in England', *Arctic*. 62, No. 1. (March 2009). See also J.K. Hiller, *The Foundation and the Early Years of the Moravian Mission in Labrador 1752–1805* (MA thesis, Memorial University of Newfoundland, 1967).

p. 93 **negotiating the establishment of a new missionary outpost:** 'Memoir or Br. Jenns Haven', *The United Brethren's Missionary Intelligencer,* 4th Qtr 1846, 151. Anonymous, *History of the Mission of the Church of the United Brethren of Labrador* (London: W. Mallalieu, 1871), 16.

p. 93 **missionaries were initially scared it was a trap:** *Journal of the Voyage of the Jersey Packet to Labrador and Newfoundland taken from the papers of Jens Haven and Chr. Drachard*, 17 July 1770, MG17-D1 Vol. I/44-a, 24, Library and Archives Canada Hiller, *Moravian Mission*, 70.

p. 93 **she maintained a traditional way of life:** *Moravian Mission,* 90, and Stopp, *Eighteenth Century Labrador Inuit*, 51 (both, see above).

p. 94 **James Hutton, wrote an excoriating letter:** James Hutton to Lord Dartmouth, 5 Jan. 1773. *William Legge, 2nd Earl of Dartmouth* fonds MG 23, A-1, H-993, Vol. 2, 2358, Library and Archives Canada.

p. 94 **another Inuit woman called Caubvick was brought to London:** Anthony Pearson, 'John Hunter and the woman from Labrador', *Annals of the Royal College of Surgeons*, Vol. 60 (1978). M. Stopp and G. Mitchell. '"Our Amazing Visitors": Catherine Cartwright's Account of Labrador Inuit in England', *Arctic* 63, No. 4 (2010), 399–413. Marianne Stopp, *Eighteenth Century Labrador Inuit*', see above. 'A Labrador Woman', Royal College of Surgeons RCSSC/P 243. http://surgicat.rcseng.ac.uk/Details/collect/43895 (accessed 17 Aug. 2022].

p. 94 **Louis-Antoine de Bougainville explicitly remarked:** Louis-Antoine Bougaineville, *Voyage autour du Monde* (Paris: Saillant & Nyon, 1771), 215. Early French descriptions of Arctic tattooing include Joseph Jouvency, *Canadicae Missionis Relatio (Rome 1710)* in Reuben Gold Thwaites (ed.), *The Jesuit Relations* (Cleveland: The Burrows, Brothers Co., 1896), 279, and Charles Pomeroy Otis (trans.), *Voyages de Sieur de Champlain*, Vol. I 1567–1635 (Boston, MA: The Prince Society, 1880), 247.

p. 94 **Banks and Cook owned:** Felicity Jensz, 'The Publication and Reception of David Cranz's 1767 *History of Greenland*' in *The Library: The Transactions of the Bibliographical Society,* Vol. 13, No. 4 (Dec. 2012), 457–472.

p. 95 **Banks also owned one of two copies of the Mikak portrait:** the claim that Banks commissioned the original portrait from Russell appears in

Jannasch, 'Reunion with Mikak', sourced to unspecified 'archives' at Göttingen, but cannot be confirmed beyond all doubt, particularly as Banks left London before Mikak arrived. Banks knew Russell, and Hugh Palliser, but the commission is not mentioned in any extant diaries or correspondence. The portrait hung in Banks's library, and was gifted to Johann F. Blumenbach at Göttingen in 1797. See *Letters to Sir J. Banks*. Vol. V, BM Add. MS 8098, 318–319, British Library, and Warren R. Dawson (ed.) *The Banks Letters* (London: British Museum, 1958), 110–118). Blumenbach wrote on the reverse '*von dem berühmten Porträtmahler John Russell 1769 gemahlt für Sir Joseph Banks von welchem ich es geschenkt erhalten*', and repeated this claim in print in his book *Beyträge zur Naturgeschichte* (Göttingen: Heinrich Dieterich, 1806), 64. The Göttingen picture appears to be the original, though Blumenbach had requested a copy on at least two occasions (Dougherty, *Correspondence of Blumenbach*, Vol. IV, Letter 869, 24 Sept. 1794, 347 (BM Add. MS 8098 219–220) and Vol. V, Letter 1022, 10 Dec. 1796, 76 (BL NHM DTC 10(1), 93–95, British Library).

p. 95 **having failed to do so when he was in Labrador:** Anne M. Lysaght (ed.), *Joseph Banks in Newfoundland and Labrador 1766* (Berkeley, CA: University of California Press, 1971), 84, 167, n111.

p. 95 **James King, who had travelled on board ship with Mikak:** Lance Bertelsen 'Revolutionary Sympathy on Cook's Resolution: The Transatlantic Education of Lieutenant James King, 1766–76', *Eighteenth-Century Life* (1 Sept. 2014), 38 (3), 64–99. The artist on Cook's third voyage, John Webber, drew a tattooed Aleut woman in 1773, and the ship's surgeon Dr Samwell described the 'tattaw' marks on Inuit women in his diary. See also J. Edge Partington, 'Extracts from the diary of Dr. Samwell (Surgeon of the 'Discovery' during Cook's Third Voyage, 1776–79)', *The Journal of the Polynesian Society* 8, No. 4 (32) (1899), 250–263.

p. 95 **not yet quite tamed:** J. Taylor Hamilton, *History of the Missions of the Moravian Church during the eighteenth and nineteenth centuries* (Bethlehem, PA: Times, 1901), 46. Barnett Richling, '"Very Serious Reflections": Inuit Dreams about Salvation and Loss in Eighteenth-Century Labrador' in *Ethnohistory* 36, No. 2 (1989), 148–69. For a meditation on a similar theme, comparing Mikak and Omai's experiences and receptions in London, see Vanessa Smith '"How Very Little He Can Learn": Exotic Visitors and the Transmission of Cultural Knowledge in Eighteenth Century London' in O. Gal and Y. Zheng (eds.), *Motion and Knowledge in the Changing Early Modern World* (Heidelberg: Springer, 2014).

p. 95 **Mikak's final years:** J. Taylor Hamilton, *A History of the Church known as the Moravian Church* (Bethlehem, PA: Times, 1900), 224. J. W. Davey, *Fall of Torngak* (London: Partridge & Co., 1903).

p. 95 **her death**: H.M. Letter, 'An Account of the Esquimaux Mikak' in *Periodical Accounts relating to the Missions of the Church of the United Brethren*, Vol. II (London: Bretheren's Society, 1797), 170–171. Anonymous, *The Moravians in Labrador* (Edinburgh: J. Ritchie, 1833), 180.

Chapter 8: 'Pricking various figures on their flesh with the point of a pin': Jane White, Mary Cunningham and The Forty Thieves 97

p. 97 **'Tattooed people who are not in prison':** 'Les tatoués qui vivent en liberté sont des criminels latents ou des aristocrates dégénérés. Il arrive que leur vie semble irréprochable jusqu'au bout. C'est qu'ils sont morts avant leur crime.' (Author's translation, from the first published version.) Adolf Loos, 'Ornament et Crime', trans. Marcel Ray in *Les Cahiers d'aujourd'hui* 5 (Paris: George Besson, June 1913), 247. Other English translations exist, based on later versions of the essay. Their versions of this sentence are less satisfactory than my own, in my view. On the dating of this essay and its publication history, see Christopher Long, 'Ornament, Crime, Myth and Meaning' in Dominique Binnamour-Lloyd and Lawrence W. Speck (eds), *Architecture, Material and Imagined: Proceedings of the 85th ACSA Annual Meeting and Technology Conference; Dallas, 1997* (Washington, DC: ACSA, 1997), 440–445. On the historical and art-historical contexts of this essay and its ideas on tattooing, see 'Critique of Ornament' in Joseph Mascheck, *Adolf Loos: The Art of Architecture* (London: I.B. Tauris, 2013).

p. 97 **'This custom is a completely savage one':** Cesare Lombroso, 'The Savage Origin of Tattooing' in *Popular Science Monthly*, Vol. 48 (April 1896), 803.

p. 97 **When the police arrived:** the narrative details of Jane and Mary's crime are taken from Old Bailey records. Henry Buckler, *Sir John Cowan, Bart. Mayor. Central Criminal Court. Sessions Paper. Twelfth Session, held October 22 1838. Minutes of Evidence taken in Shorthand* (London: George Herbert, 1838), t18381022-2327, 959–960.

p. 98 **At the gaol:** 'The Countryman Plucked', *The Era*, 7 Oct. 1838. See also 'The Forty Thieves'; *Morning Post*, 5 Oct. 1838; *Morning Advertiser*, 5 Oct. 1838; *Home Office: Newgate Prison Calendar* HO77/45/00358/60, National Archives, London; *Description Lists of Convicts* CON19-1-13, 242 & 321, Libraries Tasmania.

p. 99 **'the terror of the Borough':** 'Surrey Sessions, Tuesday', *Morning Chronicle*, 22 Oct. 1828. *Oxford Journal*, 13 Sept. 1828.

p. 100 **'Suppose that lad was to peach':** Charles Dickens, *Oliver Twist*, Vol. II (London: Richard Bentley, 1838) 186.

p. 100 **William Creamer:** *Evening Standard*, 13 Sept. 1828.

p. 100 **a dozen girls:** *The Standard*, 10 Oct. 1828.

p. 100 **Rutledge:** *Evening Standard*, 9 Sept. 1828.

p. 101 **'two little urchins':** *Morning Post*, 29 Sept. 1828.

p. 101 **thirteen-year-old arsonist:** *Evening Standard*, 10 Nov. 1829.

p. 101 **identified ... by three blue stripes tattooed on their thumbs:** *Morning Post*, 20 Sept. 1830.

p. 101 **two brothers:** *Morning Advertiser*, 18 Feb.1831.

p. 101 **John Jones:** *Morning Chronicle*, 9 April 1831.

p. 101 **George Freeman:** Henry Buckler, *Sessions Paper, Sir John Key, Bart. Mayor. Fourth Session, held at the Justice Hall in the Old Bailey, April 5 1832. Taken in Shorthand* (London: George Titterton, 1833), t18320405-278,

443. *Home Office: Newgate Prison Calendar* HO77/45/039/24, National Archives, London. *Description Lists of Convicts* CON18-1-15, 207, Libraries Tasmania. *The Digital Panopticon*, George Freeman b. 1817, Life Archive ID obpt18320405-278-defend2337 (https://www.digitalpanopticon.org/life?id=obpt18320405-278-defend2337). Version 1.2.1, consulted 22 Aug. 2022.

p. 102 **'One of them, a Rogue ':** *Daily Post*, 19 Jan. 1739; *Read's Weekly Journal*, 20 Jan. 1739; *Derby Mercury*, 25 Jan. 1739; *Stamford Mercury*, 25 Jan. 1739. The case is also reported in *Newcastle Courant*, 27 Jan. 1739, which gives the location of the theft as a 'sadler's shop', not a salter's. These publications and records are also occasionally dated 1738, in Old Style dating. Records for the Christmas Quarter Session of 1738/39 (9 Jan. 1739), which are held at the Surrey County Council History Centre (QS3/5/7 and QS2/6/Xmas 1738-9/4), are not definitive in identifying this 'rogue', perhaps the most elaborately tattooed Englishman yet described in the eighteenth century. The most plausible candidate of the four men convicted of larceny and sentenced to whippings at that Session is William Davis, a labourer from St. Saviour, charged with stealing a cheese from the shop of George Otway, a member of the Salter's Guild (Society of Genealogists, *Britain Country Apprentices 1710–1808* I(R1 16/195 National Archives, London), Vol. 10, No. 71724, 1942). I am grateful to Michael Page, Surrey History Centre, and Chris Scales, Southwark Archives, for their assistance with this research. See also Gwenda Morgan and Peter Rushton, 'Visible Bodies: Power, Subordination and Identity in the Eighteenth-Century Atlantic World', in *Journal of Social History*, 39, No. 1 (Fall 2005), 39–64.

p. 103 **'I was struck':** Gina Lombroso-Ferrero, *Criminal Man* (London: Putnams, 1911), xii.

p. 103 **Lombroso began:** full details are given in various editions of *Criminal Man* in 1876, 1878, 1884, 1889 and 1896–1897. See Ceasare Lombroso, *Criminal Man,* trans. Mary Gibson and Nicole Hahn Rafter (Durham, NC: Duke University Press, 2006). On Lombroso and tattooing see Jane Caplan, '"Speaking Scars": The Tattoo in Popular Practice and Medico-Legal Debate in Nineteenth-Century Europe', *History Workshop Journal*, No. 44 (Autumn, 1997), 106–142, and Gemma Angel, 'Atavistic Marks and Risky Practices: The Tattoo in Medico-Legal Debate, 1850–1950' in Jonathan Reinarz and Kevin Siena (eds), *A Medical History of Skin* (London: Pickering & Chatto, 2013).

p.104 **'At the sight of that skull ':** Lombroso-Ferrero, *Criminal Man* (1911), xv. See also Lombroso, *Criminal Man* (2006), 40, 47–49, 208–209, 375 fn 6.

p. 104 **'By nature marked, coted and signed':** John Mitchel, *Jail Journal* (New York: Office of the Citizen, 1854), 87. William Shakespeare, *King John* (Washington, DC: Folger Shakespeare Library, n.d.), Act IV, Scene II.

p.105 **'one of the most singular characteristics of primitive men ':** Lombroso, *Criminal Man* (2006), 58.

p. 105 **'we find the custom of tattooing diffused among classes so tenacious of old traditions':** Cesare Lombroso, 'The Savage Origin of Tattooing', *Popular Science Monthly*, Vol. 48 (April 1896).

p. 106 **Lacassagne and Havelock Ellis:** Alexandre Lacassagne, *Les tatouages: étude anthropologique et médico-légale* (Paris: J-B Baillière, 1881). See also Havelock Ellis, *The Criminal* (London: Walter Scott, 1890); Neil Davie, 'Lombroso and the "Men of Real Science"' in Paul Knepper and P.J. Ystehede (eds), *The Cesare Lombroso Handbook* (London: Routledge, 2013), 340–360.

p. 106 **frequently absconding:** *Conduct Record* CON140/1/2, 179 & CON140-1/10 178, Libraries Tasmania. *The Digital Panopticon* Jane White b. 1817, Life Archive ID obpdef1-2327-18381022 (https://www.digitalpanopticon.org/life?id=obpdef1-2327-18381022), and Mary Clifford b. 1819, Life Archive ID obpdef2-2327-18381022 (/life?id=obpdef2-2327-18381022). Version 1.2.1, consulted 22 Aug. 2022.

p. 107 **it was left to the gaoler:** *Morning Advertiser*, 5 Oct. 1838. Waddington had been dealing with these apparent gang-members for more than a decade: *Evening Standard,* 3 Jan. 3 1829. Despite the gang's uncertain existence, its reputation persisted until at least the 1860s: 'Thieves, Roughs and Idlers', *The London Review*, 8 Aug. 1868, 162–163.

p. 107 **basic error:** Mary Gibson, 'Cesare Lombroso, prison science and penal policy' in Knepper and Ystehede, *Handbook,* 30–46.

PART THREE: TATTOOING AFTER 1853 109

p. 111 **'a perfect frenzy for decalcomania':** 'The Coming Merry Christmas', *Indiana Herald*, 22 Dec. 1875.

p. 111 **OED**: 'cockamamie, n. and adj.' OED Online, June 2022. Oxford University Press. https://www.oed.com/view/Entry/35357?redirectedFrom=cockamamie& (accessed 22 Aug. 2022).

p. 112 **'the equivalent of getting your house tattooed':** Virginia Cheney, 'Use Wet Cloth or Paper to Remove Decal', *Philadelphia Enquirer,* 5 April 1947. 'Janitor solves decal problem', *Tampa Bay Times,* 22 June 1947, 15

p. 112 **'Painted strips of paper':** Arthur Kober, 'Mrs Gittleson', *New Yorker*, 24 Oct. 1931, 73.

p. 122 **'followed the craze of plastering our hands':** Frank Colby, 'Take my word for it', *Oakland Tribune*, 25 April 1947. George Currie, 'Brooklyn', *Brooklyn Daily Eagle,* 25 May 1947.

p. 122 **'could buy fuh two cends cockamamies':** Henry Roth, *Call It Sleep* (New York: Avon, 1964), 265.

p. 112 **'a 1967 issue of Playboy':** Jean Shepherd, 'The Return of the Smiling Wimpy Doll', *Playboy* , Dec. 1967, 224.

p. 113 **'one newspaper advertisement from 1866':** *Pittsfield Sun*, 28 June 1866.

p. 114 **stick them on their hands as if they were tattoos:** 'The Coming Merry Christmas',

Indiana Herald, 22 Dec. 1875.

p. 114 **1876 catalogue:** *Price List of Transfer Ornaments and Painters'*

Supplies for Sale by Wadsworth Bros & Howland (Boston, MA: L.F. Lawrence & Co., 1876).

p. 114 **Eugene Rousseau commissioned designer Félix Bracquemond:** Emily Eastgate Brink, 'Touch Codes and Japanese Taste: The Material Experience of Félix Bracquemond's Service Rousseau', *Australian and New Zealand Journal of Art* (2018), 18:1, 108–124. Sonia Coman, 'The Bracquemond-Rousseau Table Service of 1866', *Journal of Japonisme* (2016), Vol. 1, 17–40.

p. 115 **potichomania:** *Morning Post*, 21 Sept. 1854; *Cincinnati Daily Gazette*, 30 Aug. 1856; 'The Last New Mania', *Man of Ross General Advertiser*, 31 Aug. 1865; 'Classical Advertisements', *Pall Mall Gazette*, 25 July 1865.

p. 115 **tattooing was also part of this craze for all things Japanese:** Matt Lodder, '"Geijutsu-tekina" Nihon no irezumi to vuikutoria asa Ingurando no shōgyō senryaku' ['"Artistic" Japanese Tattoos and Commercial Strategy in Victorian England'], trans. Naho Onuki, in Yoshimi Yamamoto, Makiko Kuwabara and Fumihiko Tsumura (eds) *Karada o horu, sekai o shirusu irezumi tatoū no jinrui-gaku* [*Sculpt the Body, Mark the World*] (Tokyo: Shunpasa, 2022). Yoshimi Yamamoto, ''Nihon miyage' to shite no irezumi' ['Japanese tattooing as souvenirs for foreign travellers]', *Nihon kenkyū* [*Japanese Studies*] (2021), Vol. 63.

p. 115 **Many early foreign visitors to Japan were tattooed by local artists:** Norobu Koyama, 'Japanese Tattooists and the British Royal Family During the Meiji Period' in Hugh Cortazzi (ed.) *Japan: Biographical Portraits,* Vol. VI (Leiden: Global Oritenal, 2007), 72. See also John van der Kiste, *Alfred, Queen Victoria's Second Son* (Stroud: Fronthill Media, 2013); Henry Keppel, *A Sailor's Life under Four Sovereigns*, Vol. III, (London: Macmillan, 1889), 278; Charles Beresford, *The Memoirs of Admiral Lord Charles Beresford* (Boston: Little, Brown, 1914), 101.

p. 116 **Cassell's Magazine:** 'Tattooing, Savage and Civilised', *Cassell's Magazine,* Sept. 1873, 319.

p. 116 **an English-language guidebook**: Basil Hall Chamberlain, *Things Japanese* (2nd ed. London: Kegan Paul, Trench, Trübner & Co., 1891), 450.

Chapter 9: 'Gather up some good feelings, some more than merely passing pleasure, from these sacred scenes' 119

p. 119 **'an anchor to be tattooed upon his arm':** Robert Fletcher, *Tattooing among civilized people* (Washington, DC: Judd & Dettweiler, 1883), 26.

p. 119 **'I was tatooed by a Native ':** VIC/EDVIID, 1 April 1862, Royal Archives; Jane Ridley, *Bertie: a life of Edward VII* (Random House: London, 2012), 68. 'Keppel' is Lt. Colonel Frederick Charles Keppel, the Prince's equerry.

p. 120 **fashionable alligator skin boots:** Stanley Weintraub, *The Importance of Being Edward*, (London: John Murray), 2000, 79.

p. 120 **'I can say nought of Jerusalem save lamentation ':** Augusta Mentor Mott, *The Stones of Palestine: Notes of a Ramble through the Holy Land* (London: Seeley, Jackson & Halliday, 1865), 50–51.

p. 121 **'a party of Bedouin women':** Tattooed Bedouin, particularly women, were frequently remarked upon by Victorian and Edwardian travellers to the Middle East. It is clear that some Bedouin made a living as commercial tattoo artists in cities such as Baghdad, but Christian tattooers primarily worked on foreign pilgrims. One late Victorian tourist, Mrs Bishop, noted that 'The Arab women go about the streets unveiled, and with the abba covering their very poor clothing, but it is not clutched closely enough to conceal the extraordinary tattooing which the Bedouin women everywhere regard as ornamental. There are artists in Baghdad who make their living by this mode of decorating the person, and vie with each other in the elaboration of their patterns. I saw several women tattooed with two wreaths of blue flowers on their bosoms linked by a blue chain, palm fronds on the throat, stars on the brow and chin, and bands round the wrists and ankles.' See Isabella L. Bird Bishop, *Journeys in Persia and Kurdistan* (John Murray: London, 1881), 34. There is a particularly extensive description of Bedouin tattooing methods roughly contemporaneous to Bertie's visit in Edward Lane, *An Account of the Manners and Customs of the Modern Egyptians* (John Murray: London, 1860), 39–40.

p. 121 **one of his expansive reports:** Gabriel Charmes, 'Voyages en Syrie, Impressions et Souvenirs', *Revue des Deux Mondes*, 45:3 (May 1881), 753–781, 771. Matt Lodder, 'Tattoos Fit for a King', *Total Tattoo* (Feb. 2012), 60–61.

p. 121 **'five or ten francs':** This would be roughly the equivalent of 4–8 shillings, or about a full day's wages for a skilled craftsman in the period. See Arthur Bowley, *Wages in the United Kingdom in the Nineteenth Century* (Cambridge: Cambridge University Press, 1900).

p. 122 **never to have spoken of his tattoo again:** also note that despite Robert Fletcher's claim of indignant commentary about Bertie's tattoo in the press, I have not yet been able to locate any responses in any of the major newspapers or periodicals of the day.

p. 122 **'cannot but gather up some good feelings ':** Arthur Penrhyn Stanley, *Sermons Preached before His Royal Highness, the Prince of Wales during his Tour in the East in the Spring of 1862* (London: John Murray, 1863), 147.

p. 122 **tattooing on Europeans begins in the records of Christian pilgrimages:** Robert Ousterhout, 'Permanent Ephemera: The "Honourable Stigmatisation" of Jerusalem Pilgrims' in Renana Bartel and Hanna Vorholt *Between Jerusalem and Europe* (Leiden: Brill, 2015). See also Katherine Dauge-Roth, Signing the Body in Early Modern France (London: Ashgate, 2016); Mordechai Lewy, 'Jerusalem unter der Haut: Zur Geschichte der Jerusalemer Pilgertätowierung', *Zeitschrift für Religions- und Geitesgeschichte*, Vol. 55 (2003), 1–39; the oldest accounts, per Renaut (pers. comm.) are in the 1563 testimony of Alexander von Pappenheim, *Reisebericht nach Italien und ins Heilige Land (1563/64* (Hamburg: Verlag Dr. Kovač, 1564)) and the 1586 pilgrimage account of Jean Zuallart – *Les Tres devot voyage de Ierusalem* (En Anvers: Arnould s'Conincx, 1608).

p. 123 **Tattooing amongst Coptic Christians in Egypt:** Luc Renaut, 'Marquage Corporel et Signation Religieuse dans L'Antiquité' (PhD diss., École Pratique des Hautes Études, 2004), 788.

p. 123 **eighth-century, naturally preserved body of a woman:** John H. Taylor and Daniel Antoine, *Ancient Lives: New Discoveries: Eight mummies, Eight stories* (London: British Museum Press, 2014).

p. 123 **tattoos or brands of lions on their hands:** Yedida Kalfon Stillman, *Arab Dress: A Short History, from the Dawn of Islam to Modern Times* (Leiden: Brill, 2000).

p. 124 **including Loreto in Italy:** Fredrika Jacobs, *Votive Panels and Popular Piety in Early Modern Italy* (Cambridge: Cambridge University Press, 2013), 41. Guido Guerzoni, '"Notae Divine Ex Arte Compunctae": Prime Impressioni sul Tatuaggio devozionale in Italia (XV–XIX)', *Micrologus,* No. 13 (2005), 418.

p. 123 **Jan Aerts of Melchelen:** Aerts has frequently been cited as the earliest pilgrimage tattoo by Marie-Armeille Beaulieu. ('Comme un sceau sur ton bras', *La Terre Sainte*, 621, Sept. /Oct. 2012, 34–37.) 'Do you know the seal of Jerusalem?', *Jerusalme Korrespondenz* Vol. 19 (2018), 18–19. 'Like a seal on your arm', *Jerusalem Quarterly* 78 (2019), 86–92, but this is erroneous. Marc Bogaert, 'Een realistische fictie: de Heerlijcke reyse van Jan Aerts', *Verlagen & Mededelingen,* Vol. 128, No. 1 (2018). A.M. Koldeweij, 'Vrome reiziger of stoere jongen? Pelgrimstekens en profane insignes', *Transparant: Tijdschrift van de Vereniging van Christen-Historici*, Vol. 13, No. 3 (2002). For the relevant manuscript versions, see Emmanuel Neefs, *Récit de L'Expédition en Orient 1481–1484* (Louvain: Ch. Peeters, 1873), which does not include the tattoos, and Jan Aerts, *Cort verhael eender heerlijcker Reysen*, (T'Hantvverpen: Gheleyn Jansens, 1595), THYSIA 1833 & *Warachtige bescryvinge der Jerusalemsche reyse* (*c.* 1575), fol. 6v LTK 856, Leiden University Libraries.

p. 124 **German Pilgrim Ratge Stubbe**: Johann Lund, *Die alten jüdischen Heiligthümer, Gottesdienste und Gewohnheiten* (Hamburg: Liebernickel, 1704). Otto F.A. Meinardus, 'Jerusalemer Pilgerstätten auf Hamburger Armen', *Beiträge zur deutschen Volks- und Altertumskunde*, 26 (1988–1991), 117–22.

p. 124 **William Lithgow:** William Lithgow, *Totall Discourse* (London, I. Okes, 1640). For a discussion of the publication history of Lithgow's account and its description of his tattoos across several editions (1614, 1623, 1632 and 1640) see Anna Felicity Friedman, 'Custom Tattoo Work – Historical Improvisation during William Lithgow's Pilgrimage' (tattoohistorian.com, 2016). https://web.archive.org/web/20211021210117/https://tattoohistorian.com/2016/09/24/custom-tattoo-work-historical-improvisation/)

p. 124 **excised the tattoo from Lithgow's arm:** Daniel Vitkus, 'An Intrepid Scot: William Lithgow of Lanark's Travels in the Ottoman Lands, North Africa and Central Europe, 1609–1621 (review)', *Renaissance Quarterly*, Vol. 60, No. 2 (Summer 2007), 680–682.

p. 124 **paintings of tattooed pilgrims:** Katherine Dauge-Roth, *Signing the Body in Early Modern France* (London: Ashgate, 2016).

p. 126 **John Woodward and Thomas Williams:** *Proceedings at the Old Bailey on 25th, 26th, 27th and 28th February 1718[9]* (London, 1719), 6. Craig Kolslofsky, 'Self-Tattooed Servants, Soldiers, and Sailors in the British Atlantic World to c. 1750', unpublished draft manuscript (2022).

p. 126 **Jean de Thévenot:** Jean de Thévenot, *The Travels of Monsieur de Thévenot into the Levant* (London: H. Faithorne, J. Adamson, C. Skegnes and T. Newborough, 1687), Part I, 201. See also Henry Maundrell, *A Journey from Aleppo to Jerusalem at Easter AD1697* (London: W. Meadows, 1749).

p. 127 **survey by John Carswell:** John Carswell, *Coptic Tattoo Designs* (Beirut: American University of Beirut, 1958). For more on Razzouk, see Anna Felicity Friedman, *World Atlas of Tattoo* (London: Thames & Hudson, 2019); Friedman, 'Inside the World's Only Surviving Tattoo Shop for Medieval Pilgrims', *Atlas Obscura*, 18 Aug. 2016. (https://www.atlasobscura.com/articles/inside-the-worlds-only-surviving-tattoo-shop-for-medieval-pilgrims); Joshua Foer, Dylan Thuras and Ella Morton, *Atlas Obscura* (2nd edition. New York: Workman Publishing, 2019).

p. 129 **a common motif:** Brian Spencer, *Pilgrim Souvenirs and Secular Badges* (London: The Stationary Office, 1998), 13.

p. 129 **A.T. Sinclair observed:** A.T. Sinclair, 'Tattooing Oriental and Gypsy', *American Anthropologist*, Vol. 10, No. 3 (Sept. 1908), 361–386.

p. 129 **submerged in base commerce:** Mordechai Lewy, 'Jerusalem' (see above).

p. 130 **Mrs Mott:** Augusta Mentor Mott, *The Stones of Palestine: Notes of a Ramble through the Holy Land* (London: Seeley, Jackson & Halliday, 1865), 52.

p. 130 **Lacassagne:** Alexandre Lacassagne, *Les tatouages: étude anthropologique et médico-légale* (Paris: J-B Baillière, 1881) 10.

p.130 **Edward Hogg:** Edward Hogg, *Visit to Alexandria, Damascus and Jerusalem during the Successful Campaign of Ibrahim Pasha*, Vol. II, (London: Saunders and Otley, 1835), 209–210.

Chapter 10: 'Do you tattoo your children yet?' 133

p. 133 **'a lot of shillyshally usually followed':** James Joyce, *Ulysses* (Paris: John Rodker for Egoist Press, 1922), 604.

p. 133 **I am the real Sir Roger:** 'I am the Real Sir Roger' (London: Disley, *c.* 1874). Ballad Roud no. V5936, Bodleian Libraries, Oxford.

p. 133 **The trial had already gripped the country for months:** for an overview of the narrative of the case, see Rohan McWilliam, *The Tichborne Claimant* (London: Bloomsbury, 2007) and Robyn Annear, *The Man who Lost Himself* (Melbourne: Text Publishing, 2011). Where narrative details are not cited directly, they are to be found in these two texts. An account of the first months of the initial trial was published as Franklin Lushington, *Tichborne Romance: A Full and Accurate Report of the Proceedings in the Extraordinary and Interesting Trial of Tichborne v. Lushington* (London: Simpkin, Marshall & Co., 1871). *The Times* reported on the case daily. See also Henry Hawkins, *Reminiscences of Sir Henry Hawkins, Baron Brampton* (London: E. Arnold, 1904) and William Ballantine, *Some Experiences of a Barrister's Life* (London: Richard Bently & Son, 1882).

p. 134 **'Roger Tichborne was tattooed':** *The Times*, 1 Feb. 1872, 11.

p. 138 **'a mark on the arm of Roger Tichborne':** Lushington, *Romance*, 121 (see above). Twelfth Day of Trial, 29 May 1871.

p. 138 **'I have no tattoo marks'**: Lushington, *Romance*, 417 (see above). Thirty-Eighth Day of Trial, 6 July 1871.

p. 140 **'like a common sailor':** Edward Kenealy, *The Report of the Trial of Sir Richard R. C. D. Tichborne, Bart.* (London: Englishman Office, 1876), Vol. IV, 155, 169, 239.

p. 140 **'a rather strange amusement':** *The Times,* 22 Feb. 1872, 11.

p. 140 **'He was tattooed twice in his life':** *The Times*, 2 Feb. 1872, 10.

p. 141 **drew the design:** *The Times,* 23 Feb. 1872. A sketch by Bellew was reproduced during the second trial. Kenealy, *Tichborne Trial*, 300, 398 (see above).

p. 142 **Coleridge smugly noted to himself:** Ernest H. Coleridge, *Life & Correspondence of John Duke Lord Coleridge* (London: W. Heinemann., 1904), 429.

p. 142 **Roger's aunt:** *The Times,* 27 Feb. 1872, 11.

p. 142 **Roger's cousins:** *The Times,* 28 Feb. 1872, 11.

p. 142 **French tutor:** *The Times,* 5 March 1872, 11

p. 142 **'I saw those frightful marks':** The Tichborne Case (London: Harkness, *c.* 1873), Ballad Roud No. 23628, Bodleian Libraries, Oxford.

p. 142 **'We have now heard the evidence regarding the tattoo marks':** 'The Tichborne Trial: The Tatoo Marks The Case Stopped By The Jury', *The Manchester Guardian,* 5 March 1872; 'Collapse of the Tichborne Case', *The Times*, 7 March 1872; *The Times*, 4 May 1872.

p. 142 **The Claimant had lost:** *The Spectator*, 9 March 1872.

p. 142 **he now faced a criminal trial for perjury, with an almost certain outcome:** The perjury trial is serialised in *Charge of the Lord Chief Justice of England in the Case of The Queen Against Thomas Castro* (London: Henry Sweet, 1874); *The Tichborne Trial: The Summing up of the Lord Chief Justice of England* (London: Ward, Lock and Tyler, 1874), and in Kenealy, *Trial of Tichborne* (see above). Kenealy later returned to the case in *The Tichborne Tragedy* (London: F. Griffiths, 1913). See also 'The Trial of the Tichborne Claimant', *American Law Review* 8, No. 3 (April 1874), 381–456; Charles Gavard, *A Diplomat in London* (New York: H. Holt & Co., 1897); 'The End of the Tichborne Case', *Law Journal* (7 March 1874), 123; Richard Harris, *Illustrations in Advocacy* (London: Waterlow Bros. & Layton, 1881).

p. 142 **'Oh, say I am Sir Roger ':** 'The Tichborne Case, Last Scene', *Judy*, 13 March 1872, 192.

p. 142 **His supporters ... were incensed:** *The Englishman,* 16 May 1874, 84. See also *The Englishman,* 13 June 1874, 157; anonymous, *Notebooks of a Spinster Lady* (London: Cassell, 1919), 125.

p. 143 **Subscriber newsletter:** *The Tichborne Gazette* 6, 30 July 1872, 1.

p. 142 **'T stands for Tattoo Marks':** 'A new alphabet on the Tichborne Trial' (London: Disley, 1873), Ballad Roud No. V7264, Bodleian Libraries, Oxford.

p. 143 **interest in tattooing ... rose rapidly:** 'The _____'s Tattoo', *Fun*, 22 June 1872, 253. 'The Practice of Tattooing', *Manchester Evening News*, 8 March 1872.

p. 143 **'Do you tattoo your children yet?':** 'The Uses of Tattooing', *The Saturday Review*, 16 March 1872. See also Alfred S. Taylor, *Medico-legal observations on tattoo marks as evidence of personal identity. Remarks on the Tichborne Case* (London: Guy's Hospital Reports, 1874) and Alfred S. Taylor, *The Principles and Practices of Medical Jurisprudence* Second Edition (Philadelphia, PA: 1873), chapter 44. Charles Meymott Tidy, *Legal Medicine* (New York: William Wood, 1882).

p. 143 **'tattooed on the left leg':** 'A New Custom', *New York Times*, 16 Aug. 1879; *Trewman's Exeter Flying Post*, 6 Aug. 1879; *The Times*, 26 July 1897, 1.

p.143 **instructions on how to tattoo in the manner of Roger and Lord Bellew:** 'The Method of Tattooing', *Hastings & St. Leonards Observer*, 6 Sept. 1873.

p. 143 **English tattooing was compared:** 'Tattooing, Savage and Civilised', *Cassell's Magazine*

Chapter 11: 'Some memento of their heart's history' 145

p. 145 **'I had many lady visitors ':** Jane Roth and Steven Hooper, *The Fiji Journals of Baron Anatole Von Hügel 1875–1877* (Suva: Fiji Museum, 1990), 435. The narrative of this chapter is drawn primarily from von Hügel's journals.

p. 146 **He should not have been able to be tattooed:** Karen Jacobs, *This is not a grass skirt* (Leiden: Sidestone, 2019), 107. [Sydney] *Evening News*, 26 Oct. 1871, 2. Details of *liku* and *veiqia* throughout this chapter are primarily drawn from Jacobs and Juniper Ellis, *Tattooing the World* (New York: Columbia University Press, 2008), 177–184. See also Karen Jacobs, 'The flow of things: mobilising museum collections of nineteenth century Fijian liku (fibre skirts) and veiqia (female tattooing)' in Felix Driver, Mark Nesbitt and Caroline Crush, *Mobile Museums* (London: UCL Press, 2021).

p. 146 **Von Hügel's notebooks and sketchbooks of tattooing:** *Document - Drawings and notes in Anatole von Hügel's hand on Fijian tattooing: in envelope dated 30 Sept. 1921*, VH1/5/6, and *Document - Envelope containing file of scraps of journal notebooks of precis made by Beatrice Lock, letters of Baron Anotole von Hügel during trip to Fiji 1874–1877*, VH1/2/21, Museum of Archaeology and Anthropology, University of Cambridge.

p. 147 **'old hag':** Jane Roth and StevenbHooper, *Fiji Journals*, 280 (see above).

p. 147 **Lily Langtry's husband Hugo de Bathe:** *San Francisco Call*, 8 July 1904

p. 147 **Mademoiselle Heinsel:** Jean Dorsenne, *La Vie de Bougainville* (Paris : Librairie Gallimard, 1930), 210. Philippe Mazellier (ed.), *Le Memorial Polynesien 1 1521-1833* (Papeete : Hibiscus, 1978), 193. Anne Salmond, *Aphrodite's Island* (Berkley, CA : University of California Press, 2009), 120. Michel Bideaux & Sonia Faessel (eds.), *Voyage autour du monde – Édition Critique* (Paris : Université de Sorbonne, 2001), 178 fn40. Jean-Etienne Martin-Allanic, *Bougainville navigateur et les découvertes de son temps.* Vol 2. (Paris, Universitaires de France, 1964), 271

p. 148 **John Rutherford:** Lillie George Craik, *John Rutherford, White Chief* (London: Whitcombe and Tombs, 1908). Rutherford's story is covered in detail in Chapter 16.

p. 148 **Joseph Kabris:** Jennifer Tyrell, 'Joseph Kabris and his notes on the Marquesas', *The Journal of Pacific History*, Vol. 17, No. 2 (April 1982), 101–112. Anna Felicity Friedman Herhily, 'Tattooed transculturites: Western expatriates among Amerindian and Pacific Islander societies, 1500–1900', (PhD diss., University of Chicago, 2012), 200–207.

p.148 **an American naval report:** A. Farenholt, 'Tattooing in the Navy, as shown by the records of the USS Independence', *United States Naval Medical Bulletin, January 1908* (Washington: Government Printing Office, 1908).

p. 149 **Samuel Wallis of the Dolphin:** John Hawkesworth, Phillip Carteret, Samuel Wallis and James Cook, *An account of the voyages undertaken by the order of His present Majesty for making discoveries in the Southern Hemisphere* (London: Strahn & Cadell, 1773), 27 July 1767, 482.

p. 149 **he and Cook's science officer Joseph Banks were tattooed:** Sydney Parkinson, *A Journal of a Voyage to the South Seas, in his Majesty's Ship the Endeavor* (London: Charles Dilly and James Phillips, 1784), 25. The existence of Banks's tattoo is revealed in a letter from Charles Davy. J.C. Beaglehole (ed.) *The Endeavour Journal of Joseph Banks 1768–1771* (Sydney: Angus & Robertson, 1962), Vol. 1, 41.

p. 149 **Royal Navy and others began to specifically record the 'distinguishing marks':** Matt Lodder, '"Things of the Sea": Iconographic continuities between tattooing and handicrafts in Georgian-era maritime culture', *Sculpture Journal*, Vol. 24, No. 2 (2015), 195–210.

p. 149 **Henry Balfour thought:** Henry Balfour, *Evolution of a Decorative Art* (New York: Macmillan, 1893), 72–73.

p. 150 **some memento of their heart's history:** Basil Thomson, *The Fijians* (London: William Heinemann, 1908), 220.

p. 150 **'put on by some white, rather than by themselves':** J.W. Osborn, *Journal of Passages Made by the Ship Emerald of Salem* [Manuscript on microfilm] (1833–1836). Peabody Essex Museum, Phillips Library, Salem MA, as cited in Jacobs *Not a Grass Skirt*, 147–148.

p. 150 **Jacques Arago:** Jaques Arago, *Promenade autour du Monde* (Paris: Leblanc, 1822). Peter Brown, 'Jacques Arago: the Artist As Social Scientist In a World In Transition', *The Great Circle* 39, No. 2 (2017), 120–148.

p. 150 **tattooing in the Pacific can currently be dated back to at least 700**

BCE: Benoît Robitaille, 'A Preliminary Typology of Perpendicularly Hafted Bone Tipped Tattooing Instruments: Toward a Technological History of Oceanic Tattooing', in Christian Gates St. Pierre and Renee Beauchamp Walker (eds.) *Bones as Tools* (Montreal: Archaeopress, 2007), Chapter 12. Geoffrey Clark and Michelle Langley, 'Ancient Tattooing in Polynesia', *Journal of Island and Coastal Archaeology*, Vol. 15, No. 3 (2020).

p. 151 **from time immemorial:** 'Tattooing', *The Literary Gazette*, 20 Feb. 1819, 126

p. 151 **'An Ancient Custom':** *The Graphic,* 20 March 1880.

p. 151 **Martin Hildebrandt joked:** 'The Tattooing Artist', *The Sun* [New York], 18 Dec. 1872.

p. 152 **Bartholomew Savage:** *Maryland Gazette*, 27 Aug. 1761.

p. 152 **James Smith:** *Pennsylvania Gazette*, 28 Sept. 1752.

p. 152 **Richard Kibble:** *Virginia Gazette (Parks)*, 9 June 1738.

p. 152 **Henry Byam Martin:** Anne D'Alleva, 'Christian Skins: *Tatau* and the Evangelization of the Society Islands and Samoa' in Thomas, Cole and Douglas (eds), *Tattoo*, 90–108. Henry Byam Martin, *The Polynesian Journal* (Canberra: ANUP, 1981), 6 April 1847, 126.

p. 153 **permitted under British law:** G.R. Dartnell, 'Branding in the Army', *British Medical Journal* (1861), 9 Feb. 155. Peter Burroughs, 'Crime and Punishment in the British Army, 1815–1870', *The English Historical Review* 100, No. 396 (1985), 545–571.

Chapter 12: 'Elegant specimen of chromatic needlework' 155

p. 155 **'Come good Horitoyo':** 'The Tattooing Fad', *LA Times*, 23 Dec. 1900.

p. 155 **'Queen of Bohemia':** 'Prepare to be startled ...', *Philadelphia Enquirer*, 4 Dec. 1921.

p. 156 **when society wants to be tattooed:** 'Hori Toyo, Royal Tattooer in Town', *San Francisco Examiner*, 25 Nov. 1900.

p. 156 **small black bag:** 'The Orient in London', *Daily Mail*, 3 Nov. 1897, 7.

p. 156 **son of a vet:** 'Jap, with English Wife', *Brooklyn Daily Eagle*, 4 Dec. 1898, 67. Marriage Certificate Yoshisuke Kudo and Annie Ashton, GRO COL210396/2021, General Records Office, London.

p. 157 **wealthy clients across Europe:** 'Royalty Tattooed', *Dundee Courier &Argus*, 17 Jan. m1899, 4; 'All Along the Line', *LA Times*, 28 Nov. 1900; 'Frogs', *Cincinnati Enquirer*, 9 Dec. 1900.

p. 157 **prominent clients:** 'Tattooing is a new social craze', *Chicago Daily Tribune*, 8 Jan. 1899; 'He Tattooed Royalty', *New York Herald*, 1 Jan. 1899.

p. 157 **at least one advert:** *Weekly Dispatch*, 5 June 1898.

p. 157 **ejected from a Liverpool boarding house:** *Liverpool Workhouse Register* Peter Y. Kudo 353 SEL/19/55, 1896, Liverpool Record Office.

p. 157 **In New York:** *Passenger and Crew Lists of Vessels Arriving at New York, New York, 1897–1957.* Microfilm Serial T715, 1897–1957; Line: 21; Page Number: 83 *Campania*, National Archives at Washington, D.C; *Boston Globe*, 16 March 1900.

p.157 **The going rate for Japanese tattooing in New York:** 'Answers to Correspondents', *Vogue* [New York], 25 Jan. 1894.

p. 157 **'after shaving the flesh ':** 'Up-to-Date Tattooing', *Arkansas City Daily Traveller*, 16 Feb. 1898.

p. 158 **the advert proclaimed:** *New York Times*, 26 March 1899.

p. 158 **they had met ... the most famous tattoo artist in the world:** Aimee Crocker, *Without Regrets* (London: R. Hale, 1937), Chapter XIV.

p. 159 **only blossomed in the late eighteenth and early nineteenth centuries:** W.R. van Gulik, *Irezumi – The Pattern of Dermatography in Japan* (Leiden: Brill, 1982).

p. 160 **Chiyo worked out of a curio shop:** Basil Hall Chamberlain and W.B Mason, *A Handbook for Travellers in Japan* (3rd edition. New York: Charles Scribner's Sons, 1893). Yoshimi Yamamoto, *Horichiyo Report* (Tsuru: Tsurua University, March 2022).

p. 160 **Singapore, Hong Kong and Malta:** Yoshimi Yamamoto, 'Japanese Tattooists in Hongkong in the late 19th and 20th Century', *Seikei ronsō* (Political Economy Review), 85/3. 2017, 313–350. Yoshimi Yamamoto, 'Japanese tattooing as souvenirs for foreign travellers in the late 19th and early 20th century', *Nihon kenkyū* 63 (2021).

p. 160 **The princes had famously been tattooed:** Norobu Koyama, 'Japanese Tattooists and the British Royal Family During the Meiji Period' in *Japan: Biographical Portraits*. Vol. VI (ed. Hugh Cortazzi), (Leiden: Global Oritenal, 2007), 72. *Letter from John Dalton to the Princess of Wales*, 31 Oct. 1881. RA VIC/Z 474/9, Royal Archives. 'Of Interest to Her', *Vogue* [New York], 13 May 1893.

p.160 **Chiyo's fame:** Charles M. Taylor Jr, *Vacation Days in Hawaii and Japan* (London: T. Fisher Unwin, 1906), 140. 'The Apelles of Japanese Tattooers', *Pall Mall Gazette*, 7 May 1889, 3. Gambier Bolton, 'Pictures on the Human Skin', *The Strand Magazine*, April 1897, 428.

p.160 **Charles Longfellow:** Christine Guth, *Longfellow's Tattoos* (Seattle, WA: University of Washington Press, 2004).

p. 160 **William Henry Furness**: 'Artistic Tattooing', *The Oregonian*, 17 July 1894, 7. William Henry Furness, *The Home-Life of Borneo Headhunters* (Philadelphia: J.N. Lippincott, 1902), 102.

p. 161 **New York Racquet Club:** 'Tattooing is not Uncommon', *New York Times*, 18 April 1893. 'Tattooing is on Increase', *New York Times*, 24 April 1908. 'Society takes up tattooing fad', *Chicago Tribune,* 1 May 1904.

p. 161 **Martin Hildebrandt:** *The Sun* [New York], 18 Dec. 1872. See also 'Tattooing in New York', *New York Times*, 16 Jan. 1876; 'Tattooing amongst Fashionable Folks', *New York Times*, 20 Aug. 1882; Carmen Nyssen, 'Saloon-Tattoo Shops of New York City's 4th Ward', Buzzworthy Tattoo History. https://web.archive.org/web/20220606003124/https://buzzworthy tattoo.com/saloon-tattoo-shops-of-new-york-citys-4th-ward/. H. Wilson, *New York City Directory for the year ending May 1, 1859* (New York: Trow, 1858), 372.

p. 161 **Tom Riley had hosted Toyo:** *Sporting Times*, 6 Aug. 1898, 8.

p. 161 **moved to San Francisco:** *Topeka State Journal*, 12 January 1901. 'Have you been tattooed?', *Philadelphia Enquirer*, 1 Jan. 1901.

p. 161 **Alabama:** *Selma Times*, 6 Jan. 1901.

p. 162 **in full colour:** *New York Sunday World*, 16 June 1901.

p. 162 **snake-shaped paperweights:** 'Latest Fad of the tour', *New York Morning Telegraph*, 4 March 1900.

p. 162 **'elegant specimen of chromatic needlework':** 'Preposterous honeymoon triangle of our tattooed countess', *The Times* [Shreveport, LA], 22 Nov. 1925, 55.

p. 162 **'The practical joke, with its rather mean twist':** Aimee Crocker, *And I'd Do it Again* (New York, Coward McCann, 1936).

PART FOUR: TATTOOING IN THE EARLY TWENTIETH CENTURY 165

p. 167 **'O, Fashion!':** Cesare Lombroso, 'The Savage Origin of Tattooing', *Popular Science Monthly*, Vol. 48 (April 1896).

p. 167 **'Gentleman, Interested in Tattooing':** *Punch*, 11 Feb. 1920, 118.

p. 167 ***Life* Magazine:** 'The New Order', *Life*, 10 Dec. 1914, 1066–1068.

p. 168 **decadent teenage craze:** 'Les Quat'z Arts', *Le Supplement*, 23 June 1898.

p. 168 ***Deranged People of Paris*:** René Schwaeblé, *Les détraquées de Paris, Etude de moeurs contemporaines* (Paris: H. Daragon, 1910).

p. 169 **tattooing diffused into every social stratum:** 'Modern Fashions in Tattooing', *Vanity Fair*, Jan. 1926, 43.

p.170 **Thomas Chapman:** 'Death from tattooing', *Liverpool Echo*, 11 Oct. 1880.

p. 170 **'Numbers of people got tattooed':** 'Tattooing', *The Sketch*, 16 June 1897.

p. 170 **He had been an Army telegraph engineer:** Matt Lodder, 'Sutherland Macdonald, tattoo artist', *Oxford Dictionary of National Biography* (2016). https://doi.org/10.1093/ref:odnb/100996

p. 170 **visibly working:** *The Post Office Directory for London, Streets & Commercial* (London: Kelly's Directories, 1894).

p. 170 **coined the term 'tattooist':** Gambier Bolton, 'A Tattoo Artist', *Pearson's Magazine*, Aug. 1902, 175.

p.171 **usually lasted between one and six hours:** 'An English Tattooer', *Pall Mall Gazette*, May 1889.

p. 171 **one to two month's wages:** Arthur Bowley, *Wages in the United Kingdom in the Nineteenth Century* (London: C.J. Clay, 1900), 52.

p. 171 **'elevated to a place among the arts':** 'Tattooing as a fine art', *Boston Daily Globe*, 29 Dec. 1892.

p. 171 **'the most artistic tattooer in the world':** 'A Chat with a "Tattooer"', *The Sketch*, Jan. 1895, 633.

p. 171 **'I charge pretty high':** 'Tattooing as a fine art', *Boston Daily Globe*, 29 Dec. 1892.

p. 171 **cut chunks of skin out of his arm:** 'A Chat with a "Tattooer"', *The Sketch*, Jan. 1895, 633.

p. 171 **'system of disinfecting':** Gambier Bolton, 'A Tattoo Artist' (see above).

p. 172 **cocaine:** 'An English Tattooer', *Pall Mall Gazette*, May 1889.

p. 172 **'countess or two':** 'Now 'tis tattooing', *Boston Daily Globe*, May 1893, 10. 'Tattooing: Sutherland Macdonald [advertising handbill]', *Letters to W.S. Brooks* BMU 433.20.2 Spec. Coll. Archives Ernst Mayr Library, Harvard University.

p. 172 **Gamage's of Holborn:** *A. W. Gamage Ltd Sports, Cycle, Motor and General Outfitters General Catalogue* (London: A.W. Gamage, 1911), 999. I have recorded tattoo equipment in four editions: 1911, 1915, and two further earlier single undatable pages, both in private collections.

p. 174 **MacDonald's business was waning:** letters from Sutherland Macdonald to W.S. Brooks, *Letters to W.S. Brooks* BMU 433.20.2 Spec. Coll. Archives Ernst Mayr Library, Harvard University. See also 'Tattooing on the wane' *Tulsa Daily World,* 15 Sept. 1916; 'The Practice of Tattooing', *The Lethbridge Herald*, 22 Nov. 1935, 9.

p. 174 **'picture after picture':** *Daily Mail*, 16 Dec. 1921. See also 'London's new fad', *Richmond Daily Register*, 10 June 1922; 'Gossip of the day', *Sunday Post*, 6 Nov. 1927; 'Tattooing à la mode', *Daily Mail (Atlantic Edition)*, 17 March 1930, 4; 'Film fans fall for tattoo craze', *Guide & Ideas,* 7 Jan. 1939.

p. 174 **to a tiny shed perched on its roof:** Dudley Barker, 'This Tattooing Business', *Evening Standard*, Feb. 1937. 'No. 76 (and additional premises in rear)', *Crown Estate Commissioners and predecessors: Registered Files on Estates Remaining in Crown Possession after 1940* CRES 35/2108, National Archives, London. I am grateful to Malcolm Shifrin for sharing this finding with me.

p. 175 **Fukushi had a bag … stolen:** *Fukushi hakase kanreki shukuga kinen-shi* (Dr. Fukushi 60th Birthday Celebration Commemorative Magazine), (Tokyo: Commemorative Publishing Department, 1942). 'Lost and Found', *Chicago Tribune*, 5 Feb. 1928.

p.175 **undertake a collecting programme:** Fukushi's collecting began in around 1915, with his collection first exhibited at the Osaka Hygiene Expo. 'Osaka Hygiene Expo – Postcard 4' 1321/11–4, Nomura Co. Reference Room, Osaka. *Mínsú yìshù* [Folk Art], Issue 8, 1929. See also 'Speaking of pictures', *Life*, 21 Oct. 1941; Don Ed Hardy, *Tattoo Time Volume 4: Life & Death Tattoos* (Honoloulu, HW: Hardy Marks, 1987).

p. 175 **Professor Sharkey:** 'Modern Fashions in Tattooing', *Vanity Fair,* Jan. 1926, 43.

Chapter 13: 'I Just Love Sailor Boys' 177

p. 177 **'I'm having New York Pete tattoo me arms and chest':** 'She just loves sailor boys', *Detroit Free Press,* 15 Sept. 1906.

p. 177 **'pretty and exceptionally well-developed':** 'Navy = Mad Lass is Tattooed ', *Pittsburgh Press*, 20 Sept. 1906.

p. 177 **freshly tattooed design:** Madeline's tattoos are described in 'Three men held for tattooing young girl', *The Standard Union*, 14 Sept. 1906. See also 'She cannot go to sea', *Syracuse Herald*, 23 Sept. 1906; 'Brooklyn Girl with Taste for Sea Life goes to Reformatory', *New York Times*, 16 Sept. 1906.

p. 178 **'All the girls are getting it done':** 'Girl wants to be a sailor', *New York Times*, 15 Sept. 1906. 'Girl Frightfully Tattooed', *New York Press*, 15 Sept. 1906. Another young woman getting tattooed by a Bowery sailor is illustrated in 'Crazy summer fad', *Nickerson Argosy*, 3 Oct. 1901.

p.179 **'Mania to be tattooed':** 'Mania to be tattooed may cost Madeline dear', *Brooklyn Daily Eagle*, 14 Sept. 1906.

p. 179 **'A museum store in Scotland':** 'Proceedings of the Anatomical Society of Great Britain and Ireland', *Journal of Anatomy and Physiology*, Vol. 27, Part 1 (1892), ii. 'Donor. Dr Biggam. Museum Marks: Specimen consists of sheet of skin from back – depiction "Death of Aurora" and numerous other pieces of art – marine and otherwise', Anatomical Museum, University of Edinburgh 4805/4806.

p. 180 **'No pains and no money ':** New York Society for the Prevention of Cruelty to Children, *Twenty-Seventh Annual Report* (New York: NYSPCC, 1901), 6.

p. 181 **fifteen-year-old girl named Hannah:** New York Society for the Prevention of Cruelty to Children, *Twenty-Fourth Annual Report* (New York: NYSPCC, 1898). 12 May Case 115,723, 35. *Documents of the Assembly of the State of New York* Vol. II (New York: Wynkoop Hallenbeck Crawford, 1899), 43.

p. 181 **Tattooing minors was not specifically illegal:** Section 289 New York Penal Code made it a misdemeanour to 'endanger the life, health or morals of a child under sixteen years of age'. William H. Silvernail, *The Penal Code of the State of New York* (Albany, NY: W.C. Little, 1906), 126.

p. 181 **Charlie Wagner:** 'Tattooed Children astonish teachers', *Los Angeles Times*, 1 Nov. 1902. 'Tattooed Crucifix on Hebrew Child', *Morning Call*, 26 Sept. 1902.

p. 182 **imprisonment for tattooing an eleven-year-old boy:** 'To be tried for tattooing', *New York Sun*, 17 July 1906.

p. 182 **each man was charged:** *Court of Special Session*, 20 and 21 Sept. 1906 [microfilm], 65–66. New York Municipal Archives. See also 'Punish Men who tattooed girl with naval penchant', *New York Evening Telegram*, 16 Sept. 1906; 'Girl's tattooers sent to prison', *New York Times*, 21 Sept. 1906.

p. 182 **a bitter public feud with O'Reilly:** Tattoo artists at war', *New York Times*, 1 Jan. 1900. For more on Getchell and O'Reilly see Albert Parry, *Secrets of a Strange Art* (New York: Simon & Schuster, 1933).

p. 183 **heinous practice of disfiguring young girls:** *Brooklyn Daily Eagle*, 14 Sept. 1906.

p. 183 **'sea-madness':** 'Girl Sailor in Court', *Brooklyn Daily Eagle*, 15 Sept. 1906.

p. 183 **girls, some of them very young girls:** George J. Kneeland, *Commercialized Prostitution in New York City* (New York: The Century Co., 1913), 256.

p. 183 **It had the air more of a prison than an institution of care:** Cole Thompson and Don Rice, *Lost Inwood* (Charleston, NC: Arcadia, 2019).

p. 183 **a home to 107 young women:** Kneeland, *Commercialized Prostitution*, 256 (see above).

p. 184 **Annie Sigalove:** 'Heads shaved to punish', *New York Times*, 27 Oct. 1895.

p. 184 **Josephine Hall:** 'Suicide in House of Mercy', *New York Times*, 1 Nov. 1907.

p. 184 **Isabel Cowan:** 'Girl lived in the park for three months', *New York Evening World*, 29 July 1905. 'Girls Run Wild in the Park', *New York Sun*, 30 July 1905.

p. 184 **resident girls started a riot:** 'Mercy House Girls start riot, 3 escape', *New York Times*, 25 April 1915.

p. 184 **'I wish I was dead':** Morris Markey, 'Reporter at Large: Inwood', *New Yorker*, 9 Dec. 1933, 92.

p. 184 **married Frederick Perry Dickinson Jr:** 'Madeline Altman', *Marriage Indexes; Index Type: Bride; Year Range: 1904–1909; Surname Range: A – C 7/596* 1908, New Jersey State Archives. *Federal Census* 1900; Brooklyn Ward 28, Kings, New York; Roll: 1067; Page: 2; Enumeration District: 0518; FHL microfilm: 1241067. *New York State Census 1915*, Election District: 21; Assembly District: 05; City: New York; County: Kings; Page: 24, New York State Archives. *Federal Census* 1920; Justice Precinct 8, El Paso, Texas; Roll: T625_1799; Page: 31B; Enumeration District: 100.

p. 185 **Fred was dating another woman:** Fred's second wife Vera Cone hosted Fred, without Madeline, at a party. *El Paso Herald*, 26 Dec. 1922. Their engagement was announced in August 1923. *El Paso Sun Times*, 12 Aug. 1923. *Marriage Records. District of Columbia Marriages*, 9 Sept. 1923, Film 002293230, Clerk of the Superior Court, Records Office, Washington D.C.

p. 185 **'pioneer residents':** 'Cpl. C. E. Dickinson dies', *El Paso Herald*, 10 Oct. 1918.

p. 185 **He died:** *El Paso Times*, 26 Sept. 1936. *Interment Control Forms, 1928–1962*. A1 2110-B. NAID: 5833879. Record Group 92, Records of the Office of the Quartermaster General, 1774–1985. The National Archives at St. Louis, St. Louis, MO.

Chapter 14: 'Tattooing is in Fashion' 187

p. 187 **'I've simply got to tell you':** 'Dress and other vanities', *The Bunbury Herald and Blackwood Express*, SW Australia, 5 July 1929.

p. 187 **She had collected them from tattoo artists:** 'The New Beach Costumes', *San Antonio Light*, 16 June 1929. 'Novel Bathing Suits', *Newcastle Sun* [Newcastle, Australia], 23 Oct. 1929.

p. 187 **barely caused a ripple in ... *Vogue*:** 'Notes on the Collections', *Vogue* [New York], 13 April 1929, 208.

p. 188 **Their French counterparts:** *Vogue* [Paris], July 1929, 48.

p. 188 **'delicately defined designs knitted in blue navy wool':** 'Pinafore bathing suit fashion serves a dual purpose', *Daily Telegraph*, 17 July 1929. 'Dressing comfortably for sports for the sea and by the sea', *Good Housekeeping*, Jun 1929, 76–77.

p. 188 ***New York Times*:** 'Seen at Paris showings', *New York Times*, 3 March 1929. 'Paris goes for a swim', *New York Times*, 7 July 1929

p. 188 ***'amusing'*:** *Table Talk* [Melbourne, Australia], 15 Aug. 1929, 31.

p. 188 **The provincial newspapers of Virginia:** 'Fishermen inspire clothes for the beach', *Richmond Times Dispatch*, 9 June 1929.

p. 188 **'imitate the tattooing on sailors ':** 'Bathing Modes for Women' *Advertiser Adelaide*, 13 Aug. 1929. 'Ritzy Roasalie', *Des Moines Tribune Capital*, 16 May 1929.

p. 188 **'lizarding suit':** *Delineator*, July 1929, 25.

p. 189 **Elsa Schiaparelli had studied philosophy:** Meryle Seacrest, *Elsa Schiaparelli: A Biography* (London: Penguin, 2015). See also Elsa Schiaparelli, *A Shocking Life* (London: Dutton, 1954); Susan Goldman Rubin, *Hot Pink: The Life and Fashions of Elsa Schiaparelli* (New York: Abrams, 2015).

p. 190 **she had a philosophy about clothes:** Caroline Evans 'Masks, Mirrors and Mannequins: Elsa Schiaparelli and the Decentered Subject', *Fashion Theory*, 3:1 (1999), 3–31. Robyn Gibson, 'Schiaparelli, Surrealism and the Desk Suit', *Dress*, 30:1 (2003), 48–58.

p. 190 **'we arrived in bathing suits':** Elsa Schiaparelli, 'My slightly shocking life in high fashion', *Maclean's Magazine*, 15 Oct. 1954, 104.

p. 191 **'the less a man clothes himself':** Wilhelm Joest, *Tätowieren, Narbenzeichnen und Körperbemalen* (Berlin: A. Asher & Co., 1887).

p. 191 **Hermann Heinrich Ploss and Max Bartels:** Hermann Heinrich Ploss and Max Bartels, *Das Weib In der Natur- und Völkerheit*, Vol. I (Leipzig: Th. Grieben, 1905), 139–140.

p. 191 **French humourists were already posting scornful cartoons:** 'Le Train N'1880', *Le Caricature*, Supplément 53, 1881; 'L'Étoffe Manque: Comment font les Coutouriers?', *La Vie Parisienne*, 12 June, 1920; 'L'Heure du Bain', *Le Rire*, 7 Aug. 1920; *'Notes et croquis d'un vulgaire profane'*, *La Vie Parisienne*, 12 Nov. 1921, 167; 'Nouveau salon de Peinture', *Fantasio*, 1 Feb. 1927, 360.

p. 192 **speculative designs for 'lovers' and 'generals' wives':** *'La Mode (?) des Bas Pients'*, *La Vie Parisienne*, 8 March 1913, 179.

p. 192 **'Bad taste!':** 'Mauvais gout!', *Petit Journal*, 7 Dec. 1922, 6.

p. 192 **Women who had been tattooed in earlier decades:** 'Lady Londonderry's Dashion-Setting Tattooed Legs', *American Weekly*, 17 July 1938, 5. 'Tattooed Marchioness', *Life*, 18 July 1938.

p. 193 **'the effect of tattooing is produced':** Wilfrid Mark Webb, *The Heritage of Dress* (London: E. Grant Richards, 1908), 70.

p. 193 **'so delicately executed ':** René Schwaeblé, *Les détraquées de Paris, Etude de moeurs contemporaines* (Paris: H. Daragon, 1910).

p. 193 **intimate nipple piercings:** 'Wounds', *English Mechanic and World of Science*, 26 July 1889, 1270, 460–461. See also prior correspondence in Issues 1252, 1254, 1259. Mme Beaumont', the likely piercer and jeweller cited in *EMWS*, worked at 3, Rue St. Martin. *Paris-addresses*, (Paris: Ch. Avaloine et cie 1893), 2251 & (1900), 137. 'Breast Rings', *Society*, 17 June 1897. Also see *Sydney Truth*, 1 Oct. 1899; Iwan Bloch, *A History of English Sexual Morals* (London: Francis Aldor, 1936), 497; Erna Neumann, *John Bull beim Erziehen* Vol II (Dresden: Dohrn, 1901), 15, 24, 29, 55, 84.

p. 193 **scandalised tales of ... tattooed young women:** 'Les Quat'z Arts', *Le Supplement*, 23 June 1898. 'Jambes peintes', *Paris Soir*, 22 July 1925.

p. 193 **Foujita had tattooed several French women:** 'La Cena de los Burlas', *La Voz*, 3 Aug. 1929. See also Marie-Claire Dumas, *Robert Desnos Oeuvres* (Malesherbes: Gallimard, 2011), 626, 732–33; 'Chairs ornementées', *Aux écoutes*, 3 Aug. 1929, 12.

p. 194 **'Youki' Badoul, had a mermaid tattooed on her leg:** Robert Doiseneau, *Youki Desnos' Thigh Tatoo Of Foujita* (*c.* 1950). 121512237 Getty Images, Gamma Legends. Yamamoto, *Hori Chiyo Report*, 6. Bookplate included in a copy of Robert Desnos *La Liberté ou L'Amour* (Paris: Simon Kra, 197) sold at Pierre Bergé, Paris, *A Thousand Nights of Dreams – Geneviève & Jean-Paul Kahn Collection III*, 18 June 2021, Lot 141. https://web.archive.org/web/20220826100524/https://www.pba-auctions.com/en/lot/111556/15054165?offset=100& See also.

p. 194 **tattoo-themed knitwear:** 'Tatouages: Note Personelle', *Marie-Claire* [Paris], 15 July 1938.

p. 194 **tattoo designs to decorate sweaters and skirts:** *Les Modes Mensuel*, 1 July 1933, 16.

p. 194 ***Sleeping*:** *Harper's Bazaar* [New York], Aug. 1943, 110B.

p. 194 **stockings:** 'Exotica of Beauty', *Cosmopolitan* [New York], June 1959, 49. *Stockings*, 1997. 193. 5a–s, Metropolitan Museum of Art. *25th March 1959: A man examines a prototype of a new range of hand-painted stockings with a leaf motif by the designer Elsa Schiaparelli*, 3167002, Getty Images, Keystone Archive.

p. 194 **Ginger Rogers:** *Carefree,* directed by Mark Sandrich (RKO, 1938), 30:22.

p. 194 **Swanson:** 'That "Tattooed Lady" ...', *Helena Independent*, 14 July 1941.

p. 194 **LA Darling Suse**: 'Suse Sweaters', *Life Magazine*, 27 Jan. 1947, 75–78.

p. 194 **Issey Miyake:** Issey Miyake and Makiko Minagawa, *Dress 'Tattoo'* [clothing] (Issey Miyake, Autumn/Winter, 1971), Kyoto Costume Institute.

p. 194 **Sinead O'Connor:** *LOS ANGELES – FEBRUARY 22: Musician Sinead O'Connor attends the 31st Annual Grammy Awards on February 22, 1989 at Shrine Auditorium in Los Angeles, California,* 162199996, Getty Images, Ron Gallella Collection.

p. 194 **Jean-Paul Gaultier:** Adam Geczy, Vicki Karaminas and Justine Taylor, 'Sailor Style: Representations of the Mariner in Popular Culture and Contemporary Fashion', *Journal of Asia-Pacific Pop Culture*, Vol. 1, No. 2 (2016), 141–164.

p. 194 **'the ultimate in individualised body enhancement':** 'Body Language', *Vogue* (New York), 1 April 1994.

Chapter 15: 'Hurt Like Fun' 197

p. 197 **'The bright tattoo marks on her left arm':** Fred Dickenson, 'Queen Betty's Latest Conquest', *The American Weekly*, 4 May 1947.

p. 197 **'come out of the womb queer':** Kate Summerscale, *The Queen of Whale Quay* (London: Bloomsbury, 2012), 14. Much of Carstairs' biography as related here is sourced from Summerscale. See also Mark Pottle, 'Carstairs, Joe [formerly Marion Barbara] 1900≠1993', *Oxford Dictionary of National Biography* (2004), https://doi.org/10.1093/ref:odnb/65768.

p. 197 **an icon of queer history:** Barbara Grier, 'The Possibilities are staggering' [Speech delivered at 2nd Annual Lesbian Writers Conference, 19 Sept. 1975] (Chicago: Womanpress, 1976), Part 3: Feminism-International Lesbian Movement, Folder No.: 06160, Lesbian Herstory Archives, New York. 'The Queen of Whale Quay', *Outlines*, 29 April 1998, 14.

p. 198 **not butch:** Kate Summerscale, *Queen*, 73 (see above).

p. 199 **Serge Voronoff:** Serge Voronoff, *Greffes Testiculaires* (Paris, Librairie Octave Doin, 1923). See also Serge Voronoff, *Testicular grafting from ape to man* (London: Brentano's, 1930); Catherine Rémy, 'Men seeking monkey-glands: the controversial xenotransplantations of Doctor Voronoff, 1910–30', *French History*, Vol. 28, Issue 2 (June 2014), 226–240; 'Mystery Yet Surrounding Strange Transformation', *The State* (Columbia, SC), 30 Oct. 1933; *Lesbian Scrapbook (Kinsey/Katz) 1930s*, Allan Berube Papers, Series III, Box 82, Folder 28, GLBT Historical Society.

p. 199 **'a man's spirit, viewpoint and force':** Nancy Madison, 'The "Paradise" the Heiress Crusoe Found', *Ogden Standard Examiner*, 16 Jan. 1938, 22.

p. 200 **Joe once turned up to meet Marlene Dietrich:** 'The Untold Story of Marlene Dietrich', *Confidential*, July 1955, 58.

p. 200 **'tattoo things on a forearm':** Alice Hughes, 'A Woman's New York', *Shreveport Journal*, 16 April 1941, 5. John J. Vincent, 'Betty Carstairs, Major Seagrave's Successor, to race Gar Wood boat today', *Coshocton Tribune*, 30 Aug. 1930.

p. 200 **'strong, tattooed arms, gripping the wheel':** Hardin Burnley, 'Sports Features', *Clarion-Ledger* [Jackson, MI], 29 Aug. 1930, 10.

p. 200 **'not exactly delicate epidermis':** Maury Paul, 'Metropolitain Smart Set', *San Francisco Examiner*, 31 March 1941.

p. 200 **blue and red designs dear to sailors:** 'Betty Carstairs will make final try for prize', *Press and Sun Bulletin*, 13 Aug. 1930, 27.

p. 201 **'hurt like fun':** Nancy Madison, 'Heiress Crusoe' (see above).

p. 201 **Norman 'Sailor Jerry' Collins:** Don Ed Hardy, *Sailor Jerry Collins,*

American Tattoo Master (Honoloulu, HW: Hardt Marks, 1994). Nick Schonberger, *Homeward Bound: The Life and Times of Hori Smoku Sailor Jerry* (Sailor Jerry Ltd., 2010).

p. 201 **Domingo Galang:** Carmen Nyssen, 'Domingo Galang', *Buzzworthy Tattoo History* (2017). https://web.archive.org/web/20170817041907/https://buzzworthytattoo.com/tattoo-artists-tattooed-people/domingo-galang/

p. 202 **'a young woman of striking appearance':** 'E.J.S.', 'Motor Boat Notable', *Harrisburg Telegraph*, 9 March 1932, 6. A Pennsylvania newspaper went with 'stout-hearted' Bob Considine, 'On the Line', *The Scranton Tribune*, 11 March 1940.

p. 202 **Mathilde and Mathias Vaerting:** Mathilde and Mathias Vaerting, *The Dominant Sex* (London: George Allen & Unwin, 1923).

p. 203 **'vogueish unisex adornments':** Melanie Phillips, 'Seeing tattoos makes me feel physically sick', *The Times,* 8 Feb. 2022.

p. 204 **'The arts of the toilet become a pastime':** Mathilde and Mathias Vaerting, *Dominant Sex*, 91–94 (see above).

p. 205 **overemphasised her masculinity:** Harry Benjamin, 'Transsexualism and Transvestism as Psychosomatic and Somato–Psychic Syndromes', *American Journal of Psychotherapy*, Vol. 8, Issue 2 (1954), 219–230.

p. 205 **'a most unconvincing woman':** Erickson Educational Foundation 'Counseling the Transexual' [pamphlet] (Baton Rouge, LA : Erickson Educational Foundation, *c.* 1974), *Leaflets and Pamphlets for Transsexuals and Transvestites*. Albany Trust 14: Other Organisations, 1962–1985 (1967–1974) 14/44 Reel 47, London School of Economics and Political Science Library.

p.205 **unable to wear a sleeveless dress:** Anonymous, 'Tattoos Anyone?', *Femme Mirror*, Vol. 6., No. 5, Oct. 1981, 5.

p. 205 ***Rites of Passage*:** 'Dick on Jane', *Screw,* 15 March 1990, 14. *Transgender*, 15 March 1977–30 August 2002 and undated, Part 6: Spinsters-Youth Folder No.: 14730, Lesbian Herstory Archives, New York.

p. 206 **Modern social science research:** Laura Ragmanauskaite, Jin Kim, Qi Zhang et al., 'Self-reported tattoo prevalence and motivations in transgender adults: a cross-sectional survey', *Dermatology Online*, Vol. 26, Issue 12 (2020).

p. 206 **'I'm planning tattoo sleeves':** Halo Jedha Dawn, 'Gender Creative Parenting and Me' in Laura Kate Dale (ed.), *Gender Euphoria* (Unbound, 2021).

p. 206 **'tattoos bring gender home':** Emmett Nahil, 'Epidermis: Tattoos and Transmasculine Selfhood' in Dale, *Gender Euphoria* (see above).

p. 207 **'fuck-awful cold':** Kate Summerscale, *Queen*, 187 (see above).

Chapter 16: 'Blue All Over' 209

p. 209 **'PART MAN! PART MONSTER!':** 'The Great Omi' [handbill], verso, Private Collection. An example of this card was sold on eBay by Vasta (vastaimagesbooks), April 2020. 'AMERICAN 1940 THE GREAT OMI FACIAL TATTOO SIGNED PITCH CARD ~ VASTA ARCHIVE'.

Worthpoint.com, https://web.archive.org/web/20220826160828/https://www.worthpoint.com/worthopedia/american-1940-great-omi-facial-tattoo-2056004684. An alternate version of the card was published in 'The Omi Letters', *Tattoo International* Issue 184 (Spring 2013), 41–42. See also *The Great Omi* (Winston Salem, NC: The Tattoo Archive, 2021).

p. 209 **'two handwritten letters':** Judy Tutle, 'Omi, you were great', *Tattoo Historian* 10 (Fall 1986), 17–23, 32–36.

p. 210 **'his father William':** 'Knaresborough Road, Ecclesall Bierlow, Yorkshire & Yorkshire (West Riding), England', *1891 Census of England, Wales & Scotland,* Eccleshall 65, RG12/3812, 16, PRO, National Archvies, London. Max O'Donnell, 'True Blue', *Evening Argus*, 7 May 1948.

p. 210 **private school:** *The Elstonian Association Register*, Bedford Middle Class Public School (1898) X271/5/2 Bedfordshire & Luton Archive Services. 'Tattooed from head to foot', *Evening Telegraph*, 19 Jan. 1933, 4.

p. 210 **tutored by his father's groom:** 'Mystery Man', *Sussex Daily News*, 19 Aug. 1935.

p. 211 **he was a handsome, upstanding, regular Army officer:** Max O'Donnell, 'True Blue' (see above).

p. 211 **machine gun squadron of the Westminster Dragoons** 'Horace Leonard Ridler', *Medal Index Cards* WWI, Army Medal Office (In the Care of the Western Front Association Website); London, England.

p. 211 **invested ... in a chicken farm:** 'The Blue Major' [Press clipping, source unknown], *E.H. Cookridge Fonds*, Box 1, File 8, McMaster University Library and Archives.

p. 211 **Horace urgently needed an act:** 'Le Grand Omi, le suel homme bleu', *Comoedia*, 16 June 1935.

p. 212 **John Rutherford:** James Drummond (ed.), *John Rutherford: The White Chief* (Christchurch, NZ: Whitcombe and Tombs, n.d.).

p.212 **Very little of Rutherford's account can be corroborated:** W.L. Williams, 'The Story of John Rutherford', *Transactions and Proceedings of the Royal Society of New Zealand 1890,* Vol. 23 (1890), 460. See also Leonard Bell, 'A portrait that asks questions', *Journal of New Zealand & Pacific Studies*, Vol. 7, Issue 1 (2019), 7–17; Annie Werner, 'Savage Skins', *Kunapipi,* Vol. 27, Issue 1 (2005), 11–25.

p. 213 **Westminster Royal Aquarium:** John Murchison Munro, *The Royal Aquarium* (Beirut: American University of Beirut, 1971). See also 'London Music Halls: The Aquarium', *The Era*, 3 Sept. 1898; Alistair O'Neill, *London after a Fashion* (London: Reaktion, 2007), 36.

p. 213 **Captain George Costentenus**: Caroline Arscott, *William Morris and Edward Burne-Jones: Interlacings* (London: Yale University Press for the Paul Mellon Centre, 2008). See also Robert Bogdan, *Freak Show* (Chicago: University of Chicago Press, 2104), 243; 'Royal Aquarium Westminster' [handbill], *Human Freaks 3* (65), John Johnson Collection, Bodleian Library, Oxford.

p.213 **In some versions:** 'A Tattooed Man and a Spotted Boy', *Morning Post*, 22 Nov. 1881.

p. 213 **in others:** 'Tattooing Extraordinary', *Liverpool Albion*, 24 June 1876.

p. 213 **tattooed slowly and tortuously:** 'The Tattooed Man at Vienna', *Morning Post*, 2 Feb. 1872.

p. 215 **Tattooed ladies were very popular:** Amelia Klem Osterud, *Tattooed Lady: A History* (London: Taylor Trade, 2014).

p. 215 **Frank and Emma de Burgh:** R.J. Stephens, 'Tattooed Royalty. Queer Stories of a Queer Craze', *Harmsworth Magazine*, Vol. I (1898), 472.

p. 215 **'Living Gallery of Japanese Art':** Handbill sold at Stride & Son, Chichester, 24 June 2021 and is now in a private collection. *Sporting Times*, 30 April 1898, 6.

p. 215 **Professor Williams:** *The Era,* 11 Jan. 1890, 21. 'Tattooers and Tattooed', *Pall Mall Gazette*, 9 April 1892.

p. 215 **best places in London to get tattooed:** 'Boys Aquarium Spree', *Western Mail*, 22 Nov. 1898.

p. 215 **Tom Riley and ... Alfred South:** 'Westminster', *The Standard*, 16 July 1898.

p. 215 **A rare photograph of Ridler:** A negative of this image acquired from George Burchett is included with another photo from the tattooist, in a collage originally erroneously attributed to Dora Maar ('Reproduction de deux photographies représentant une femme et un homme tatoués. Vers 1935'. AM2004-0163(1063), Centre Pompidou, Paris). Damarice Amaro (ed.), *Dora Maar* [ex. cat.] (Paris: Centre Pompidou, 2020), Obj X76801. Burchett's positive print original is in a private collection. Dora Maar was in London in 1935 and likely acquired the photos directly from Burchett's Waterloo Road shop. The model in the second picture can be seen in 'Human Picture Galleries', *Britannia and Eve*, Sept. 1935, and the overdrawing evokes similar work in *E.H. Cookridge Fonds*, Box 1, File 11, McMaster University Library and Archives.

p. 215 **He was cultured:** 'I tattooed the famous' [press clipping, source unknown], *E.H. Cookridge Fonds*, Box 2, File 2, McMaster University Library and Archives. These quotes are in published extracts taken from George Burchett, *Memoirs of a Tattooist* (London: Oldborne, 1958). In *Memoirs*, ed. Peter Leighton (aka Edward Spiro and E.H. Cookridge) ventriloquises George and copies from newspaper sources, and so the *Memoirs* must not be considered true direct citations. For example, 'I was cultured', here, is adapted from Max O'Donnell, 'True Blue'. For more information, see Jon Reiter, *King of Tattooists: George Burchett* (Milwaukee, WI: Solid State, 2012), 212, and Matt Lodder, 'George Burchett: The Man, The Myth, The Legend', *Total Tattoo*, Feb. 2013.

p.215 **'150 Hours':** 'Tattoo Man', *What's On*, 21 Jan. 1938.

p. 215 **thousands of hours:** 'Tattooing that took years', *Derby Evening Telegraph*, 17 April 1937. 'Sensational Novelty Act on Empress Stage', *Medicine Hat Daily News*, *28* Aug. 1942.

p.217 **'Omi is blue all over':** Max O'Donnell, 'True Blue', *Evening Argus*, 7 May 1948.

p. 218 **World's Fair in New York:** 'Epidermic Art Gallery', *Laurel Outlook*, 19 July 1939. See also *Richmond Times-Dispatch*, 8 July 1939, 8; 'He's Different', 6 July 1939; 'Tattooed from head to toe' [press clipping, source unknown], *E. H. Cookridge Fonds*, Box 1, File 8, McMaster University Library and Archives.

p. 218 **Ripley's *Believe it or Not!*:** 'The Great Omi', *Southern Weekly News* [Brighton], 7 Sept. 1935.

p. 218 **sideshows and fairs in Toronto and in Vancouver:** '"Blue Man" Makes an Appearance Here', *Vancouver Sun*, 9 Aug. 1941. See also *Windsor Star*, 15 May 1941; *Ottawa Citizen*, 18 Dec. 1942; 'L'Homme plus tatoué au monde', *Petit* Journal, 25 April 1943.

p. 218 **The strangest man in the world!:** *The Province*, 15 Aug. 1941.

p. 219 **Horace passed away:** 'Horace Leonard Ridler. Burial Date 23 December 1965', Burials in the Parish of Chalvington, Sussex, 1965, 40, *Sussex Parish Registers,* East Sussex Record Office; Brighton, England. 'Gladys Jessie Ridler', *Deaths Registered in October, November and December 1969 RID-RIG*, Vol. 5, 1965, 1391, General Register Office.

p. 219 **'To live, he died':** 'The Great Omi', *Southern Weekly News* [Brighton], 7 Sept. 1935.

p. 219 **'FAMILY NAME: GREAT':** 'Omi Great, 1 July 1940, Buffalo, NY', *Records of the Immigration and Naturalization Service, 1787–2004*, 85/M1480; Roll Number: 048, The National Archives at Washington, D.C.

PART FIVE: TATTOOING TOWARDS THE MILLENNIUM 221

p. 223 **'The practitioners of the prickly arts':** Harold Hughes, 'Harbor's Tattoo Art Colony Vanishes', *The Oregonian*, 15 June 1955, 17.

p. 223 **'Necrophilia, narcissism, sex'**: 'On her back was the Union Jack', *The Economist*, 28 Dec. 1963.

p. 223 **public information campaign:** 'Your permanent number', *New York Times*, 15 April 1937. 'Hand-lettered sign advertising Social Security number tattoo styles, 1936', SY1936/120 Patricia D. Klingenstein Library, New-York Historical Society. 'Social Security' [film] (British Pathé, 1936), 1154.1. See also 'Social Security brings boom to tattoo artists', *The Gastonia Daily Gazette*, 13 April 1937; 'Seems very few have SS numbers tattooed on them', *Helena Daily Independent*, 1 Feb. 1937; 'Needlework', *Literary Digest*, 27 March 1937; 'Security Number is tattooed', *New York Times*, 13 Jan 1937.

p. 223 **As the Second World War began:** Derin Bray and Margaret Hodges, *Loud, Naked and in Three Colours* (Portsmouth, NH: Rake House, 2020). See also 'Tattooists kept busy', *Evening Telegraph,* 4 Nov. 1939; 'Girl Tattooist', *Auckland Star,* 2 Nov. 1946.

p. 223 **Those left at home:** 'Tattooed ATS Girls', *Nottingham Evening Post*, 3 Feb. 1945. 'Service Girls get Tattoo Minded', *The People*, 4 Feb. 1945.

p. 223 **thousands of people come in:** Elsie Marshall, 'Designs on People', *Illustrated*, 17 April 1943. See also William Hickey, 'Something Up My

Sleeve', *Daily Express*, 13 March 1940; 'Leaves his mark on thousands', *Dundee Evening Telegraph*, 21 July 1948.

p. 223 **'they just went around me and I was never wounded':** Lars Krutak, 'Shamanic Skin', *Lars Krutak: Tattoo Anthropologist*, 27 May 2013, https://www.larskrutak.com/shamanic-skin-the-art-of-magical-tattoos/

p. 223 **'magic ... prevents you from being ... hurt by torture':** John Maloy, 'Cambodian Soldiers Use Tattoos to Protect Them from Bullets', *Huffington Post*, 19 Oct. 2009.

p. 226 **'The right hand has the mark of an anchor':** 'Korean Marine Identification Marks', *Central Intelligence Agency Information Report*, 23 Oct. 1951. RDP82-457R008900430008-3, Central Intelligence Agency Archives.

p. 226 **forcibly tattooed with anti-communist slogans:** Charles S. Young, *Name, Rank and Serial Number* (Oxford: Oxford University Press, 2014), 42–43, 102–103. See also Catherine Churchman, 'Victory with Minimum Effort' in Tessa Morris-Suzuki (ed.), *The Korean War in Asia* (Lanham: Rowman and Littlefield, 2018), 92–93; David Cheng Chang, *The Hijacked War* (Stanford, CA: Stanford University Press, 2020), Chapters 8, 10, 11 and 15.

p. 226 **'favourite haunt of London's fashionistas':** 'Tattooing makes an indelible mark at Selfridges', *Financial Times*, 17 June 2003.

p. 227 **banned on under-18s:** 'Introduction of the Tattooing of Minors Bill', *Records of the Children's Division*, BN 29/1427, National Archives, London. 'Tattooing of Young Children: Home Office memorandum; report 'The Incidence of Tattooing in Approved Schools and Remand Homes', *Records of the Children's Division* BN 29/1680, National Archives, London. See also 'Wave of tattooing among children', *The Times*, 13 July 1956; 'More tattooing of teenagers', *The Times*, 3 Aug. 1962; 'Serious and risible tattoos', *The Times*, 1 Feb. 1969. *Burrell v Hammer* (Divisional Court, 1966) 1966 WL 22058.

p. 227 ***completely* illegal in New York City:** David N Silvers and Harry Gelb, 'Dermatopathology in Historical Perspective: The Prohibition of Tattooing in New York City'. *The American Journal of Dermatopathology*, Vol. 13, Issue 3 (June 1991), 307–309. Michael McCable, *New York City Tattoo* (Honoloulu, HW: Hardy Marks, 2013). Spider Webb, *Pushing Ink* (New York: Simon & Schuster, 1979).

p. 227 **Massachusetts:** Bobby G. Frederick, 'Tattoos and the First Amendment – Art Should Be Protected as Art: The South Carolina Supreme Court Upholds the State's Ban on Tattooing', *S C L Rev*, Vol. 55, Issue 1 (2003), 231–235. 'Judge throws out 38-year ban on Massachusetts tattoo artists', *Seattle Times*, 8 Nov. 2000.

p. 227 **Denmark:** A.E. Laumann and N. Kluger, 'History and Epidemiology of Tattoos and Piercings: Legislation in the United States and in Europe' in Christa De Cuyper and Maria Pérez-Cotapos (eds), *Dermatologic Complications with Body Art* (Cham: Springer, 2018).

p.227 **Eastern bloc:** Maria Alina Asavei, 'Engraving Portraits in the Skin: Vernacular Commemorative Tattoos for Ceaușescu, Tito, and Stalin', *Nationalities Papers* (2022), 1–20.

p. 277 **'small, neat design on the shoulder':** 'Lucky Spider Tattoos', *Hull Daily Mail*, 3 June 1950, 4. 'Women', *Hull Daily Mail*, 9 June 1950.

p. 278 **the old skin game:** 'Tattoos Flourish', *The Oregonian*, 26 Sept. 1965.

p. 228 **'renaissance' of tattooing:** Matt Lodder, 'The myths of modern primitivism', *European Journal of American Culture*, Vol. 30, Issue 2 (2011). See also Arnold Rubin, *Marks of Civilization: Artistic Transformations of the Human Body* (Los Angeles, CA: University of California Press, 1986), 236; Juliet Fleming, 'The Renaissance Tattoo' in J. Caplan (ed.), *Written on the Body – The Tattoo in European and American History* (Princeton, NJ, Princeton University Press, 2000), 61–82; Margot Mifflin, *Bodies of Subversion* (New York, NY: Juno Books, 1997); Clinton Sanders, *Customizing the Body* (Philadelphia, PA: Temple University Press, 2008).

p. 228 **Museum of American Folk Art:** Sanka Knox, 'Heyday of Tattooing Recalled at Folk Art Museum', *New York Times*, 8 Oct. 1971. Jamie Jelinski, 'Tattoo! at the American Museum of Folk Art', *Sang Bleu*, 12 April 2014, https://web.archive.org/web/20210901000000*/https://magazine.sangbleu.com/2014/04/12/tattoo-at-the-american-museum-of-folk-art/

p. 228 **Les Skuse:** Russell Miller, 'Works of art in the flesh', *The Observer,* 6 Feb. 1972. See also Matt Lodder, *British Tattoo Art Revealed* [exhibition], National Maritime Museum Cornwall (2017); Briony Fer, 'Photographs and Buildings (mainly)' in Ian Borden (ed.), *Forty Ways to think about Architecture* (Chichester: Wiley & Sons, 2014), 66; 'Les Skuse The Champion Tattoo Artist of All England, Camden Arts Centre, 13 February–5 March' [handbill] (1972), NMWA23777 National Museum of Wales.

p. 228 ***Vanity:*** *Vanity* [ex. cat.], Brighton Museum and Art Gallery, 9 May– 31 Aug. 1972, obj A182, 12.

p.228 **'The Renaissance of Tattooing':** 'The Renaissance of Tattooing', *This Week*, dir. Ian Fordyce (Associated Radiodiffusion, 8 May 1958), 389649, British Film Institute.

p. 229 **Black Eyes and Lemonade:** Barbara Jones, *Unsophisticated Arts* (London: Little Toller, 2013). See also Gillian Whiteley, 'Kitsch as Cultural Capital: Black Eyes And Lemonade and Populist Aesthetics In Fifties' Britain', *Kitsch* (Newcastle upon Tyne: Cambridge Scholars Press, 2013); Catherine Moriarty, '"The museum eye must be abandoned": Figureheads as Popular Art', *Sculpture Journal*, Vol. 24, Issue 2 (2015); *Black Eyes & Lemonade* [ex. cat], Whitechapel Gallery, 1951, Objs. M16–17.

p. 229 **Bristol Tattoo Club:** R.W.N. Scutt and Christopher Gotch, *Art, Sex & Symbol* (2nd edition. London: Cornwall Books, 1986). See also Paul Sayce, 'A History of British Tattoo Clubs', *Tattoo International,* Issue 185 (*c.* 2015); Ron Ackers, *Tattoo Artist* (Bottrop: Peter Pomp, 1997).

Chapter 17: 'Songs of my heart' 231

I am extremely grateful to Ian Thompson, who loaned me his copy of Charlie Dick's memoir during the preparation of this chapter.

p. 231 **'Girls tattooed us '**: Anthony Pitch, *Our Crime was being Jewish* (New York: Skyhorse Publishing, 2015). Susan Eisdorfer Beer, *Oral History,* 16 May 1995, RG-50.030.0326, United States Holocaust Memorial Museum.

p. 231 **'I had never known a client so unflinching'**: Charles Dick, *POW: True Prison Camp Horrors* (London: Digit, 1958), 41–45. The main narrative for this chapter is adapted from this text. Further details are in Ossie Jobson, 'Charles Dick', *Tattoo International*, Issue 185 (*c.* 2015), reprinted from *Tattoo Life*, June 1985.

p. 231 **pages of lyrical verse:** Charles Dick, 'The Poems of a Prisoner of War' (Morpeth: Charles Dick/*Northumberland and Alnwick Gazette*, 1946). 'Skilled "character" dies, aged 84', *The Journal* (Newcastle, UK), 28 June 2003.

p. 235 **Scouse POW Ginger:** 'Ginger's Tattooing: It Undermined Nazi Discipline' [Press clipping, source unknown], *E. H. Cookridge Fonds*, Box 1, File 8, McMaster University Library and Archives.

p. 235 **Dr Eric Wagner:** Erich Wagner, 'Ein Beitrag zur Tätowierungsfrage' (PhD diss., Universitätsanstalt für gerichtliche Medizin und naturwissenschaftliche Kriminalistik, Jena, 1940). English translations from an unpublished translation by Kenneth Kipperman.

p. 235 **tattoos at Buchenwald were recorded from 1938:** Alexandra Przyrembel, 'Transfixed by an Image: Ise Koch, the "Kommandeuse of Buchenwald"', *German History*, Vol. 19, No. 3 (2001). *Conduct of Ilse Koch War Crimes Trial*, Part 5, 28 Sept., 8 and 9 Dec. 1948 (Washington D.C: Government Printing Office, 1949), 1040.

p. 236 **tattooed Frenchman ... 'disappeared':** *Koch Trial*, Part 5, 1025.

p. 236 **morbidly routine:** Gemma Angel, 'The Tattoo Collectors: Inscribing Criminality in Nineteenth-Century France', *Bildwelten Des Wissens*, 9.1 (Special Issue: Prepared Specimens) (2012), 29–38. Gemma Angel 'Recovering the Nineteenth-Century European Tattoo. Collections, Contexts, Techniques' in Lars Krutak and Aaron Deter-Wolf (eds), *Ancient Ink* (Seattle, WA: University of Washington Press, 2017), 107–129.

p. 237 **Werner B testified:** Przyrembel, 'Transfixed' (see above).

p. 237 **Edgar Krasa:** Pitch, *Our Crime* (see above). Edgar Krasa, *Oral History*, 7 Sept., 1991RG-50.243.0044, United States Holocaust Memorial Museum.

p. 237 **Joyce Wagner:** Pitch, *Our Crime* (see above). *Oral History*, 23 Jan. 1991 RG-50.004.0001, United States Holocaust Memorial Museum.

p. 238 **George Burchett:** Kathleenn Lyon, 'Slave girl freed of Nazi brand', *Daily Mail*, 2 March 1948, 3.

p. 238 **Christian Warlich developed a tincture:** Ole Wittmann, *Christian Warlich: Tattoo Flash Book* (London: Prestel, 2019). Erich Andres, *Warlichs Methode der Tattoo-Entfernung* [photo] (1936) CW-174-178. State Historical Museum, Hamburg.

p. 239 **his recipe:** *Akte zur Überprüfung von Wahlichs Praxis der Tattoo Entfernung*, CW-185, -186, -189, -191, -192. Hamburg State Archives. Ole

Wittmann, *Tattoolegenden: Cristian Warlich auf St. Pauli* [exhibition], 27 Nov. 2019–25 May 2020, State Historical Museum, Hamburg.

p. 239 **blood-type markers on … Waffen SS:** Earl F. Ziemke, *The U.S. Army in the Occupation of Germany* (Washington DC: Center of Military History, United States Army, 1975), 293–294.

p.239 **Adolf Eichmann:** Isser Harel, *The House on Garibaldi Street*, ed. Shlomo Shpiro (London: Routledge, 2013). Guy Walters, *Hunting Evil* (London: Bantam, 2009).

p. 239 **Josef Mengele:** Neal M. Sher and Eli M. Rosenbaum, 'In the Matter of Josef Mengele' (Washington DC: US Department of Justice, Oct. 1992), 42–53.

p. 240 **'Operation Tat-Type':** 'Tattooing could save your life', *Science Digest*, Oct. 1952, 71–73. Elizabeth K. Wold and Anne E. Laumann, 'The Use of blood-type tattoos during the Cold War', J. Acad Dermatol, Vol. 58 (2008), 472–76.

p. 241 **The best people are tattooed:** Ossie Jobson, 'Charles Dick', Tattoo International Issue 185 (*c.* 2015), 60.

Chapter 18: An Artistic Hammer and Sickle 243

I am grateful to my friend Louise Hamilton for her help with Icelandic translation, and to Valur Inigmundarson (University of Iceland) and David Sheinin (Trent University, Ontario) for helping me make sense of the contexts of this story.

p. 243 **'Art is a lie':** Pablo Picasso, 'Picasso Speaks', *The Arts Magazine*, May 1923.

p. 243 **the story:** 'Uw vuðri veröid – Pólitískt stórhneyksli í Buenos Aires' ['Out of this world: Major Political Scandal in Buenos Aires'], *Frjals þjóð* [Free Nation], 16 May 11954, 1–4. The narrative of this chapter is adapted from this article.

p. 244 **that month:** Ted Morgan, *Valley of Death* (London: Random House, 2010). See also Stephem Schlesinger, Stephen Kinzer and John H. Coatsworth, *Bitter Fruit* (Cambridge, MA: Harvard University Press, 2005); Vina Lanzona, *Amazons of the Huk Rebellion* (Madison, WI: University of Wisconsin Press, 2009).

p. 246 **the article is not written in a tone that suggests absurd humour:** I am indebted to Louise Hamilton and Valur Inigmundarson for their independent assessments of the article's tone in Icelandic.

p. 247 **'Satyr, Faun and Centaur with a Trident':** Pablo Picasso, *Satyr, Faun and Centaur with a Trident* [painting] (1946), Antibes, Musée Picasso.

p. 247 **nude dancer … had to abandon her career plans:** 'Couloirs et Coulisses', *La Vie Parisienne,* 4 Jan. 1936, 388.

p. 247 **elaborately tattooed woman picnicking:** Pablo Picasso, *Love in the Afternoon with a Tattooed Woman* [pastel] (1968). Private collection.

p. 247 **Marcelo and Hortensia Anchorena:** John Klein, *Matisse and Decoration* (New Haven, CT: Yale University Press, 2018). Pierre Barillet, *À la ville comme à la scene* (Paris: Fallois, 2004), 105.

p. 248 **Eva Perón ... copied Hortensia's haircut:** Alicia Dujovne Ortiz, *Eva Peron* (Paris: Grasset, 1995).

p. 248 **French Communist Party:** Gertje Utley, *Picasso: The Communist Years* (New Haven, CT: Yale University Press, 2000).

p. 248 **kept a portrait of Adolf Hitler in his library:** Brigitte Benkemoun, *Je suis le carent de Dora Maar* (Paris: Stock, 2019).

p. 248 **named Communist sympathisers within the Argentinian government:** David M.K. Sheinin, 'Cold War and the End of Argentine Democracy, 1947–1961' in *Argentina and the United States: An Alliance Constrained* (Athens, GA: University of Georgia Press, 2010). See also Sam Pope-Brewer, 'Anti-US Sentiment Rising in South America Countries', 27 April 1953; Mario Rapoport, 'Argentina and the Soviet Union: History of Political and Commercial Relations', *Hispanic American Historical Review*, Vol. 66, Issue 2 (1986); 'National Intelligence Estimate', 9 March 1954. *Foreign Relations of the United States, 1952–1954, The American Republics,* Volume IV, Document 125 NIE-91-54, Office of the Historian, Washington D.C.

p. 248 **a new trade deal with Argentina:** *Soviet Bloc Economic Penetration of Underdeveloped Countries, c.* 1955. RDP79-T01149A000400110003-8, Central Intelligence Agency Archives. 'Soviet bids Latins to talks ontrade', *New York Times,* 1 May 1954.

p. 248 **the previous year:** 'Argentina halts meat exports', *New York Times,* 27 March 1953. See also 'Peron Threatens Seizure of Cattle', *New York Times,* 2 April 1953; 'Peron Aides Seek Living Cost Cuts', *New York Times,* 3 April 1953; 'General Peron's Beef', *New York Times,* 3 April 1953; 'Shortage of meat vexing Argentina', *New York Times,* 13 Sept. 1953; E. Louise Peffer, 'The Argentine Cattle Industry under Peron', *Food Research Institute Studies,* Issue 1 (1960), 151–184.

p.249 **cultural cold war:** C.L. Sulzberger, *New York Times,* 17 Jan. 1954. This mirrors a similar concern a year earlier: 'Icelanders warm to Soviet Culture', *New York Times,* 31 Oct. 1953.

p.250 **CIA-backed propaganda campaigns:** 'The Ambassador in Argentina (Nufer) to the Department of State', 5 Feb. 1953. *Foreign Relations of the United States, 1952–1954, The American Republics,* Volume IV, Document 114, 611.35/2-553, Office of the Historian, Washington D.C. 'Memorandum by the Secretary of State to the President', 19 Nov. 1953, *Foreign Relations of the United States, 1952–1954,* The American Republics, Volume IV, Document 123, 735.00/11-1953, Office of the Historian, Washington D.C.

p. 250 **'cultural activities':** 'Working Group in Iceland', *Memorandum for the Operations Coordinating Board'*, 2 March 1954. RDP80-R01731R003000050007-1, Central Intelligence Agency Archives. 'Activities of the Operations Coordinating Board', 24 March 1954, RDP80-R01731R003000170002-3, Central Intelligence Agency Archives.

p. 250 **increasing American prestige in Iceland:** 'Quarterly Status Report', *The Foreign Information Programme*, 30 Oct. 1952, Central Intelligence Agency Archives. See also Valur Ingimundarson, 'Immunizing against the

American Other', *Journal of Cold War Studies*, Vol. 6, No. 4. (Fall 2004), 65–88; Valur Ingimundarson, 'Buttressing the West in the North: The Atlantic Alliance, Economic Warfare, and the Soviet Challenge in Iceland, 1956–1959', *The International History Review*, Vol. 21, No. 1, 80–103.

p. 250 **encourage Icelanders to read US-friendly literature:** *The Icelandic Book Publishing Business*, 9 March 1954. RDP62-00865R000100120002-8, Central Intelligence Agency Archives.

p. 250 **heavily reliant on foreign exports:** 'Current Situation in Iceland', *NSC Briefing Western Divivion*, 26 July 1954. RDP79-R00890A000300040047-9, Central Intelligence Agency Archives.

p. 252 **Roald Dahl's ... Skin:** Roald Dahl, 'Skin', *New Yorker*, 17 May 1952.

Chapter 19: 'A bit more on his arse' 255

p. 255 **'Hi, Alan? It's Dave here ...':** *Moths to a Flame*, dir. Roger Earl (Marathon Films, 1988), 82 mins.

p. 255 **Alan was born in Liverpool:** Simon Fraser, 'Obituary: Mr Sebastian', *The Independent*, 22 May 1996. Paul King (ed.), *Alan Oversby: Documentary Evidence* (San Francisco, CA: Association of Professional Piercers, 2022). 'Tattoos and Piercings' in Simon Dwyer (ed.), *Rapid Eye* (Brighton: Rapid Eye, 1989).

p. 255 **first pierced:** Jim Ward, 'Meet Mr Sebastian', *Piercing Fans International Quarterly*, No. 4 (Summer 1978), 6–9. The audio of this interview is at the Body Piercing Archive, San Francisco.

p. 257 **'He is a teacher ...':** Anna Motson, 'The Heart under the Sleeve', *Daily Telegraph*, 1 March 1975, 46.

p. 257 **'Not in the least bit erotic':** Jim Ward, 'Meet Mr Sebastian', *Piercing Fans International Quarterly*, No. 4 (Summer 1978), 6–9. The audio of this interview is at the Body Piercing Archive, San Francisco.

p. 257 **integral part of the subcultural ... gay scenes:** Emmanuel Cooper, 'Skin Deep', *HIM* [Press clipping, source unknown] (*c.* 1992), Private Collection. 'Indelibly Inked', *Gay Times* March 1992.

p. 258 **Cliff Raven, Sid Diller and Dave Slack:** Marcus Podlichuk, 'Mr Sebastian Ink', *Tattoo International* 52 (1982), 9.

p. 258 **Doug Molloy & Jim Ward:** Jim Ward, *Running the Gauntlet* (San Francisco: Gauntlet Enterprises, 2011).

p. 258 ***Adventures of a Piercing Freak*:** Doug Molloy, *Adventures of a Piercing Freak* (Sacred Debris, 2019). *The Art of Pierced Penises* (United States: Calston Industries, 1976).

p. 259 **Cliff Raven:** Tattoo Archive, *Life & Times of Cliff Raven* (Winston Salem, NC: Tattoo Archive, 2013). Dale Grande, *Original Cliff Raven Designs* (Chicago: Chicago, 2013). Nick Collella, *Cliff Raven Travel Book* (Chicago: Great Lakes Tattoo, 2021).

p. 259 **Phil Sparrow**: Justin Spring, *Secret Historian* (New York: Farrar, Straus & Giroux, 2010). Jeremy Mulderig (ed.), *The Lost Autobiography of Samuel Steward* (Chicago: University of Chicago Press, 2018). Samuel

Steward, *Chapters from an Autobiography* (United States: Grey Fox Press, 1981).

p. 259 **'feast the eyes on male beauty':** Mulderig, *Lost Autobiography*, 201.

p. 259 **Hardy made a pilgrimage:** Ed Hardy and Joel Selvin, *Wear Your Dreams* (New York: Thomas Dunne, 2013), 49.

p. 259 **pushed tattooing:** Karin Breuer, *Ed Hardy: Deeper than Skin* [ex. cat.] (San Francisco: Fine Art Museums of San Francisco, 2022). Ed Hardy, *Tattooing the Invisible Man* (Santa Monica, CA: Smart Art Press, 1999).

p. 260 **kept meticulous records of his clients:** Justin Spring, *An Obscene Diary* (New York: Antinus Press, 2010).

p. 260 ***Bad Boys and Tough Tattoos*:** Samuel Steward, *Bad Boys and Tough Tattoos* (New York: Harrington Park Press, 1990).

p. 260 **his portfolio:** Excerpts published in King, *Alan Oversby*. Private collection.

p. 261 **Greville Hallam:** Heather Mills, 'Killers joined legion, court told', *Daily Telegraph*, 18 April 1985, 3.

p. 261 **'Gay skins':** Murray Healy, *Gay Skins* (United Kingdom: Bread & Circuses, 2014).

p. 261 **other, more predatory tattooers:** Chris Salewicz, 'Scratching the Skin, Scarring the Soul', *Time Out* [London], 5 November 1982.

p. 262 **parodic or even Freudian response:** David Bell, Jon Binnie, Julia Cream & Gill Valentine, 'All hyped up and no place to go', *Gender, Place & Culture* Vol. 1, Issue 1 (1994), 31-47. Moya Lloyd, 'Performativity, Parody, Politics', *Theory, Culture & Society* Vol. 16, Issue 2 (1999), 195–213.

p. 262 **Some psychotherapists:** The literature on this issue is summarised in Kevin Borgeson and Robin Valeri. 'Gay Skinheads: Negotiating a Gay Identity in a Culture of Traditional Masculinity', *The Journal of Men's Studies* 23, no. 1 (March 2015), 44–62. Alison Moore, 'Visions of sadomasochism as a Nazi erotic', *Lesbian and Gay Psychology Review* Vol. 6, no. 3 (November 2005).

p. 262 **their fascist fashions:** Robert Forbes & Eddie Stampton (eds.), *The White Nationalist Skinhead Movement* (London: Feral House, 2015), 259, Chapter 12.

p. 262 **American Nazi Party advertised ... in Drummer:** Jack Fritscher, *Gay San Francisco, Eyewitness Drummer* Vol. I (San Francisco: Palm Drive, 2008). *Drummer* Volume 1, No. 1 (1976), 26. 'Dear Sir', Vol. 1, Number 3, *Drummer* (1975), 12.

p. 262 **Nicky Crane:** 'Nazi Nick is a Panzi', *The* Sun, 30 July 1992.

p. 262 **London Apprentice:** 'LA Faces Anti-Racist Picket', *Capital GayI*, 2 July

1993, 4. S. Kidman, 'The Stench of Racism', *Capital Gay*, 14 May 1993, 2. Vicky Pengielly, 'Racism will not be tolerated', *Capital Gay*, 28 May 1993. 'London Apprentice Picketed', *Black Lesbian and Gay Centre Newsletter* (August–September 1993), 4. 'We're not Fascists, say Skinheads', *Capital Gay*, 23 October 1987, 11.

p. 262 **John Hudspith:** 'Masochistic homosexual was kicked and punched to death', *The Independent*, 15 March 1990.

p. 263 **'Cut Here':** Michael Morley, *The Dennis Nilsen Tapes* (London: Hodder & Stoughton, 2021).

p. 263 **spate of ritual murders:** Michael Hames, *The Dirty Squad* (London: Little Brown, 2000).

p. 263 **Alan was charged and convicted:** 'Brigade of the Dungeon', *The Sun*, 21 December 1990. 'Torture Vice Gang Sentenced', *Daily Telegraph*, 20 December 1990. *R v Oversby* (1990). Law Commission, 'Consent in the Criminal Law: A Consultation Paper' (1995), 139.

p. 264 **'draws the blood of customers':** Bob Corfield, 'Ban on gay tattoos', *The Sun* (*c.* May, 1985), reprinted in *Tattoo Buzz* (May/Jun 1985), 33.

p. 264 **'would not touch a homosexual':** 'The Great AIDS Debate', *Tattoo Buzz* (May/Jun, 1985), 32–34.

p. 264 **'to warn common needle users':** William H. Buckley, 'Identify All the Carriers', *New York Times*, 18 March 1986.

p. 264 **zero publicly reported cases ... definitively be attributed to tattooing:** P. R. Cohen, 'Tattoo-Associated Viral Infections: A Review', *Clinical, Cosmetic and Investigational Dermatology*, Vol. 14 (2021), 1529–1540.

p. 265 **'He insisted ...':** 'Fritscher & Earle: Two Filmmakers in Conversation' in Marc Siedelmann (ed.), *California Dreamin'* (United States: Editions Mustache, 2016).

Chapter 20: 'Pain Doesn't Scare Me' 267

p. 267 **'Pain doesn't scare me':** Dennis Rodman and Tim Keown, *Bad as I Wanna Be* (New York: Delacorte Press, 1996), 166.

p. 267 **It was time to show them ...':** Dennis Rodman, *I should be Dead by Now* (New York: Sports Publishing, 2013).

p. 267 **Erik finishes a long, ravishing stroke:** Scott Raab, 'Wild Thing', *GQ* [United States] (January 1995), 94–101. The primary narrative of this chapter is drawn from Raab's article.

p. 268 **first tattoo after he joined the San Antonio Spurs:** Rodman, *I Should Be Dead*. (See above)

p. 268 **'this year, there's a series of tattoos':** Anthony Cotton, 'Not All Fun, Games for Rodman ...', *Washington Post 3* December 1992, B1.

p. 268 **Images of him in a Detroit Pistons jersey**: Michael Layton, 'LANDOVER, MD - DECEMBER 26: Dennis Rodman #00 of the Detroit Pistons ...' [photo], 26 December 1992, 1291717294, Getty Images Sport.

p. 268 **'I was still too scared to let loose ...':** Dennis Rodman and Michael Silver, *Walk on the Wild Side* (New York: Delacorte Press, 1996), 10–11.

p. 272 **Rodman has a problem:** Michael Wilbon, 'The Worm has Turned', *Washington Post*, 3 November 1997, B7.

p. 273 **Fanatix:** Jake Malooney, 'The Untold History of the Dennis Rodman Tattoo T-Shirt', *Rolling Stone.com*, 27 April 2020. https://www.rollingstone.com/culture/culture-features/dennis-rodman-tattoo-tshirtuntold-history-bulls-basketball-990275/. *Dennis Rodman v Fanatix Apparel, Inc.*, case no.96–2103 (D.N.J., May 28, 1996). Shontavia Johnson, 'Branded: Trademark Tattoos, Slave Owner Brands and the right to have "free" skin', *Mich. Telcomm. & Tech L. Review* Volume 22 (2016).

p. 273 **precise legal status of tattoos:** Matt Lodder, *Body Art: Body Modification as Artistic Practice* (PhD Diss, University of Reading, 2010). C. A. Harkins, 'Tattoos and Copyright Infringement: Celebrities, marketers, and businesses beware of the ink'. *Lewis and Clark Law Review* 10 (2006), 313–332. Yolanda M. King, 'The Challenges Facing Copyright Protection for Tattoos', *Oregon Law Review* 92, no. 1 (2013), 129–162. Arianna D. Chronis, 'The Inky Ambiguity of Tattoo Copyrights: Addressing the Silence of U.S. Copyright Law on Tattooed Works', *Iowa Law Review* 104, no. 3 (March 2019), 1483–1522.

p. 274 **several cases:** *S. Victor Whitmill v. Warner Bros. Inc.*, No. 4.11-CV-752 (ED Mo. April 288, 2011). *Reed v. Nike, Inc.*, No. 05-CV-198 BR (D. Or. Feb. 10, 2005).

p. 274 **Kat von D.:** *Sedlik v Drachtenberg* No CV-21-1102 DSF (MRWx) (D Ca. 30 August 2021).

p. 275 **An activist called Rich:** Shannon Larrat, 'Takedown This!', *Modblog*, 3 May 2007, https://web.archive.org/web/20181211151119/https://news.bme.com/2007/05/03/takedown-this/. 'Takedown This', *The New Freedom*, 2 May 2, 2007, https://web.archive.org/web/20070505051600/http://www.thenewfreedom.net/wp/2007/05/02/takedown-this/

p. 276 **his tattooed legacy:** Harry Cheadle, 'A Brief History of Tattoos in the NBA', *Vice*, 27 May 2011 https://www.vice.com/en/article/8gmmm4/a-brief-history-of-tattoos-in-the-nba. Andrew Gottlieb, *In the Paint* (United States: Hyperion, 2003).

p. 276 **Jacci Gresham:** Karen L. Hudson, *Chick Ink* (Avon, MA: Adams, 2007). Beverley Yuen Thompson, *Covered in Ink* (New York: NYU Press, 2015). Mifflin, *Bodies of Subversion*, 62.

p. 276 ***Color Outside the Lines*:** *Color Outside the Lines*, dir. Artemus Jenkins (Jenkins & Bailey, 2013), 90 minutes.

p. 276 **After Rodman's very public embrace of tattooing:** George James, 'From Back Alleys to Beauty Queens', *New York Times*, 29 July 2001.

p. 276 ***Ebony* magazine:** Melissa Ewey, 'Who has a tattoo, and where?', *Ebony* (July 1998), 76–82.

Conclusion 279

p. 279 **'It's a pleasant profession':** *Frisco Skin & Ink* (Metamorphosis II Productions, 1990), 1h52m.

p. 280 **every three years, a tattooing craze:** Eddy Gilmore, 'Tattoos Flourish', *The Oregonian* 26 September 1965.

p. 280 **'no Tugboat Annies':** 'Tattoos give body sexy something', *Naples Daily News* (Florida), 11 March 1973.

p. 280 **all sorts of people are doing it:** 'Tattoo You?', *City Limits*, 5 February 1982, 35.

p. 280 **Kate Moss was tattooed by … Lucian Freud:** 'True Story of Lucien Freud Tattoo', *Mail on Sunday* 24 July 2022, 14–15.

p. 280 **tattoo studio opened in Selfridges:** 'Tattooing makes an indelible mark at Selfridges', *Financial Times*, 17 June 2003.

p. 280 **tattoos conquer modern art:** 'Tattoos conquer modern art as needles and ink replace brushes', Paul Harris, *The Observer*, 23 January 2011.

p. 280 **the artform of sailors, bikers and assorted deviants:** John Henley, 'Rise and Rise of the Tattoo', *The Guardian*, 20 July 2010.

p. 281 **Harris Interactive:** *Harris Poll* #12, February 10, 2016. #22, February 23, 2012. #58, October 6, 2003.

p. 282 **Vladimir Franz:** Matthew Day̌, 'Tattooed from Head to Toe: the Czech who would be president', *Daily Telegraph*, 8 December 2012, 24.

p. 282 **first tattoo convention in China:** Dominic Morgan, 'Tattoos Make Mark', *China Daily* 13 September 2017. Aleksandar Carevic, 'Shanghai's First Tattoo Convention, in Pictures', *Smart Shanghai*, https://web.archive.org/web/20151015034638/https://www.smartshanghai.com/articles/activities/shanghai-tattoo-2015.

p. 282 **Supreme Court … ruled definitively that tattooing could continue:** Hikari Hid, 'Discreetly, the Young in Japan Chip Away at a Taboo on Tattoos', *New York Times*, 23 April 2022.

p. 282 **Nanaia Mahuta:** Bernard Lagan, 'Tattooed Minister Makes Her Mark', *The Times*, 3 November 2020.

p. 282 **Justin Trudeau:** Charlie Mitchell, 'Troubled Trudeau Comes Out Fighting', *The Times*, 4 October 2019.

p. 282 **one newspaper:** All these headlines taken from the *Daily Mirror* at mirror.co.uk during March 2022. The list is not exhaustive.

p. 283 **tattooing robots:** S.C. Stuart, 'Are You Brave Enough to Get a Tattoo From a Robot?', *PCMag*.com, 9 March 2021.

p. 283 **QR codes:** Olivia Solon, 'This Tattooing Robot Draws Perfect Artworks on your Skin', *Mirror.co.uk*, 29 October 2014; Shamani Johsi, 'People keep getting QR Codes Tattooed on Their Body', *Vice* 21 October 2021.

p. 283 **non-fungible tokens:** Tony Bradley, 'NFTs And Tattoo Art Collide with Launch of Indelible', *Forbes.com*, 2 June 2022.

p. 283 **'as ancient as time, as modern as tomorrow':** *Tattooing as you like it: The Legacy of Milton Zeis* (Colorado Springs, CO: Yellow Beak Press, 2012). Zeis sold a flyer with this slogan as part of a tattooing kit in the late 1930s and early 1940s.

ACKNOWLEDGEMENTS

This book is dedicated to Lal Hardy. My curiosity about traditional tattooing serendipitously led me into his shop in 2003, and I never could have anticipated the wisdom, support, kindness, generosity, friendship and patronage he would go on to give me over the twenty or so years that have followed. A special dedication also goes to Alex Binnie, another friend and legend of the industry without whose support and knowledge this book would be greatly impoverished.

The research for this book spans more than a decade, and thus this list of acknowledgements will doubtless be incomplete. Nevertheless, particular thanks must go to the following people, whose knowledge and work have made *Painted People* possible.

I stand on the shoulders of my fellow tattoo historians. Amongst academic specialists, I am particularly grateful to Gemma Angel, Aaron Deter-Wolf, Anna Felicity Friedman, Sebastian Galliot, Lars Krutak, Sean Mallon, Luc Renaut, Benoit Robitaille, Maya Sialuk Jacobsen, Jamie Jelinski, Yoshimi Yamamoto and Ole Wittman, who I am proud and humbled to call my peers and colleagues. Work of industry historians including Derin Bray, Rich Hardy, Paul King, Manfred Kohrs, Terry Manton, Carmen Nyssen, Paul Roe, Nick Schonberger, Brett Stewart, Nick York and the members of the *Knights of the Round Shader* Facebook community, amongst others, has also been crucial in underpinning this book.

This book builds on my exhibitions, particularly *British Tattoo Art Revealed* at the National Maritime Museum in Cornwall. Thank you to my co-curators Derryth Ridge and Stuart Slade, and to the incredible collectors who lent objects, time, and considerable expertise: Neil Hopkins-Thomas, Paul Ramsbottom, Willie Robinson and Jimme Skuse.

Thanks to the students and researchers who have assisted the project in various ways over the years, including Julia Amigo, Jeanne Barnicaud, Julie Bréthous, Ingrid Marvin, Naho Onuki and Kaede Ose.

Thank you to every tattoo artist whose work I wear or who has supported my research, and in particular to Becca Marsh, Aaron Hewitt, Claudia De Sabe, Yutaro, Mo Coppoletta, Doug Hardy, Dan Smith, Jack Watts, George Bone, Julie Clarke-Edwards, Mick of Zürich and Maxime Büchi, who have been especially enthusiastic and kind over the years. Thanks too to Perry Rule at *Total Tattoo* magazine.

Thank you to public historians including Fern Riddell, Amber Butchart, Eleanor Janega, Hallie Rubenhold, Lindsey Fitzharris, Adam Rutherford, Dan Snow, Caroline Pennock, Phoenix Andrews and in particular Alexandra von Tunzelmann, who introduced me to my agent, Max Edwards and who thus lit the spark which led to this book. Thank you to my editors, Grace Pengelly and Hazel Eriksson, to Alex Gingell, and to all at HarperCollins for graciously putting up with my disorganisation, my missing of deadlines, my doubtless infuriating work, and for making this book something worth reading.

Thank you to all my colleagues at the University of Essex, including Gavin Grindon, Diana Bullen Presciutti, Wayne Martin, Jane Hindley, Ellisif Wasmuth and Paola Guiseppantonio Di Franco for motivation, writing support and tolerance. In the same vein, thank you to Sue Malvern, my PhD supervisor.

Thank you to Kate Bird, the best person I know. Thank you, too, to Kevin Ingham, Geraint North, Sara Wallace and Shell Grayson. Tim Winch, you are missed.

I could not have completed this book, or become the person I am today, without the unending love and support of my parents, Christine and Mike. I love you both.

Above all else, I want to thank my partner and true love Layla Boyd, who has seen and endured the production of this book up close. She is a bedrock. Layla, I literally could not have done this without you.

PICTURE CREDITS

Page	Credit
vi	Keystone / Stringer / Getty Images
xii	Unknown source, collection of Lal Hardy
8	Granger Historical Picture Archive / Alamy Stock Photo
16	© Wolfgang Neeb / Bridgeman Images
24	Alex Segre / Alamy Stock Photo
31	© Anne Austin
34	From *Griechische Geschichte* by M. von Witzleben (Meidinger Jugendschriften Verlag, Berlin, 1908), plate 3
41	*Fort Wayne Sentinel*, 11 September 1915
44	Ana Lo / Shutterstock
56	The Artchives / Alamy Stock Photo
64	zhang jiahan / Alamy Stock Photo
74	Granger Historical Picture Archive / Alamy Stock Photo
77	From *Warhafftige Contrafey einer Wilden Frawen/ mit irẽ Töchterlein : gefunden in der Landschafft/ Noua terra genañt/ vnd gehn Antorff gebracht/ vnd von menigklich alda offendtlich gesehen worden/ vnd noch zusehen ist [True story of a wild woman / with her little daughter: found in the countryside/ called Noua Terra/ and brought to Antwerp / and publicly seen by many people / and can still be seen]* by Matthäus Franck (durch Mattheum Francken, Antwerp, 1567), Zentralbibliothek Zürich, PAS II 7/4, https://doi.org/10.7891/e-manuscripta-92246
86	The Picture Art Collection / Alamy Stock Photo
96	Tasmanian Archives: CON19/1/13, image 321
110	Unknown source, collection of Stephan Schomowski
118	Hulton Archive / Stringer / Getty Images
124	From *Heiligdommen Godsdiensten en Gewoontens der Oude Jooden [Shrines Religions and Customs of the Ancient Jews]* by Johannes Lundius (Nicolaas ten Hoorn and Antoni Schoonenburg, Amsterdam, 1726)

125 Private collection, photograph by Andy Olenick, with the portrait owner's kind permission

132 From *The Report of the Trial of Sir R.C.D. Tichborn, BART, edited by Dr Kenealy* ('Englishman' Office, London, 1876), vol.1, page 91, Internet Archive

141 Ibid., page 409

144 Museum of Archaeology and Anthropology, Cambridge: 693839_D.100193.VH

154 © Crocker Art Museum

166 Magite Historic / Alamy Stock Photo

173 From A. W. *Gamage Ltd Sports, Cycle, Motor and General Outfitters General Catalogue* (A.W.Gamage, London, 1911), page 999, collection of Dr Matt Lodder

176 *The Nickerson Argosy* (Nickerson, Kansas), 3 October 1901

180 Photographed by the Anatomical Museum, University of Edinburgh

186 Sasha / Stringer / Getty Images

189 © British Library Board. All Rights Reserved / Bridgeman Images

196 Everett Collection Historical / Alamy Stock Photo

208 Daily Herald Archive / National Science & Media Museum / SSPL / Getty Images

214 Public domain image sourced from the Wellcome Collection

216 Dora Maar, 1935, Musee National d'Art Moderne, Centre Pompidou, Paris. © 2022 Rmn Grand Palais / George Burchett / Dist. Photo SCALA, Florence

222 Public domain image sourced from cia.gov, general CIA records

224 Popperfoto / Contributor / Getty Images

225 Public domain image sourced from the (US) National Archives and Records Administration (NARA)

230 © British Library Board. All Rights Reserved / Bridgeman Images

238 *Daily Mail*, 2 March 1948, image courtesy McMaster University

242 *Frjáls þjóð* [Free Nation] (Reykjavík, Iceland), 16 May 1954

254 Alan Oversby Archive, collection of Jeremy Castle

266 Jussi Nukari / Shutterstock

278 From the collection of Dr Matt Lodder

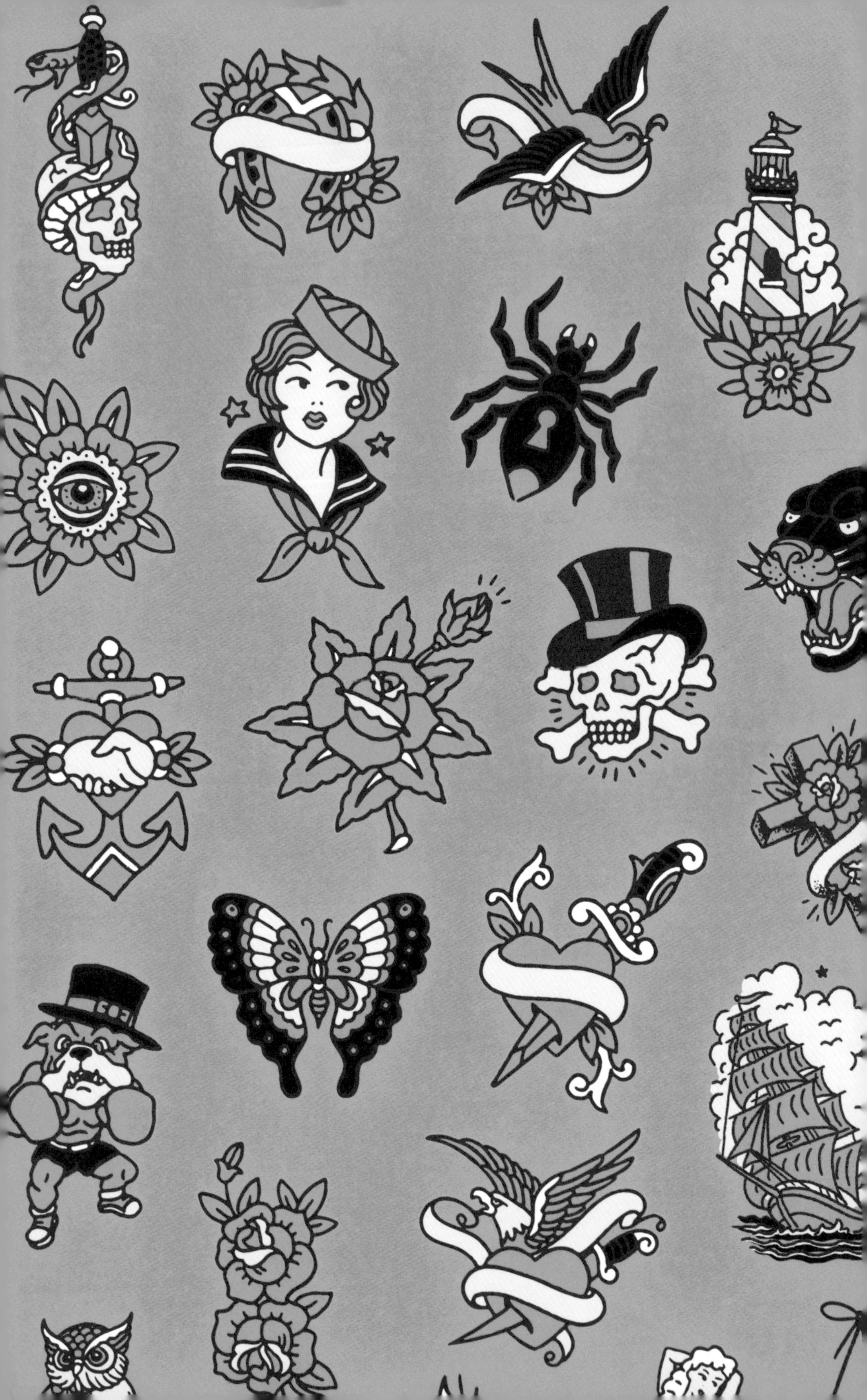